Seeking Bāuls of Bengal

'Bāuls' have become renowned as wandering minstrels and mystics of India and Bangladesh, and are known through their beautiful and often enigmatic songs. They are recruited from both Hindu and Muslim communities, privileging the human being over such identities. Despite their iconic status as representatives of the 'spiritual East', and although they have been the subject of a number of studies, systematic research with Bāuls themselves has been largely neglected. Jeanne Openshaw's book is new, not only in analysing the rise of Bāuls to their present revered status, but in the depth of its ethnographic research and its reference to the lives of composers and singers as a context for their songs. The author uses her fieldwork and oral and manuscript materials to lead the reader from conventional historical and textual approaches towards a world defined by people called 'Bāul', where the human body and love are primary, and female is extolled above male. This is a compelling story of creativity and dissent even in the face of persecution.

Jeanne Openshaw is Lecturer in Religious Studies at the University of Edinburgh.

University of Cambridge Oriental Publications 60

Seeking Bāuls of Bengal

A series list is shown at the back of the book

Seeking Bāuls of Bengal

JEANNE OPENSHAW
University of Edinburgh

CAMBRIDGE
UNIVERSITY PRESS

PUBLISHED BY THE PRESS SYNDICATE OF THE UNIVERSITY OF CAMBRIDGE
The Pitt Building, Trumpington Street, Cambridge, United Kingdom

CAMBRIDGE UNIVERSITY PRESS
The Edinburgh Building, Cambridge CB2 2RU, UK
40 West 20th Street, New York, NY 10011-4211, USA
477 Williamstown Road, Port Melbourne, VIC 3207, Australia
Ruiz de Alarcón 13, 28014 Madrid, Spain
Dock House, The Waterfront, Cape Town 8001, South Africa

http://www.cambridge.org

First published 2002

Printed in the United Kingdom at the University Press, Cambridge

Typeface Times 10/12 pt. *System* LaTeX 2ε [TB]

A catalogue record for this book is available from the British Library

Library of Congress cataloguing in publication data

Openshaw, Jeanne.
Seeking Bāuls of Bengal / Jeanne Openshaw.
p. cm. – (University of Cambridge oriental publications, 60)
Includes bibliographical references and index.
ISBN 0 521 81125 2
1. Bauls – India. 2. Bauls – Bangladesh. I. University of Cambridge oriental publications, no. 60.
BL1284.84 .O74 2002
294.5′512 – dc21 2001052403

ISBN 0 521 81125 2 hardback

For my parents and sister

I have made the world my home
And my home the world,
I have made ‘others’ my own people,
And my own people ‘others’.

Ghar kainu bāhir
Bāhir kainu ghar
Par kainu āpan
Āpan kainu par

Caṇḍīdās

As long as you judge in terms of high and low you are deluded;
All are the same to one who knows reality . . .

Yābat ucca nic bicār
Kara tābat bhrānti tomār
Tattva jñāne sab ekākār . . .

Rāj Kṛṣṇa (Khyāpā)

CONTENTS

ILLUSTRATIONS

ACKNOWLEDGEMENTS

Many people, initiated and non-initiated, academic and non-academic, have assisted me in my work. My greatest debts are twofold: first to the followers of Rāj Khyāpā, and other friends and acquaintances among the *bartamān panthī*; secondly to Dr Śakti Nāth Jhā, Krishnanath College, Berhampore, West Bengal. I am also greatly indebted to my supervisor at the School of Oriental and African Studies, Dr Audrey Cantlie, for her constant support and advice during the long years of my work, as well as to Dr Christopher Pinney (University College, London) and Dr Julius Lipner (University of Cambridge), examiners of the doctoral dissertation on which this book is based, whose suggestions and encouragement have been invaluable. I should also like to thank Professor Rajat Ray (Presidency College, Calcutta), Professor C. A. Bayly (University of Cambridge), Dr Carol Salomon (University of Washington), Professor Veena Das (University of Columbia), Professor Dr Rahul Peter Das (University of Halle) and Professor Soumyendra Nath Mukherjee (University of Sydney) for their comments on this work, most of which I have endeavoured to incorporate. Apart from my official supervisors in India, Dr Surajit Sinha (CSSS, Calcutta) and Professor Ashin Dasgupta (National Library, Calcutta), others who offered comments, assistance and inspiration include Professor Richard Burghart, Professor A. Piatigorsky (SOAS), Professor Trevor Ling, Professor Debiprasad Chattopadhyaya, Dr Samita Sen (University of Calcutta), Dr Subho Basu (SOAS), Dr Ranjit Bhattacharya (Indian Anthropological Survey, Calcutta), Dr Kumkum Bhattacharya (Visva Bharati, Santiniketan), Dr Sutapa Bhattacharya (Visva Bharati, Santiniketan), Dr Martin Kämpchen, and Sri Pradip Bhattacharya IAS (Calcutta). I am grateful to artists Sri Kiron Sinha and Smt. Shyamali Khastgir for allowing me to reproduce their representations of 'Bāuls', and to the Rabindra Bharati Society who hold the original Abanindranath Tagore painting of Rabindranath as the 'Blind Bāul'. Thanks are also due to Crystal Webster, University of Edinburgh for her technical assistance.

I should like to express my gratitude to SOAS (London), ICSSR (Delhi), CSSS (Calcutta), and the National Library (Calcutta) and Rabindra Bhaban, Visva Bharati (Santiniketan) for providing me with facilities for my research, as well as to the Royal Anthropological Institute (London) and the University of London for financial assistance during my doctoral research. Thanks are also due to Clare Hall and Lucy Cavendish College, University of Cambridge, where I held the

Spalding Trust Visiting Fellowship in Comparative Religion, and the Alice Tong Sze Research Fellowship in the Humanities respectively during the writing of this book.

Portions of this book have been published earlier in: 'Rāj Kṛṣṇa: perspectives on the worlds of a little-known Bengali guru', in *Mind, body and society: life and mentality in colonial Bengal,* ed. Rajat Kanta Ray, 1995; 'The radicalism of Tagore and the "Bāuls" of Bengal', *South Asia Research*, 17.1, 1997; 'The web of deceit: challenges to Hindu and Muslim "orthodoxies" by "Bāuls" of Bengal', *Religion*, 27, 297–309, 1997; ' "Killing" the guru: anti-hierarchical tendencies of "Bāuls" of Bengal', *Contributions to Indian Sociology,* 32.1, 1998.

TRANSLITERATION

The standard system of transliteration (as exemplified by J. D. Anderson 1962) has been modified in the following ways: *anusvar* is transliterated *ṅ*, rather than *ṁ* or *ṃ*, to avoid such infelicities as Bāṁlādeś. This in turn has entailed a further modification: the 'n' transliterated *ṅ* by Anderson and others is here rendered *ń*: thus Śańkar, not Śaṅkar. In general, 'v/b' is written '*b*' when thus pronounced in Bengali, and '*v*' when not. However, on occasion Sanskritic '*v*' has been retained: thus 'Vaiṣṇava' (and 'Vaishnava') is found as well as 'Baiṣṇab'. In the case of some relatively familiar proper names, conventional spellings without diacritical marks have often been followed, for example, 'Vaishnava', and 'Tantric'. In general, place names are without diacritical marks. For inconsistencies in transliteration, I ask the reader's indulgence. Quotations from Rāj, Hem and other composers retain the spelling of the original. Where secondary sources are cited, the diacritical mark system (or lack of it) of these sources is reproduced.

Texts

Unless otherwise stated the translations of Bengali texts are my own. Song numbers follow the original handwritten manuscripts. (The numbers of Maṇi Gõsāi's songs are different in this book from those in my thesis and earlier articles. They are now numbered according to Maṇi's handwritten manuscript.)

ABBREVIATIONS

BBBG	*Baṅlār bāul o bāul gān* (Bāuls and Bāul Bengal) by Upendranāth Bhaṭṭācārya 1388 BS, first published in 1364 BS (1957–8 CE), Calcutta. References to *BBBG* are to the revised edition.
BBUS	*Bhāratābarṣīya upāsak sampradāy* (Religious sects of India) by Akṣay Kumār Datta, ed. Binay Ghoṣ, 1969.
BS	Bāṅgālā San (Bengali era). The difference between BS and CE is 593–94 years. Thus 1400 BS is 1993–94.
HYP	*Haṭha Yoga Pradīpikā*. The Bengali edition used here is Sarasvatī 1987.
PS	Police Station area (Bengali: *thānā*). Administrative units into which Districts are subdivided.
SBED	*Samsad Bengali English Dictionary.*

INTRODUCTION

> Who then are the Bauls? The word itself means 'mad'. When Bengalis use the term, they usually mean to indicate a type of mendicant religious singer who, dressed in tattered clothes deliberately made up of the garments of both Hindus and Muslims, wanders from village to village celebrating God in ecstatic songs, existing on whatever his listeners choose to give him. Although today he is possibly a householder . . . traditionally he has 'only the wind as his home'. His hair is long and his beard matted, and as he sings he accompanies himself on a one-stringed instrument . . .

Thus Edward C. Dimock Jr (1959:36), one of the few non-Bengali authorities on the subject, broaches the hazardous task of describing 'Bāuls', a category of person inhabiting the Bengali-speaking region of South Asia, that is West Bengal (India) and Bangladesh. As will become clear, authorities on Bāuls agree on very little, and several contradictory images persist. While the passage cited accurately reflects the perceptions of some Bengalis, virtually all Dimock's assertions would be contradicted by one or other specialist in this topic. Indeed one of the arguments of the present volume is that this lone male minstrel with 'only the wind as his home' is a relative newcomer in the history of 'Bāuls'.

It was during preliminary library research that the divergence in perceptions of Bāuls in the secondary sources first struck me.[1] Studies on 'Bāuls' have based themselves on two sources considered to be primary: first, persons (typically male) who call themselves or are called, with varying degrees of coincidence, '*bāul*'; second, and more usually, songs written down by non-'Bāuls' and published in various collections as 'Bāul songs' (*bāul-gān*).[2] Criteria for classification as Bāul songs are rarely if ever explicit. Some appear to be defining a Bāul song with reference to Bāuls (equally difficult to define). Thus whatever a 'Bāul' writes or sings is a Bāul song, a procedure which is sometimes reversed so that whoever

[1] By secondary sources are meant writings on Bāuls and/or Bāul songs by non-Bāuls. Although the category Bāul is contested and problematic, most people are clearly not Bāul in any sense.

[2] Another potential source, scarcely used until recently, is hand-written manuscripts (and occasionally printed versions of these). For such manuscripts, see, for example, Āhamad Śarīph on manuscripts collected by his father, Ābdul Karim. M. M. Bose (1930) also based his work on manuscripts, but classified his subject as the 'post-Caitanya Sahajiā cult'.

composes Bāul songs is a Bāul. For others, '*bāul*' is reduced to a form, a style of song, or an idiom, so that the same person may compose in various styles, of which '*bāul*' is only one.

From their general absence, it would seem that details of the collection of such songs, and indeed their context as a whole, are considered irrelevant by the authors of studies on Bāuls. Despite, or perhaps because of, the inevitable transformation they suffer in being transcribed from usually oral sources and put in collections, the songs are seen as things in themselves, and are, in the presentation, severed from their origins. As their source is obliterated they become a source in themselves. In such studies, most of the knowledge claimed concerning those called *bāul* is in fact derived from these collections of songs, which can be used selectively to support a wide variety of theories for several reasons: first, their sheer volume (amounting to several thousand songs); secondly, their heterogeneity – including a veritable bricolage of terminology, Sufi, Tantric, Vaishnava and so on; thirdly, the latitude afforded the interpreter by the assumption of 'intentional' (coded) language (*sandhā-bhāṣā*) as a feature of Bāul songs.

Both these sources, Bāuls and Bāul songs, tend to be seen as solid and unambiguous by the authors of such studies. They are also thought to provide information about the same 'thing', due in part to the assumption that a word (*bāul*) necessarily corresponds to some clear-cut phenomenon, dubbed 'Baulism' by some (e.g. Ashraf Siddiqui 1976). This reification, the assumption that there is something to be discovered, inevitably means that the paths by which the secondary sources approach this 'thing' become irrelevant. There is a continual presentation of views as fact – a rapid descent into stereotype in which assertions are made about 'Baulism', 'the (typical) Bāul', 'Bāul religion' etc. As will be clear by now, the word *bāul* has functioned as both noun and adjective, sometimes ambiguously or simultaneously, especially in Bengali, where articles are attenuated, and no distinction is made in writing between upper and lower case. It is not without significance that the adjectival dimensions are more in evidence in Bengali, especially rural, less Anglicised usage.[3] Reification is related to a wider phenomenon, the essentialising of the term Bāul. While everyone, including those called Bāul, tends to essentialise – in the sense of assuming that the word *bāul* has *some* essential meaning, even if this is obscure – those calling themselves *bāul* would usually reject the originary essentialism of the secondary sources discussed in chapter 2.

In view of all this, it is hardly surprising that several differing images of Bāuls are found in the secondary sources. Recent perceptions may be broadly divided into two categories: first, Bāuls as a class of heterodox mystics in eternal pursuit of the 'Man of the Heart', or the 'unknown bird' within, Rabindranath Tagore and

[3] For example, a Bengali phrase (used in this case by a local would-be singer): '*Āmi bāul haye thākba*' should be translated adjectivally as 'I shall be *bāul*', but is almost invariably translated as 'I shall be **a** Bāul'. Most English-language sources speak of 'the Bauls'. In some cases I have omitted the definite article and the upper-case 'B', in order to suggest the adjectival possibilities of the word *bāul*. For aesthetic reasons, the word Bāul does not appear within inverted commas in this book, although they should always be understood. The same is true of terms such as 'Hindu' and 'Tantric'.

K. Sen being the chief exponents of this approach. Second, Bāuls as a *sampradāy* (tradition), or even sect, entry to which requires initiation, and which consists of practitioners of arcane 'sexo-yogic' rites. (This is argued with a negative gloss by A. K. Datta, and more empathetically by Upendranāth Bhaṭṭācārya, for example.) To these may be added: Bāuls as disreputable, low-class entertainers (as related in the writing of J. N. Bhattacharya, for example), an image which, at any rate among scholars, has been superseded by the more elevated one of Bāuls as performing artists of consummate skill (e.g. Majumdar and Roberge 1979). Related to this is an image derived from 'the West', that is, Bāuls as Bengali hippies. This is familiar to anthropologists from a chapter in V. W. Turner's *The ritual process: structure and anti-structure*, called 'Bob Dylan and the Bauls', in which music and itinerancy are emphasised, Turner concluding that 'this is the authentic voice of spontaneous communitas' (1969:165–6). Finally there is the divergence of views dependent on situating Bāuls against a Hindu or Muslim background, thus creating a fundamentally Hindu or Muslim identity, whether or not this is then considered to 'spill over' to include the other community.

The significance of a study of Bāuls

What is the significance of a study of Bāuls? After all, however they are defined, people called Bāul comprise only a small fraction of the populations of greater Bengal (West Bengal and Bangladesh) (see chapter 4). As already mentioned, Bāuls are primarily known to others through their often beautiful and enigmatic songs, and it is these that, especially from the end of the nineteenth century, have given them an influence far wider than their numbers would suggest. Since that time, Bāul songs, and notions of what it is to be Bāul, have become increasingly important to urbanised, educated Bengalis, and more recently to Euro-Americans. In the process, Bāuls assumed the guise of bearers of an authentic indigenous heritage, albeit construed in startlingly different ways, as Bengali, Indian, Hindu, Muslim, materialist or secular. The emergence of these perceptions and the concomitant rise of a class of semi-professional Bāul performers so familiar in Bengal today is dealt with in the first part of this book. Nowadays, as national and international representatives of South Asian folk culture or indigenous spirituality, the iconic status of Bāuls is firmly established.

Of no less significance to students of Bengali religion, culture and history is another less conspicuous class of people called Bāul. These are initiates into esoteric practice who, although they know and sometimes sing songs, do not depend on music (and patrons) for their livelihood. My anthropological fieldwork with such Bāuls constitutes the core of this book. Nor can it be said that such Bāuls are only of relevance to Bengali studies within the field of Indology. A study of Bāuls is clearly important in the wider contexts of South Asian Buddhist, Tantric, Vaishnava, Nath, Sufi, Fakir and Siddha traditions. Parallels with the north-Indian Sant movement, related to both Hindu and Islamic traditions, and the Nath tradition have frequently been drawn (K. Sen *c.* 1935, *BBBG*, etc.). Most scholars are of the view that Bāuls form part of pan-Indian 'yogic', 'tantric', 'devotional' or 'mystical' movements. These connections have been discussed elsewhere and will be briefly considered in Part I in connection with secondary sources on Bāuls. Here a cursory consideration of one such parallel, with Bengali Tantra, is given.

Although Bāuls are generally concerned to differentiate themselves from Tantrics, parallels will immediately strike the reader, especially in the field of esoteric practice, and attitudes to the material world and the female. Bāul divinisation of the human being, an implicit characteristic in many areas of Hinduism (Fuller 1992: 72ff.), finds unambiguous expression in Tantra (Denton 1991). One of the more radical inferences of the present volume, concerning notions of the completeness or autonomy, and therefore superiority, of women, is not without echoes in Tantric traditions (Gupta 1991: 207–8). Indeed Bāuls are often identified with Vaishnava Tantra, an association which obscures the greater radicalism of many called Bāul. Unlike Shaiva and Shakta Tantrics, those called Bāul may be recruited from Muslim as well as Hindu communities. They tend to reject the orthopraxies and orthodoxies of both religious traditions, including the worship of images and transcendent deities, the authority of scripture and indeed any other knowledge which is not one's own.

The significance of a study of Bāuls is no longer confined to the South Asian context. Recent years have witnessed an immense expansion of the Bāul role as representative of South Asian spirituality and folk culture. Bāul musicians regularly take part in cultural export drives such as the government sponsored Festival of India, and participate in a range of workshops, concerts and other inter-cultural encounters centring on music, dance, poetry, drama, yoga and meditation (not to speak of marijuana and sex). The rapid absorption of the famed 'Bāul emperor', Pūrna Dās, into popular American culture – he features on the front cover of one of Bob Dylan's albums (Ganguly and Ginsberg 1994) – as well as Ginsberg's own espousal of the Bāul song in his poetry, marks their apotheosis as global hippies.

Outline of contents

The first section of this book is concerned with the treatment of Bāuls by scholars, writers and other authorities, such as contributors to the Census of India. The evolution of the various images of Bāuls, outlined above, is initially considered from an historical point of view. This is followed by a brief discussion of the ways in which differing identities of Bāuls are constructed by their proponents in the secondary sources, for example, through a search for the ancestry and birth of 'the Bāuls', and by means of selection of themes derived from Bāul songs. A subsidiary aim of this part of the book is to introduce the reader to the materials at issue in Bāul studies.

After an initial period of library research, I began fieldwork in West Bengal, India. People called Bāul had already attracted my attention during a previous research project, with devotees of the Bengali goddess Kālī. Perhaps as someone with no firm roots herself, I felt I could identify with the liminality of the

Bāuls of my acquaintance, their suspicion of boundaries and their fascination with transcending them. Was it really possible, I wondered, to realise 'roots in the void'?[4] Not untypically, initial fieldwork was characterised by confusion. It soon became apparent that one of my few advantages was that, unlike almost every Bengali I met (and not a few foreigners), at least I recognised my ignorance of what it is to be *bāul*. The bulk of my anthropological fieldwork with people called Bāul was conducted from 1983 to 1990. It covered five central districts of West Bengal and eventually focused on the descendants by initiation of Rāj Khyāpā (1869–1946 CE), most of whom inhabit areas of central West Bengal adjacent to the Bangladesh border. Originally from an upper-caste, educated background, Rāj had left householder life after a series of devastating personal losses. After some years wandering India as a renouncer (*sannyāsī*), he settled down in central Bengal, where he made disciples. Among local non-initiates, Rāj is remembered for his scandalous love affair and elopement with a lower-caste woman, who not only was married with young children, but was also probably his disciple. In view of the quality of Rāj's writings, which include many songs, as well as a verse autobiography, it seems reasonable to attribute his past obscurity to this scandal and his adamant refusal to compromise with convention. The reason for my selection of the 'lineage' of Rāj Khyāpā as the focus of fieldwork was its elaboration of and emphasis on elements which are present but relatively unstressed in other lineages of the area. Apart from an unusually strident denunciation of divisions between person and person in favour of the human being (*mānuṣ*), another distinctive feature was the high value conferred by their songwriters (probably all men) on 'woman' (and even particular women), as guru and epitome of the human being.

Whereas the first section deals with representation of Bāuls in the secondary sources, the rest of the book is based almost entirely on primary sources, that is, ethnographic and manuscript materials. After providing a brief account of the fieldwork areas, and the process of fieldwork, Part II introduces various kinds of people called Bāul either by themselves or by others. Unsurprisingly perhaps, their opinions concerning what it is to be *bāul* reveal almost as much diversity as do the secondary sources. It soon seemed evident that the term Bāul is used in such radically different ways in different areas and by different people as to be of little use from an analytical point of view.

From Part III onwards use of the word *bāul* is largely abandoned, and another term (*bartamān*) is introduced into the discussion, one with which those such as Rāj and his followers among others would more readily identify as their 'path'. They say they are in *bartamān*, from which the short-hand term *bartamān-panthī*, that is, 'followers of *bartamān*' is derived. The connotations of this term will be discussed more fully in chapters 4 and 8. Here suffice it to say that the category *bartamān* is defined in opposition to another, *anumān*, which connotes, among other things, 'orthodoxy', in the sense of ideas and practices legitimised by reference to authorised scripture (Hindu or Muslim). These are rejected as

[4] The title of a book on Bāuls by A. Dasgupta and M. A. Dasgupta (1977).

based on 'hearsay' or 'conjecture' (standard meanings of the word *anumān*) by *bartamān-panthīs*. *Bartamān-panthīs* claim to depend instead on the 'existent' or 'here and now' (*bartamān*), by which is meant, among other things, what can be ascertained through one's senses and what is based on one's own knowledge and judgement rather than that of others. Such oppositional tendencies have elicited the interest of historians of the Subaltern Studies school. Their contribution to the subject of Bāuls and other 'minor religious sects' is considered in the conclusion.

If one were to take the widest definition of Bauls, that is, all those called Bāul by themselves or others, then the subjects of my research (and even more those who comprised its final focus, that is Rāj and his followers) obviously constitute a narrower category than what is perhaps best viewed as a shifting and often contradictory collocation of categories, all called Bāul. If nothing useful can be said, especially at this stage, about the term Bāul, can any preliminary generalisations be made about the subjects of my focused research? One crucial characteristic is that the latter are not born *bartamān-panthī*, but are recruited as adults from the wider society. Such structures as are invoked derive from guru–disciple rather than father–son ('blood') lineages. Some are householders, others renouncers, and most attempt to evade, transcend or mediate between such distinctions with varying degrees of success. Disciples recruit from Hindu and Muslim communities. Some lineages are mixed, with gurus of Hindu origin taking Muslim disciples and vice versa (a practice found in the Rāj Khyāpā lineage), although this pattern is increasingly under strain from Hindu–Muslim 'communal' polarisation in South Asia. While technically anyone may follow the path of *bartamān*, and wealthy or (usually declassed) upper-caste people, especially men, are found in their ranks, in practice this is largely a movement of the rural poor. There are necessarily as many women as men, for esoteric practice involves a partner of the opposite sex. These body-focused, Tantric practices are central in the lives of *bartamān-panthīs*. Their language (including songs), ideas and practices (*sādhanā*) are in many contexts subversive of conventional structures and distinctions. For this and other reasons, they are often vilified and even persecuted (see Jhā and Ghaṭak 1997 for a detailed account of this; also Isherwood 1990).

One factor hindering analysis of those called Bāul was the virtual absence of detailed, contextual studies. It was partly to rectify this situation that I concentrated my fieldwork on one particular lineage, that of Rāj Khyāpā. In time it was possible to supplement synchronic views with diachronic perspectives of the lineage, drawn from oral historical and manuscript materials. It is regrettable that, owing to problems of length, aspects of this material dealing with the lives of Rāj and his immediate followers will have to be considered in a separate volume. In the present work, a summary of the autobiography of Rāj Khyāpā has been included. Rāj and his followers are then situated in the context of the scholarly and indigenous categories of householder versus renouncer. Attitudes to the structures (of caste, guru lineages etc.) which inform these two realms are also considered. Whereas other scholars have rightly emphasised the primacy of the guru, an additional dimension is highlighted in this book, namely the ambivalence towards the male institutional guru, and the undermining of his authority in a variety of ways. In this connection, the *bartamān-panthī* view of womanhood as an ideal is also discussed, as well as the ways in which the practical and theoretical importance conferred on women by them tend to destabilise the patrilineally derived structures of Hindu and Muslim (and renouncer) communities. Such distinctions between person and person are subverted by a focus on the human being (*mānuṣ*), interpreted either generically, or in terms of the perfected human being. In Part IV, affective and ideological dimensions are explored. It is argued that those such as Rāj make an association between *hiṅsā* (envy, discrimination) and the structures of both householder and renouncer worlds on the one hand, and love (*prem*) and the absence or transcendence of such structures on the other. The important concept of the human being is once again taken up here, as is the identification of woman/women with love and non-discrimination or 'non-dualism' (*advaita*). This in turn connects in interesting ways with practices involving male and female partners, as well as the notorious 'four moons' practices. Esoteric practice (*sādhanā*) and talking about such practice are central concerns of those such as Rāj and his followers. Possible connections between notions of completeness (or autonomy) and women, and the idea that women epitomise the human being are explored. These topics are considered in Part V.

Method

Within social anthropology and related disciplines, criticism of the antiquated notion of a bounded Subject (the anthropologist) analysing a bounded group of Others has been largely directed against the latter part of the equation, leaving the autonomous, individuated researcher intact. It is paradoxical that, in the context of academic preoccupations with the decentring of the sovereign subject, the once transparent academic researcher has assumed an unassailable and monolithic presence, solipsistically engulfing an entire world of his or her creation. As Hobart (1990) has pointed out, in demonstrating how we distort the Other, even the textual criticism of Clifford and others ultimately privileges the anthropologist and Western academic cultures at the expense of the supposed subjects of research. As a result 'the Other' becomes more remote than ever.

The assumption of an encapsulated, virtually impervious researcher reflects a biological or psychological essentialism, according to which an individual's genetic inheritance or early conditioning are determinant, and to a corresponding exaggeration (in my view) of the power of the individual fieldworker to sail intact through the vagaries, bewitchments and ruptures of fieldwork. How is it, I wonder, that some anthropologists present themselves as a constant before, during and after their fieldwork? Is it attributable to culture – to a consciousness of self as 'individual' rather than 'dividual' (Marriott, Strathern) – or to personality or gender? Is it a result of a different theoretical climate in the time when people had the luxury of long-term fieldwork, and to the fact that researchers now are able to spend so little time in the field? Is it connected with that illusion of mastery required to write up one's material in an academic style? Whatever the reason, the persisting assumption that academic writing issues from a single unwavering view-point which somehow encompasses all others has certainly been a source of personal strain.

In recent years considerable attention has been paid to the inescapable subjectivity of anthropological fieldwork and writing. The ethnographer is expected to include personal detail in an attempt to situate the fieldwork and ethnography. This clearly constitutes an advance on a situation where the fieldworker or writer's training (or some other assumed superiority) was considered to endow the capacity for immaculate perception, and where inevitable biases masqueraded as the truth. However, to state some personal information at best solves little while pretending to solve much, and at worst introduces a new kind of essentialism into the situation.

It may be thought that my presence as a researcher and fieldworker is not sufficiently salient in this book. Several factors may account for this, mostly deriving from the nature and length of my fieldwork. At the beginning of fieldwork the inter-relation between researcher and 'informants' is paramount, and writing after a short period in the field is therefore conducive to self-representation and related theories. Unfortunately a situation deriving from the compulsions of contemporary academic life also involves an implicit assumption of the easy penetrability (or total impenetrability and therefore irrelevance) of 'other' cultures. My own research simply passed the point where this particular interface was paramount. I stayed on in India for a good number of years, often living and travelling with the people I worked with. In time my research expanded to include their manuscripts – I was ignorant even of the existence of these at the beginning of the work. Much of the thesis on which this book is based was written in Bengal, where the chasm between living and writing seemed less marked than in Britain.

Throughout my work, and despite the problems inherent in such an approach, I have endeavoured 'to know the people in their own image' (A. Sen 1987:235). For that reason, my approach has been informed by the ideas and theories of my research subjects. Sometimes this operated in a negative fashion. For example, it would have been more problematic to eschew the essentialist obsession with origins which dominates Bāul studies were it not for the prevalent rejection of such procedures by those I worked with. Similarly, what might be thought my cavalier treatment of structures elaborated by Indological scholars and others would be less justified were it not for the fact that generally these are either not known or are denied validity by the subjects of my research.

More positively, the influence of those I worked with altered the direction of the research. Although I knew something of esoteric Bāul practices before beginning fieldwork, my intention was to avoid this potentially exoticising topic. After all, an important initial aim of the research was to challenge another kind of exoticisation, the notion of the Bāul as epitome of the Spiritual East. At that point, my interest lay rather in Bāul attempts to renounce distinctions of caste, religious community etc., and the relation of this endeavour to perceptions of Bāuls as mad. As work progressed, however, *bartamān-panthīs* persuaded me of the centrality of esoteric practice. Omission of this crucial subject surely amounted to the imposition of an external agenda, and a gross distortion of the material. Not only that, in a more general way, my own monomania (D. Chakrabarty 2000:275) became apparent. The focus of research shifted to an exploration of the links which I now discerned between such practices and social radicalism. One of the intentions of this volume is to delineate some of the connections between social radicalism and the personal cultivation of body, mind and emotions, especially in terms of love.

It has not been my purpose to present those called Bāul through a seamless narrative, but rather to bring different perspectives to bear on the varied types of material at issue. The attempt in Part 1 to lay bare the differing paths by which the subject has been approached by scholars and writers is followed by a parallel endeavour to evoke, at least in part, the paths travelled by myself on the one hand, and some of those called Bāul on the other. In this respect, I would distance myself from the ethnosociological project, which also purports to 'know the people in their own image'. In his recent reformulation of this creative and inspiring enterprise, entitled *India through Hindu categories*, Marriott concedes that:

> The model . . . is undoubtedly biassed in the direction of its sources, which are mostly Hindu, more north Indian than southern, more learned than popular, more of *sāṁkhya-yoga* than of any other *darśana*, more *āyur-vedic* than astrological, more orthodox than devotional, more high caste than low, and more male than female. (1990:32)

This has not prevented Marriott from envisaging a 'Hindu world' within which 'varied people' operate (1990: xiii), a timeless realm comprehensively mapped from the superior vantage point of the ethnosociologist. Although a strength of the model is its allowance for varied perspectives (1990: xiii), the possibility that there may not be a niche for every eventuality is not in general entertained. In the final analysis, authority is denied South Asians and instead vested in the master-designer, the ethnosociologist. In the present volume, an overarching panorama viewed and mapped from a superior stance is not assumed. Instead, pathways are temporarily illumined as one proceeds. A parallel may be drawn with the fluid rhetorical patterns deployed with such skill and artistry by many so-called Bāuls. These combine conventional, even clichéd sequences with new and unexpected combinations of elements and thus meanings. In emphasising the creativity of those called Bāul, any attempt to define or enclose them in the analyses presented here has been renounced. Of course I am aware that my position as author militates against this aim.

Grand schemes such as ethnosociology are notoriously unconvincing at the periphery, and the material concerning Bāuls and *bartamān-panthīs*, liminal in relation to householder and renouncer culture, as well as to 'Hinduism' and 'Islam,' is of particular significance in challenging the equation drawn between Hindu and South Asian culture by ethnosociologists and others. It also calls into question the imposition of mutually exclusive and exhaustive religious categories, such as Hinduism and Islam, whether it be on individuals, groups or, in its crudest manifestation, geographical areas, on the pattern of nation states. While it is demonstrably possible to view Bāuls through the prism of Hinduism or Islam, both these approaches involve neglect of a radicalism which, however compromised, especially in these days of resurgent 'communalism' in India, most certainly merits representation.

The terms 'syncretism' and 'eclecticism' are often used in connection with Bāul studies. These notions entail a privileging of the structures of the traditions from which such syncretism or eclecticism is considered to draw, Hinduism and Islam, for example. Such traditions are viewed as coherent structures in contrast to a collection of unstructured contents resulting from various kinds of bricolage. Other assumptions may follow from this: that the perpetrators of and participants in such 'cults' (as Bauls are often called) lack rigour or display confusion. Their ideas and practices are often seen as the result of accident rather than design, of lack of understanding rather than different understanding. They are seen as passive and misled consumers, rather than producers of culture (see Chartier 1984:234). They are, in fashionable words, deprived of agency. Yet possibly there is as much, or as little system in thinking and practice here as in the ostensibly more systematised entities from which they are considered to derive. As Romila Thapar has pointed out, the strength of a tradition lies first in its adaptability rather than its rigidity, but secondly and equally in the effectiveness with which the traces of this strategy are subsequently covered over by appeals to tradition. In the case of many called Bāul, such traces are largely left uncovered, partly because of the lack of stable group formation and authority structures, partly because of a suspicion of system itself. Whether conceived of as operating synchronically or diachronically (see below), system and structure are often seen as a trap, or as disempowering in other ways. A positive valuation of eclecticism is found, for example, in the importance conferred on the experience of the living human being and whatever suits her or him, rather than tradition. One has only to see a devotee, or even a researcher of literalist leanings, substantialise certain Bāul notions, and then to trace the fate of that substantialisation, to understand the truism that system, in the sense of the privileging of certain connecting paths over others, is primarily a matter of prestige and power. As Chartier says: 'We must replace the study of cultural sets that were considered as socially pure with another point of view that recognizes each cultural form as a mixture, whose constituent elements meld together indissolubly' (1984:233). Indeed, where Bāuls and *bartamān-panthīs* are concerned, the question of who appropriates from whom can be far from unproblematic.

Whereas scholars may see Bāuls as passive and uncomprehending recipients of elements of 'great traditions', the argument here is that they are often engaged in an active and intentional appropriation of elements, whether at the level of terminology, ideas or practice. Various kinds of appropriation are combined with oppositional precipitates from the orthodoxies and orthopraxies against which those in *bartamān* to some extent define themselves, in an array of subversions, transformations and hybridisations. Parallels may be drawn here between Bāuls and Gypsies (Okely 1983:77). This book aims to bring out the creative appropriation and adaptation of contents and structures (Chartier 1984). O'Hanlon emphasises in her critique of the subaltern studies project, 'the creative practice of the subaltern ...

[the] ability to appropriate and mould cultural material of almost any provenance to his own purposes and to discard those . . . which no longer serve them' (1988:197).

In fact, where the present subject is concerned, another more generous approach to syncretism is also found among scholars: that Bāuls equate Hindu and Islamic (usually Sufi) contents, from the superior perspective of a pan-Indian mysticism. While this kind of positive unifying procedure – reminiscent of the Hindu notion that all paths lead to the same goal – is indeed found in 'Bāul songs', there is also a more radical negative trend, rarely presented in studies on Bāuls. In the latter, the contiguity of two systems (Hindu and Islamic) arguably operates to produce a critique of both. While in the first case both systems are endorsed, here they are identified with each other in order to be collectively rejected. I would contend that the assimilation of syncretic or eclectic tendencies with Dumont's characterisation of Hinduism as inclusive and hierarchising has obscured this other more radical tendency: that of rejection and equalising; more specifically, identifying and rejecting Hindu and Muslim orthopraxy and orthodoxy, and equating all as human beings (*mānuṣ*).

The famed patchwork garment of the iconic Bāul is often taken to symbolise syncretistic, eclectic and anti-structural tendencies (e.g. Turner 1969). In practice it comes in a variety of forms, from the poor 'tatters' referred to by Dimock, to the immaculately tailored patchwork coat, with strategically incorporated 'Bāul symbols' (the fish, the bird, the one-stringed lute and so on), increasingly worn by semi-professional Bāul singers. A very different kind of garment was put together by some of Rāj's followers, as part of a practice called *behāl-sādhanā*, often associated with Fakirs in Bengal. According to this, every day for twelve years the disciple stitches a new patch of cloth on to an original tunic provided by the guru. The disciple wears only this increasingly colossal garment throughout the entire period. When finally it is taken off, it is never worn again. As with syncretism, the patchwork garment may mean many things.

While I trust that this book will be of interest to Indologists and historians of South Asia, this is a work primarily grounded in anthropological fieldwork. Although historical sources for Bāuls are briefly considered in the first section, colleagues in other disciplines may object to the fact that to some extent I approach the various histories of Bāuls as constructions, without arbitrating between them. The decision to incorporate this material in the first place was partly in order to present the reader with some of the material at issue on Bāuls. As will be argued in chapter 2, historical materials are used to construct a variety of often contradictory identities for Bāuls, at times for ideological reasons. Given limitations of space and my own specialism, it seemed preferable to focus on this neglected aspect. Also, as mentioned above, concern with the origins or even history of Bāuls is partly avoided because of the fierce rejection of such procedures by many of my research subjects, albeit not in all contexts.

One crucial characteristic of most *bartamān-panthīs* (and Bāuls) is that they rarely define themselves in terms of personal or group origins. First, they are initiated as a couple (or less usually as an individual) into a new life at some point in adulthood. The resulting relativisation of birth group has been remarked on in connection with renouncers by Dumont (1960). It will be argued here that many of those in *bartamān* go one step further than this, in their attempt to renounce renunciation. Just as Hinduism and Islam are relativised by being equated, so many of those I worked with identify and reject the structures (primarily of caste and religion) of both householder and renouncer life. All these are dismissed as products of discrimination (*hiṅsā*), and denied in favour of the human being.

People called Bāul thus inhabit or pass through more social contexts than others of their socio-economic class. Associated with this liminality is a great sophistication about the perils of identity, and how 'history' creates or shores up these allegedly false concepts. What the individual knows from his/her own experience becomes paramount, everything else being suspect as 'hearsay' (*anumān*). Especially during fieldwork, a tendency to view a preoccupation with the past and history as bleeding the present (*bartamān*) of its significance became apparent. 'History' is thus classifiable as *anumān* (conjecture, inference, or, more significantly in the present context, others' knowledge, as opposed to one's own). It is tantamount to dead men's leftovers. An intent to claim agency and gain autonomy, to escape the definition of others, thus defining (or refraining from defining) oneself, is a characteristic of many different kinds of people called Bāul. This evasion of definition relates to the notion of 'Bāul' as mad. In this connection a quote from the work of K. Sen is of interest. Sen reports 'a Bāul' mocking the habit of accumulating texts and so on from the past: 'Are we dogs, that we should lick up these leftovers? As long as words are necessary, new words will arise. They will never be wanting. But through lack of faith human beings store up plates of leftovers like dogs. Even a dog discards a plate of leftovers in time. But human beings are more lowly. They take pride in the antiquity of this or that leftover' (K. Sen 1993:67).[5]

In general, the present work therefore aims to reflect as far as possible the categories and perceptions (including, by the criteria of certain 'high' traditions, 'misperceptions') of those with whom I worked. According to one reading, the fluctuating structures and identities discernible during fieldwork indicate intermediate, and equally fluctuating, positions between different (inferred) traditions. Had this book been written at an earlier period of scholarship, I should probably have felt obliged to resolve the contradictions in the material (thus substantialising the term Bāul in one way or another), but, having agonised over the appropriateness or otherwise of judging people by the standards of traditions of which they are either unaware or opposed to, it seemed to me that this would constitute a distortion. As has been observed, the paradigm of centre versus margins itself tends to hierarchise (Kumar 1994:10). Moreover, as stated above, emphasis on any one structure is necessarily exclusive of others. An emphasis on creativity and multiplicity forestalls or sabotages the crystallisation of any one structure. Not only this, as

[5] My translation. Even if this account is embroidered or apocryphal, it does ring true for many of those called Bāul. There are contrary tendencies, but these are relatively unstressed, at least in the people I worked with. This will be discussed later.

will be argued in Part II, there is a sense in which the more any one structure is emphasised, the more other identities tend to override being Bāul. In consonance with the generally emic orientation of this work, it should be pointed out that, at least after chapter 4, the use of terms such as 'yoga', 'tantra' etc., generally reflects the common perceptions of these systems I found in the villages, held by 'folk' practitioners and non-initiates alike, rather than the yoga and tantra of the texts and of scholarship based on these.

As stated above, all this is not to deny strong resemblances between movements categorised by scholars and others as Tantra (Buddhist and Hindu), Sahajīyā (Buddhist and Vaishnava), Lokāyata (Materialist), Sufi, Nāth, Siddha or Sant on the one hand and the terminology, ideas and practices of many of those called Bāul. It is simply to assert that the use of these conventional categories to structure historically Bāul contents not only detracts from and renders derivative the structuring and anti-structuring practices of Bāuls, it also necessarily privileges certain traditional lineages over others, an ideological exclusivity which is, I would contend, seriously at odds with the general position of my research subjects.

Lest it be thought from all this that those in *bartamān* are thoroughgoing postmodernists, it should be pointed out that in many contexts theirs is a metaphysics of presence. While opposing an historically based or originary essentialism, notions of 'non-dual' substance are affirmed, especially in the context of refuting distinctions between person and person. Substance or matter (*bastu*) – not necessarily exclusive of subtle aspects such as mind, emotion and consciousness – is favourably contrasted to names and words (*nām*). Whereas the latter may connote scripture, others' knowledge (as opposed to one's own) and even deception, *bastu* is identifiable with *rajaḥ-bīj*, the generative essences of male and female, as well as with the 'I' (*āmi*). This last notion, familiar from Hindu philosophy, is elaborated by some *bartamān-panthīs* as an anti-structural device to subvert divisions among human kind. Along with more individualistic interpretations of the 'I' (involving actual or potential difference as an individual), it is crucial for notions of agency.

Much has been written on the tension between the political project of 'restoring agency' to the 'subaltern' (including women) through writing, and the avowed aim of decentring the Enlightenment subject, along with notions of humanism, agency and autonomy (O'Hanlon 1988; O'Hanlon and Washbrook 1992:150ff.; Ahmad 1992:100, 104). The suspicion of such notions relates to the presentation as universal truths of constructions produced in specific historical and geographical contexts with unacknowledged biases of class, gender, race and so on. This sleight of hand has contributed to the effectiveness of such discourse in marginalising and subordinating Others: subalterns, women, Orientals, the Third World, and so on. The self-determining subject-agent of Western liberal humanism, with its covert Euro-American, upper-class, male bias, has historically been associated with naive voluntarism. Such a philosophy justifies the status quo by assigning responsibility to individuals for their destinies, and all too easily leads to a devaluation or even dehumanisation of non-whites, women and the lower classes. However, the

Foucauldian reaction to this philosophy, which in its extreme form suggests totalising and inescapable systems of power, is equally paralysing from the political point of view. Both outlooks are in effect deeply conservative and have thus been argued to deprive 'others' of agency.

Agency is clearly a matter of concern to those in *bartamān*. Not only do they endeavour to evade and challenge spheres of discourse which marginalise them; they are also intent to claim and develop an agency which they consider every human being to possess. However, they would generally be bemused at the idea that their agency required restoration, or that they needed to be represented by anyone else. Bāuls and *bartamān-panthīs* generally display great skill in song and speech, not only in their mother tongue, Bengali, but also in various kinds of ever-evolving coded Bengali, often restructuring, reinterpreting and appropriating in various ways the speech of the dominant cultures, Hindu and Muslim. If they are unclear in their speech and writing, it is intentional. After working with Tantrics, a few of whom are as likely to throw missiles as words at the hapless researcher, it was a great relief to work with people for whom talking about esoteric practice is second only in importance to practice itself. Apart from the mastery of rhetorical skills, agency, in the sense of the power to mobilise body, mind and emotion to transform one's own destiny is strongly asserted. From a more pessimistic perspective, I was inspired but occasionally appalled at the sheer scale of ambition of those I worked with. Esoteric practice restores to the individual or couple the power to transform their destiny in desirable ways, enabling them eventually to attain perfection, however that is conceived. In comparison with all this, paltry endeavours such as the writing of this book were rightly considered of little import. In their attitudes to my research, the knowledge that others have much to learn from a *bartamān* approach vied with a caution born of a history of opposition and persecution. With the exception of a few individuals who for different reasons seek publicity (two have written their own books in Bengali), names of living *bartamān-panthīs* and some place names have been disguised in this book.

Agency is considered by *bartamān-panthīs* to reside primarily in the two mouths possessed by all human beings, the upper and the lower (the genitals). While men are said to be more competent in speech (and most gurus are male), women are more powerful in the lower mouth. So far so familiar, except that in most contexts words are less highly valued than substance, the preserve of the lower mouth. A primary aim of male practitioners is to acquire female substance and qualities. Moreover the notion prevails that esoteric practice is oriented to the male, not because of his strength, but because of his weakness. As in many communities, women are variously construed by male *bartamān-panthīs* in terms of shifting combinations of (male) 'self' and 'other'. As a result there are more contradictions in notions of womanhood than in those of manhood. Alongside more conventional views of women are the following: that women are the epitome of the human being; that it is women not men who are naturally complete and autonomous; that women are agents by nature, whereas men are merely potential agents.

The fieldwork on which this book is based was conducted with both women and men called Bāul. In mixed company, it was usually, although by no means always, men, with their confidence in their developed upper mouth, who dominated conversation. I talked exclusively with women when alone with them, mainly at night, when some took the opportunity to instruct me in esoteric practice. The songs and manuscripts used here were usually written by and for men.[6] Whether such materials concern theory, esoteric practice or the discriminatory structures of social life, the general view of their authors is that men, with their divisive we–they categories, have much to learn from women, who epitomise love.

The myth of the Spiritual East, of which the iconic, etherealised Bāul at the beginning of this introduction constitutes a major incarnation, is rarely evaluated in relation to its presumed indigenous base. Part I of this book concerns what might over-simplistically be judged a contribution to, or creative appropriation of the myth by sections of the Bengali élite. However, the major focus of the present work is the immensely varied and largely rural mass of musicians, initiates, adepts and gurus, whose cultural forebears provided a focus for this particular version of the myth. Readers less interested in the background material and élite perceptions of Bāuls may wish to begin the book from Part II. My aim in these subsequent sections is to highlight elements that were eventually masked by the overweaning figure of the iconic spiritualised Bāul. I thus hope to contribute to scholarly work which demonstrates the continuing influence of notions of the Spiritual East on our understanding of South Asia. Euro-American based scholars and élite South Asians have all too often acquiesced in the idea that values such as humanism and equality, including gender equality, were introduced into South Asia by 'the West', thus encouraging the rejection of such values as foreign by chauvinist and fundamentalist elements in South Asia. The material on Bāuls supports the notion that humanism,[7] non-discrimination between person and person and the high valuation of women also have indigenous roots, even if the triumph of the image of the lone, wandering Bāul, indifferent to worldly concerns (*udāsīn*), has at times obscured such values.

[6] At times, song 'signatures' comprise the names of a man and woman, although the name of the woman tends to be concealed, for outsiders, through masculinisation or through inclusion as a suffix of the man's name. For example, many songs in Rāj's hand have as their idiograph 'Rāj–Rājeśvar', Rājeśvar being a male name given to his female partner. For insiders at least, such songs clearly acknowledge the contribution of a female partner.

[7] The connotations of this term as used by Bāuls will become clearer in the course of the text.

I

Background: literature on Bāuls and Bāul songs

1

What's in a name? The advent of 'the Bāul'

In this chapter[1] the evolution of different perceptions of Bāuls is considered from an historical point of view; in particular, the advent of variously inflected, idealised, 'gentry' (*bhadralok*) images of 'the Bāul' from the nineteenth century, which is when the word *bāul* began to emerge in the sources as the name of a class, group, tradition (*sampradāy*) or even sect. The following account traces a trajectory from near total obscurity relieved only by the odd reference to Bāuls as godless and debased entertainers of the common folk, to their apotheosis as bearers of a glorious indigenous heritage.

This radical change of perceptions has been neither uniform nor total, however. At the beginning of what were to be long years of fieldwork with so-called Bāuls, a (*bhadralok*) Tantric guru of Calcutta cautioned me: 'Whatever you do, don't become a Bāul!' And perhaps to appeal to common class loyalties he added: '*Bhadralok* never become Bāul, they become Tantric!' Almost a century earlier, similar attitudes were expressed by the eminent jurist and president of the Brahmin Sabhā of Bengal, J. N. Bhattacharya, *bhadralok* par excellence, whose tolerance of Tantric gurus, in so far as they were learned and confined themselves to Brahmin disciples, contrasted with a scathing attack on Vaishnava gurus (among whom Bāuls may be included) for their illiteracy and proselytisation among the 'lower classes' (1896:26, 29).

While definitions of the word *bhadralok* vary, along with preferred English renderings of the term (see glossary, p. 254), there is general agreement that the *bhadralok* did not constitute a homogeneous group. Scholars such as Broomfield emphasise the overt opposition between conservatives and reformers (or liberals). In the case of the former, Broomfield associates a desire to preserve a closed (*bhadralok*) society with nostalgia for the golden age of classical Brahmanism, whose decline was predictably attributed to precisely those mediæval cults, especially Vaishnavism, of which popular contemporary Hindu beliefs were felt to be degraded survivals (1968:16f.). This he contrasts with another more outward-looking *bhadralok* school of thought, one ready to espouse European ideas and values such as secularism, liberalism and rationalism, and thus implicitly abandon

[1] Shakespeare's words in the chapter heading are an excellent translation of the first line of a Bāul song composed by a disciple of Rāj Khyāpā, Maṇi: '*Nāme ras kise* . . . '. See p. 194.

high-caste dominance of the elite (1968:17–18). On the other hand, S. N. Mukherjee has convincingly argued that these ideological divisions between groups of *bhadralok* were of less importance than their solidarity as a class in opposition to the lower orders (1993:146ff.). All agree that neither of these apparently opposing ideologies was calculated to narrow the vast gap between *bhadralok* and *choṭalok* (the common people) (Broomfield 1968: 153–4, 322–3, S. N. Mukherjee 1993:73). On the other hand, they supported a positive disapproval of those such as Bāuls, ostensibly on the grounds of perceived sexual and other depravity, a matter on which all were in agreement, including the British. Even on what might be seen as the margins of *bhadralok* culture proper, Bāuls had been castigated as agents of Kali (personified as the presiding deity of the last age) along with Buddhists, Tantrics, lecherous orthodox pundits, *kulīn* polygamists, Anglicised young men, and even notables such as Rammohan Roy and Vidyasagar.[2]

Early perceptions of Bāuls

The degree of consensus on such matters is revealed by a perusal of early source material, including official texts, to which I shall turn first. Before considering these sources, a few preliminary remarks are called for. The dearth of references to Bāuls in the early imperial sources, in contrast to their increasing prominence in more recent official texts, is here taken to be indicative of their insignificance in earlier *bhadralok*, and hence British perceptions of Bengali society (see below). Official sources reflect not only the increasing prominence of Bāuls, but also a radical change in perception of the term *bāul*. They also demonstrate the difficulties involved in the application of conventional British classifications of Indian society ('caste' versus 'sect', Hindu versus Muslim, and so forth), especially where those such as Bāuls are concerned. Bāuls are most often classified as a sub-set of Vaishnava in the early official sources. There is considerable confusion and contradiction between one source and another and even within the same source where Vaishnavas are concerned, the latter being variously dubbed class, caste, sect, or even more than one of these at the same time.[3] Risley and Hunter regard caste and sect as mutually exclusive (the term sect not being applied to those who remain within their caste) and exhaustive (those who reject their caste are automatically in a sect). This caste/sect distinction rests on the assumption of sectarian ascesis, or rather lack of progeny, as those who reproduce inevitably begin to look like a caste again, given the terms of the discussion. In an attempt to resolve such difficulties, coinages such as 'open caste' (Risley) and 'sectarian caste' (Blunt) arose, such hybrids demonstrating the inadequacy of the original classification.

[2] In a Bengali drama by Nārāyaṇ Chaṭṭorāj, '*Kali kautuk nāṭak* . . .' (S. Sarkar 1989c:44). See also Jayanta Gosvāmī (1974:1115ff.) for a slightly different account of this farce. Sarkar tentatively traces the provenance of such works to the 'depressed upper-caste literati, within a . . . preindustrial middle class' (1989c:38).

[3] Risley 1891:339–48; Hunter 1875a:65, 1876a:55, 289, 1876e:57, 1877:56–7, 287.

One can attribute much of this confusion to what Partha Chatterjee calls the 'traditionalisation' of South Asian society, a process effected by the 'freezing of the categories of social classification, such as caste, and privileging of "scriptural" interpretations of social law at the expense of the fluidity of local community practices' (Chatterjee 1994:31). However, Chatterjee's further argument of the 'creation by colonial rule of a social order that bore a striking resemblance to its own caricature of "traditional India"...' (1994:32) is harder to endorse, as is Inden's similarly Saidian statement that 'the intellectual activities of the orientalist have even produced in India the very Orient which it constructed in its discourse' (Inden 1990:38). Such assertions have provoked accusations of complicity in the very denial of agency which these scholars purport to criticise. Among others, Aijaz Ahmad (1992), O'Hanlon (1991) and Peabody (1996) have argued for the attribution of some autonomy to the intelligentsias of colonised countries, as opposed to their portrayal as passive victims of colonial formulations. Such authors have advocated a more nuanced treatment of what Ahmad has called 'a wilderness of mirrors' in describing the complex interplay of 'brahminical and Islamic high textualities, [and] the orientalist knowledge of these...' (Ahmad 1992:105). In the case of Bāuls, it would be my contention that, imperial classificatory crudity aside, whatever material is found in official sources – as well as its relative paucity in earlier as opposed to twentieth-century sources – largely constitutes a reflection, albeit retrospective, of the level of interest, knowledge and attitudes of educated Bengali informants.

None of this is to deny the profound, if indirect, effects of British imperialism on *bhadralok* perceptions of Bāuls from the mid-nineteenth century onwards. As will be shown below, when those alienated by the processes and effects of imperial domination searched for their roots, they found, among other iconic figures, 'Bāuls'. Moreover, the exoticisation of Bāuls by the *bhadralok*, for whom they came to represent both 'other' and 'self' in an array of complex configurations, may arguably be seen, in part and with many qualifications, as a deflection of, or displaced acquiescence in European orientalisation of 'India' as a whole.

By now it is a commonplace that each version of an Other is also the construction of a Self (Clifford and Marcus 1986:23), or, as Inden has argued in the case of South Asia, that 'Euro-American Selves and Indian Others have ... dialectically constituted one other' (1990:3). In addition to the positing of opposing essences emphasised by Inden and Nandy (1983), Peabody has focused on an additional mode of 'Othering', one based on the assumption of a single essence for humankind, in which differences are elaborated according to degree not kind, and are mapped on to an evolutionary or historical scale (1996:188–9; see also Inden 1990:43). This allows for the production of a multiplicity of Others and, especially pertinent in the present context, shifting boundaries between Self and Other (1996:190). The notion of different modes of Othering (not necessarily confined to these two) is illuminating in the context of evolving *bhadralok* perceptions of Bāuls.

Essentialising and Othering strategies are not confined to European cultures. As Ahmad points out, it was the power of colonial capitalism which directly or indirectly rendered European essentialisations so widely devastating (Ahmad 1992:105). These crucial economic and socio-political factors lie outside the scope of this work. However, in moving from Orientalist essentialisations concerning India to élite Bengali perceptions of Bāuls, it is important to emphasise a fundamental distinction deriving from these factors. While Orientalist discourses have been characterised as entailing 'attempts by Selves to displace the agency of Others and thus rationalise various interventionist agendas' (Peabody 1996:189), this was hardly the case with *bhadralok* perceptions of Bāuls. Questions of identity were crucial to the colonised élite, and, to oversimplify what follows, Bāuls were variously coopted in this cause as Other to the Self, as a lost Self, or as a true Self.

Bearing in mind the limitations of British imperial sources,[4] I now propose to turn to the material itself. To begin with the earliest relevant source, Bāuls are mentioned only twice in the entire series of Hunter's *Statistical Account of Bengal*, published from 1875 CE. In both cases, they are classified as Hindus, but apart from being identified as Bairāgī (see Glossary) in one case, and Vaishnava but not Bairāgī in the other, nothing more is said of them (1875a:65–6; 1876d:51). According to Risley, 'Baolas' are 'separated from the main body of Vaishnavas'. They comprise a number of 'disreputable mendicant orders' and recruit mainly from the lower castes. Flesh and alcohol are forbidden but fish is eaten; hemp is smoked; they 'never shave or cut their hair, and filthiness of person ranks as a virtue among them'. They are believed to be grossly immoral, he maintains, and are 'held in very low estimation by respectable Hindus' (Risley 1891:347).

It is interesting to note that while later writers were to emphasise critical attitudes of Bāuls towards distinctions of caste and religion, as well as to the scriptures which legitimise these, such characteristics are not mentioned by early writers in English or Bengali.[5] In general, Bāuls are conspicuous by their absence in these early sources – they do not appear even in the first series of *District Gazetteers* (1910 to 1925) – and by the vagueness and contradictions which characterise the references that do occur (Openshaw 1994:13–14). Even more significant is the omission in these sources of a feature which was later to predominate to the exclusion of almost everything else, that is, 'Bāul songs'.

Not that glimpses of Bāul songs were absent from Bengali sources of this and even earlier periods.[6] However, they tended to be disparaged as entertainment,

[4] Apart from the inherent slant of census material, its variable quality, even within its own terms of reference, should be borne in mind. Where the districts of Bengal are concerned, the type of information provided depended largely on the local District Officers' interests and competence, whether they themselves were responsible for authorship or provided information for another (as was often the case with Hunter's *Statistical Account of Bengal*).

[5] An apparent exception to this is the first known description (in 1872 CE) of the composer and guru Lālan, subsequently elevated to the status of archetypal Bāul, in which his opposition to divisions of religion and caste (*jātibhed*) is cited (in the Bengali journal *Grāmabārttā*; see A. A. Caudhurī 1990:92). Significantly, however, Lālan was not categorised as a Bāul in this context, nor, as far as we know, at this period.

[6] '*Bāul*' seems to have featured as a category of rural song from at least the eighteenth century (S. K. De 1962:350, 394).

often for the purpose of soliciting alms. Consonant with this, emphasis was on form, rather than content, as seen in J. N. Bhattacharya's condescending dismissal of the songs on grounds of their 'queerness', 'quaint allegories' and 'rustic philosophy' (1896:482–3). Where actual texts of Bāul songs do figure in early Bengali sources, it is often in the context of dramatic or satirical works, where the author employs the form of the Bāul song as a vehicle for his own contents and agenda.[7] In an example from the early 1860s, Kālīprasanna Siṅha's 'Sketch of Hutom Owl' (*Hutom Pyācār Nakaśā*) depicts 'Bāuls' singing songs to 'non-Bāuls' in Calcutta. The text of one Bāul song is 'signed' with the author's own pseudonym (Hutom), and conveys his satirical comments on the life and inhabitants of contemporary Calcutta.[8] It seems that light banter and irreverent satire (often with conservative undertones) gradually gave way to more serious and even reformist messages.[9] Whether the Bāuls in such writings are portrayed as mendicants, as lampooners of the new vices of Calcutta, or serious critics of more established practices such as dowry, they all share with the reprehensible Bāuls of the official sources the characteristic of being outsiders. As we shall see, this is a persistent theme.

Risley's views on Bāuls were endorsed by J. N. Bhattacharya, who included them in the class 'disreputable Chaitanyite [Vaishnava] sects of Bengal'. Here too they are characterised as low class and deliberately dirty. As mentioned above, it is the entertainment value of Bāuls and their songs which is emphasised. Everything about them – their dress, musical instruments, dancing and songs – is 'queer' and 'amusing'. Their 'deplorable moral condition' (that is, sexual indulgence as a 'religious exercise' and the alleged drinking of solutions made from human excretions) is given as the reason for their exclusion from the pale of humanity by Brahmanism. Finally, Bhattacharya questions their classification as Vaishnavas, on the grounds that they are a 'godless sect' and (the only praiseworthy feature) worship no 'idols' (1896:482–3).

Perusal of these sources for the word Bāul is little more than an arbitrary entrée into a very complex area. Of the many names of 'sects' listed and described, not a few are in some way identified with Bāuls in other contexts. Such names include: Sahajīyā, Darbeś (Dervish), Neṛā, Kartābhajā, Sā̃i and Bairāgī. In the opinion of the authors quoted, these 'groups' tend to share with Bāuls sexual immorality (bracketed with prostitution) and/or consumption or other use of human excreta. Such sects are almost invariably placed on the Hindu side of what is seen as the great Hindu–Muslim divide. Apart from this general agreement, the way each of these named groups is described and classified is variable, as with Bāuls themselves. Here, as in many sources on Bāuls, one finds the assumption of a one-to-one

[7] A notable exception to this pattern is the academic work of A. K. Datta, who appended some songs to his section on Bāuls.

[8] Hutom is the name of a large, ugly owl. The other sketch features a 'Bāul' group begging from door to door, singing the names of Krishna and a light song mocking piety, of which the text is provided (Nāg 1398 BS:107, 116).

[9] By 1876, in a drama called *Corer opar bāṭ-pāṛi* (A swindler robs a thief) by Amṛtalāl Basu, we find a so-called Bāul group singing songs against dowry (Nāg 1389 BS:85; also Rāmākānta Cakrabartī 1997:57).

equivalence between name and thing, an issue treated with considerably more sophistication by many of those called Bāul, as will be shown below. Many types of confusion are involved: of tradition (*sampradāy*) with sect, of name with tradition, and of important gurus with founders.

In his monumental work on Bāuls,[10] Upendranāth Bhaṭṭācārya assigns the blame for much of this confusion to Akṣay Kumār Datta (1820–86), who was, accordingly to Bhaṭṭācārya, the first to write of *bāul, āul, neṛā, sahajī, kartābhajā, sā̃i, darbeś* and so on (*BBBG*:56). Datta produced the first volume of his pioneering Bengali work 'Religious traditions of India' (*Bhārat-barṣīya upāsak sampradāy*) as early as 1870 CE, that is, even before the census sources discussed above. He deals briefly with about thirty *sampradāy* under the rubric 'branches of the Caitanya *sampradāy*' (*BBUS*:110–50).[11] Speaking from his fifteen years' field experience in both parts of Bengal, Bhaṭṭācārya accuses Datta of sitting in Calcutta and basing his text on hearsay.[12] He emphatically denies the status of *sampradāy* to these named categories, except for '*bāul*', the others being assimilated in some way or other to the '*bāul sampradāy*'.[13] It should be noted here that, while Datta may well have been the first to have 'substantialised' such names into *sampradāy*, lists of similar names had apparently been emerging from the Vaishnava community from the late eighteenth century. A particularly baroque example, of about a hundred names, including *bāul, āul* etc. is furnished by the *Baiṣṇab bratadin nirṇay*.[14]

Datta is also criticised by Bhaṭṭācārya for ignoring the great traditions (*sampradāy*) of Fakirs of East and West Bengal, an omission shared to an overwhelming extent by the sources in English cited, and one inevitably entailed by Datta's inclusion of Bāuls and so forth as off-shoots of the Caitanya *sampradāy*.[15] Bhaṭṭācārya's contention is that Datta was blindly followed on these matters by subsequent authors. Without speculating on whether Datta's work directly or indirectly influenced writers of official texts or whether they all had access to similar sources of 'hearsay', it is interesting to note that, in addition to the general exclusion

10 The first edition of *Bāṅlār bāul o bāul gān* (Bāuls of Bengal and their songs) came out in 1364 BS (1957 CE), although the author had been working on this subject since the nineteen thirties (*BBBG*:*ja*), or even twenties (*BBBG*:533). The revised and enlarged edition usually cited in this book is dated 1378 BS (1971 CE).

11 Caitanya was a charismatic, early sixteenth-century Vaishnava leader, commonly regarded as the founder of Bengali Vaishnavism.

12 *BBBG*:57. While this may not be entirely true (see the biography of A. K. Datta by Mahendranāth Rāy *c.* 1292 BS), there is no doubt that Bhaṭṭācārya's fieldwork was considerably more extensive than that of Datta, who suffered from poor health and died prematurely.

13 One difficulty is that Bengali terms with their own denotations, connotations and mode of operation are often made to function additionally as equivalents of English terms. Thus, in indeterminate fashion and without necessarily losing its old associations, the word '*sampradāy*' is coopted as a direct translation for the English term 'sect' (and indeed '*Religious sects of India*' might be a more appropriate rendering of Datta's Bengali title).

14 S. Cakrabartī 1989:17. Unfortunately, no date is given for this work.

15 In fact, recent editions of Datta's work do append a cursory section on Fakirs, based on material received subsequently by the author from another (*bhadralok*) source. According to this they are very localised, of recent origin and, although mainly Muslim, possibly Kartābhajās in disguise (*BBUS*:334–5).

of fakirs from their consideration, they all tend to assume that such names as *bāul*, *āul*, *neṛā* and so on correspond to *sampradāy* or to sects, depending on the language used. The fact that Datta modelled his text on H. H. Wilson's significantly entitled *Religious sects of the Hindus*, first published in *Asiatik Researches* from 1828 CE, provides a further twist to the story. In the light of this connection, it is interesting that Bhaṭṭācārya accuses Datta of projecting scandalous attributes on to Bāuls, and decries his tendency to depict them as 'strange' (*adbhut*) and 'disgusting' (*bibhatsa*) (*BBBG*:58–9). Yet while some of Datta's allegations, for example, that Bāuls eat human flesh and wear clothes from corpses, are indeed sensationalised, they are probably based on misunderstanding rather than pure projection. In fact, many attributes reported by Datta, namely the reabsorption into the body of the 'four moons' (semen, menstrual blood, urine and faeces), bodily practices with women and an association with the practice of medicine of various kinds, suggest to a fieldworker that Datta's pioneering work was not fabricated. As we shall see, this kind of material was soon to be swept aside in a tide of idealistic constructions of Bāuls.

The assumption of an exclusively Hindu identity for Bāuls should be seen in the context of developments within Bengali Muslim society from the last quarter of the nineteenth century. In association with the rise of a series of Islamic reform movements,[16] a stream of hostile tracts was unleashed against the perceived heterodoxy of Muslims called '*fakir*' or '*bāul*'. Such tracts, generally written by Islamic scholars and clerics, include 'Fake fakirs' (*Bhaṇḍa phakir*) and 'Mandate for the destruction of Bāuls' (*Bāul dhvaṁsa phatoyā*) (R. K. Ray 1995: 22–3; Jha 1997:32ff.). Sources disagree on the effects of such movements on Bāuls or Fakirs. Most suggest that their numbers were severely reduced due to persecution by 'reformist' tendencies (Haq 1975:300; Śariph 1370 BS:29), which included violence as well as social oppression (R. K. Ray 1995:21ff.). Ahmed, however, inclines to the view that the actual effect was small (1981:33). However that may be, the exclusion of these Muslim Bāuls (or Fakirs) from *bhadralok* and imperial accounts considered above is intriguing. Is it simply a reminder that the *bhadralok* consisted overwhelmingly of Hindus who by and large were unaware of, or indifferent to, Islam and Muslims? Is it yet another indication of the enormous gulf between the urban life of Calcutta and rural Bengal? Both these factors have a clear role to play in this and other aspects of Bāul studies. However, another possibility is that the word Bāul only began to be used substantively for communities more usually called Fakir from the very end of the nineteenth century. Elucidation of this issue requires further research, especially on the Islamic anti-Fakir/Bāul tracts. At present I confine myself to noting that tracts containing the word Bāul in the title date only from the twentieth century. Moreover, as far as we know, Lālan, who came to epitomise the traditional Bāul, and who was also vilified by reformist Islamic elements, never called himself Bāul, nor was so called by his contemporaries. In his songs, he usually 'signs' himself Fakir Lālan and refers to

16 Such as the Fara'idi and the Muhammadiya (Haq 1975:299–300, Ahmed 1981:39–71).

his guru Sirāj as Sā̃i or Darbeś ('Dervish') (Jhā 1995:153). It seems likely that the substantive use of the word 'Bāul' in a non-Muslim context also began much later than is usually thought, albeit earlier than for Muslim communities. Writing in the first half of the nineteenth century, Wilson mentioned numerous groups, including 'seceders' from the main body of Vaishnavas such as 'Kartabhajas' and 'Sahujas'. Bāuls are not mentioned.

Elite and orthodox Muslim views on Bāuls will be considered further below. To return to those of the largely Hindu *bhadralok*, initially hostile or disdainful attitudes towards Bāuls may be seen partly as a deflection of negative Orientalist constructions of India and its people in general on to those such as low-caste Vaishnavas and Bāuls, who thus became incomprehensible and despicable Others. This no doubt coincides with the withdrawal of the elite from a shared, or overlapping, popular culture, a process beginning with the increasing influence of Western education and ideas from the middle of the nineteenth century (S. Banerjee 1989:83). Alongside negative projections (of cannibalism, bodily filthiness, prostitution etc.), the intent to expose Others, and thus define the Self, drew attention to established esoteric practices which were perhaps as repugnant to the majority of rural Bengalis as to the *bhadralok*. Ironically, the reformist persecution of (especially Muslim) initiates called Fakir and Bāul fuelled by this greater awareness was more or less contemporaneous with the increasing idealisation of 'the Bāul' by the urbanised élite, to which we shall now turn. With the advent of the Bāul as the embodiment of indigenous wisdom and spirituality, such inconvenient characteristics as esoteric practices were forgotten by Hindu and Brahmo *bhadralok*, or elided from their accounts.

Changed perceptions of Bāuls

Towards the end of the nineteenth century, a new *bhadralok* attitude to the rest of Bengali society begins to be discernible alongside the others – one of interest and even, at times and at least in theory, identification. This development is associated with the growth of national and more especially regional consciousness,[17] along with a reevaluation of Bengali language and culture *vis-à-vis* Sanskrit and classical Hindu culture. One manifestation of this was the search of Calcutta based *bhadralok* for historical and geographical roots in the idyllic rural life of 'Golden Bengal' (*sonār bāṅlā*). With the conflation of temporal and spatial distance, the idealised village was to become the locus of old values in the present time (S. Sarkar 1989a:35, 41). The same period witnessed an upsurge in the popularity of the Bāul song as an indigenous Bengali folk form, as well as the emergence of the idealised Bāul of the (Hindu and Brahmo) *bhadralok*, and, usually much later, of the Bengali Muslim élite.

[17] From the late nineteenth century onwards, the word *deś*, which originally meant place of origin, or place in a geographic, social or cultural sense, increasingly came to mean 'nation' (especially in reference to 'Bengal'), in *bhadralok* parlance. At the same period, regional or Bengali referents came to predominate in the use of the term *jāti* (birth group) (Gordon 1974:10–11).

Two aspects of this complex development which are pertinent to the present topic will be considered here. For convenience of presentation I shall first look briefly at the reassessment of Bengali language, literature and culture *vis-à-vis* Sanskrit, encouraged by the discovery in 1907 of the Caryāpadas and Dohās, old Bengali songs and couplets which came to be considered the direct ancestors of Bāul songs. This reappraisal, as well as the transcription, composition, and publication of Bāul songs by and for the educated Bengali classes, had begun even before the retrieval of the Caryāpadas and Dohās. However, it was after this discovery, and especially through the efforts of Rabindranath Tagore and K. Sen, that the popularity of Bāul songs reached its acme, and the Bāul as the embodiment of ancient indigenous wisdom came to the fore. Second, the advent of variously inflected images of the idealised Bāul of the *bhadralok* is considered, along with a brief consideration of parallel but later developments in the case of the Bengali Muslim élite.

In the early part of the nineteenth century, Orientalist-inspired Indologists had focused almost exclusively on India's classical heritage,[18] while Bengali, despite its rich literary heritage, was demoted in favour of Sanskrit to the status of a spoken vernacular. Although the attitude to Bengali began to change around the 1860s (Clark 1967:87), even that great advocate of his mother-tongue, the Bengali littérateur Bankimcandra, displayed considerable ambivalence towards Bengalis, especially the majority non-Aryans and their culture (Van Meter 1969:65–6). One of the factors contributing to a reevaluation of Bengali language and culture *vis-à-vis* Sanskrit and classical Hindu culture was the discovery of old Bengali songs known as the Caryāpadas and Dohās by H. P. Śāstrī.[19] This inspired new research into the origins of vernacular Bengali literature.

The Caryāpadas (or Caryā songs) and the Dohās (distichs), written by the Siddhas (perfected ones) between the eighth century and the twelfth century CE, are generally considered to belong to the Tantric Buddhist school of thought and literature known as Sahajiyā or Sahajayāna (S. B. Dasgupta 1969:9, 13). The term *sahaj*, from which these labels derive, literally means 'being born together with', and by extension 'congenital, innate, hereditary, original, and natural', although Kvaerne prefers 'co-emergent' (following Guenther) or 'simultaneously arisen' (1977:61–2). In modern Bengal, *sahaj*(*a*) also means 'easy', 'simple' and 'plain'. *Sahaja* constitutes an ontological as well as a psychological category, and emphasis is placed on realisation rather than ritual or scholarship. Indeed formalism and convention of any kind, lay or religious, Hindu or Buddhist, seems to have been rejected (S. B. Dasgupta 1969:53–4). Condemnation was therefore not confined to Vedic ceremonial and the four 'class' (*caturvarṇa*) ideology, especially the alleged superiority of Brahmins. Yogis and devotees of almost every kind were mocked and criticised, renunciation and austerity were scorned, as were the formalism and

[18] See Kopf 1969:22–41. The term 'Orientalist' here refers to a specific movement associated with the cultural policy of British colonialists in India at the end of the eighteenth and beginning of the nineteenth centuries.

[19] As early as 1897 CE Śāstrī had published *Discovery of living Buddhism in Bengal*, University of Calcutta.

ceremonialism of Tantric Buddhism – *mantra, yantra and tantra* (S. B. Dasgupta 1969:54–8; R. C. Majumdar 1971:535). This spirit of heterodoxy and criticism is related to a wide variety of traditions: Buddhist, Jain, Hindu, and perhaps especially the Materialist schools (called Cārvāka or Lokāyata) (S. B. Dasgupta 1969: 61–77).

These details have been provided here not only because of their relevance to Bāul studies, but because of the attraction such themes held for *bhadralok* beleaguered by the onslaught of aggressive European rationalism. Here, from within Bengali culture itself and dating back to a period far preceding the European Enlightenment, was a critique of traditional Hindu practices very like the attacks formulated by the colonialists themselves, which had thrown the Bengali intelligentsia on the defensive. Moreover, the fact that the Caryās were written in Bengali rather than Sanskrit, coupled with their literary quality and antiquity, placed the recent developments in Bengali literature during the nineteenth-century Bengal 'Renaissance' in a new context, and contributed to the re-evaluation of Bengali in relation to Sanskrit. Scholars have discerned striking resemblances between Caryās and Dohās on the one hand and some Bāul songs on the other, especially in respect of the antinomianism and anti-formalism outlined above, the common usage of enigmatic language, technical terms and some important terminology, such as the word '*sahaj*' itself,[20] and the fact that the Caryās were also meant to be sung (Kvaerne 1977:8). The question of the alleged persistence of 'Sahajiyā Buddhism' in the Bāuls will be considered later.

As will be shown below, as early as 1883 CE, the poet, writer and artist Rabindranath Tagore was advocating a return to the language and literature of rural Bengal, of which he considered Bāul songs to be the epitome. Nevertheless, the general assumption that it was Tagore and his associates alone who brought Bāuls to the attention of the *bhadralok*, or elevated them in their eyes,[21] is an exaggeration. To begin with, Tagore was not the first to publish songs of Bāuls.[22] Second, the sporadic appearance in earlier Bengali sources of the 'Bāul song' form as a vehicle for increasingly idealistic authorial agendas (see p. 23) indicated the development of more positive images alongside that of the disreputable Bāul. By the last part of the nineteenth century it had become highly fashionable for poets and songsters to compose and perform in a *bāul* style. Such was the popularity

[20] See, for example, K. Sen 1952: 296–7. It goes without saying that continuities of meaning are not necessarily involved here.

[21] According to Sukumār Sen, Rabindranath 'discovered' *bāul* songs (1948:992). See also Dimock 1966:253, 1989:76; S. B. Dasgupta 1969:157–8.

[22] Apart from a short review of a book of collected 'Bāul songs' in the family journal *Bhārati* in 1883 (see below) from which he quotes a few songs, Tagore first published songs of Bāuls in the journal *Prabāśi* in 1322 BS (1915 CE). Twenty years previously in 1302 BS (1895 CE), however, his niece Saralā Debī and Akṣay Kumār Maitreya had published eight Bāul songs of Lālan and one of Gagan, also in *Bhārati.* Asit Kumār Bandopādhyāy is of the opinion that Harināth Majumdār (alias Kāṅgāl Harināth or Phikir Cā̃d) first drew the attention of *bhadralok* to Bāul songs (1990:249) and Harināth certainly published a song of Lālan in his *Brahmāṇḍabed* in 1292 BS (1885/6 CE) (S. Cakrabartī 1992b:22). Akṣay Kumār Datta's treatise on *sampradāy*, which includes some Bāul songs, first came out in 1870.

of these works that one mofussil writer bemoaned the fact that they had virtually eclipsed those of the more traditional exponents of the genre.[23] The scholar Sukumār Sen was later to comment disdainfully on the absence of literary merit in these fashionable, fake (*kṛtrim*) Bāul songs (1948:995). Upendranāth Bhaṭṭācārya deplored the appropriation by such urban educated 'amateur bāuls' (*śakher-bāul*) of the Bāul song, the cooption of this latter in the service of conventional religiosity, and the inclusion of such songs with others by the same composers on almost every topic under the sun, for example, the benevolence of Queen Victoria, the characteristics of the Indian woman, current affairs and social problems (*BBBG*:103–4).

Before turning to an examination of Rabindranath's attitudes to Bāuls, it is appropriate to consider the phenomenon of these amateur Bāuls (*śakher bāul* or *saker bāul*), who in one form or other continue to play an important role in the Bāul scene to this day. The term 'amateur Bāul' has had a variety of shifting connotations, which emerge in contrast to equally labile figures or qualities which include the 'professional' and 'traditional' Bāul. In the latter part of the nineteenth century, the typical amateur Bāul was a middle-class literate Hindu male. Although wearing the label 'Bāul' at times, his primary identity and occupation lay elsewhere.

The most famous of the alleged amateur Bāuls was (Kāṅāl) Harināth Majumdār (1833–96 CE), who often 'signed' his songs 'Phikir Cā̃d'. Significantly, both Harināth and Lālan, with whom he was acquainted, inhabited that area of central Bengal in which the Tagore family had large country estates. Born into a middle-caste Hindu family, Kāṅāl's early life was marked by the death of his parents, and his struggle to gain an education. His nickname 'Kāṅāl' (indigent) was a true reflection of his condition. After an abortive attempt to make his way in Calcutta, he returned home to embark upon a varied career as teacher, writer and editor of a local journal. His championship of the downtrodden against their oppressors, irrespective of whether they were British or Indian, received little support, and indeed alienated powerful vested interests, including the Tagores. It is said that Lālan and his disciples were among the very few to defend him against the threats of the strongmen of the Tagore family. Whereas Kāṅāl had earlier been associated with the reformist Brahmo movement, in later life he turned towards Tantra, and, apparently owing to the serendipity of some literary followers, to writing and performing songs which at first were published as 'Fakir' and subsequently as 'Bāul'. Despite the group's casual beginnings, Kāṅāl himself seems to have taken the enterprise more seriously. He and his group were in demand all over Bengal, and a host of similar groups sprang up in surrounding towns and villages. Such performers dressed up in long robes, strapped anklets to bare feet and at times wore false beards and long curly hair. Their largely mofussil town audience greatly appreciated their performances, which traversed a spectrum from

[23] Mīr Mośāraph Hosen in *Saṅgīt Lahiri* (1887:56, cited in Sudhīr Cakrabartī (1992b:142, 160)). Hosen specifically mentions the neglect of Lālan and Pāglā Kānāi in favour of 'amateurs' such as Phikir Cā̃d (that is, Harināth Majumdār), the well-known 'amateur Bāul', of whom more below.

banter and mimicry, through light sentimental ditties, to idealistic religious songs (J. N. Bhattacharya 1896:483; S. Cakrabartī 1992b:142). As Cakrabartī points out, the neglect of Harināth the social radical is in striking contrast to the lionisation of this later peddler of the 'opium of fake Bāul songs' (1992b:171). More pertinent in the present context is the marginalisation of traditional singer-composers such as Lālan by the more accessible, even anodyne songs of the amateur Bāuls, a pattern which continues to this day.[24]

As suggested by the comments of the scholars cited above, the label 'amateur Bāul' has long carried derogatory connotations. Nor is this simply because, however enthusiastic and well-meaning, an amateur is considered marginal and therefore less committed and competent (see Sukumar Sen's literary criticism of 'amateur Bāul' songs). Dressing up as 'a Bāul' for performances easily takes on the complexion of acting a part, and hence of imitation and lack of authenticity. In the case of Bāuls there is also, as mentioned above, the issue of 'appropriation' of a musical form, a supposed ideology and a label (Bāul), a charge which has more recently been modified into one of exploitation of poor, uneducated rural Bāuls by the powerful. As I shall argue, these nuances have now completely overridden any positive associations, with the result that these days the term 'amateur Bāul' is only used to denigrate others.

Where the original 'amateur Bāuls' differ from those of today is that they accepted this label and even wore it with pride. The last quarter of the nineteenth century witnessed the publication of not a few collections of songs by self-proclaimed amateur Bāuls (Karim 1980:200ff.). In part this testifies to a *bhadralok* concern not to be confused with 'professionals' (*peśādārī*), a sensitivity not uncommon in artistic circles of the time.[25] Where Bāuls in particular are concerned, one may also presume a wish to dissociate from more 'traditional' Bāuls, indicative of the lingering influence of their disreputable image. The status of amateur effected a distance between esoteric and other allegedly heinous practices of such Bāuls, and the respectable classes who found them so offensive. Finally, the label '*śakher bāul*' could carry positive connotations of being Bāul through fancy or inspiration (*śakh*), and there may be parallels between favourable connotations of the term 'amateur Bāul' and new notions of art and the artist inspired by nationalism, according to which inspiration (*śakh*) is valued above training (*śikṣā*) (Guha-Thakurta 1996:77, 79). This is in interesting contrast to most of those called Bāul with whom I did fieldwork, whose primary emphasis is precisely on training (*śikṣā*).

The emergence of such amateur Bāuls awaits further research. However, many of them might tentatively be identified as 'less successful *bhadralok*', to use Sumit Sarkar's phrase, consisting of rural or small town traditional literati, increasingly

[24] Material on Harināth Majumdār was taken largely from Cakrabartī (1992b:161–75). See also Jaladhar Sen 1320 and 1321 BS, A. A. Caudhurī 1988 (ed.), 1998; Parijāt Majumdār (ed.) 1999.

[25] The distinction between 'amateur' and 'professional' is of considerable vintage in Bengal. It is said that a young Brahmin Kabiwālā (singer-poet) Haru Ṭhākur (1738–1812), who had formed an 'amateur group' (*śakher dal*), was insulted when a patron treated him as an indigent professional. (Kabiwālās were generally of inferior class.) Later however he was persuaded to form his own professional group (*peśādārī dal*) (De 1962:322–3, 333).

marginalised by the dominance of 'Renaissance' culture, and the less successful products of English education (Sarkar 1998:172, 305–4). As such, they occupied a variety of intermediate positions between the rural masses and the Calcutta Bengali élite. Continuities, even if tenuous, are therefore to be inferred between these 'amateur Bāuls' and an older and thriving tradition of village poets, to which those we consider traditional Bāul composers are far more central. Still less is known about this older tradition of rural poets than that of the amateur Bāuls, even after the development of print culture permitted the recording of new voices, either as authors or presumed recipients of texts. What is of interest in the present context is why composers in these broader traditions (rural or urban) began to wish to identify themselves and their songs as 'Bāul'.

The 1880s saw a decline in *bhadralok* scepticism and rationalism, along with the growing appeal of the great saint Ramakrishna, himself from a traditional rural literati background (Sarkar 1985:106; P. Chatterjee 1992:41ff.). In connection with folk-drama (*yātrā*), Sarkar remarks on the transformation during the last part of the nineteenth century of initially despised figures such as the wandering mendicant Vaishnava and 'holy fool' into symbols of hope (Sarkar 1990/91:113, 121). This period marked a hiatus between 'two dominant myths – the "renaissance" dream of improvement . . . in a modernising direction under British tutelage, and the vision of patriotism solving the country's ills by overthrowing foreign rule' (Sarkar 1985:106). Sarkar dates disillusion with the first myth from the 1870s and early 1880s, while the new patriotism came into prominence around 1905 (1990/91:102). He associates the intervening period with resort to 'a series of logically distinct but often intermingled "Others": past as contrasted to present, country versus city, a deliberate feminization as opposed to active masculinity, the attractive playfulness and irresponsibility of the child and the *pagal* [loosely 'mad'] as against the goal-oriented instrumental rationality of the adult male' (Sarkar 1998:300). From the 1880s too, the epic style of poetry was displaced by the romantic poetry of nature of Biharilal and Rabindranath (Sarkar 1990/1:102), both of whom also composed songs called Bāul. Interestingly, Biharilal, whose work was admired by the young Rabindranath, specifically characterised his songs as those of an 'amateur Bāul',[26] a matter in which he was apparently inspired by Harināth Majumdār (S. Cakrabartī 1992b:169).

It is against this background that the increasing renown of Lālan Śā, most esteemed of 'traditional' Bāul composers, takes on significance, a process which probably began, ironically, with the writings of his associate, amateur Bāul Harināth Majumdār.[27] Lālan was taken up by the Tagore family, in the area of whose Śilāidaha estates both he and Harināth lived. He died in 1890 CE, and was reputed to have had many thousands of disciples, in several districts of Bengal. Although, as mentioned above, Lālan never seems to have applied the name 'Bāul' to himself, one of his disciples, Duddu, wrote a song identifying himself as 'Bāul'

[26] See the introductory verse to his collection of twenty songs entitled '*Bāul biṅśati*' (1307:139). The collection was written in 1887 (Pāṇḍā 1388 BS:14).

[27] A. A. Caudhurī 1990:92f.; also see notes 5 and 22.

(see pp. 108–9). As a song-writer of great power, and, unusually it seems, a guru beyond moral reproach (Jhā 1995:177), Lālan constituted an ideal focus for the promotion of new and favourable images of that Other, 'the Bāul', whose charisma lit a path back in space and time to the traditional culture of golden Bengal. These images were largely to displace the older disreputable Bāul, who survived only as a 'degenerate' or 'fake' counterpart of the new exemplar.

Bāuls and patriotism

Probably the first indication of what was to be Rabindranath Tagore's life-long fascination with Bāuls and their songs was his review of a collection of 'Bāul songs' (*Bāuler-gāthā*) in 1883 CE, in which he made an impassioned plea for renewed acquaintance and identity with the 'uneducated, authentic heart' (*aśikṣita akṛtrim hṛday*) of Bengal, and specifically, the language and literature of the villages. In this context, the Bengali language is contrasted with both English and Sanskrit, as well as styles of Bengali corrupted by these.[28] He argues that, just as it is imperative that an individual poet speak with his own voice, rather than that of others, so it is with nations (*jāti*). Yet we Bengalis, he continues, know neither the language nor the spirit (*bhāb*) of Bengal (1290 BS:34ff.). In the review, the word *bāul* scarcely occurs, and then only as an anonymous, disembodied source of indigenous wisdom.[29] 'Bāul songs' are by implication elided with 'village songs' (1290:40), and Tagore ends with three songs of 'alms-gatherers and fishermen' from his own collection. In his account of the alienation of the educated, urban elite from their Bengali roots, Tagore marshals a 'Bāul song' from the collection under review to support his argument:

> I haven't discovered who I am, brother,
> I keep saying 'I', but the 'I' hasn't really become mine.
> . . .
> Do I ever enquire where 'I' have come from?[30]

As will be seen later, the theme of the 'I', coopted here by Tagore in the service of a kind of Bengali patriotism, tends to be glossed very differently by more traditional rural songwriters called Bāul, for whom it is a device to erase rather than constitute specific identities. Tagore's patriotic concerns are unlikely to have been of interest to any but *bhadralok* Bāuls: the theme of *jāti* or *jāt* as regional or national identity is absent from more traditional Bāul songs. *Jāt* figures prominently in these in the sense of caste or religious (communal) identity, but

[28] Ṭhākur 1290 BS:34–41. It seems likely that at least some of the 'Bāul songs' in the collection reviewed were composed by 'amateur Bāuls', since Rabindranath implies that some are new, and complains about the inclusion of songs of 'English wallahs' and of the Brahmos, a reformist religious group recently founded by the urbanised elite.

[29] Phrases such as '(the) Bāul says' or '(the) Bāul replies' preface a couple of songs from the collection which are germane to Tagore's own argument (38).

[30] '*Āmi ke bhāi āmi jānlem nā/ Āmi āmi kari kintu āmi āmār ṭhik haila nā/. . . Kothā haite elām āmi, tāre kai guṇi!*' (1290:36).

the 'I' theme is used by them to demolish, not establish, *jāt* in these senses.[31] Before leaving the subject of Tagore's review, it is worth pointing out that the phenomenon of the urban *bhadralok* (Hindu or Brahmo), divorced from his (rural) home (*deś*)[32] and his Bengali heritage, persists to this day, as does the attraction of the Bāul as a symbol of the reclamation of both: the Other which is the alienated Self.

Rabindranath's patriotic sentiments took on a specifically political hue for the period of his brief involvement with the nationalist movement, which marked the advent of the second of the dominant myths mentioned above. Thus the year of the partition of Bengal in 1905 also saw the appearance of a booklet of nationalist (*svadeśī*) songs by Rabindranath, entitled 'Bāul' (Ṭhakur 1312 BS). Most of the songs in this volume (and indeed most of Tagore's *svadeśī* songs) were given a Bāul melody (*bāul-sur*), or in some cases another kind of folk-melody, in order, comments P. Mukhopādhyāy, to touch the masses (1355:125). In these songs, the idea of the country as Mother is prominent, and Golden Bengal (*sonār Bāṅlā*), Mother Bengal (*Baṅgamātā*), the soil of (my) country (*deśer māṭi*), the soil of Bengal (*Bāṅlār māṭi*) also figure (ibid.).

Shortly after Rabindranath's disillusionment with the nationalist movement, his association began with the scholar K. Sen, who was to have a profound influence on his ideas about Bāuls. From 1915 CE, Tagore began to publish Bāul songs of Lālan, Gagan and others in the journal *Prabāśi* (1322 BS). Around the same time, he played the part of the 'blind Bāul' (*andha-bāul*) in his own dance-drama *Phālguṇi*. Benevolently wise, the blind Bāul is nevertheless characterised by his remoteness. Not only is he indifferent to worldly affairs, he is devoid of background, kith, kin or indeed specific social context of any kind. Even the unpredictable appearances (to sing songs) of this emblematic figure occur at one remove, in a play within the play. Tagore was painted in this role more than once by his nephew Abanindranath Tagore (see Fig. 1). Whereas Tagore's Bāul had earlier been identified with Bengali village life and folk culture, from now on his ties with society are virtually severed. In addition to Tagore's disillusionment with nationalism, this is attributable to the influence of K. Sen, a classical scholar primarily interested in 'sects' and 'cults' of India in general, rather than Bengali village life (*BBBG*:95).

Before continuing with Rabindranath and K. Sen, it is of interest to note the appearance, long after Rabindranath had withdrawn from the nationalist movement, of a '*svadeśī* (nationalist) Bāul' in the folk-drama, *Karmakṣetra*, written by Mukundadās at the time of Gandhi's Non-Cooperation Movement (1920/21).[33]

[31] An interesting example of a wider possibly patriotic concern by a 'traditional Bāul' is found in a song by Duddu Śā, disciple of Lālan (see Jhā 1991: song 18). However even here, *jāt* refers to communal religious, not national or sub-national, identity, and constitutes the obstacle not the aim.

[32] Even today, most Calcation *bhadralok* trace their origins to a specific *deś* in rural Bengal.

[33] Gosvāmī 1972:117. Mukundadās Cakrabartī (1878/9–1934 CE), a Kāyastha of humble rural and mofussil town origin, was initially a grocer and singer of *kīrtan*. He was jailed by the colonial authorities after producing his first and very outspoken folk-drama (*yātrā*), completed in 1907. Mukundadās's folk-dramas were known as '*svadeśī yātrā*', because they embodied the ideals of the Nationalist Movement (Gosvāmī 1972:337).

Figure 1. *Rabindranath Tagore as a Bāul (original in Rabindra Bharati Society, Calcutta).*

In contrast to Rabindranath's blind Bāul, this fervently patriotic figure is firmly rooted physically and psychologically in his native land. Whereas earlier sources present the Bāul as, if anything, broadly Vaishnava, Mukundadās's Bāul – as befits a devotee of the mother country – is Shakta; he even worships an image of the Goddess (one of the few constants in fluctuating perceptions of Bāuls is their rejection of image worship). Mukundadās's Bāul advocates education for girls, albeit mainly to train them for their role as housewives. In Gandhian fashion he supports aboriginal cottage industries, such as the spinning wheel, while abhorring the British–Indian life-style of Calcutta (characterised by the perverse use of fans in winter and hot tea in summer), as well as foreign medicine and so forth. In short, the Bāul is a much revered, charismatic and wise commentator, inspiring all around him to cooperation and self-sacrifice in the nationalist cause. Despite Mukundadās's undeniable contribution to the spread of political ideas in Bengal (Gosvāmī 1972:338) and possibly to the further popularity of the Bāul figure, his socially and politically concerned Bāul has been of little long-term significance. The fact that he strikes one, certainly nowadays, as a transparent vehicle of nationalist propaganda is a tribute to the dominance of alternative images of the Bāul. Significant in the present context is Mukundadās's assimilation of the Bāul figure to such a role. Despite the differences, he was probably inspired by Tagore's 'blind Bāul', who himself was the descendant, albeit under another name, of a whole theatrical host of wise renouncers and wandering madmen.[34] Subsequently too the Bāul was to assume a similar role as choric commentator (*vivek*) in many films (Majumdar and Roberge 1979:9).

The later Bāul of Tagore and Sen

In contrast to the rapid demise of the 'nationalist Bāul', the image of the wandering, unattached (*udāsīn*) Bāul of Tagore has triumphed over all rivals, and exerts its influence even on scholarly opinion to this day. However, in contrast to earlier images of Bāuls as disreputable buffoons worthy only of revulsion or derision, all these images (of Mukundadās and Tagore/Sen) are of remote, idealised, even semi-divine figures, commanding the deepest reverence. Still exclusively male (and often elderly), their lone Bāuls are all without female associates. Moreover, while each of their images of Bāuls has its own distinctive characteristics, Tagore, Sen and Mukundadās all view the Bāul as a fount of non-sectarian wisdom, capable of offering an indigenous alternative to orthodox divisiveness. In contrast to earlier sources, all emphasise the Bāul as the meeting-place of Hindu and Muslim, but while Mukundadās is concerned with combating contemporary social evils including communal divisions, the Bāul of Tagore and Sen, 'indifferent' to worldly affairs, embodies a stage pre-existing such divisions.

[34] Within Rabindranath's œuvre itself, the blind Bāul was himself foreshadowed by the Fakir in an earlier play, *Ḍākghar* (1912), and the Grandfather (Ṭhākurdā) in *Śārodotsab* (1908). For 'ancestors' of the 'blind Bāul' outside Tagore's work, see S. Sarkar 1990/1:113, 121.

Rabindranath Tagore was not only fulsome in his praise of Bāul songs, philosophy and 'spirit', he frankly acknowledged his own debt to them. He adopted Bāul melodies and imagery and admitted to being profoundly influenced by Bāul mysticism (Tagore 1971:78ff.; 1931:110ff.). He even signed himself on occasion 'Rabīndra Bāul' and, as we have seen, took the role of Bāul in his own plays. In turn, as will be discussed below, others frequently depicted him as a Bāul. In short, he shared many characteristics with the 'amateur Bāuls'; and, as we have seen, he began to take an interest in Bāul songs and collect folk-songs in the 1880s, the hey-day of the amateur bauls. In 1925, a group of staff and students from Rabindranath's educational institution in Santiniketan made an excursion to the Jayadeb Bāul/Vaishnava festival to perform Rabindranath's Bāul songs, wearing for the occasion long white robes and turbans, and carrying the emblematic Bāul one-stringed lute (*ektārā*), a quintessentially amateur Bāul enterprise.[35] Yet, although some followers of Lālan apparently alleged that Rabindranath owed his greatness as a poet to Lālan (*BBBG*:533), the label 'amateur Bāul' was never, to my knowledge, associated with Tagore, either by himself or others. Of course, Rabindranath's creative genius would render ridiculous any suggestion of imitation – an important connotation of the label 'amateur Bāul'. Moreover it could be argued that by the time Rabindranath began to be identified as 'Bāul', the new idealised image of 'real' Bāuls had begun to hold sway, thus obviating any need for differentiation from them. In any case, his social status was sufficiently elevated to prevent any possible confusion with either professionals, or the older disreputable Bāuls. As suggested above, the situation was different for some 'less successful *bhadralok*', for whom a line of demarcation between themselves and 'traditional' Bauls was probably felt necessary to avert the danger of being completely de-classed.

Tagore's early interest in Bāuls, shared by others of the Tagore family, and his willingness to identify with them, is perhaps partly attributable to his Brahmo background.[36] Indeed resemblances between Lālan and the Brahmos had been discerned, as early as 1872 CE, in Harināth Majumdār's journal *Grāmabārttā*, albeit consistently denied by Lālan himself (Jhā 1995:175). Brahmoism, an élite reformist faith, had come into conflict with conservative sections of the Hindu community, which tended to denounce them as 'denationalised'. One of the issues of debate was the relative merit of worshipping God without form (*nirākār*), a key tenet of Brahmoism, as opposed to God with form (*sākār*), and especially Hindu image worship. In 1895 CE, an article by Rabindranath's niece, Saralā Debī, extolled Bāuls as examples of 'low-class' (*nimnastar*) espousal of the *nirākār* position. Bāuls could thus be taken as providing an indigenous Bengali base for the Brahmo side in this debate (Saralā Debī 1302 BS:275). Such differences as there are in the

[35] Information contributed by Śāntideb Ghoṣ, for an exhibition on 'Rabindranath and Bauls' prepared by Dr Sutapā Bhaṭṭācārya. Materials in Rabindra Bhaban, Santiniketan.

[36] Subsequently Tagore was to associate the Bāuls with his departure from the Brahmo faith (1931: 110–11).

views of Tagore and Sen concerning Bāuls may be related partly to their different backgrounds, Brahmo and Hindu respectively.[37]

Despite slight differences of emphasis, the Bāul of Tagore and Sen is profoundly unworldly. His search is for the Man of the Heart (*maner mānuṣ*), for the Unknown Bird (*acin pākhi*), which enters and departs from the cage of the human body, themes which were already attractive to Tagore and many others by the 1880s (Ṭhākur 1290 BS:38–9, S. B. Dasgupta 1969:161–2). One of Tagore's favourite Bāul songs (attributed to Gagan Harakarā) begins (in the translation of K. Sen):

> Ah, where am I to find him, the Man of my Heart?
> Alas, since I lost Him, I wander in search of Him,
> Thro' lands near and far.[38]

In Tagore's view, this song expresses 'the longing of the singer to realise the infinite in his own personality', and the phrase 'Man of my Heart' means that 'for me, the supreme truth of all existence is in the revelation of the Infinite in my own humanity' (1971:78–9). The phrase '*maner mānuṣ*', usually rendered 'Man of the Heart', literally means the 'person of the heart and mind'. It also has the following dictionary meanings: 'a favourite, a minion, a lover' (*SBED*), and during fieldwork among those called Bāul, I frequently found it used in the conventional sense of 'a/the person (suitable) for me' or 'a person one finds particularly attractive'. In all these senses, it refers as often to a woman as a man, as indeed does the word *mānuṣ* itself. For example, a woman initiate said that, after the death of the adept with whom she had had a relationship for many years, 'I couldn't find anyone who suited me' (*maner mānuṣ pelām nā*), a phrase taken from a well-known Bāul song. A male initiate remarked to me, in the context of lamenting the difficulty of finding a suitable partner for esoteric practice: 'it is difficult to find the right person' (*maner mānuṣ pāoyā bhāṛ*) – another phrase from a song. Unusually among Indian adepts, a partner of the opposite sex is considered essential to such practitioners, and a male practitioner without a woman is ridiculed. These issues will be discussed at more length later.

While any English translation of the phrase *maner mānuṣ* would be woefully inadequate in one way or another, Tagore and Sen's spiritualised and masculinised rendering (as seen, for example, in the capitalised 'Man' and 'Him') reveals their own preconceptions. Because there is no differentiation of upper and lower case

[37] Tagore's use of Sen's work on Bāuls was understandably selective. Although both writers tended to emphasise the same aspects of the material in their publications, Sen, a scholar knowledgeable about renouncers and adepts of various kinds, did not exclude from his writings other, even contrary, features of Bāuls. However these elements are usually either omitted from his writings, or subsumed in the interests of a generalised and etherealised pan-Indian mysticism.

[38] Appendix on Bauls by Sen in Tagore 1931:216. Tagore discusses the song (translated slightly differently) in *Creative Unity*, first published in 1922 (Tagore 1971:78ff.). While Tagore himself brought out this song (in the original Bengali and in two different versions) in *Prabāśi* (1322 BS vol. I, nos. 1 & 2), it had been published previously by Saralā Debī and Akṣay Kumār Maitreya in *Bhārati* 1302 BS. In fact Tagore seems to have amended his first truncated version of the song in accordance with the *Bhārati* version.

in Bengali, nor any pronominal distinction of gender, the following is also a technically feasible (although equally distorted) translation of Gagan Harakarā's verse:

> Ah, where am I to find her, the woman of my heart?
> Alas, since I lost her, I wander in search of her,
> Thro' lands near and far.

In fact Sen's spiritualised rendering may not constitute too great a distortion in the case of this particular song (see below), but serious problems arise when the translation of *maner mānuṣ* as 'Man of the Heart' is extended to all contexts.

It is no doubt significant that, in his reprint of Sen's account of Bāuls, Rabindranath omitted the section hinting, with great delicacy and many provisos, at Bāul 'ideas in regard to the love of man for woman'.[39] This relationship is ignored by Tagore, and in general by Sen himself, in favour of what the latter calls 'the mutual love of the individual and Supreme self', between the lone (male) Bāul and the 'Man of the Heart' (K. Sen *c.*1935:226; Tagore 1931:217). Thus an almost inevitably (male) hierarchical relationship is given priority over the potentially equalising love relationship between a man and woman.[40] This image of the Bāul emerges clearly in a later poem of Rabindranath's, often quoted in connection with studies on Bāuls.[41] In this, Tagore empathises with the lone wanderer in nature, identifiable as Bāul by his one-stringed lute. An outcast from society and conventional religion, this perennial outsider wanders on his lonely life's path, singing and searching for the *maner mānuṣ*. The Tagorean image was endorsed as authentically Bāul by the respected scholar S. B. Dasgupta, who credits the Bāuls with 'deviation and innovation' with respect to their 'genealogical' predecessors, the Buddhist and Vaishnava Sahajiyās. While the Sahajiyās conceived of the *sahaja* (see p. 27) as the unity of two opposites on the same level (*prajñā-upāya,* Rādhā-Kṛṣṇa, or woman-man), realisable through sexo-yoga or bodily love, for the Bāuls, he asserts, the *sahaja* was the Divine, the Beloved within, the *maner mānuṣ* (1969:165–6).

While *maner mānuṣ* normally does have internal as well as external referents for so-called Bāuls, these are not necessarily 'spiritual'. Despite its manifold problems, a questionnaire handed out by A. Mukhopādhyāy (1988:112) to certain Bāuls is of interest here. It is clear that respondents had to choose between several set options. Responses to the question concerning the identity of the *maner mānuṣ* reveal that, along with the '*ātmā*' (Self) and '*bhagabān*' (conventionally 'God'), the 'guru', 'semen' and 'Rādhā' are also popular choices. One's partner

[39] K. Sen *c.* 1935:223. His 1929 article in the *Visvabharati Quarterly* was reprinted in K. Sen *c.* 1935:202–33. For Tagore's abridged version, see Tagore 1931:209–21. See V. C. Mishra 1987: 174–8 for an account of a similar tendency in Tagore's translation of Kabir.

[40] The model used by many adepts called 'Bāul' is that of an equal extramarital relationship (*parakīya*) rather than the unequal marital one (*svakīya*).

[41] For example, Sudhīr Cakrabartī uses a line from the poem as the title of his book *Gabhīr nirjan pathe* (1989). Rabindranath's poem, 'Orā antyaja, orā mantra barjita', written in 1936, is No. 15 in the collection *Patraput̤* (Ṭhākur 1395:56ff.). The first part of the text is translated below.

in *sādhanā* is not among the options. What this kind of procedure obscures is, for example, that Rādhā may refer to the female partner, that *ātmā* may be equated with semen (among other things), and *bhagabān* with the male and female in union (*bhaga* = vagina; *bān* = arrow, i.e. penis). Also worth mentioning is the fact that the phrase *maner mānuṣ* figures in only a tiny minority of collected Bāul songs (of whatever provenance), despite the *bhadralok* assumption of the inseparability of this theme and Bāuls.[42] In the 1992 festival of Pauṣ at Santiniketan, the elderly doyen of Tagore songs who presided over the folk culture section berated visiting Bāuls as 'fake' (*nakal*) because they omitted to sing songs about the *maner mānuṣ*.

In his 1883 review *Bāuler-gān*, Tagore cited a song from the collection concerning the search for the *maner mānuṣ*, remarking that this was a popular theme in contemporary English poetry, and one moreover which had begun to be adopted by Bengali poets. Conceding that the song he cites may indeed be of recent origin, Tagore nevertheless legitimises it as authentic on the grounds of its 'plain Bengali' and 'straightforward spirit' (Ṭhākur 1290:37–8), and laments that, while everyone is agog to hear foreign words of 'Universal Love', no one pays any attention when such words are sung by a Bengali mendicant going from door to door. Where Gagan Harakarā's *maner mānuṣ* song is concerned, Upendranāth Bhaṭṭācārya is reluctant to call it a Bāul song, instead categorising it as a song of devotion to God (*BBBG*:95). A further irony is that Gagan Harakarā, a mofussil postman, may have been an associate or follower of Harināth Majumdār, the well-known 'amateur Bāul' mentioned above (Jhā 1995:176).

The aim of this discussion has been to account, at least in part, for the popularity of this phrase among the *bhadralok*, as well as to indicate the kind of interpretation they might have conferred on it. My argument is not that the *maner mānuṣ* theme is attributable to *bhadralok* inspired by the English Romantic poets. After all, this phrase is found in the songs of the famous Lālan (e.g. Jhā 1995:42, 90), who died in 1890, and for whom other influences were undoubtedly formative. Diverse sources were no doubt operative in the case of the earlier poet and journalist, Īśvar-candra Gupta (1812–59 CE), who also wrote on the *maner mānuṣ*, along with other themes, such as the guru, which would later be identified as Bāul (a term not used by Īśvar-candra himself). As remarked above, Lālan seems not to have called himself Bāul. It seems that both the Bāul exemplar, Lālan, and archetypical Bāul themes, such as the *maner mānuṣ*, only became identified as Bāul by a process of retrospection.

An archetypal wanderer, the Bāul of Sen and Tagore is unconfined by context – historical, geographical or social. Just as he floats without trace on the river of time (see p. 57), so he is the wise minstrel drifting sporadically in and out of the lives of those conditioned by location (*deś*) and birth-group (*jāt*). Thus, for example, the free, asocial Bāul unconfined by *jāt*, of Tagore's poem *Patrapuṭ*

[42] Almost all the songs quoted in S. B. Dasgupta's section on Bāuls and the 'Man of the Heart' are by the 'amateur Bāul' Harināth Majumdār, his disciples, or by Lālan.

no. 8.[43] Tagore's stereotypical encounter with Bāuls is that of the physically and metaphorically confined householder attracted by the song of a Bāul outside – on the road, or in nature (e.g. Ṭhākur 1397a:52ff.; 1397b:15; 1383:7). Removed from his temporary village context and indeed human society in general, the lone Bāul is once more the perennial outsider, but now seeking the *maner mānuṣ* beyond all confines and barriers. As Sen puts it: 'ever on the move, removed from all traditional ties, the Bāuls are free as the wind' (K. Sen 1961:103). Since it involves being 'spontaneously individual', and 'natural' (*sahaj*) (Tagore 1931:111, 215), becoming Bāul thus requires no initiation (*dīkṣā*) and no cultivation (*sādhanā*). Decontextualised and spiritualised, his timeless essence is potentially accessible to all, even *bhadralok*. As an outsider he calls especially to his own, and by 1936, Tagore was to claim 'I am one of them':

> They are untouchable, without initiation,[44]
> Priestly touts bar their way
> To the temple, abode of the gods.
> They seek the divine in its own place
> Beyond all confines,
> In the splendour of simple devotion,
> In the star-studded sky,
> In the flower-strewn wilderness,
> In the deep agony
> Of separation from one's companion.
> These fabricated visions, cast in a mould,
> Behind closed doors in enclosing walls
> Forever elude them.
> Long have I seen their practitioners (*sādhak*)
> Alone at dawn by the Lotus [Ganges] river –
> She who destroys without a thought
> The solid foundations of ancient temples.
> I have seen them, one-stringed lute in hand,
> Floating on a stream of song,
> On a secret lonely path
> In search of the Man of the Heart.
>
> I, a poet, am one of them –
> I too am outcast, without initiation,
> My offerings did not reach
> That jail imprisoning the gods [the temple].
> The smiling priest emerges from the temple
> Enquiring, 'Did you see your god?'

[43] '*O āche anādarer acihnita svādhīnatāy, jāte bā̃dhā paṙe ni/ O bāul o asāmājik* . . .', 'Oh Bāul, forever unconfined by birth-group and society, yours is the unmarked freedom of neglect . . .' (Ṭhākur 1395:36).

[44] Literally 'without *mantra*', that is, the *mantra* which confers twice-born status, and therefore the right to enter temples. *Patrapuṭ 15, 'Orā antyaja, orā mantrabarjita . . .'* (Ṭhākur 1395:56ff.), my translation.

'No', I say.
Astonished he asks: 'Don't you know the path?'
'No', I say.
Then the question: 'So you have no birth identity (*jāt*)?'
'No', I say.

It is the fate of colonised élites, including the Bengali *bhadralok* to which Tagore belonged, to suffer alienation of various kinds: from their compatriots, their heritage, their expected role as leaders of their country and their colonial overlords. This common repertoire of dislocation and estrangement was inflected in various ways for different groups and individuals. In the poem quoted, Tagore presents himself very much as the outsider. Whether because of his Brahmo background, his family's 'degraded' (Pirāli) Brahmin status, his personal upbringing (Kripalani 1980:38ff.), the immense sensitivity of his nature, or, most probably, a combination of these, Tagore's sense of isolation and alienation from the structures of society was no doubt exceptional, leading in the end to a deeply felt identification with those iconic outsiders, Bāuls. The theme of transcending structures and boundaries, of being an outsider and indeed mad (a meaning often attributed to the word *bāul*), will be taken up in subsequent chapters in connection with very different kinds of Bāul.

Visual images of Bāuls

The impact of Tagore and Sen's ideas was profound, not only among the *bhadralok* classes in general, but among scholars and artists. Especially revealing in this connection are visual representations of Bāuls, the most seminal of which has been mentioned above, a portrayal not, significantly, of a Bāul, but of Tagore playing the role of Bāul in his play *Phālguṇi* (see Fig. 1). In conformity with the text of the play, this mystical sage-like figure, whirling with half-closed eyes in self-absorbed ecstasy, is devoid of background or context of any kind. The defining features, as with gentry perceptions of Bāuls in general, are music and dance performed by an isolated male. The frequency with which this image has been replicated and inflected is indicative of its profound significance for the Bengali gentry. And indeed, in many respects the Tagorean Bāul has become the authentic Bāul, the standard by which all Bāuls are judged. In a mutually reinforcing pattern, those of the new semi-professional class of Bāuls who most closely replicate this image are lauded as authentic Bāuls and receive further patronage. Certain features of the image of the Tagorean Bāul, from the voluminous robe (inaccessible to the poor) to the position of the emblematic lute high above the head, where it is played only with difficulty, have been adopted in part by successfully 'authentic' semi-professional Bāuls such as Sanātan Dās (Fig. 2). The search for authentic (as opposed to commercial or 'filmy') Bāuls has led to the re-siting of the Tagorean Bāul in the paddy fields of Golden Bengal (Fig. 3). Hovering above the iconic Bāul is the 'unknown bird', a theme beloved of the gentry. Interestingly this image suggests a combination of Tagore and Sanātan Dās.

Figure 2. *Sanātan Dās Bāul.*

Figure 3. *A portrayal of a Bāul on a literary magazine cover (Deś).*

After Tagore made them popular, Bāuls were frequently depicted by Bengali artists. Representations which at first sight seem to depart from the Tagorean exemplar in fact retain many of its key features. The Santiniketan artist Kiron Sinha still depicts the elderly, lone, male Bāul, but this time in nature, rather than against a blank background (Figs. 4 and 5). An example by a woman artist, Shyamali Khastgir, reproduces the stance of the Tagorean Bāul, along with standard accoutrements – the bird and the one-stringed lute – while reflecting the androgynous appearance of local (male) Bāuls (Fig. 6). The inclusion of female elements, either through androgyny or the presence of a female partner, contrasts with the lone, elderly Bāul, who exemplifies an exclusive, sexless, masculinity. All these representations are other-worldly, intoxicated by music or dance, or removed from mundane life through sleep. A recent reproduction of fifty representations of Bāuls confirms these trends (S. Cakrabartī 1997). Diverse though they are, the vast majority of these (forty-five) figure a lone male Bāul, of which all but two are presented without any background or context. (One of the exceptions is in a natural background.) There is also the expected emphasis on singing, dance and music (especially the emblematic *ektārā*), and again, except in one case, the Bāul is self-absorbed with eyes averted or closed.

The partiality of these beautiful images, and of gentry perceptions of Bāuls, will become clearer in the course of this book. At this point, it may be of interest to consider a few contrasting representations by Bāuls organised by themselves, without respect to patrons or researchers.[45] These remind us that contrary to the romantic image of the lone Bāul, removed from worldly connections, Bāuls of whatever kind are, not surprisingly, related in manifold ways to others in society, and, more important in the present context, are concerned to represent themselves as such. The first of these shows Rāj Khyāpā and his partner in esoteric practice seated on a dais, with their disciples, Hem and his wife, below (Fig. 7). The fact that the Tagorean Bāul is so frequently an elderly lone male is no doubt related to the concern to avoid the sexual dimension discussed above. Here, by contrast, this dimension is explicitly recognised, with the woman in each case seated on the same level as the man. The second photograph shows an older Rāj (perhaps in the late 1930s or early 1940s) wearing a turban, and encircled by patrons and disciples (Fig. 8). Intended for disciples and other associates, and figuring partners, disciples and friends, such representations are far removed from the lone Bāul lost in a mystic trance, whose eyes are closed or averted. On the contrary, these subjects gaze directly at the viewer. Even where a lone Bāul is depicted, the subject (Maṇi, a disciple of Rāj) confronts and even challenges the onlooker, as, I understand, he always did in life (Fig. 9). It is significant that, although Rāj and his immediate followers were avid song-writers who also performed their music, they did not have photographs of themselves taken in this role.[46]

[45] Although this lineage, that of Rāj Khyāpā, was the one I primarily worked on, the photographs were taken long before my arrival, and all of those represented were deceased. For reasons of confidentiality, none of the many photographs I took of living Bāuls are reproduced in this volume. The exception to this is Sanātan Dās (see Fig. 2) who expressed a wish for his views and identity to be published.

[46] I am indebted to Dr Christopher Pinney for pointing out that contemporary artistic and photographic conventions no doubt influenced the structure of these representations.

Figure 4. *Singing Bāul (oil painting by Kiron Sinha).*

Figure 5. *Reclining Bāul (oil painting by Kiron Sinha).*

Figure 6. *A Bāul (pen and ink by Shyamali Khastgir).*

Figure 7. *Rāj Khyāpā, Rājeśvar and disciples.*

Figure 8. *Rāj and company, in later life with a group of male associates.*

Figure 9. *Maṇi Gõsāi, a disciple of Rāj.*

Recent perceptions of Bāuls

The change of attitude towards Bāuls in the wake of the efforts of Tagore and Sen is discernible in official sources. In the 1931 Census, Bāuls appear in an appendix entitled 'Indigenous dances of Bengal' by G. S. Dutt, in which emphasis is placed on Bāul songs. As we have seen, in earlier official accounts of Bāuls, the songs were scarcely mentioned, and if they were it was in dismissive or even derogatory terms. While J. N. Bhattacharya (1896) had focused his attention on form ('quaint allegories' for example), Dutt now speaks in admiring tones of the perceived content of the songs, notably their otherworldliness and tolerance (Dutt 1931:539).

From 1901 Tagore had begun to found an indigenously inspired educational institution at a site called Santiniketan, in Birbhum District, in Western Bengal. One of his many aims was to narrow the gap between *bhadralok* and non-*bhadralok* by a variety of means (Das Gupta n.d.: 21, 36–7). Yet, ironically, a significant legacy of the Tagorean idea is to be found in the transformation of Bāuls into an object of 'culture', thus rendering anodyne and placing at a suitable distance those with whom Tagore claimed to have identified. Bāuls have come to figure prominently in Santiniketan life, and perform annually, largely to *bhadralok* audiences from whom they hope to elicit patronage, at the increasingly commercial festival of the month of Pauṣ. The degree to which Bāuls have become a cultural icon can be assessed by the inclusion of a separate section on the 'Bauls of Birbhum' in the 1961 *District Census Handbook* (Birbhum) and several entries in recent District Gazetteers (Birbhum). The early Birbhum Gazetteer had none (O'Malley 1910). The situation of Tagore's Santiniketan in Birbhum District is doubtless the reason for the identification of Bāuls with this area. Rabindranath himself had specifically mentioned, not the Bāuls of Birbhum, but those of Śilāidaha (greater Nadia) as 'genuine' (*khā̃ti*) (letter dated 3 Jyaiṣṭha 1345 BS). Recent scholarship has also tended to assert a close association of Bāuls and other 'minor religious sects' with Nadia, rather than Birbhum District (S. Cakrabartī 1980). Interestingly, while Bāuls were mentioned twice in Hunter's *Statistical Account of Bengal* (see p. 22), neither citation features Birbhum or Nadia Districts. One reason for this may be that Nadia District is also now associated with Bāuls because of Tagore, albeit to a lesser extent than is the case with Birbhum District.

Where most educated Muslims were concerned, a change of attitude towards Bāuls, Fakirs, and so forth, had to await Independence and partition in 1947. Whereas the alienation of nineteenth-century (Hindu and Brahmo) *bhadralok* had led to a search for roots and an indigenous base for their ideas in 'Golden Bengal', many Muslims of the period were for various reasons searching for theirs in Islam. Their notions of the fundamental, true Islam originated outside Bengal, in Arabia and North India (R. K. Ray 1995:23), and strenuous attempts were made to purge Bengali Islam and Muslims of elements considered non-Islamic in terms of this model. As proclamations and tracts against them reveal, those called Fakir or Bāul looked non-Muslim, 'other' and therefore 'Hindu' to reformist Muslims

(Jha 1997:33–4). However, the situation changed after 1947 when the eastern section of Bengal became part of Pakistan. In the newly formed East Pakistan (now Bangladesh), the struggle against West Pakistani domination found expression in the language issue; and the Bengalis of the eastern wing strenuously resisted the imposition of Urdu rather than Bengali as their national language and the suppression of Bengali culture in the name of Islam. The resulting 'Bangladesh Renaissance' embraced the entire literary and cultural tradition of Bengal, especially 'folk' elements such as Bāuls and Bāul songs (G. P. Bhattacharjee 1973:81–2). The early 1960s saw the re-establishment of the famous Bāul, Lālan Śā, perennially popular in West Bengal. A mausoleum was built for him at the place where he lived and died, in Kushtia, which is visited by thousands on the anniversary of his death and during the annual festival (A. A. Caudhurī 1992). The institutionalisation of Lālan and Bangladeshi Bāuls in general has been aided by the founding of the Lālan Centre for Folk Literature (later the Lālan Academy) with its associated seminars, films, articles and books.[47] Considerable disillusionment has recently been expressed concerning this institution, and its appropriation by 'non-Bāul' elements (A. A. Caudhurī 1992:23, 30).

The increasing prominence of Bāuls, itself resulting largely from the efforts of Tagore and Sen, in turn encouraged more detailed research into the subject, and eventually provoked a scholarly reaction against the Tagorean representation itself, notably from Upendranāth Bhaṭṭācārya. Thus, while on the one hand taking A. K. Datta to task for sensationalising Bāuls, Bhaṭṭācārya also criticises K. Sen for spiritualising them, attributing Sen's aversion to what he called 'cheap sensuality' to *bhadralok* prejudice (*BBBG*:80–1). In a parallel way, Bhaṭṭācārya's assertion that Bāuls constitute a 'religious tradition' (*dharma sampradāy*) should be seen in the context of his opposition to the notion that *bāul* is just one of many *sampradāy* (A. K. Datta) on the one hand, and, on the other, to the contrary view that it is not a *sampradāy* at all (K. Sen). Arguing that Sen's 'true' or 'pure' (*sāccā*) Bāul, the wandering spiritual seeker, is the construction of an imaginary ideal, Bhaṭṭācārya maintains that such Bāuls are non-existent in Bengal (*BBBG*:80, 93–4). He not only suggests that the Bāuls Sen met were not 'genuine', he suspects the authenticity of the songs collected by Sen (*BBBG*:74), casting doubt on their style, and maintaining that he was unable to find such songs in his own research (*BBBG*:101–11). The assumption that a modern or well-educated style and use of language disqualifies a song from being Bāul has been shared by many subsequent scholars.

Despite Bhaṭṭācārya's trenchant, if somewhat exaggerated, critique, the resistance to any challenge to the Tagorean image is considerable. Even nowadays, the persistent need to spiritualise continues largely unabated. To take an example at random, a reviewer of a recent Bāul performance scarcely touches on the individual performer or performance, but prefers to indulge in a reverie of a lone wanderer on a dusty road, with long hair, flowing robes and a one-stringed lute, whose face,

[47] Tofayell 1968:103; A. A. Caudhurī 1990:101. For a brief survey of the vast quantity and variety of products of the Lālan industry, see Caudhurī 1990:92–121; 1992:30.

significantly, is not discernible (Jay Gosvāmī in *Deś* 16.1.93:107–8). In the case of academic writings, June McDaniel has demoted the 'ordinary Bāuls' she met in favour of what she calls 'the perfected Bāul', that is, the Bāul of K. Sen and Tagore (1989:161–2). Most astonishingly, R. M. Sarkar, in a glossary entry on 'four moons' practices, has 'semen, menstrual flow, stool and urine' being exchanged 'of course psychically' (1990:225)! Even a scholar of the stature of S. B. Dasgupta, clearly discomfited by Bhaṭṭācārya's critique, continued to defend the Tagorean position and, indeed, to style Tagore 'the greatest of the Bāuls of Bengal'.[48] Dasgupta's refutation of alternative views rests on the distinction he draws between a 'restricted' and a 'general' denotation of the word Bāul. On the basis of what is in effect a definitional fiat, he is thus able to exclude esoteric cults involving sexo-yogic relations as applying only to Bāuls in the 'general' sense.[49] Bāuls in the true, restricted sense are the remainder when such elements are subtracted from Bāuls in the general sense. Predictably, the themes that remain as 'most striking features' are those of the 'Man of the heart' and the 'unknown bird', precisely those which appealed most to Tagore, K. Sen and earlier poets of the nineteenth century who, Dasgupta hastens to add, were in no way attracted to secret sexo-yogic practices (1969:161f., 166). As suggested earlier, this is the key to much of the confusion in Bāul studies. Only exclusion of these sexo-yogic elements would render Bāuls a suitable object of *bhadralok* identification or appropriation, and Dasgupta is far from alone in labouring to effect a distinction between *bhadralok* Bāuls, such as Tagore and the amateur Bāuls on the one hand, and non-*bhadralok* Bāuls, characterised by disreputable body-centred practices, on the other. Upendranāth Bhaṭṭācārya, the first to do extensive fieldwork, accommodated these problematic sexo-yogic aspects by classifying them as religious. His attitude is in interesting contrast to that of earlier scholars such as A. K. Datta and J. N. Bhattacharya, who experienced no difficulty in portraying Bāuls and the like as godless and depraved. Of course, U. Bhaṭṭācārya did nothing to challenge the opposition between *bhadralok* and non-*bhadralok* Bāuls. He simply reversed the values so that the latter became the 'real (*āsal*) Bāuls' and the former imposters.

Bhaṭṭācārya's resistance to the monopolisation of the Bāul field by *bhadralok* (however well-meaning) is understandably shared by other fieldworkers, for our research reveals the immensity of worlds thereby excluded. But this should not blind us to the ultimate untenability of a dichotomy between 'real' and 'fake' Bāuls, however constructed. The difficulties involved in establishing such a divide are revealed by a consideration of individuals such as Harināth Majumdār and Mukundadās (see pp. 29, 33), both of whom are firmly on the 'amateur' side of

[48] Dasgupta 1969:160–2, 187. In this revised version of the first (1948) edition, Dasgupta made significant additions in an attempt to defend his position against Bhaṭṭācārya's arguments. In another context, Dasgupta was prepared to give a little more credence to Bhaṭṭācārya's views (Dās and Mahāpātra 1958:ix). See also Dimock's article entitled 'Rabindranath Tagore – "the Greatest of the Bāuls of Bengal"' (1959).

[49] Dasgupta concedes: 'There is truth in the assertion of Dr Bhaṭṭācārya inasmuch as, in a general way, the *sādhakas* of the Vaiṣṇava Sahajiyā order, and orders akin to it, with their secret practices involving the "four moons" (*cāri candra*) were also known as the Bāul' (1969:161).

the divide, according to Bhaṭṭācārya. Bhaṭṭācārya's chief criterion for 'real' (*āsal*) Bāuls was precisely what disqualified them in the eyes of others, namely, esoteric practices (*sādhanā*) focusing on the body and its products. In this connection it should be mentioned that Mukundadās had been initiated first as a Vaishnava, and subsequently as a Shakta (Gosvāmī 1972:35, 56), although it is not clear from the sources what practices these initiations entailed. Where Harināth is concerned, apart from being an associate of Lālan, a 'real' Bāul par excellence, he too was initiated into Tantra in later life. Not a few contemporary *bhadralok* were involved surreptitiously in esoteric body-centred practices similar to those of 'Bāuls', but under the more respectable banner of Tantra.[50] Nor can relative openness or secrecy about such practices be taken to be diagnostic, for those considered to be real Bāuls also took pains to conceal such practices, through the use of 'intentional language' (*sandhā-bhāṣā*). As we have seen, a related criterion for distinguishing real from fake Bāuls is the subject matter and style of their songs. Bāul songs will be considered in more detail below.

A further possible set of criteria for distinguishing real and fake Bāuls, namely caste, education, occupation and class, is at first sight equally unpromising. While Mukundadās was indeed high caste (Kāyastha), Harināth was born into a middle-ranking caste, Tili. More significantly, some of the best known of Bhaṭṭācārya's 'real' Bāuls were born into high-caste families, for example, Hāuṙe Gõsāi and Gõsāi Gopāl, both Brahmins. Although most 'traditional' Bāuls' are indeed of low caste and/or class origin, and relatively uneducated, this is far from being invariably the case. Many, especially successful songwriters, were relatively well educated, for example, Hāuṙe Gõsāi, Duddu Śā and Rāj Khyāpā. Occupation as a criterion is closely connected to that of class, and both are related to the issue of whether someone is thought to be Bāul full time or part time. While Lālan is known only as a Fakir or Bāul, Mukundadās and Harināth both had other primary (*bhadralok*) occupations. In fact, as will be shown in subsequent chapters, the vast majority of rural initiates called Bāul continue to earn their living through various (albeit not usually high-status) occupations. Even renouncers who live from alms, and gurus supported by disciples, sometimes require additional means of livelihood.

It is clearly the case that, in differing ways, issues of class inform first the agreement on the part of writers and scholars that there are real and fake Bāuls, as well as their disagreements as to which is which. Fieldwork and textual sources do indeed suggest that the few high-born Bāuls accepted as 'traditional' are almost invariably de-classed in some way; often along with technical or *de facto* renunciation of worldly life and social identity. Although they clearly had a wide range of connections, the primary milieu of Mukundadās and Harināth was not the lower (subaltern) classes. Inevitably constrained by their associates and their presumed audience, talented *bhadralok* such as these domesticated a perennially radical

[50] It seems quite likely that Tagore and Bihārilāl, as well as Harināth, were not ignorant of such 'Bāul' practices, but deliberately disguised or excluded these from their presentation. This is even more certain in the case of K. Sen, who was all too aware of persecution of those called 'Bāul' and the danger of too much research on the subject (1953:72–3).

message in the cause of nationalism and conventional spirituality. The predicament of Bhaṭṭacāryā, shared by many committed researchers, is that in erecting boundaries around Bāuls – for the purpose of excluding the hosts of *bhadralok* pretenders, aficionados and imitators – he risked substantialising and even ghettoising people characterised by the uncompromising rejection of definition and identity as such. Despite his shortcomings as an in-depth researcher on Bāuls, K. Sen (and Rabindranath Tagore) should be credited for stressing precisely these characteristics, and for presenting them as a resource, not only for India but for the world (Sen 1961:103; Tagore 1931, 1971).

The descendants of the amateur Bāuls have continued to flourish, although no longer calling themselves such. Not a few middle and upper-class Bengalis sing and write Bāul songs, or simply take pride in calling themselves Bāul, a term which variously connotes a generalised spirituality, non-attachment, eccentricity and a proclivity for wandering. Nor is this phenomenon confined to Bengal. Consonant with the universalism of Tagore (and most of those called Bāul for that matter, albeit of different kinds), non-Bengali speakers and even Western admirers, such as Alan Ginsberg, compose and sing 'Bāul songs' (Ganguly and Ginsberg 1994). Such has been the triumph of the Tagorean image of the Bāul in many areas of Bengal, that the amateur Bāul no longer needs to differentiate himself from the 'real' Bāul. On the contrary, the claim to be an authentic Bāul is at times fiercely contested. This situation remains unaltered despite the considerable research now carried out on Bauls. As pointed out above, it survives partly to the extent that the gulf between lower-class rural Bāuls and *bhadralok* Bāuls is sustained. But also, at least among some of the educated class, changing mores have rendered more acceptable esoteric practice (or at least its sexo-yogic aspects). Indeed the paradoxical situation has arisen where, in addition to those who perform esoteric practices while denying it, nowadays not a few affirm that they do, but in fact do not. Aspects of this complex situation will be dealt with in later chapters.

The Tagorean image of Bāuls predominates in areas of *bhadralok* dominance in West Bengal, especially Calcutta and its hinterland, the Santiniketan area and some district towns. It does so not only because the *bhadralok* continue to be isolated from the realities of rural life, but also because the assumptions of upper-class patrons of folk music and indigenous spirituality have themselves precipitated a variety of cultural phenomena. Those Bāuls encountered by urbanite Indians and foreigners are almost invariably brought to visibility in the first place by non-Bāul patrons or middlemen, and it goes without saying that such Bāuls succeed in proportion to their sensitivity to the varied expectations of their patrons. Even in the case of the most successful Bāuls of this type, proximity is generally destructive of the Tagorean ideal. First, the transcendence of boundaries, so appealing in the Tagorean Bāul, ultimately poses a threat to conventional society; class mechanisms and idealisation re-establish the necessary distance. Moreover, even such *bhadralok*-oriented Bāuls are doomed to violate the unrealisable image of the 'disinterested' (*udāsīn*) Bāul in other ways. After all, the very act of responding to a patron, however subtly, is hardly compatible with the spirit of the autonomous *udāsīn* Bāul, indifferent to worldly concerns. Far from being alone, such Bāuls are usually encumbered by an array of kith and kin through blood, marriage, initiation and music. Rather than following a random, spontaneous trajectory through life, they tend to move from house or ashram to predetermined places, in order to perform songs for fixed remuneration, or in serial attendance of an established chain of festivals.

Despite the radical transformations in images of Bāuls described in this section, my argument is not that any of these perceptions of Bāuls by non-Bāuls were or are entirely false, even by the standards of those Bāuls I worked with in rural Bengal. In particular, it would be inappropriate to view them as Orientalist perceptions of the sub-continent passed intact like the proverbial parcel from the *bhadralok* on to Bāuls. In the analysis of such stereotypes, the degree to which, at every stage, they are a product of negotiation and mutual creation, however uneven the contributions, should be borne in mind. They are constituted more through a process of exclusion and exaggeration than pure projection or fantasy. They thrive on the 'otherness' of 'the Bāul', for historical, geographical and social specificity constitute an ever-present threat to this decontextualised and spiritualised essence. An attempt will be made to introduce some of these specificities in the following chapters. However, before turning to my own pursuit of Bāuls in the field, a brief consideration of scholarly views on Bāul history and identity is called for.

2

The making of the Bāuls: histories, themes, Bāul songs

Authorities on Bāuls, convinced that the name *bāul* denotes a sect, a *sampradāy* (tradition), a cult, an order of singers, a community, a spirit, a class of mystic, a religion – in short an entity of some kind – attempt to demonstrate and confirm this presupposition by a variety of means. Thus the birth or origin of the Bauls is discussed and their ideological ancestry and history is traced. Their identity is revealed through classification of distinguishing features (themes) of Bāul songs, and through etymological research into the name Bāul. Here the first two of these, the historiographic and thematic methods, will be briefly considered.[1]

Scholars have constructed their different histories of Bāuls in the face of considerable odds. As might be expected from the elusiveness of Bāuls themselves, their past is wrapped in obscurity. First, scholars agree that no founder has been acknowledged either by Bāuls themselves or by others. This is particularly inconvenient for those who wish to assert that Bāuls are a sect, since founders and sects are considered to be mutually reinforcing. Second, there is the alleged lack of written Bāul literature. After a search in many districts of Bengal, Bhaṭṭācārya concluded that there is no uniquely Bāul text (*BBBG*:289; also Dimock 1966: 253–4). Indeed it is widely held that Bāul tradition was entirely oral until Bāul songs were transcribed and preserved in written form (by non-Bāuls) at the end of the nineteenth century. In fact, the practice of keeping notebooks of songs (as well as other writings usually not classifed as Bāul), even if transcribed or copied by village scribes, is well attested, but these often ephemeral products rarely reached the eyes of those writing 'history'. It is also difficult to date the songs. Not only have they changed in being passed down through what may be centuries, but they are usually written in village Bengali (and in various of its many dialects at that), a language whose antiquity cannot be assessed, since texts were generally not written in this language (Dimock 1959:38).

Dimock has drawn our attention to another difficulty: namely, that while the word *bāul* does frequently appear in medieval literature and after, its usage continues to be ambiguous, since it is not clear when the term *bāul* (as 'mad' etc.) began to assume its sectarian significance (1966:254). To complicate matters still further,

[1] Examples of etymological research into the word Bāul include S. B. Dasgupta (1969), Dimock (1966), Haq (1975), Sukumar Sen (1971), Karim (1980), Jhā (1985:112–67, 1999:57–114).

he comments on the association 'for many centuries' of 'the Bāuls' with the 'more easily definable Vaiṣṇava or Sahajiyā groups, to whom they bear conscious similarities'. He continues: 'It is indeed possible that the term *bāul*, which as we have seen means "mad", was a term descriptive of these groups, which made a practice of moving against the current of accepted societal custom. It is at best unclear when the term began to be applied to the particular type of mendicant which it is now used to indicate' (1959:37–8).

A consideration of Muhammad Enamul Haq's seminal work on Sufis in Bengal only increases the confusion. Haq divides Bāuls into many named groups (Pāgal Nāthi, Khuśi Biśvāsi, etc.), each owing allegiance to various named Hindu or Muslim gurus (1975:300). In addition he speaks of the Darbeśi who became 'identified' with the Bāuls, the Neṙā who 'afterwards affiliated themselves' to the Bāuls, and the Kartābhajās of whom two 'sub-sects', Āul and Sā̃i, characterised by independence of thought and freedom from the trammels of 'sectarian laws and regulations', were in every respect identical with the Bāuls (1975:283ff.). In this account it is difficult to ascertain who exactly were Bāuls apart from these other named groups. And indeed, in other passages Haq himself concludes that Bāuls are a 'class of mystic' rather than a sect (1975:298, 300), and that *bāul* is the 'generic name of a community formed out of the incorporation of individual mystics who cared for no sect, society or religion' (1975:300). Their only creed, he tells us, is that of 'emancipation from thraldom of all description' (1975:311). The significance of this remark will emerge in due course.

In conformity with his presentation of Bāuls as timeless mystics, K. Sen emphasises their specific historical obscurity. While partly accounting for the lack of written records on Bāuls in terms of their lowly origins and illiteracy, he was also impressed by their lack of concern for the 'history of their sect' (1961:105). Sen reports that he held the following conversation with a Bāul on a river bank in Vikrampur, East Bengal:

> 'Why is it', I asked [the Bāul], 'that you keep no historical record of yourself for the use of posterity?' 'We follow the *sahaj* (simple) way' he replied, 'and so leave no trace behind us.' The tide had then ebbed and there was little water in the river bed. Only a few boatmen could be seen pushing their boats along the mud, leaving long grooves behind them. 'Do the boats' the Bāul continued, 'that sail over the flooded river leave any mark? It is only the boatmen of the muddy track, urged on by their petty needs, that leave a long furrow behind. This is not the *sahaj* way. The true endeavour is to keep oneself afloat in the stream of devotion that flows through the lives of the devotees, and to mingle one's own devotion with theirs. There are many classes of men amongst the Bāuls, but they are all just Bāuls; they have no other achievement or history. All the streams that fall into the Ganges become the Ganges.' (1961:104–5).[2]

The attraction of this account can be gauged from the fact that it was produced, in slightly different versions, in at least three of Sen's publications, and in Tagore's appendix to his 1930 Hibbert Lectures.

[2] The probable Bengali base for this English rendering is in Sen (1993:67), given as a lecture in 1949.

The wandering, mystical Bāul of K. Sen and Tagore is fixed neither spatially nor temporally. Where the former dimension is concerned, Sen is concerned to relate Bāuls immediately to the Sant mystics of north India, and, in the wider context, to the 'soil' of India in general (Sen 1961:105). Tagore was to universalise them still further, in the context of his 'Religion of Man' (1931). Where the temporal dimension is concerned, Sen's attempt (1952) to place Bāuls in the context of the Vedas (including the Upanishads), emically eternal in the sense of existing outside time, is of significance. Since this genealogy contradicts Bāul opposition to scripture as reported by Sen himself (*c.* 1935:209ff.), it is tempting to interpret it as a way of conferring legitimacy on Bāuls, as well as an encompassing Hindu identity. The fact that Sen then attempts to establish parallels between Bāuls and Buddhism, Jainism and the mediæval Sant movement also, is indicative of the author's view of Hinduism as a kind of pan-Indian mystical consensus (1952; *c.* 1935:211ff.). Sen's unifying strategy, where present-day Bāuls are assimilated to the ancient Vedas (as well as their heterodox opponents), low-class 'illiterate' minstrels to a poet from the élite (Rabindranath), and Bengal to the rest of India, is conducive not only to a wider Indian nationalism (as opposed to a narrower Bengali version), but also to the familiar notion of a natural, universal mysticism, which finds its clearest articulation within the wider Hindu tradition. Sen quotes 'a Bāul' as follows: 'Only the artificial religions of the world are limited by time. Our *sahaja* (simple, natural) religion is timeless, it has neither beginning nor end, it is of all time' (*c.* 1935:211). On this evidence it would appear that Bāuls not only reject 'the interpretive notion of "history" ' (Larson 1980:305), but also the far more familiar notions (to South Asians) of *sampradāy* '(living) tradition' and *paramparā* (serial succession of gurus).

In contrast to Sen's Bāuls, however, most authorities on Bāuls are deeply concerned with history, and use it in various different ways to construct Bāul identity. First, there is the search for the 'birth' of the Bāuls, which presupposes the coming into being of some entity which did not exist before, and which since that time has remained essentially the same. Another related type of search is for the antecedents of the Bāuls: those 'sects' or *sampradāy* who between them gave birth to 'the Bāuls', who thus differ from each of these selected forebears in some ways, and resemble them in others. This procedure is rendered transparent by the different ancestries allotted to Bāuls, each of which in turn relates to differing conceptions of Bāuls themselves, presumably on the different parents, different progeny principle.

Convinced that Bāuls are an entity of some kind, be it religious or social, authorities understandably become concerned with their origin or their birth. Disagreement is wide: Brajendranāth Śīl and others date the birth of the Bauls towards the end of the fourteenth or the beginning of the fifteenth century CE (Dimock 1966:254). Sukumār Sen recognises their existence as a definable group in the early sixteenth century (1948:396), Bhaṭṭācārya sees *bāul dharma* as having reached its completed form somewhere between 1625 and 1675 CE (*BBBG*:289), while Qureshi prefers 1700 CE (1977:18). Several authors then envisage a considerable expansion, although again the date varies (e.g. Dimock 1966:254; Haq 1975: 298–9). Haq views corruption as an inevitable nineteenth-century consequence of 'expansion of the creed among the uncultured low-class masses' (1975:299). Most authors agree on a decline (S. K. Bose 1961) or a change of form (Capwell 1974) in the twentieth century, often attributed to Hindu and Muslim reformist tendencies (Haq 1975:299–300; Qureshi 1977:15). This idea of the degeneration or actual demise of the Bāuls, the relegation of their 'completed form' to the past, is conducive to the untrammelled perpetration of each author's image of Bāuls in the face of contradictory material.

As mentioned earlier, several scholars see in 'the Bāuls' the persistence of 'Sahajiyā' Buddhism. Winternitz speaks of 'novel, monistic doctrines, which were called Sahajayāna . . . (and are) even today prevalent among the Bāuls in Bengal' (1933:393). Radhakamal Mukherjee speculates that 'Bāuls . . . inherited the tradition of Buddhist Sahaja Samādhi' (1966:104), while R. C. Majumdar opines that the 'rational spirit and freedom of thought' of the Buddhist Sahajiyā was 'continued by the Bāuls in Bengal throughout the Medieval Age', and even discerns its influence in the nineteenth-century Bengal Renaissance (1971:535). Bhaṭṭācārya presents Sufi and Vaishnava contributions as mere influences which virtually left untouched a Buddhist Sahajiyā core, preserved in secret through the centuries (*BBBG*:50–1). This assessment is consonant with, and in fact necessitates, the author's assertion that Bāuls are a *sampradāy*. Indeed a *sampradāy* of continuous and exceptional fidelity to the line of gurus (*paramparā*) must be envisaged as the minimum requirement for the preservation over centuries of this core, on such a wide scale and, moreover, in secret. Bhaṭṭācārya sums up a lengthy section on the evolution of *dharma* in Bengal (*BBBG*:133–290) with a genealogical table of *sampradāy*, showing the descent of the Bāuls through various ancestors from the original forebear, Tantric Buddhism.

Conferring on Bāuls a fundamentally Buddhist identity is in interesting contrast to those sources, especially early official and *bhadralok* sources, who classify them, if anything, as Vaishnava. Later official sources tend to agree, S. K. Bose claiming that the 'sect' is an offshoot of the Vaishnavism of Sri Caitanya (1961:52–3), and Durgadas Majumdar hesitantly opting for Vaishnava Sahajiyā in his characterisation of Bāuls (1975:156). On the other hand, some Muslim writers confer on Bāuls a Sufi identity, albeit corrupt or degenerate (Karim 1980:50), a conclusion underwritten by historical comments. Haq emphasises the Sufi contribution to Caitanyite Vaishnavism itself (1975:272) and in any case denies that Bāuls are a Vaishnava sect (1975:296). In dubbing Bāuls a 'degenerated Muslim Sufi sect' (1980:5), Karim also denies their association with Vaishnava Sahajiyās (1980:95). Karim's somewhat fanciful efforts largely consist in demonstrating similarities between early (imported) Bengali Sufi orders and Bāuls, and he concludes that Bāuls were a religious sect with a Muslim mystic bias by the fourteenth or fifteenth centuries CE. Any Buddhist influences that may be discerned are probably due to the 'later' conversion of Buddhist mystics into Islam (1980:98), and in any case, he adds, Buddhists were influenced by Sufis from Persia (1980:111). The various ancestries ascribed to Bāuls have more recently been supplemented by another: in diametric opposition to K. Sen's image, Bāuls have been aligned with South Asian traditions of materialism (Lokāyata), especially by S. N. Jhā (1985/6, 1999).

This brief summary does no justice to the wealth of complex and detailed material brought to bear on the history of Bāuls, often by scholars of great skill and dedication. Nor will any attempt be made here to evaluate these various accounts of Bāul history. This is not simply the evasion of a non-historian, nor because all such accounts are to be considered equally plausible or implausible. While this can be said for several accounts (for reasons to do with the lability and increasing cachet of the word Bāul), some accounts can definitely be ruled out of court. An extreme example is the use of spurious manuscripts to argue a high Sufi background or definitively Muslim ancestry for Lālan.[3] One problem with many of these histories of Bāuls lies in their assumptions of singularity and therefore mutual exclusiveness (cf. P. Chatterjee 1994:113ff.). This in turn largely stems from the essentialised and substantialised category 'Bāul'.

I now propose to turn to an ahistorical mode of constructing Bāul identity, whereby scholars substantialise the term Bāul through an enumeration (in fact, a selection) of 'contents' or defining features gleaned from collections of songs, the implication being that these contents, often presented as 'beliefs', characterise all Bāuls. The circularity of such arguments is obvious, yet the game of definition where selected themes are grouped and regrouped in an attempt to aggrandise what are often preconceptions is hard to resist. 'The Bāuls' are then seen as differing from or similar to other named groups in terms of these themes. What is Bāul thus emerges as a unique thematic configuration. In turn, Nāths, Buddhist Sahajiyās, Vaishnava Sahajiyās, Vaishnavas, Tantrics and Sufis each have their own configuration according to how they perform on the thematic checklist. One feature of this approach is that it includes, along with terminology, and on the same level, ideas, practices, attitudes and so on, all inferred from songs, as if these are all 'things' of the same kind, to be shared or passed on. Scholars and other sources emphasise different Bāul characteristics, each selection being consonant with that author's perception of Bāuls.

To illustrate this approach, the five themes selected by the most authoritative writer on Bāuls, Upendranāth Bhaṭṭācārya, will be briefly considered. While Bhaṭṭācārya, in the course of his refutation of K. Sen and elsewhere, suggests that Bāuls are characterised by practices with a female partner and those using the 'four moons' (*cār-candra bhed*), he tends not to define them with reference to these characteristics. One reason for this is that, by his own account, not all Bāuls do 'four-moons' practices, nor do Bāuls at all stages practise with a female partner. Moreover, it is not only Bāuls who carry out these practices (*BBBG*:81–2, 85). In order to define Bāuls, Bhaṭṭācārya resorts to the usual practice of the selection of themes, literally 'the materials of Bāul *dharma*', drawn directly from songs

[3] Thus, for example, S. M. Lutphar Rahmān (1983) and Md. Ābu Tālib (1976) whose arguments rely in large part on a manuscript biography of Lālan judged spurious by leading authorities (R. K. Ray 1995:37 n.42).

(*BBBG*:291–368). The five he selects are:

(i) Antinomianism: literally, 'a spiritual path which contravenes or lies outside authorised scripture (Hindu and Muslim)' (*bed-bahirbhūt dharma*).[4]
(ii) The doctrine of (the primacy of) the guru (*gurubād*).
(iii) The value of the physical human body – the doctrine of the universe and the receptacle (body), (*sthūl mānab-deher gaurab – bhāṇḍa-brahmāṇḍa*). The usual aphorism associated with this runs: 'Whatever is in the universe is in the receptacle of the body' (*Yā āche brahmāṇḍe, tāi āche ei deha bhāṇḍe*).
(iv) The person of the mind/heart (*maner mānuṣ*).
(v) The truth concerning form and essence (*rūp-svarūp tattva*). The central notion here is that the physical body (*rūp*) of each man and woman is identifiable with his or her essence (*svarūp*), usually equated with Kṛṣṇa and Rādhā respectively. In esoteric 'sexo-yogic' practice, the supreme joy of union of the divine lovers is attainable.

These five themes are clearly not of the same order. *Maner mānuṣ*, for example, is a phrase found in some songs, considered by many to be synonymous with others such as 'the elusive person' (*adhar-mānuṣ*), 'the natural person' (*sahaj mānuṣ*), 'the golden person' (*sonār mānuṣ*), 'the lord' (*sā̃i*), 'the unknown bird' (*acin pākhi*) and so on, the list varying according to the source. The notion that all these have the same referent is vitiated by disagreement as to what that is. The other four contents are presented as operating at different levels of inferred meaning. This is fraught with difficulties, for clearly no one-to-one correspondence operates in the songs. Apart from the assumption that several terms may have the same referent, it is clear from the sources that terms often have several referents (Qureshi 1977:35ff.). Support could be found for innumerable themes in such a huge and heterogeneous body of literature as the combined collections of so-called Bāul songs. A certain arbitrariness of selection is therefore unavoidable in the thematic approach to Bāuls. Authors tend to infer ideas, values or practices which in turn are thought to characterise earlier and presumably contributory cults or sects. Hence there are cultural precedents for all Bhaṭṭācārya's contents except for the *maner mānuṣ*, a phrase which occurs only in a tiny fraction of the collected songs. Where innovation is occasionally conceded it is only on the more intractable surface level of terminology, as in this case.

These themes will not be discussed here. Antinomianism and the guru will be dealt with at length in later chapters, especially in relation to Rāj Khyāpā and his people. One may simply note here that, understandably, some authors have found these two themes contradictory (e.g. R. C. Majumdar 1971:536). Moreover, those who argue that Bāuls are a sect or *sampradāy* allow general antinomianism less scope than those who emphasise spontaneity, individualism (A. Dasgupta and M. A. Dasgupta 1977: Introduction) or creativity (K. Sen 1961:104–5). On the

[4] '*Bed*' (Veda) means the *śariyat* for Muslim Bāuls and Fakirs.

other hand, Sen's mystic Bāul tends to transcend and encompass orthodox thinking, rather than actively oppose it; indeed, as remarked above, Sen relates his Bāuls to the Vedas. As we shall see, the mordant anti-orthodoxy found among Rāj and some of his followers is far too combative to be in any sense 'mystical'. The third and fifth themes both involve the attribution of supreme value to the human body, conflating it on the one hand with the external universe and on the other with internal essence. The crucial importance of the body and body-centred practices will be considered later.

Bāul songs and 'intentional' language (*sandhā-bhāṣā*)

Before proceeding to a description of fieldwork and my own pursuit of Bāuls, some consideration is required of the material on which virtually all scholars have based their work, namely 'Bāul songs'. First, in order to counteract the impression of self-evident authenticity which the presence of published collections of such songs tends to confer, it is pertinent to recall the problems associated with the definition of Bāul songs. As mentioned above, while Bāuls are sometimes defined in relation to Bāul songs (whoever composes Bāul songs is a Bāul – the case of Rabindranath and the amateur Bāuls), the reverse is often taken to be true (only Bāuls can compose Bāul songs, or, in the extreme case, whatever a Bāul composes is a Bāul song).

Although everyone is sure that they know who is a Bāul[5] and what is a Bāul song, in fact there is little agreement on this.[6] For those who start from the Bāul song rather than the Bāul, the defining characteristic of Bāul songs may be formal or stylistic. Here again, what is called Bāul song varies, musically speaking, from area to area (S. N. Jhā 1985:561; S. Cakrabartī 1992a:38). At times a song may also be judged to qualify as a Bāul song on the basis of theme (for example, the Man of the Heart, the Unknown Bird, or, for Bhaṭṭācārya, esoteric practice). Even more commonly, certain songs are excluded on this basis. This degenerates into another circular process (on the pattern of the ambiguous relationship of Bāul songs to Bāuls), whereby initial selection for collections of Bāul songs is in part determined by thematic criteria, and subsequently the collection is used as a basic source from which to elucidate the 'themes' of Bāul songs.

As we have seen, Bhaṭṭācārya argues that the term Bāul song (and, by implication, the word Bāul) has been used too loosely from the latter part of the nineteenth century onwards. Only those songs which express and are rooted in the philosophy (*tattva-darśana*) and practice (*sādhanā*) of 'Bāul religious tradition' are authentic Bāul songs. Therefore, only Bāuls can compose them (*BBBG*:103). While this assertion has the merit of reflecting the opinion of many traditional practitioners called Bāul, who tend to the view that words and actions (*sādhanā*) inevitably

[5] For example, Dimock writes: 'Despite all the doctrinal and historical vagueness, however, everyone knows a Bāul when he sees or hears one' (1989:76).

[6] There is considerable disagreement as to whether particular known individuals are or are not Bāuls. Even apart from the problem of Tagore and the amateur Bāuls, one may cite the case of Pāglā ('mad') Kānāi, who is a Bāul to Tofayell and Siddiqui (author of the *Kushtia District Gazetteer* 1976), but not to others (see Dasgupta 1969:160).

go in tandem,[7] it assumes a continuous tradition of authentic Bāuls in exclusive relationship with a clearly defined genre of 'real' Bāul songs. I should like to propose an alternative, albeit less emic, scenario for the composition of these songs, one which avoids such essentialist assumptions, and thus the dichotomy between so-called real Bāuls and amateur Bāuls.

As pointed out earlier, the amateur Bāuls cannot be entirely divorced from a thriving rural tradition of composition and versification, in which, of course, Bhaṭṭācārya's 'authentic Bāuls' play a far more central and continuing role. It seems clear that such composers and versifiers, whether called Bāul or not, would compose on all important aspects of their lives, subject to the constraints of current and evolving genres, permissible themes, and the wishes of patrons and presumed audience or readership. While the songs of a renouncer confining himself to ashram life reflect that dedication (and some of these are Bhaṭṭācārya's Bāuls), the wider range of concerns of a householder initiate and guru such as Śarat Candra Nāth (Dīn Śarat) is expressed in compositions with a broader range of themes (Nāth 1341 BS). Even Rāj Khyāpā, who had a female partner but no children, and who ultimately lived a fairly isolated life, did not always confine himself to themes Bhaṭṭācārya would regard as Bāul.

Communities of Vaishnavas and Fakirs, including those called Bāul, fostered oral and written traditions of great complexity, which included the composition of songs. Gurus who were gifted composers of songs often attracted disciples inspired to do likewise. (This was the case with Lālan and some of his disciples, Rāj Khyāpā and several of his immediate disciples, and even the 'amateur Bāul' Harināth Majumdār.) In contrast to the emic model, this does not mean that all initiated (or even 'perfected') Bāuls can compose songs, and in this connection it is unsurprising that many of the most skilled Bāul songwriters were relatively well educated. Nor, of course, does this mean that all these rural composers were necessarily initiated into a lineage which might be called Bāul. In a situation where the majority of those who wrote songs classifiable as Bāul also composed songs which would not be so classified, the rise of the amateur Bāul song is indicative of the different concerns (from patriotism, imperialism and social problems, to romantic love) of composers who increasingly chose to call themselves Bāul, and their presumed audiences. In other words, the ascendancy of such songs constitutes a difference of degree rather than of kind. Above all, as stated above, it indicates the lability and increasing cachet of the label Bāul, from a certain period. The fact that Kāṅāl Harināth's songs were initially published as Fakir songs, and only much later as Bāul songs (P. Majumdār 1999:136), is an indication of a more general trend.[8] The question of why, from a certain period, uninitiated composers found the notion of 'the Bāul' and the 'Bāul-song' so attractive that they tried to write in a 'Bāul' style and assume that identity has been addressed above.

[7] On the non-dualistic principles outlined by Marriott and Inden (1974, 1977), Marriott (1976), Inden and Nicholas (1977).

[8] Even as late as 1919 CE, the scholar S. K. De clearly considered Bāul songs, unlike *yātrā, kabī* and *pā̃cāli*, to be unworthy of separate treatment (1962).

Published collections of Bāul songs, normally transcribed (edited and 'corrected') from oral sources, invariably obscure such complexities. Those collections, or more usually parts of collections, which do derive ultimately from manuscripts in the possession of so-called Bāuls have also usually suffered selection, 'correction' and editing in the process.[9] Where they exist, song collections in the possession of Bāuls have often themselves been traditionally written down by village scribes. An example of this is the manuscript of Bholāi Śā, disciple and adopted son of the famous Bāul Lālan (see Jhā 1995). An exception to this is the collection of songs composed and written down, along with other kinds of material, by Rāj Khyāpā (Openshaw 1994). However, where one or two of his songs have found their way into published form (e.g. *BBBG*:869, 844), discrepancies between these and Rāj's handwritten text lead one to presume another source. In the case of Dīn Śarat and Rāj Khyāpā, we are fortunate to have a published volume and manuscript (respectively) of songs compiled by the composer, as opposed to a collector or editor. Such rare collections reveal the slippage between the categories 'Bāul' and 'Bāul-song' obscured by other compilations.

Partly because of the disagreement concerning which criteria to use, the number of songs classified as Bāul by one scholar or another is vast, and there is immense heterogeneity of style, form and terminology in the songs thus compiled. Terminology associated with Vaishnava, Hindu Tantric, Sufi and Sahajiyā literature is found in different songs and sometimes within the same song. There are even songs, included in collections of Bāul songs, which may convincingly be glossed in a straightforward neo-Vedantic or orthodox Muslim sense. When such potentially inconvenient contents appear to be deconstructed or voided within the song, no problem is experienced by commentators, but otherwise this provokes a search for 'intentional meanings' in an attempt to impose uniformity on the material. The very format of a collection of songs suggests uniformity and continuity and tends to lull doubts concerning their status and the criteria used in their collection.

In the collections, songs are usually ordered according to theme (see above) or composer (e.g. *BBBG*). The identity of the latter is gleaned from the collophonic idiograph or 'signature' found towards the end of many Bāul songs. This idiograph usually consists of the name of the composer ('Lālan says . . . '). Although such claimed authorship is clearly connected to the affirmation of personal experience and creativity as opposed to traditional knowledge (cf. Granoff 1986–92:300), notions of creativity deriving from uniquely individual events and experience are not always appropriate. Consonant with Hawley's (1988) notion of the signature as a sign of authority rather than authorship, disciples and other followers or admirers of a famous 'Bāul' may compose in his name. It seems clear that Lālan's name was also used as a signature by others (S. Cakrabartī 1992b:107). An unambiguous case, cited by S. B. Dasgupta, significantly concerns the 'amateur Bāul', Harināth Majumdār, whose disciples composed songs in their guru's name (S. B. Dasgupta

[9] A conspicious recent exception is Jhā 1995.

1969:184).[10] A common practice is to include two names in the signature, that of the composer and his guru, which may indicate consonance between personal experience and enlightened authority. More easily discernible to the researcher than composing in someone else's name is the contrary practice, where would-be composers insert their own name into a pre-existing song, for collections reveal the same song with several different signatures. Although this is sometimes done for self-aggrandisement and/or to attract disciples or patrons, it is removed only in degree from the established traditional practice of bricolage in which materials from songs are recycled in various combinations and inflections. In the case of the guru, this may be explicit, as when Maṇi Gõsāi ends one of his songs with: 'Maṇi cites the words of Rāj [his guru] . . .'.

Whether scholars and writers on Bāuls emphasise the continuity of traditional forms and contents or instead highlight individual authorship in association with Western derived notions of creativity, almost all are preoccupied with a search for the unique and definitive text. The presupposition is that a song composed by one individual must imply one correct version of which others are 'corruptions'. Written versions tend to carry more weight, especially in *bhadralok* eyes. Indeed, collections of written, decontextualised songs often become the yardstick by which a song performed by a 'Bāul' is evaluated. The problematic existence of discrepant written versions of the same song is almost invariably accounted for in terms of error in transmission, or transcription (by the collector from an oral source). Yet, as Qureshi suggests, differing recensions seem to be the rule rather than the exception. Sometimes different versions directly contradict each other, he adds (1977:43), although he is not prepared for that reason to abandon his quest for the definitive text. Editors of Bāul songs also have a tendency to 'correct' the songs in the light of their own understanding, to use those versions which most appear to support their argument, and so on. The approach of many authorities in this and related matters encourages the idea of a system, the tyranny of text over performance, of tradition over creativity in the sense of constant reworking and choice of interpretation. As a result, contextual studies relating songs or song series to particular performances and the exegeses of those performers are virtually non-existent.[11]

In a similar way, meaning is thought to be single, or if double, unambiguously so (providing the code is known), and to inhere in the text itself, hence the irrelevance of context for such writers. The assumption is that there is a correct interpretation of the songs, just as there is a correct version, even if we and possibly some Bāuls are not aware of it. Thus sources engage in combat on the correct interpretation of certain 'symbols'. The possibility that there may be several different

[10] The extent of this practice is unknown, since it is not readily detectable in the sources. It will be argued later that this degree of self-negation *vis-à-vis* the guru is not typical of rural practitioners called Bāul. Perhaps the chief reason for writing in the name of a famous Bāul, such as Lālan, is to give a song credibility and cachet.

[11] Salomon's article (1979) on Sanātan Dās's performance and exegesis of a song cycle is an exception. However, in other contexts, Salomon too argues for a definitive text.

or even simultaneous interpretations is often not entertained.[12] This brings us to an all too brief consideration of *sandhā bhāṣā* or *sandhyā bhāṣā*, a complex topic usually discussed in the context of what is called 'Tantra', Hindu and Buddhist.[13] In connection with his work on the Caryā songs and Dohās (see p. 27), Haraprasād Śāstrī used the term *sandhyā bhāṣā* (literally 'twilight language'), meaning half concealed, half revealed (1959:8). However, Vidhuśekhar Bhaṭṭācārya and others have argued that the correct term is in fact *sandhā bhāṣā* 'intentional language', that is, language literally and apparently meaning one thing, but aiming at a deeper meaning (or meanings) behind it.[14] In the context of Bāul and other Bengali 'obscure religious cults', Dasgupta divides *sandhā-bhāṣā* into technical jargon, where some words are infused with meanings known only to initiates, and 'enigmas' or riddles which, when interpreted literally, yield an absurd meaning (1969:414–15, also T. Mukherji 1963:11–12). Amusing enigmatic verses are common in rural Bengal, where they are generally known as the songs of the *ulṭā bāul*. And indeed this is a style frequently found in collections of Bāul songs.[15] Sometimes such songs are posed as a riddle, with the composer asking 'does anyone know the secret?' (Dasgupta 1969:423–4). For present purposes the important point is that a spectrum of phenomena is included under the rubric *sandhā bhāṣā*. For example, as stated above, language with presumed 'intended meaning(s)' may make literal sense or not. Thus a non-initiate listening to a song or a conversation may not even suspect the existence of anything other than conventional surface meanings. However, there are Bāul songs which deliberately point to the existence of some other meaning(s), while witholding clues as to what these might be.[16]

[12] A notable exception to this is S. N. Jhā (1995, 1999).

[13] For a recent discussion of *sandhyā/sandhā bhāṣā* in relation to the 'Bāul' Lālan, see S. N. Jhā (1995:295ff).

[14] Vidhuśekhar Bhaṭṭācārya's argument is outlined in S. B. Dasgupta (1969:413). See also P. C. Bagchi (1975:27ff.) and Eliade (1958:249ff.). Although most scholars agree with Bhaṭṭācārya on this issue, A. Wayman and S. B. Dasgupta have also defended the use of the term *sandhyā-bhāṣā*.

[15] An example of this style, chosen at random from English translations of 'Bāul songs', is the following song by Gopāl (D. Bhattacharya 1969:62):

> . . . The land talks
> In paradox
> And the flowers devour
> The heads of fruits,
> And the gentle vine,
> Roaring,
> Strangles the tree.
> The moon rises in the day
> And the sun at night . . .

[16] For example, the following song of Gõsāi Gopāl leaves the non-initiate wondering what the 'moon' 'means' here (D. Bhattacharya 1969:65–6):

> Where is the home
> of the moon?
> And what makes
> the cycle of the days
> wander encircling
> the moving nights?
> . . .

These songs sometimes serve to demarcate the boundary between initiated and non-initiated, or between initiates at different 'stages'. Where they issue a challenge to answer the riddle, the song is usually part of a verbal duel (*pāllā*) in which another (initiated) singer is expected to respond appropriately. Other songs do provide the outsider with clues to a meaning which will make sense of the song.[17]

As to the purpose of such twilight or intentional language, several possibilities have been suggested. Many scholars argue that its function is to keep certain practices secret, either from the more conventional or orthodox, or from non-initiates in general. Such secrecy in turn is seen either as protecting the practitioner from persecution, or the uninitiated from knowledge and practices which they might misuse (Eliade 1958:250). A second and contrary idea is that its purpose was to attract people away from 'orthodox' religion towards Tantra. A third explanation is connected with the idea that higher experiences cannot be expressed in ordinary language (Govinda 1959:46). Eliade further argues that *sandhā bhāṣā* serves to

> project the yogin into the 'paradoxical situation' indispensable to his training . . . It is not only to hide the Great Secret from the noninitiate that he is asked to understand *bodhicitta* at once as 'thought of awakening' and *semen virile;* through language itself (that is, by creation of a new and paradoxical speech replacing the destroyed profane language) the yogin must enter the plane on which semen can be transformed into thought, and vice versa. (1958:250–1)

Finally Agehananda Bharati has suggested that intentional language might have been used as a 'mnemonic device' or even at times facetiously (1970:170–1).

The relation of these first two accounts with what Bharati terms 'efferent' and 'afferent' *sandhā-bhāṣā* respectively may be noted. While an efferent term employs abstract theological or philosophical language and intends an objective entity, action or event, afferent refers to the use of object-language intending conceptual

> He who is able to make
> the full moon rise
> in the sky
> of the darkest night,
> has a right to claim
> the glory of the three worlds . . .

[17] As for example in this song by Yādubindu (D. Bhattacharya 1969:76):

> Plough-man
> are you out of your wits
> not to take care
> of your own land?
> A squadron of six birds
> is picking at the rice,
> grown golden and ripe,
> in the field of your limbs.
> Farming the splendid,
> measured land
> of this human body,
> you raised the crop . . .

In this song, references to the limbs and the human body enable the translator to interpret retrospectively the six birds as the six adversaries (*rīpu*) – lust, anger, greed, ignorance, pride and envy.

or mystical realities.[18] The fact that Bharati feels able to assert that the latter 'overwhelmingly outnumber' the former (1970:173) suggests the certainty of an established system, where intended meanings are transmitted with the same regularity as texts themselves, although this can hardly be said for the whole of Tantra (Granoff 1986–92:300; Shaw 1994:149). Systematisation and uniform sources of authority tend to eliminate dissent and alternative interpretation, and in any case, it is these former aspects which are more apparent in textual and therefore historical sources.[19] To retain Bharati's terminology for the moment, one might say that in the context of Bāul studies, by contrast, the preponderance of afferent versus efferent depends on the disposition of the commentator, and, in the case of those called Bāul, on their assessment of their audience. Commentators such as K. Sen, Tagore, H. C. Paul and so on tend to infer more subtle, spiritual and respectable intended meanings, while others, such as Bhaṭṭācārya, would infer more 'gross', ostensibly 'material' and less respectable ones. In the former case, the assumption is that overtly erotic language is an expression, however inadequate, of experiences which are inexpressible directly in words. In the latter, practices are inferred which in the view of the commentators require concealment.

Without wishing to pre-empt a later discussion, it is worth noting here that, while many rural practitioners (*sādhak*) called Bāul may in some contexts produce conventional 'spiritual' interpretations of their songs, in general, and especially for insiders, the efferent predominates over the afferent, contrary to what Bharati affirms for Tantra. These contrasting situations should be considered in relation to several other factors. The most important of these is the ultimate concern of most such Bāuls with direct sense-perception (*bartamān*), as opposed to the universe of conventional religiosity or idealist spirituality, which is generally dismissed as hearsay (*anumān*). As one guru told me: 'Our interpretation (*byākhā*) is different from other interpretations. Everything must be seen in relation to the body and (material) substance (*bastu*).' Whereas rural Bāul practitioners would generally be classified as 'subaltern' or at least 'declassed', both Hindu and Buddhist Tantra have at times been favoured with upper-caste and even, occasionally, state patronage. For Bāuls, secrecy has a vital role to play in averting verbal, written and even physical attack from established religious groups. Whereas many Tantric texts

[18] An example of the former (efferent) is where *bodhicitta* (thought of enlightenment) is taken to mean 'semen virile' (Bharati 1970:173). An example of the latter (afferent) is where *lalanā* (woman) is taken to mean *nirvāṇa* (enlightenment). In fact, the situation is more complex than this, as seen by Bharati's example (of efferent *sandhā*) of the sun (not an obvious philosophical or theological term) 'intending' the menstrual fluid (Bharati 1970:176).

[19] It goes without saying that scholarly assessments are dependent on the nature of sources available. Dissent and alternative meanings are thus more easily accessible to a contemporary fieldworker than to an historical or textual scholar. It should also be remembered that scholars differ as to the degree of systematisation in Tantra, Padoux, for example, stressing rigid sectarianism (*Encyclopaedia of Religion*: 76 quoted in Granoff), whereas Granoff emphasises a tension between the validity of the new, based on personal experience, as opposed to authoritative scriptures and the line of teachers. Needless to say, the characterisation of 'Tantra' in the present context concerns the more systematised end of the spectrum, and certainly not the Caryā songs, which bear many resemblances to Bāul songs: for example, they were probably addressed to both insiders and outsiders, and similarly tended to contain the name of the author or other *siddhācārya* (perfected teacher).

are confined to initiates, songs of those called Bāul are usually directed at both insiders and outsiders, traditionally for the collection of alms and also, nowadays, for remuneration from concerts. This acts as a partial determinant of overt content, and tends especially to exclude scandalous surface meanings such as are found in some Tantric contexts.[20] As Sukumar Sen suggests, it is appropriate to consider the more 'external' meanings and connotations, which often lend themselves to orthodox religious (idealist) interpretations, in the context of alms gathering (*bhikṣā*) (1948:4). Whereas some scholars have argued that the secrecy of esoteric language deprives it of rhetorical or persuasive function (Thurman 1988:125), this is scarcely the case with Bāul songs. Indeed their appeal may wean people away from more conventional forms of religiosity, and even induce them to take initiation from a guru. It may also be noted here that while a common idea of *sandhā bhāṣā* as involving one intentional meaning in addition to the conventional meaning tends to void the latter of significance, this is not the case where multiple or indefinite meanings are intended, or where the act of intending itself is crucial. Connected with this is the obvious point that these glosses operate against a background of conventional language. This is not only because the encoded meanings retain links with either the sound or conventional sense of their terminology, but also because only certain words and phrases are encoded in any way, being embedded in portions of text in straightforward standard (or dialect) Bengali. Another ramification of the fact that songs are sung to a wide variety of people is that a song is usually transmitted without an interpretation. This conduces to a multiplicity of meanings and to the fostering of talent for creating meaning or meanings. Confronted with a previously unknown song, an older, skilled initiate will be able to conceive of many more meanings than a novice. The extent to which this multiplicity is retained, or collapsed in order to privilege one particular meaning, depends on a variety of factors, especially context, but also on the personal disposition of the individual expounder.

Both textual and fieldwork sources on Bāuls reveal polysemy or polyvalence (Eliade) to be more common than any clear one-to-one equivalence between conventional and intended meaning (although the latter may well be attempted in the context of a particular person explicating a particular song). Within the ambit of Tantric studies, a variety of phenomena is described, ranging from such one-to-one equivalence (Snellgrove 1959:99–100), to the attribution of several fixed meanings, depending on the practitioner's level of realisation (Thurman 1988:130), and finally to polyvalence culminating in ambiguity (Eliade 1958:250f.). Kvaerne argues that Eliade's representation of *sandhā bhāṣā* as conducing to a state of paradox is even more clearly expressed in the Buddhist Caryā songs (1977:39ff.), which bear a relationship to Bāul songs. Kvaerne's assertion that the same image may have both an absolute and a relative referent – a challenge to Bharati's afferent–efferent classification – is also true of Bāul songs in one sense. However, rural Bāul practitioners, who tend to privilege body-focused meanings, are unlikely to be even-handed on this issue. Whether this reflects different source

[20] Bharati quotes an extreme example: 'inserting his organ into the mother's womb, pressing his sister's breasts, placing his foot upon his guru's head, he will be reborn no more' (1970:171).

material,[21] or a difference of view between the Siddhas and practitioners called Bāul is a matter of speculation. In the context of the fifteenth-century north Indian sage, Kabīr, Hess proposes the analogy of three-dimensional molecular clusters, where individual symbols are connected to multiple meanings, which in turn are connected to other symbols. Exploration of texts and glossaries only permits a shifting illumination of structures and worlds – total comprehension is ever elusive (Hess and Singh 1986:138–9). Such an approach is useful in the context of Bāul songs also, with the added complication that meanings themselves may become symbols, and vice versa. Moreover, except for instances of (temporary or flexible) 'sectarian' closure (where different interpretations may be associated with different groups, or different stages within a group), new interpretations are often readily accepted and added to the repertoire.[22] Many songs can be read at several different levels, and meanings proliferate or condense, accumulate or oppose each other, in what Eliade referred to as a 'destruction of language' (1958:150). In no respect is rigid adherence to a symbolic code evident from those who compose, sing and explain Bāul songs. However, while meanings are multiple and shifting, they are not infinite. For example, although the 'four moons' (*cāri candra*) is variously interpreted by rural Bāul practitioners, 'meanings' fall within the parameters of male and female sexual fluids (including menstrual blood), urine and faeces. Spiritualised interpretations of the 'four moons', such as that of H. C. Paul (1973a), must at present be ruled out of court (S. N. Jha 1995:66–7).[23]

This discussion of Bāul songs might usefully be concluded with a consideration of the hazards of translation. While translations can obviously be more or less accurate, they are at best misleading, since, without an extremely lengthy commentary (which would itself impose an unwarranted fixity), they exclude not only nuances but other levels of meaning. Written or sung with at least two different audiences in mind (non-initiates and initiates, with the latter being at various stages), translation often amounts to butchery. For example, the word *caitanya* may refer to the historical figure (the saint Caitanya), to 'consciousness' (a literal meaning), and to the menstrual flow (among several meanings for initiates), with each meaning having the potential for varying degrees of presence or absence in different contexts and for different people. Even if it were possible to put several translations side by side, following a 'conventional' gloss with one (or more) for initiates, this would impose an unwarranted closure and misleadingly lineal structure on the meanings. In any case, meanings are far from being uncontested, even at the same level of initiation. Different groups, and even different individuals, may create or perpetuate particular meanings (just as they might practices), partly, but only partly, as

[21] Kvaerne's work is necessarily confined to textual and other historical sources, including a Sanskrit commentary on the Caryā songs. On the other hand, the primacy given to body-focused meanings only emerges clearly in fieldwork, where explanations of songs may be forthcoming, rather than from texts, where one is confined to surface meanings.

[22] Thus meanings from different parts of Bengal, which I occasionally 'traded' for others, were often readily and seamlessly incorporated by those receiving them. Hess reports a similar experience (Hess and Singh 1986:146).

[23] Of course, it is possible that such meanings will have to be taken more seriously in future.

a boundary creation or maintenance exercise. Even this last statement imposes an erroneous rigidity on what is in fact a fluid process, for, in the course of one conversation, new nuances, connotations and even denotations may be created. Every new exegesis (offered, for example, by an initiate from another locality) may alter the parameters of connotations and denotations. At the same time, it should be pointed out that ideas relating to structure are not excluded. Within a vast repertoire of possibilities, one finds robust notions concerning the authenticity of songs, correct recensions and true meanings, held by both initiates and performers.

In this book, I have deliberately avoided the usual focus of Bāul studies, namely Bāul songs. Apart from the fact that the great majority of studies are concerned with these to the exclusion of everything else, reasons for this decision included the availability to a serious fieldworker of a mass of alternative material, as well as the enormous hazards involved in treating the songs, especially in translation, as outlined above. However, we shall have occasion to return to the subject of language, in addition to songs as such, for the various phenomena which have here been included under the rubric of *sandhā bhāṣā* are by no means confined to songs or written texts. Of particular importance in this connection is *hari-kathā* which literally means 'god-talk', *hari* being a name of Viṣṇu. However *hari* also means 'woman' to many initiates, and *hari-kathā* refers to discussions concerning esoteric practices. This will be considered later.

Recent studies on Bāuls

These preliminary chapters have focused on earlier (and formative) secondary sources on Bāuls. The purpose of dealing with these older sources was to outline the evolution of present views of Bāuls held by the *bhadralok*, as well as to present the reader with some material relevant to Bāul studies. Subsequent studies have all too often reproduced, in varying combinations, the same perceptions as their antecedents, any original contribution consisting of new insights being brought to bear on old collections of songs. While more recent works in English are written from various perspectives – Bengali literature (e.g. Dimock 1966; Salomon 1979), ethnomusicology (e.g. Capwell 1986), performing arts (e.g. Majumdar and Roberge 1979), anthropology (e.g. R. M. Sarkar 1990) and folklore (e.g. A. Karim 1980) – serious studies in Bengali emerge, almost without exception, from the institutional stable of Bengali literature (for example, works by S. N. Jhā and Sudhīr Cakrabartī). In studies written in both Bengali and English, the overwhelming emphasis is on songs, and there are, in addition, innumerable collections and translations of Bāul songs. While this is in itself a perfectly valid approach, it has led to a one-dimensional perspective on the subject. Certain modern scholars, in particular S. N. Jhā, have based their studies on in-depth fieldwork, in the pioneering tradition of U. Bhaṭṭācārya.

It would serve no useful purpose to enumerate the multitude of articles on Bāuls, or the plethora of collections and translations of Bāul songs, produced in West Bengal, Bangladesh and abroad. Some of these are listed in the Bibliography.

An indication of the volume and recent escalation of works on Bāuls is provided by A. A. Caudhurī's work on the famous Bāul, Lālan Śā. Here the section on the history of research into Lālan alone, by no means discussed in depth, occupies fifteen pages, while an incomplete list of works on Lālan takes up a further fourteen (1990:92–121).

An attempt has been made in this part to show how Bāuls have been variously constructed by the indigenous (and colonial) élite. For all these authorities, Bāul is seen as some kind of entity or essence, rather than a vehicle for negotiable and disputed meanings. At times, the essentialised category 'Bāul' has served unacknowledged ideological purposes, for example to appropriate the Bāuls as part of a esteemed indigenous heritage, Hindu or Indian in the case of West Bengalis, Islamic (or at least non-Hindu) in the case of Bangladeshi writers. From being wholly 'Other', Bauls also came to be seen as the 'Self', in various and complex ways, by an increasingly alienated Bengali élite.

In striking contrast to the invisibility of Bāuls in early sources, nowadays they not only exist, they matter. Indeed, in some senses they exist because they matter. The phenomenon of *bhadralok* expectations precipitating certain ways of being Bāul (see p. 41) is only the most concrete manifestation of this. Operating on a more general level is the ever-widening ascription of the name Bāul, irrespective of its differing connotations. Despite the kaleidoscopic incarnations of Bāuls, the Bāul as outsider (whether as Other, Self or a combination of these) is a recurring feature. The theme of transcending or eluding structures and categories, of being an outsider and indeed 'mad' (a meaning often attributed to the word 'Bāul') will be taken up in subsequent chapters in connection with very different kinds of Bāuls.

In the course of outlining evolving *bhadralok* perceptions of Bāuls, I have at times felt it necessary to adumbrate my fieldwork findings in order to place such perceptions in a wider context. However, just as the amateur or idealised Tagorean Bāul should not be dismissed as entirely false, by the same token the presence of a continuous, authentic Bāul tradition, underlying or contrasting with these various 'invented traditions' (Hobsbawm and Ranger 1983), should not be assumed. This issue is considered in the following chapters, in which I turn to my own pursuit of Bāuls through fieldwork.

II

In search of Bāuls

3

Fieldwork in Rarh

On one matter, authorities on Bāuls agree: whatever their provenance, Bāuls are a Bengali phenomenon. Although in practice this is seen in geographical terms, it is more accurate to say that songs collected and classified as Bāul songs are composed in Bengali. Definition and classification of Bāuls and Bāul songs thus tend to proceed from within the broad context of the history of Bengal and Bengali literature, and this is despite the difficulty of the peripheral relation of things *bāul* to mainstream Bengali history. 'Bengal' has meant different things at different times, and not infrequently several things at the same time (Hunter 1881:1). For the purposes of the present work, Bengal comprises present-day West Bengal (India) and Bangladesh (formerly East Pakistan). This is the area where, with some notable exceptions, Bengali is the first language of a majority of people. Fieldwork for this book was conducted in West Bengal.

Bengal lies on the Tropic of Cancer, bounded by the Bay of Bengal to the south and by various ranges of hills and mountains for much of the rest of its border. A large part of the area consists of the linked deltas of the Ganges and Brahmaputra rivers which inundate the plain annually during the monsoon. The centre for fieldwork connected with Rāj Khyāpā and his followers was a largely moribund section of this delta area, known as Bagri (Bāgri). However, the initial phase of fieldwork was conducted in another region known as Rarh (Rāṙh), which lies to the west of Bagri on slightly elevated ground. In view of the importance of rivers in Bengal, the staple diet is predictable (rice and fish), as is the main cash crop (jute). Since partition, West Bengal has become heavily industrialised in certain areas. The partition of Bengal in 1947, for the second time, one part (West Bengal) going to India and the other becoming the eastern wing of Pakistan (subsequently Bangladesh), largely on the basis of majority religious allegiance (Muslim or Hindu) has had incalculable consequences for both sides, economic, political and cultural.

I began fieldwork in 1982 from a base in Santiniketan, Birbhum District, in the Rarh area, where I have had Bāul acquaintances since 1973. Initially the work was confined to Birbhum District itself, but I soon moved out on Bāul networks to other parts of Rarh, namely the districts of Burdwan, Bankura and Purulia. Subsequently my scope broadened to include the Bagri area of Murshidabad and Nadia Districts. I first came across those associated with Rāj Khyāpā, whom I call Rāj's followers or Rāj's people[1] in 1985, and began detailed fieldwork with them in 1986, mainly in the Krishnapur Police Station area (PS) of Nadia District, but also in Murshidabad and, in connection with Rāj's history, in a part of Birbhum far from Santiniketan, where he spent the last decades of his life. From 1988 I combined fieldwork with translation and analysis of manuscripts of the Rāj Khyāpā people, and began to write up the material as a thesis in 1991.

This section primarily concerns ideas of what it is to be *bāul*. Ideas held by those who would claim or admit to this identity, by those who would not, and by those who would not but are thus called by others are all included. Information from both areas of fieldwork is considered and contrasted. One area centres on Santiniketan (in Bolpur PS), the other on Krishnapur. Since each fieldwork area radiates out from these centres and is considerably larger than either Bolpur or Krishnapur, I also use the short-hand terms 'Rarh' and 'Bagri' respectively. This does not imply either that the responses described below are unique to either geographical area, or that they are to be found uniformly throughout that area. While the intention is to demonstrate the variety in use of the name Bāul, there is no attempt to describe the whole range of responses. The main aim is to delineate two contrasting sets of responses. The first of these predominates in the Santiniketan area and is centred on performers of Bāul songs, these ranging from alms-takers to professional performers. Here complex responses to the perceptions of Bāuls held by *bhadralok*, and others on whom they are economically dependent, are operative. In this situation, *bāul* identity is often thought highly desirable and is even subject to competition, not only by Bāul performers themselves, but even by others who reject and resent their predominance. The second of these responses predominates in Krishnapur, where *bāul* tends to be an identity with variable but distinctly undesirable connotations, imputed to others in an ever-receding pattern.

In dealing with each area, I begin with non-Bāul perspectives on what it is to be *bāul*, and then move inwards to a consideration of various insider views. In this section I also include sketches of a few of the hundreds of musicians and initiates I met in the course of my research. For a variety of reasons, these cannot be considered representative. When starting fieldwork in Birbhum District, my Bāul acquaintances and friends struck me as highly individual, in a variety of colloquial senses. The fact that they appeared to differ considerably in their theoretical and practical orientation to the world clearly relates to problems of the category Bāul itself. But this is not the whole story. Many wore their individuality on their sleeve, espousing an ideal of autonomy and non-conformity. Later I was to conclude that those called *bāul* do indeed tend to be more 'individual' than the renouncers to whom Dumont applied the term (1960:46), partly because they inhabit the boundaries of different worlds, including that of renouncers. This and other issues will be discussed in more detail below.

[1] '*Rājer lok*' ('Rāj's person' or 'people') refers to those who wish to link themselves with Rāj Khyāpā, or are thought to be so linked. Such linkage is usually expressed in terms of initiation.

Although Birbhum District is popularly known as the 'Home of Bauls', 'Land of Bauls' or 'seat of... Bāul philosophy' (D. Majumdar 1975:156), modern scholars have considered Nadia District a more plausible candidate. Birbhum was the adopted home of both Tagore and K. Sen, and the presence there of many well-known, self-proclaimed Bāul singers should perhaps be seen in this light. Along with most researchers on Bāuls, I began my fieldwork among these singers in Birbhum. Subsequently I found it more conducive and interesting to shift focus to the Bagri area in general, and eventually to the 'Rāj Khyāpā people' in particular. (Although Rāj himself was an inhabitant of another part of Birbhum District for the last part of his life, I know no one in Rarh who would now call himself or herself one of Rāj's people.)

Birbhum District lies to the west of the delta area of West Bengal, on slightly elevated terrain. It forms part of the wider area called Rarh, which lies to the west of the Bhagirathi river, a distributary of the Ganges, as opposed to Bagri (the moribund delta to the east of that river) which includes much of Murshidabad and Nadia. Because the land is elevated, better drained and drier in general, Rarh has traditionally been considered more salubrious, although less fertile, than Bagri. While the rivers, the older mode of transport, run eastwards across the district to join the Bhagirathi, the main railway line, built around 1860, runs north–south through the district. Its construction led to the growth of new towns along its route, at the cost of the older river settlements. Bolpur is one such new town, lying on the railway line in the southern part of the district. Santiniketan, a mile away from Bolpur, was originally founded as an ashram in 1862 by Maharṣi Debendranāth Ṭhākur (Tagore). From 1901, his son Rabindranath began a series of educational experiments in Santiniketan. Despite strong associations with Vaishnavism through the poets Jayadeb and Caṇḍīdās, and, more recently perhaps, through the Bāuls, the district has even stronger affiliations with Shakta Tantra, oriented to Goddess worship. Several 'seats' of the goddess (*pīṭhasthānas*) are located within its boundaries (D. Majumdar 1975:154–60). Despite points of resemblance between some Shakta Tantric practices and those attributed to Bāuls by some scholars, self-proclaimed Bāuls are usually concerned to differentiate themselves from the former. A Shakta-Vaishnava opposition may be articulated here, or the view that Shaktas are more socially and religiously conformist. However that may be, Shakta traditions are well established among the dominant and upper castes of the district, and certainly Rāj Khyāpā, whose story will be summarised below, found Shakta Birbhum an alien environment.

Non-*bāul* views on Bāuls (Rarh)

Popular views concerning Bāuls, especially those of the *bhadralok*, have not been unaffected by scholarship. More significant here than the pioneering work of A. K. Datta or U. Bhaṭṭācārya's vast and little-read tome are the inspiring sentiments of K. Sen and Rabindranath, still quoted in lectures and talks all over Bengal. This influence is especially discernible in Calcutta, the Santiniketan area, and some district towns of West Bengal. A scholarly provenance (or legitimation) may be detected in certain analogies concerning Bāuls, current especially among the educated upper castes. What is of interest here is which of many original analogies survive, and the form in which they do.

One popular analogy – 'mud mixes with mud, but bricks never merge' (*kādāy kādāy mele, iṭe iṭe melenā*) – was attributed to Kabir by K. Sen, the mud referring to Kabir and his followers, and the bricks to religious scholars.[2] Several times I came across this analogy applied in relation to Bāuls versus non-Bāuls, or even, significantly, to low versus upper-caste Hindus. It was elaborated for my benefit that the Bāuls (or low castes) are *kā̃cā* (raw, upripe), whereas non-Bāuls (or upper castes) are *pākā* (ripe, cooked, prepared). In further explanation of the mud and bricks analogy, I was often told by *bhadralok* informants that Bāuls mix with everyone: 'they don't respect caste, or differences between Hindu and Muslim', 'they make *par* (others, "them") into *āpan* (one's own people, "us")'. Another related analogy, attributed to Tagore, is one in which Bāuls (or alternatively *sādhus* or even Vaishnavas) are likened to leaves shed from the two great trees of Hinduism and Islam. These fallen leaves are shed automatically, by a natural process, I was told, and thus the tree suffers no harm. Moreover, the leaves, from whichever tree they fall, mingle together and become indistinguishable.[3] Here loss of caste and religious identity (first and second analogy respectively) combined with an identification with nature take on an ambiguous quality not present in their sources (Tagore and Sen). In this alleged denial of distinctions, this entropic disintegration of boundaries (D. P. Bhattacharyya 1981:37) is also discernible one of the many connections between being Bāul and being mad. In the context of affirming that Bāuls do indeed disregard distinctions between Hindu and Muslim, Muhammad Mansur Uddīn adds, in an illuminating phrase: 'Indeed they mix together like madmen' (*pāgale pāgale milan ghaṭe*) (1383 BS:10).

Echoes of the ideal Bāul of K. Sen and Tagore are especially discernible when wandering is emphasised as a Bāul characteristic, together with the associated qualities of 'divine' madness and spontaneity. One may be told, for example, that 'a Bāul never knows where he will be tomorrow'. As is the case with scholars, etymologies are marshalled in defence of these notions. Thus *bāul* may be rendered *be-ul* (without (*be-*) discipline or restraint (*ul*)), or as *bāundule* (vagabond), or as deriving from *bātul* (crazy). Other related ideas are that Bāuls do not discriminate between persons and situations; they have no commonsense, no mental balance (*digbidik jñān*, literally 'knowledge of direction'). People may joke '*āmi bāulā haba*', which refers to an intention to simply wander about aimlessly.

[2] Sen's Kabir adds: 'too much writing hardens their hearts. When stones strike against each other, sparks fly. Being ignorant we are like clay. Clay mixes easily and indistinguishably. The Mullah and Pundit will never agree' (1952:299).

[3] It is interesting that the category 'Vaishnava' (generally regarded as firmly within 'Hinduism') is included here. This no doubt reflects the view, sometimes found in rural areas, that because Vaishnavas recruit from all castes and communities (i.e. including Muslim), they cannot be Hindu.

Interestingly, alternative scholarly views, such as those of A. K. Datta and Upendranāth Bhaṭṭācārya, have scarcely impinged on *bhadralok* consciousness in this area, although a few of the latter's findings occasionally percolate through via less significant but more accessible sources. However, increased mixing with so-called Bāuls, on however superficial a level, has presented another kind of challenge to the Tagorean stereotype. Thus one sometimes hears that Bāuls are promiscuous, addicted to hashish and, increasingly – perhaps because of the commercialisation of Bāul and *bhadralok* relations – that they are greedy for money. The gulf between these two stereotypical complexes is often rationalised, as it is in the case of *sādhus* in general, by relegating the 'pure' (*sāccā*) Bāul to the past ('there used to be real (*āsal*) Bāuls, but now we do not see them', etc.). Otherwise, in similar fashion to such scholars as S. B. Dāsgupta (1969), Haq (1975) and Dimock (1966), Bāuls are seen as falling into two classes: one genuine (and usually conveniently inaccessible), one degraded (by other influences).

Many educated Hindus of Birbhum regard Bāuls with an ambivalence similar to their attitude to *sādhus* in general: as an ideal never to be emulated. Despite voicing envy for those free of the bonds of worldly life (*saṅsār*), and admiring the courage of renouncers in extricating themselves from the web in which they feel enmeshed, householders would usually spare no effort in discouraging a relative from pursuing such a vocation. Indeed, where Bāuls are concerned, the ambivalence is even sharper, for it is precisely the lack of boundaries so attractive in the idealised Bāul of K. Sen and Tagorean provenance which ensures lowly status. Nevertheless it is not entirely false to say that, especially in Santiniketan – this being a somewhat unique *bhadralok* enclave – being Bāul is a 'good thing'. At least from the time of Rabindranath who often, as we have seen, posed as a Bāul and was represented as such by others, it was the fashion for the boys of well-to-do families to be photographed dressed as Bāuls. A regular part of *bhadralok* musical education is learning Bāul songs, and indeed several *bhadralok* of the locality compose 'Bāul-songs', one or two going so far as to dress as Bāuls on occasion. A highly respectable but independent and eccentric widow claims to be Bāul, and I even heard a young woman undergraduate of the university at Santiniketan cite becoming Bāul as her ambition.[4]

Bhadralok attitudes to Bāuls can also be said to parallel the attitude of Bengali urbanites to rural life in general. On the one hand, villages are idealised and identified with a golden past (Bengali families usually trace their roots to a rural area). On the other hand, they are regarded as alien, and infested with snakes, dacoits, ghosts and revolutionaries. Bāuls have been cast in the shape of various ideals, sometimes inspired by nationalist sentiment, but these same perceived qualities render them threatening to conventional, caste-based society. Friends and well-wishers often combined a fascination for my research topic with considerable apprehension at the prospect of my doing fieldwork.

[4] It should be added that this is unusual, and provoked mild amusement in others, as well as unvoiced suspicions concerning her common sense and respectability. Such indigenising strategies pose no risk to the more established.

However, it should not be thought that the ideal Bāul of some scholars and local popular perception is entirely reducible to a figment of the *bhadralok* imagination. Nor is this only due to the clear tendency of the *bhadralok* stereotype to accentuate and even precipitate certain ways of being *bāul*. Another factor is the consonance of the Tagorean ideal with Bāuls as seen from the point of view of those in conventional householder life. The connection between the presentation of the renouncer as an unattached individual and reliance on texts of Brahmin householder provenance will be discussed later. In the specific case of Bāuls, the contexts in which *bhadralok* meet people called *bāul*, that is, at festivals, as collectors of alms from houses or shops, on trains, in concerts (all situations in which women are absent or less visible), do little to discourage perceptions of Bāuls as permanently itinerant lone spirits, in short as the idealised, unattached (*udāsīn*) Bāul. Aspects such as ashram life, female partners and networks of 'kin' connections generated through initiation are less visible from this perspective. The ideal Tagorean Bāul also resembles someone who is *in the process of* moving out of householder life (*saṅsār*), or is on its fringes, someone, in short, who not only is likely to have a greater degree of connection with the world of householders, but also who has perhaps not yet been initiated, transferred his allegiance to guru-kin, or become established in esoteric practice with a partner. I should add here that, to the extent that the more commercially successful Bāuls increasingly travel in troupes, the idea of Bāuls as bands of professional musicians is gaining ground.

Bāuls on being *bāul*

In view of the results of my library research, it was not entirely a surprise to find that the first problem was one of identifying Bāuls. My intention of combing the villages of Bolpur PS for Bāuls, conceived out of a desire to be systematic, was rapidly abandoned. Instead I came to prefer a method more consonant, I presumed, with the *bāul* way of doing things: that is, accompanying Bāul friends (some of whom I had known from the 1970s) on excursions that promised to be interesting – trips to festivals or to other homes or ashrams – where I met other people called *bāul*, and in turn followed up those I liked or found interesting. Bāuls of the Santiniketan area were always impressing on me the importance of following one's inclination. This in turn is related to a concept of the Bāul (favoured by those patrons who are influenced by K. Sen and Tagore) as a spontaneous, 'natural' mystic in pursuit of the *maner mānuṣ* (literally the 'person of the mind/heart' or 'a person of one's liking'). This concept can be used to justify not going against one's inclinations in general (on the grounds that one should not hurt the person (*mānuṣ*) within), or to argue for mixing, on any level, with those one likes. Later on I was to identify this latter pattern of fieldwork with another prescription, more common among those in Bagri – that of the practice of 'associating with adepts' (*sādhu-saṅga*).

This method held another advantage for me. Despite my familiarity with Bengal, where I had previously done research, and the Bengali language, the hardships of initial fieldwork, and indeed my resistance to it, were considerable. At first everything seemed difficult: the food (which later I came to relish), the total lack of privacy, the lack of bathrooms and toilets, sleeping on hard floors with no mosquito net, the perpetual exhaustion from staying up all night listening to performances or conversing, and the frustration of coping alone with linguistic usage even more complex than I had anticipated (my first and only research assistant[5] having rapidly succumbed to the temptations of the ever available hashish). Through these difficulties, I hung on to the thread of affection of my Bāul (and Fakir[6]) friends, allowing it to nourish and support me. Its genuineness rarely seemed to be compromised by the obvious truth that sophisticated social skills in a wide variety of contexts were essential to the livelihood of these initial Bāul friends of mine. A foreign associate not only enhanced their status in most situations in Bengal, but also, one way or another, promised some alleviation of the appalling uncertainties which threatened to sabotage the joy (*ānanda*) and love (*prem*) of life. The lives of even relatively successful Bāul singers seemed to be blighted by memories of grinding poverty, seasonal fluctuations in 'programmes' (paid concerts) and perpetual competition from Bāuls 'popping up like monsoon frogs', in the words of a jaded old pro. This increase in would-be Bāuls is attributable to the impact of *bhadralok* expectations, backed by their money and prestige. It is largely *bhadralok*, and to a lesser extent foreigners, who make donations to Bāul singers for performing on trains or in private houses, who hire them for private and public concerts, and who send them abroad. Thus there has been a diversion of the ideal of *bhikṣā* (alms for singing) into a more commercial, contractual arena. Despite this transformation (and its degree may well be exaggerated), the old ideal exerts a powerful and complex influence, even, paradoxically, in this new contractual sphere. After all, it forms an integral part of the *bhadralok* image of the unworldly (*udāsīn*) Bāul. The ideal is expressed by *bhadralok* and Bāul alike: 'a Bāul never asks for anything'; 'when a Bāul sings, if people give they give, if they don't he simply moves on'. The necessity to embody such an ideal is hardly calculated to enhance the ease of drawing up contracts.

My first contacts during fieldwork were Bāuls who endeavour to live from their music, and thus inhabit this immensely contradictory world. Apart from technical and dramatic prowess, success in this field is partly a matter of sensitivity to context, and, specifically, skill at fulfilling conflicting expectations. For example, the idea of the Bāul as entertainer (as seen in J. N. Bhattacharya's account), while superseded in the case of scholars and *bhadralok*, still persists in many villages of the Rarh area. Thus a Bāul musician whose performance in the Santiniketan context is a model of sober 'spirituality', with restrained elegant gestures and delicately ornamented vocal style, adorned with just a touch of *bāul* madness, may completely switch style in non-*bhadralok* village contexts. In the latter, his repertoire may stretch to witticisms, mimicry, obscenities and histrionics. He will tend to make greater use of folk and popular musical styles and accompany his singing and playing with

[5] A Brahmin 'younger brother' whom I had known from previous visits.

[6] The term 'Bāul' tends to apply to Hindus only in Rarh. In Bagri, on the other hand, '(Muslim) Bāul' and 'Fakir' are often identified.

wild leaps and whirlings, much to the relish of the audience. (Subsequently, he may feel obliged to decry the necessity to indulge the villagers' taste for colour (*raṅ*) to the accompanying fieldworker.) An audience with mixed expectations creates a dilemma. Sometimes the leader or older member of a troupe will begin the show with a dignified, restrained and 'spiritual' performance. He may perform songs with obscurely 'intentional language' (that is, language which points away from surface meaning to another non-explicit level), thus enhancing his spiritual prestige and creating an aura of otherness. This contributes to authenticity at a time when the attention of the audience is easier to command. Subsequently sons or disciples[7] of the first performer will 'colour' the proceedings, and here language with explicit pointers to meanings of interest (the mysteries of the female body etc.), which others would disdainfully dub 'raw verses' (*kā̃cāpad*) may be served up, along with popular, even risqué songs. This will then be excused by the leader of the troupe to those with more gentrified expectations on the grounds of the inexperience and youth of performers or the demands of the audience. It is interesting in this connection that a large number of Bāuls of the Santiniketan area have a background in folk-drama (*yātrā*) or other performing arts.[8]

Like the skilled performers described above, a great number of Bāuls of this area are of the Jat Vaishnava community. Jat Vaishnava is a complex category, broadly speaking comprising those for whom the label Vaishnava functions, either positively or despite themselves, as their caste identity. They may be differentiated from those for whom the identity Vaishnava coexists with a separate caste identity, such as Brahmin or Kayastha. They also differ from those Vaishnavas who have renounced householder life and along with it caste identity of any sort. Jat Vaishnavas are traditionally associated with singing and music, and living from alms.

Many established and relatively successful Bāul performers in the Santiniketan and Calcutta areas are Jat Vaishnavas.[9] They include the most famous of them all, Pūrṇa Dās, 'Returned from Abroad,[10] Bāul Emperor and TV and Radio Artist'. It seems reasonable to assume that the numbers of Jat Vaishnavas of Rarh and Calcutta claiming Bāul identity has increased considerably in the past few decades. While there are many successful singers who sing Bāul songs without claiming to be Bāul in Calcutta and Dacca (Bangladesh), Pūrṇa Dās is one of the few self-proclaimed Bāuls to have achieved this degree of fame and success.

7 In the context of performers, the guru is almost always an instructor of music and perhaps dance.

8 One skilled and well-respected performer of this kind was completely out of his depth when he ventured into Bagri, only to be booed into silence by initiates at a gathering of *sādhus*.

9 It should not be thought that Bāuls who are Jat Vaishnava are somehow united through this common identity. There is often rivalry among the few singers of reputation, both in respect of obtaining 'programmes' and the attentions of potential patrons. Rivalry may be temporarily forgotten in order to defend common interest against external threat. The selection of musicians for the group seems to be a matter of weighing all sorts of delicate considerations: whose playing or singing would enhance the group without upstaging the main singer, who would show proper deference to the main singer, and so on. Often other less-well-known Jat Vaishnavas were selected, and sons (if available).

10 '*Bideś pherot*', occasionally rendered on visiting cards 'Returned Foreign'. Nowadays trips abroad are a source of prestige rather than shame.

More typical than Pūrṇa Dās in some ways are B. N., a Jat Vaishnava singer, his wife M., and their three sons, who live in the town Bolpur, adjacent to Santiniketan. I had met them (as well as some other Jat Vaishnava Bāuls) in 1973 at the famous Bāul festival of Jayadeb Kenduli. B. N., a talented musician, also used to sing in people's houses in Santiniketan for small donations, and in the hope of meeting potential patrons, *bhadralok* or foreign. Now he usually goes abroad once a year. B. N.'s father was a Brahmin who had 'married' a Vaishnava woman, herself a musician of considerable talent, and B. N.'s 'visiting card' encapsulates both these identities in schizoid fashion, despite the aspersions the combination casts on his legitimacy. On one side is written 'B. N. Mukherji' (a Brahmin title) and on the other 'Mad Lord (*Pāgal Ṭhākur*) B. N. Dās Bāul' ('Dās' denoting his Vaishnava origins). M. is of Jat Vaishnava origin, and in the locality, B. N. and his family are generally known as (Jat) Vaishnava or by a more derogatory term for this, 'Bairāgī'.[11] However, 'Bāul' is also used, especially in connection with B. N.'s singing. B. N.'s own tendency has been increasingly to accentuate a whimsical *bāul* side of his identity over the years, in response not only to the impulses of his personality, but also to the taste of his Santiniketan patrons. His appearance has also undergone several transformations. At first he was clean-shaven, with long oiled hair and dressed in white (in Vaishnava manner). Later he grew a beard, and began to wear what he called 'Bāul dress', that is, a turban and patchwork robes. In recent years he has adopted saffron robes and turban and is again clean-shaven (another notion of Bāul dress). His wife is even more versatile: in addition to Bāul (and Vaishnava) idioms, she is possessed each year by the goddess Bhabatāriṇī ('She who takes one across the ocean of this world'), who is identified with Kālī, and whose worship is said to be traditional in her husband's paternal family, and requires a Brahmin priest. Despite his various changes of garb, B. N. has never abandoned the basic renouncer style, that is, long hair and loose flowing robes. He and his wife were also initiated by a much respected teacher of *sādhanā*, whose identity is said variously to be Vaishnava, Bāul or Darbeś (Dervish). (In the present context, *sādhanā* refers to various esoteric body-centred practices, including those involving a partner of the opposite sex, of which the ability to control orgasm is an important feature.) Realising that I had heard of *sādhanā*, M. (and B. N. less coherently through the perpetual haze of hashish) gradually told me of their guru and his teachings. Among other initiates of the area, however, B. N.'s interest or ability in *sādhanā* is questioned (because of evidence that he does not practise retention of semen[12]), although his interest in women is indubitable. Two of their three sons are talented musicians, taught to sing and play several instruments by their father and paternal grandmother. The eldest is also initiated into *sādhanā*, although a conventional marriage (arranged by his mother) has perhaps hindered his development in that direction. The second son's interest is confined to music. The youngest son initially eschewed both music and *sādhanā*, and went abroad

[11] *Bairāgī* is also applied to renunciate Vaishnavas.
[12] The fact that his wife has been sterilised, and that he has fathered a child by someone else is cited.

with a foreign wife, from where he has now returned. M., articulate and relatively independent, was one of those with whom I travelled to meet her friends and relatives (by blood or through various gurus), as well as to festivals, households and ashrams. In the course of this I met many other people calling themselves Vaishnava or (particularly if they were musicians) Bāul. My failure to conform to the stereotype of the Westerner obsessed with music, hashish or sex sometimes caused confusion. Such expectations derive from the limited experience of a few Bāuls, such as B. N., whose foreign acquaintances tend to be wedded to the notion of Bāuls as Bengali hippies. Despite my failings on this score, I was usually in demand, if only as a potential patron.

Would-be Bāuls also include poor, often Scheduled Caste (formerly 'Untouchable') men, and occasionally women, of musical and dramatic talent. They may be attracted to what they presume to be the *bāul* way of life, as well as the possibility of earning a living in this way. For example, G. and B., of different Scheduled Castes, would often sing together at small local festivals for little or no money, without the elaborate dress of someone like B. N. They had no initiation (not even the first stage of *dīkṣā*, which many ordinary householders take), and no guru of any kind except an upper-caste amateur musician who could read music. Family life held little attraction for them, even apparently in their childhood, during which they had often run away from home. G. had been involved in folk drama as a child. Neither knew about esoteric practices with a partner, although G. seemed to know of its existence. By chance, G. eventually settled with his family in an isolated place, ceased to be *bāul* in most senses, and took to cultivation. B. eventually left his village and family (mother, father, wife and children) and came to settle in Santiniketan with another woman. Nowadays he looks very much the Bāul, a token of his success being his acceptance as authentic by an expatriate Bengali expert on Bāuls, who shall be nameless.

In a continuation of the earlier 'amateur Bāul' phenomenon, members of higher castes, including *bhadralok* dressed up in quasi-Bāul fashion, are still to be seen singing 'Bāul songs'. These range from a Brahmin lecturer at a teacher training college, to the son of a pious tea-shop owner of middle-ranking caste. (A far greater number of middle and upper-caste Hindus write Bāul songs, as do a whole range of renouncers. The former category includes the owner of a shoe-shop, and an ex-principal of a college.) Nowadays, these are disparagingly referred to as 'gentlemen Bāuls' (*bābu Bāuls*), or 'artists' and 'performers' (*śilpī*) by those who claim a more traditional base, notably those of the Jat Vaishnava community. For example, a prosperous man of Nepali origin writes 'Bāul songs' – in Bengali and English (of a kind) – this latter no doubt to attract the interest of foreigners. These he sings himself, and persuades others to sing. Like Pūrṇa Dās, another more widely acclaimed 'Bāul Emperor', he cherishes grand schemes for founding a hostel for old or ailing Bāuls, a school for Bāuls and so forth.[13] Generally treated with amused tolerance or resignation by semi-professional Bāul

[13] See Manas Ray (1994:93–4) for a translation of a speech by Pūrṇa Dās on this issue and a common reaction.

singers and esoteric practitioners, and with awe by parvenus, I once heard his claim to be Bāul Emperor vociferously challenged by an outraged elderly *sādhu*: 'Who gave you the title Bāul Emperor? Who the hell are *you*?' These more educated and powerful members of society plagiarise from older songs, and use encoded language on the surface level, being in many cases ignorant of its more hidden meanings. At times, their Bāul songs degenerate into an anodyne version of neo-Hindu idealism, a litany of praise for past Bengali (*bhadralok*) heroes, or, perhaps prompted by political parties, a vehicle for social or political messages, such as national integration or family planning. Such songs, coupled with their connections, knowledge of *bhadralok* rhetoric, some English, and economic advantage enable these would-be Bāuls to attract attention and funds from *bhadralok* and foreigners alike. This appropriation of the field is usually viewed as participation by the appropriators, for with the assurance of their background, they assume they understand and are in a position to correct and re-establish the 'true Bāul tradition'.

Largely helpless in the face of this appropriation, other self-proclaimed Bāuls react with a mixture of acquiescence and resistance. 'Gentleman' or 'artist' rivals are dismissed by them as preaching castelessness while retaining their high-caste titles and privileges. Other tokens of resistance include privately singing songs composed by 'gentleman Bāuls' in slightly different versions, so as to mock the author.[14] The term 'amateur Bāul' (*śakher bāul*) is still sometimes applied to part-timers, who temporarily don Bāul garb, particularly when performing Bāul songs. Connotations of acting and lack of authenticity override all others in the use of the term nowadays, and it is therefore used only of others. On the other hand, these same 'gentleman Bāuls' will claim superiority over those whom they allege are interested in money alone, or are Bāul as a profession rather than from conviction, and so on, another echo from the past. Similarly, new entrants from poor families are derided on various grounds by the more traditional Jat Vaishnava singers. It may be said that they have no family background, they are not initiated, they do no esoteric practice, they are only interested in money, they are too inferior to pursue this path and so forth. These new entrants themselves will argue that such criticism is motivated by a desire to forestall competition and by caste bias – true Bāuls should treat everyone equally, they point out.

Similarly, a small minority of self-proclaimed Bāuls may attempt to command respect in terms of esoteric practice (*sādhanā*), especially in opposition to those who live from their music, whom they deride as mere performers. Such Bāuls may either be failed performers, or non-performers who resent the value given to those who specialise in 'externals'. In the midst of such relativism, *sādhanā*, albeit understood in widely differing ways, commands near universal respect, except for the few who are ignorant of its existence, regard it as an aberration, or (in the case of a few élite Bāul aficionados) who demote the Bāul as practitioner (*sādhak*) in favour

[14] A young Jat Vaishnava Bāul was instructed to perform the Bāul songs of a respected shop-keeper owner (called K. Sen) by his father (also a performer). On a private occasion I heard him pervert the 'idiograph' of one of these so that it went: 'So stupid is K. Sen. . . . '.

of the Bāul as artist. However, it would be a mistake to conclude from this that there is some general agreement that those who do *sādhanā* are more *bāul* than others. As will be shown later, an emphasis on the category of the human being (*mānuṣ*) is frequently invoked by so-called Bāuls to deny not only differences of birth group (caste and religion), but also any sort of distinction between human beings, including that derived from stages of achievement in *sādhanā*. The ideological equivalent of the bricolage of the patchwork garb worn by some Bāuls reveals itself in a readiness to accept new ideas or meanings and incorporate them seamlessly into their rhetoric (cf. Hess and Singh 1986:146). But the more one becomes involved in a *system* of *sādhanā*, associated with a lineage structure and authority, the more other identities tend to over-ride *bāul* identity.

Nowadays, Birbhum District is advertised as a tourist destination largely in terms of its Bāuls. The West Bengal state government has taken over the running of what is perhaps the main Bāul festival (at Jayadeb Kenduli). At Jayadeb, as well as at the Santiniketan festival of the month of Pauṣ, the composition and performance of songs on 'appropriate' themes, such as family planning, national integration, anti-communalism and so forth is encouraged. Winners of Bāul competitions held by the state government are paid a monthly stipend in return for singing with their troupes at appointed places in West Bengal on similar set themes. The state government has also made films on Bāuls. Even outside West Bengal, Bāuls have become part of the folk-culture industry, and nowadays frequently travel all over India and abroad.

The patronage of (largely Western) foreigners has become increasingly important in some circles. Bāul singers often hanker for trips abroad, which later enhance their visiting cards along with other qualifications such as 'radio artist', or – even better – 'TV artist'. The image of Bāuls as Bengali hippies predominates for some Westerners, and is assiduously fed back to Western patrons by at least one Bāul singer. For example, Pūrṇa Dās, the most successful Bāul in *bhadralok* terms, opined: 'You know, Bob Dylan is a sort of a Bāul. And so are the hippies . . . All over the world we have met Bauls.'[15] A few *bhadralok*, and even fewer foreigners, have become cultural brokers in the business of exporting Bāul singers to the West, Japan etc. In turn this means that the tide of *bhadralok* heading for Bāul festivals such as Jayadeb Kenduli and the Santiniketan festival of Pauṣ is swelled by foreigners also in quest of their ideal. Despite the mutual attraction of some foreigners and some Bāuls, the intellectual influence of the former is minimal, since their linguistic interaction with Bāuls and knowledge of the wider phenomenon are far more limited than those of the *bhadralok*.[16]

One place where all these various kinds of Bāul come together, if only to perform on the same stage, is at the Santiniketan festival of Pauṣ, organised by Visva Bharati, the educational institution originally founded by Tagore. It was here that

[15] Interview (translated into English) in the *Telegraph* (Colour Magazine), 5 December 1982, Calcutta.

[16] In other ways the influence of foreigners can be considerable. Their patronage may bring sudden affluence; occasionally sexual relationships of foreign women with Bāul men may disrupt relationships and lives.

I also met local Fakirs, one or two of whom sing semi-professionally, as well as Fakirs from Bagri (Muslim Bāuls). It should be mentioned here that, in Birbhum, Fakirs are quite separate from (Hindu) Bāuls, and are not called *bāul* either by themselves or others. This is in contrast to other areas of Bengal, especially Bagri, where mixed Hindu and Muslim lineages are common, and where in any case the term *bāul* is applied as much to Muslim lineages as to Hindu ones.[17] One reason for this separation in Rarh is the long-standing identification of Bāuls as Vaishnava or Hindu in the eyes of the (Hindu) *bhadralok*. This in turn leads to 'Hinduisation' of the Bāuls of the area, who have increasingly incorporated more conventional (Hindu) religiosity as part of their repertoire.

Definitions

As shown above, it is not only writers on Bāuls who argue about who Bāuls are; those called Bāul disagree on what it is to be *bāul*, and who is or is not Bāul. Not infrequently this takes the form of an animated and acerbic debate. In the competitive climate around Santiniketan, there are several ways of justifying one's claim to being Bāul, while simultaneously discrediting the claims of others. While a small minority of self-proclaimed Bāuls of the area may attempt to legitimise their claim by the standards of esoteric practice (*sādhanā*), a far greater number do so on the grounds of initiation by a guru. Whereas esoteric practice implies development through one's own endeavours, appeal to a guru often amounts to no more than an attempt to place oneself in a tradition – be it a musical tradition, a conventional religious tradition (through the usual mantra-initiation by a guru of the family lineage, a *kul-guru*), or a tradition of esoteric practice. Alternatively, or additionally, musicians may nowadays appeal to householder hereditary principles to claim authenticity as Bāuls. Such claims have been made by a few Jat Vaishnavas, for whom being *bāul* is often related to the purely musical aspect, in addition to being Vaishnava. One well-known Jat-Vaishnava Bāul claims that Bāul is becoming his *jāt* (birth group, or 'caste'), because he, his father and his father's father were singers. In an autobiograpical sketch, the famous Pūrṇa Dās establishes his credentials with the claim that 'we have been Bāul for seven generations' (Pūrṇa Dās 1986:6). Such people may be thrown on to the defensive by others who maintain that no Bāul should procreate in the first place! Most commonly, however, Bāul performers echo the Tagorean ideal in their emphasis on life-style (wandering), attitudes (having no plans, no discrimination) and above all emotion (*bhāb*) as crucial to being Bāul. *Bhāb* may be seen as more or less inhering in an individual: an emotional tone present from birth, one gradually cultivated perhaps through esoteric practice, or, more usually, something elusive yet spontaneous, which comes and goes, as does the Unknown Bird. This emphasis on spontaneous

[17] Throughout this book terms such as 'Hindu lineage' and 'Muslim lineage' are short-hand for lineages recruited primarily from Hindu or Muslim communities, identities which are subsequently invoked, inflected and denied in varying ways and degrees. The same applies to 'Hindu/Muslim Bāul' and (later) 'Hindu/Muslim *bartamān-panthī*' etc.

emotion, especially in the context of the artistry of performance, is opposed to that of esoteric practice, which involves sustained effort towards a goal. Perhaps to echo their several constituencies, the better-known Bāul performers, such as Pūrṇa Dās, Sanātan Dās and B. N. tend to avail themselves of all these claims: several gurus, esoteric practice, descent through the patrilineage (and at times through the mother's line) and even *bhāb*.

Bahiraṅga (outer aspects)

In urban centres, at least among the *bhadralok*, and around Santiniketan, the definition of *bāul* as a particular kind of singer associated with other external characteristics holds sway. In the popular perception, what distinguishes a Bāul from, for example, a singer whose repertoire includes Bāul-songs, are certain observable characteristics, of which dress is perhaps primary. Although Bāul dress in Rarh is far from uniform (flowing robes may be yellow, pink, ochre or patchwork), it invariably draws on images of the renouncer, eschewing the entire gamut of householder styles.[18] The fact that this is less true of Fakirs is no doubt connected with the unimportance of renunciation as an institution within Islam. However Fakir musicians in Rarh are increasingly adopting stray items of Bāul dress, especially at festivals. While cannibalising the garb and emblems of renunciation, those who live from Bāul identity usually take care not to be confused with non-Bāul renouncers. Distinguishing features may include various musical instruments, anklets with bells (for dancing), oiled hair rolled into a top-knot, and so forth. Also, items from different types of dress may be combined – an echo of the patchwork garment itself. Patchwork traditionally signifies lack of ego (*ahaṅkār*) and poverty, especially in the Fakir tradition (and indeed *fakir* is often taken to mean 'one who has nothing'). While yellow, pink or ochre robes are associated with (Hindu) renunciation, patchwork has either Islamic or (more usually) non-sectarian resonances, consonant with its potential negation of uniform through explicit bricolage. Pūrṇa Dās, unique among self-proclaimed Bāuls in his degree of commercial success, remarked of his own immaculate saffron coloured garb: 'I am actually supposed to wear a patchwork robe, but think of the reaction when the public sees me dressed up so poorly.'[19] It is perhaps not without significance that Pūrṇa Dās, who was patronised by the (*bhadralok* dominated) Communist Party of India as a young singer, subsequently took to flirting with B.J.P. (chauvinist Hindu) politics along with the likes of film-star Victor Banerjee. Indeed the Islamic connotations of patchwork (the quintessentially fragmented, sewn garment) possibly provide a sub-text to Pūrṇa Dās's avoidance – cut and stitched garments being traditionally regarded by the Hindu orthodox as having lost their integrity and liable to trap impurities (Bayly 1986:295). Another Jat Vaishnava Bāul exploits the growing *bhadralok* awareness of the existence of 'dressed up' (*sājā*) Bāuls. The patchwork he wears

[18] Male householder styles include 'modern' trousers, traditional white 'pyjamas' and the *dhoti*, a length of white unstitched cloth drawn up between the legs.

[19] Interview in the *Telegraph* Colour Magazine, Calcutta, 5 December 1982.

as the authentic Bāul dress is, however, carefully tailored from new pieces of cloth, some in the shape of significant Bāul emblems, such as the fish, the one-stringed lute, and so forth.

At the very least, some token element from the broadly construed idea of Bāul dress is thought *de rigueur* by those claiming a Bāul identity, whether it be an orange cummerbund, a patchwork waistcoat or a fluorescent turban or scarf. Some may even don a Bāul persona on particular occasions. On a visit to a Bāul festival, a young male singer, dancing with immense enthusiasm and in full Bāul regalia (smart ochre robes and turban), turned out to be none other than a Scheduled Caste peon from the university at Santiniketan, a (usually) quiet, deferential young man in shirt and trousers.[20] As mentioned above, other Bāuls who claim a more traditional base (such as Jat Vaishnavas) may attempt to maintain boundaries by deriding such part-timers who only wear this outer dress (*bahirbās*) during performances, as 'dressed-up Bāuls' or 'amateur Bāuls'. The former assert their own genuineness in terms of their constant use of 'outer-dress', a practice which may indeed be restrictive of occupation and other activities. My afore-mentioned research assistant, a Brahmin who eventually took to the dress of a Shakta *sādhu*, once remarked: 'How can I go to the cinema or visit my sister's family dressed like this? All I want to do is stay in the cremation ground with the goddess.'[21] Alternatively, Jat Vaishnavas or renouncers claiming to be Bāul may describe as authentic (*āsal*) only the 'inner-dress', the loin cloth (*doṙ-kaupīn*), which is the sign of Vaishnava renunciation (*sannyās* or *bhek*).[22]

Emblems of outer dress, and even inner dress (the loin-cloth), may all be relativised in certain contexts. This may be the case with the garland of wooden beads signifying initiation, allowing all one's hair to grow (being *śarbakeśi*), or, alternatively, combining a clean-shaven face and long hair, reminiscent of female appearance. Once during a particularly hirsute phase, B. N., whose transformations of appearance have been described above, argued in some detail that being *śarbakeśi* is essential to being *darbeś*, another of his identities. Later I was to remind a B. N. shorn of all facial hair of this conversation. His first reaction was a lightly dismissive comment that he'd shaved because his beard and moustache had begun to itch. He paused, 'How would it be if I became shaven-headed (*neṙā*) as well?' he proposed mischievously. (The reference was to my enquiries about the equation, made in some of the literature, of *bāul* and *neṙā*. He was teasing me – certainly nowadays being shaven-headed lies outside any *bāul* repertoire, and that of Bengali renouncers in general.) 'If you do that, will you remain *darbeś*?', I asked. 'I shall remain "I" ',[23] he said twice, suddenly serious and almost defiant. I was later to encounter a more clearly articulated appeal to the 'I' as a way of demolishing

20 In time, such 'part-time' Bāuls may dispense with their Bāul persona; or alternatively grow increasingly into that role.

21 Significantly he added: 'There is great joy (*ānanda*) in being here at the bottom, sister. You have nowhere further to fall.'

22 As a rule, *bhek* is taken by all Jat Vaishnava males before they marry. *Bhek* here has structural parallels to the sacred thread (*paite*) ceremony of Brahmin boys.

23 '*Āmi āmi-i thākba.*'

identities (and distinctions of any kind) in connection with the Rāj Khyāpā people. As mentioned earlier, in the Santiniketan area, a significant proportion of Bāuls have a background in folk drama and *kīrtan* (song-cycles narrating the tales of Rādhā and Kṛṣṇa etc.). Another Jat Vaishnava Bāul performer was perhaps drawing on his extensive performing experience when he chose to relativise life-styles, and avoid criticising other Bāuls, with the words: 'Everyone has their own role to play, their own place.'

Definitions of *bāul* may thus be divided into the external (*bahiraṅga*), which includes singing (and speech) and appearance, and the internal (*antaraṅga*) including *bhāb* and esoteric practice. Views on the relation of inner state and outer form, held by those called Bāul, are of interest as they relate to possible recognition of other Bāuls. Some say that the inner state is consonant with appearance and action, thus rendering interpretation possible, at least by the one who 'knows'. Thus, one can be judged *bāul* or not, or *siddha* (perfected, realised) or not, by the songs one composes. This equation may be extended to singing in general, although this idea is losing ground in the face of commercialisation of Bāul songs in certain areas of West Bengal. Some say external appearance and action may eventually transform and bring into line one's inner state, that is, one 'imitates' at first, but in time this imitation becomes one's nature (*bhāb* becomes *svabhāb*). This is one of the reasons given for men dressing as women, in what is termed *sakhī-bhāb* or *Rādhā-bhāb*. It is also one of the reasons given for imitating one's guru in dress and action. Yet others see appearance as potentially in inverse relation to the inner state; thus a Bāul who dresses over-carefully or who shows too slick a mastery of Bāul gesture or rhetoric may be derided as an artist (*śilpi*), that is, a mere performer.

Antaraṅga (inner aspects)

In the course of time, I began to meet more people (called *bāul* by others), who earned their living in ways other than music. This partly occurred because I had stopped asking *bhadralok* to identify Bāuls (these were almost invariably performers), and instead relied on Jat Vaishnava Bāul acquaintances to introduce me to those adept at esoteric practice.[24] The latter then launched me into other networks. As mentioned above, I began my research with an interest in ideas (and practices) concerning differences of caste, religion, gender and so forth. It was only gradually and somewhat unwillingly that I began to take an interest in esoteric practice. The fact that, however fervently held, unorthodox attitudes were considered derivative of esoteric practice and its effects had gradually impinged on me. (As pointed out earlier, esoteric practice here refers to a more or less systematised set of body-centred practices, usually involving a partner of the opposite sex.) Even in the case of those for whom such esoteric practice was of primary importance, its practice was sometimes difficult to infer from external appearances (*bahiraṅga*). These might be intentionally misleading, since esoteric

[24] Performing and esoteric practice are not necessarily incompatible, but for various reasons, it is difficult to devote time to esoteric practice while earning a living from performance.

practice is an inner matter (*antaraṅga*), and since, as I was often told, it was necessary to conceal it from the uninitiated. There was the added complication that while some Bāul performers are genuine advocates of esoteric practice (which they conceal from orthodox patrons), many others display an interest in esoteric practice only with those who expect this of them. The main problem was to distinguish the more orthodox Vaishnavas, for whom the term *sādhanā* bore entirely different connotations, from unorthodox Vaishnavas who might be concealing their identity. Gradually some rules of thumb emerged. First, whether the person concerned was a householder or renouncer, one would look for evidence of a partner of the opposite sex. Another reliable indicator was that while orthodox Vaishnavas are vegetarian, these unorthodox Vaishnavas are fish-eaters. The latter would also dissociate themselves from image worship, importance being conferred instead on a guru.[25] In fact, these two features are related, since fish cannot be offered to the images of Kṛṣṇa and Rādhā, but must be offered to the guru – in the many senses of that word (this issue will be discussed later). In the Muslim context, one would look for an avoidance of beef, and perhaps other meat and also eggs. In other words, identical food habits were unorthodox in quite different ways in a vegetarian Vaishnava and a beef-eating Muslim context. In the Muslim case, an emphasis on the guru was favoured as opposed to Islamic practices such as prayers at the mosque (*namāj*) and fasting (*rojā*).

One person who convinced me of the impossibility of separating antinomian attitudes from esoteric practice was D. D., an ex-Brahmin adept who lived alone with his partner in a densely wooded ashram, surrounded by land which they gave out to share-croppers. Pot-bellied, with a wild mass of hair, D. D.'s enthusiastically slurred words and exuberant laughter emerged from a cloud of marijuana smoke. 'If you're going to smoke this stuff', he said, 'you've got to do it full-time!' He was one of the most vehemently and coherently unorthodox *sādhus* I met in Rarh, yet would always return to the same point: 'The main thing is the practice: that is, to retain the *bastu* (bodily substance in general, and especially semen) . . . The supernatural (*alaukik*) or spiritual (*ādhyātmik*)[26] get you nowhere. What counts is retention of substance (*bastu*), and then the rest of the esoteric practice.'

Method

Partly through travelling on ever-widening and overlapping Bāul networks, my scope extended to five central districts of West Bengal: Birbhum, Bankura, Purulia, Murshidabad and Nadia. It should not be thought, however, that all those called Bāul are on the same or even interlinked networks. Many of those called Bāul by others share as few common links as would any two Bengalis taken at random.[27]

[25] There might be an image in an ashram as a 'cover', but it would almost certainly be tended by someone else.

[26] An educated man, D. D. used this word in the conventional sense, as relating to *ātmā*, the Self. Many initiates use the term to refer to their own practice, and indeed to the body.

[27] Bengalis are known for their ability to establish relationship with any other Bengali, through a combination of kin or affinal links, plus those based on locality and friendship, for example.

It would therefore be incorrect to infer common or overlapping networks from the somewhat artificial encounters between Fakirs, Muslim Bāuls and various types of (Hindu) Bāul introduced by *bhadralok* who organise the Santiniketan festival of Pauṣ.[28] As mentioned above, it was at this festival that I met some Fakirs of Rarh, whom I subsequently followed up at their homes and at other festivals (where there were sometimes no Hindu Bāuls). It was also here that I met some Muslim Bāuls from Bagri, a different network again from the Fakirs of Rarh, although there are points of overlap. Some of the most significant encounters happened by chance. For example, the first time my feet touched the ground in Nadia District, I noticed a *sādhu* crossing the empty road in a cloud of red dust from the disappearing bus. He had a renouncer's loose robes dyed with brick-coloured earth (*geruyā*), long white hair in a bun, a beard and moustache. Most striking was the red dot in the centre of his forehead and the vermilion he wore in the parting of his hair, after the fashion of a married woman. It was my first meeting with B.G., one of Rāj's people.

At times my pattern of movement was almost frenetic. I often travelled each day to a new place – by bus, cycle, pony-cart, rickshaw, boat or on foot – only to talk through the night, dragged out of exhaustion by the riveting discussions known as *hari-kathā*. These itinerant habits were in conformity with the expectations of many of my new friends and acquaintances. 'At first everyone is restless and roams around doing *sādhu-saṅga* (associating with adepts)', I was often told. 'A time will come when you'll just want to stay in one place.' A sign of this desirable outcome, or perhaps a means of ensuring it, would be to take formal initiation from a guru, a move especially favoured by those who wished to fulfil this role themselves. However, others discouraged me. Once someone complained to me that, after initiation, his guru had become more tight-fisted with his teachings rather than less, presumably in order to perpetuate the benefits of his dependence. At the same time, he lamented, other practitioners deflected his queries by telling him to go to his own guru. For a woman of my conditioning, the ideal of giving up everything to the guru (although this is variably operative, and sometimes actively opposed) was particularly daunting. It was reassuring to learn that these doubts were common among initiates and would-be initiates. The tendency to take an old guru (or even to affiliate oneself retrospectively to a deceased guru), the multiplicity of informal (*upadeś*) gurus, and the tendency to collect and change (even formal) gurus, may all usefully be seen in this light.

At this stage, my fieldwork was characterised by alternating emotions of elation and disorientation. It often seemed that I had come so far that even my Santiniketan life was irretrievable, let alone the person I had been in England. Only the obsessive act of writing notes provided a link with the past. Before me stretched the thread of love of the people I was now with, to which I clung like someone drowning, and which would surely, to use their idiom, take me across to the other shore.

[28] At this festival these different Bāuls and Fakirs may perform on the same stage, and are even encouraged to accompany each other for certain set pieces. Off-stage, significantly, accommodation is divided into Bāul and Fakir, which in practice denotes Hindu and Muslim respectively.

The magical intensity of those days, the sense of being favoured by some kind of grace (*kṛpā*), and, on a more mundane level, the gift of initial 'capital'[29] with which to begin trading, however humbly, in *hari-kathā* – all this reinforced an earlier decision not to go against my feelings for the sake of research. In time I had sufficient 'capital' not only to effectively counter queries concerning formal initiation, but also to argue for its irrelevance. (Notions of the guru will be discussed in more detail below.)

Several factors contributed to my decision to shift the focus of fieldwork away from Rarh to Bagri: the fact that practitioners (*sādhak*), as opposed to performers, were the norm in the latter area; the fact that such practitioners (and that part of Bagri where most of Rāj's people live) had been little studied; lastly, the not unreasonable expectations of some Bāul performers of Rarh that I would share with them my perceived wealth, just as they shared everything with me,[30] encouraged me to shift the focus of fieldwork towards this new area. Eventually, as a way of providing a focus to what seemed a vast and alarmingly heterogeneous mass of information, I decided to concentrate my efforts on the descendants by initiation of Rāj Khyāpā, who live primarily in the remoter parts of the districts of Nadia and Murshidabad. The selection was made partly because of certain unusual emphases which I discerned in the Rāj Khyāpā 'tradition', especially their attitude to women and their critique of the institutional guru. Shifting my centre to Nadia I spent the later phase of fieldwork working with the Rāj Khyāpā people, as well as other initiates of the locality.

[29] Here 'capital' (*pũji*) refers to knowledge (of practices and intentional language – *hari-kathā*). In other contexts it refers to the accumulation or acquisition of substance within the body. Many initiates have a background in petty trade.

[30] It is a short step from singing for money to giving information for money. In Bagri I could work with people earning their living in other ways.

4
Fieldwork in Bagri

In West Bengal, Rāj Khyāpā people are found mainly in the Krishnapur PS of Nadia District, the Kadampur PS of Murshidabad District, and to a lesser extent in other parts of Nadia and Murshidabad Districts. While conducting fieldwork in the area, my base was Krishnapur PS, and most work was done in that area.[1] Murshidabad and Nadia Districts lie in the Bagri area of West Bengal. This consists of the delta area of the Ganges lying east of the Bhagirathi river, on which Calcutta lies, and west of what is now the main distributary, the Padma. An area latticed with moribund rivers, bils and swamps, Bagri was until quite recently an unhealthy, relatively underpopulated area. British rule ended in 1947 with the traumatic partition not only of Bengal, but of Nadia District itself. This and the later Bangladesh war of independence from (West) Pakistan brought huge influxes of refugees, especially to the newly constituted border regions of Nadia and Murshidabad. All the older people I worked with inhabit a totally different world from that of their childhood, either because they themselves were refugees, or because of this transformation of their natal area.

Demand for land for agriculture and settlements has virtually eliminated the once vast expanses of water and jungle. The trauma of partition was perhaps most acute in the vicinity of the new 1947 border, and communal tensions between Hindu and Muslim are still never far from the surface. Proximity to the Bangladesh border encourages smuggling, and the mushrooming village of Krishnapur, dominated by the new rich, thrives on 'black' money. Living near the border is hazardous owing to depredations of increasingly armed raiders from Bangladesh, and hardly a night passes without the sound of bombs and gun-fire. This is not entirely new. Nadia had been notorious for dacoits, anti-socials and cattle rustling for at least a century (Majumdar 1978:299ff.). Despite increased prosperity and communications, the continuing remoteness of Krishnapur PS should not be underestimated. Even in the 1981 Census, the settlement of Krishnapur itself had not achieved the status of

[1] 'Krishnapur' and 'Kadampur' are pseudonyms. Kadampur PS of Murshidabad District, where some of the Rāj Khyāpā people live, resembles Krishnapur in many respects, as regards terrain and agriculture. It also shares a border with Bangladesh, with all that that implies. One difference lies in the fact that Kadampur has a large Muslim majority, while Krishnapur has a majority of Hindus. Fieldwork was not carried out in Bangladesh, where, at least before partition in 1947, there were many followers of Rāj Khyāpā.

a town. The nearest railway station and large town is 3 hours away by express bus. Before the construction of two metalled roads after independence, communications in the area used to come to a complete standstill in the monsoon months, and this is still true of much of the area. Agriculture is the primary (legal) occupation of the area. The land is fertile, and rotation of a variety of crops is widely practised with the help of irrigation.

Krishnapur has significantly lower rates of literacy than Nadia district as a whole (S. N. Ghosh 1981d). Although many of those known locally as Bāul are illiterate or semi-literate, my impression is that their general level of literacy is greater than that of non-initiates of their respective socio-economic classes. This may be related perhaps to the desire both to read and copy written sources and to write down songs and other materials available orally. Ramakanta Chakravarti argues for the effectiveness of low-caste gurus particularly Sahajiyās in spreading literacy among the low castes, a phenomenon already noted by Ward in 1811.[2] Chakravarti points out that 'of the 492 Vaiṣṇava works which were composed between the seventeenth century and the first half of the nineteenth . . . the great majority were written by Vaiṣṇavas who were, in all probability, independent of the Gauḍīya Vaiṣṇava order'. The frequent employment of Vaishnava women as teachers of aristocratic women in the eighteenth and nineteenth centuries is also of note in this connection (1985:341).

According to the 1981 Census, Hindus were 58.66 per cent and Muslims 41.34 per cent of the total population in Krishnapur PS, a considerably lower percentage of Hindus than Nadia District as a whole, where they are assessed at 75.20 per cent.[3] Scheduled Castes formed 26.21 per cent of the population of Nadia district in 1981, of which Namasudras are by far the most numerous (Majumdar 1978:95). In Krishnapur PS, Brahmins are few in number, and the dominant caste is Mahishya, who claim a higher place in the caste hierarchy than is acceptable to the upper castes (Majumdar 1978:94–5). It is often said that the Mahishyas are actually Halia (from *hāl* meaning 'plough') or Chashi (ploughmen) Kaibartas, who, having abandoned traditional Kaibarta pursuits, such as fishing, for agriculture, subsequently laid claim to a higher status (S. Bandyopadhyay 1990:101ff.). In Krishnapur it is also said that many people managed successfully to change their caste affiliation in the turmoil of partition, one of the most popular choices being Mahishya. Among Hindus, Vaishnavism of various kinds is dominant. One indicator of this is that, unusually in West Bengal, collecting alms (*bhīkṣā*) is a viable source of livelihood in the area.[4] Caitanya, the main figure in the Vaishnava revival

[2] W. Ward (1811, vol. IV:71), cited in Chakravarti (1985:341). Sahajiyā is a term often used synonymously with Bāul.

[3] S. N. Ghosh 1981d. This is hardly surprising for an area sandwiched between Muslim dominated Bangladesh and Kadampur PS (Murshidabad District), which has a Muslim majority of 86.43 per cent. Both Kadampur PS and Krishnapur PS have much larger percentages of Muslims than do their respective districts as a whole.

[4] One elderly widow of my acquaintance obtains not only sufficient rice from alms, but is able to sell the surplus to buy oil, pulses and salt, and even put something aside for going on pilgrimage. Only her room and *sāṛis* are provided by her daughter.

in Bengal in the early sixteenth century, was himself from Nabadvip in Nadia. The undivided district was the stronghold of Brahmin dominated Vaishnava orthodoxy, as well as the source of several anti-Brahminical 'minor religious sects', dating from the eighteenth century (Sudhir Chakravarti 1980). It is the latter kind of Vaishnavism which predominates in Krishnapur, remote as it is from Nadia centres of Vaishnava orthodoxy, such as Nabadvip and Santipur.

Perceptions of being *bāul* in Krishnapur

As in the case of Rarh, I began work in Bagri by asking a wide variety of local people to identify Bāuls they knew, why they thought they were Bāul, what *bāul* meant, etc. My enquiries were made of scholars, government officials, shop-keepers, teachers, peasants, artisans, priests, menials, vendors, rickshaw drivers, *sādhus* of various kinds, and so forth. The first point to strike me was that the disagreement in the Santiniketan area concerning who is or is not Bāul is found in this area also, but in an inverse sense. As remarked above, in Santiniketan, Bāul was generally a coveted if contested identity. Moreover, Bāuls kept materialising in unexpected places: thus it transpired that the father of a university lecturer, my research assistant, and on occasion even I myself were 'revealed' to be Bāul. In the Krishnapur area and much of Bagri, however, *bāul* virtually amounts to a term of abuse. Even those who in some contexts may not disown a Bāul identity will typically deny it in public. Bāuls are continually vanishing, as those one was authoritatively told were *bāul* present themselves in terms of other identities. In this section, perceptions of what it is to be *bāul* are divided into two: first, perceptions of householders (or renouncers) of the Krishnapur area whom no one would call *bāul;* and second, those of householders or renouncers often called *bāul* by others.

In contrast to areas such as Santiniketan, Bāuls are not primarily associated with Bāul songs in Krishnapur. Far from the romantic notions found in Santiniketan concerning Bāuls, non-Bāul householders of Krishnapur tend to regard those they call *bāul* as promiscuous (*caritrahīn*), indulging in filthy (*noṅrā*), obscene practices, and as a general threat to social order. Early on in fieldwork I was at the house of B.G., a disciple of Maṇi Gõsāi, himself a disciple of Rāj Khyāpā. To my query about Bāuls, one of B.G.'s disciples, an inhabitant of a village in which Maṇi Gõsāi spent his last days, lamented: 'nowadays everyone chases away Bāuls with a stick as they would a snake'. Although R. N., B.G.'s wife, attempted to sabotage this conversation, her disciple disclosed that these Bāuls were none other than the disciples of Maṇi Gõsāi. 'They call us Bāul because we don't observe distinctions of caste or religion', he explained. The reality of these attitudes came home to me when an irate Vaishnava Brahmin waylaid me at a bus-stop to harangue me for studying these (as he saw them) degraded, lecherous, anti-social Bāuls. His life mission, he said, was to exterminate them. In his view, Bāuls are responsible for the break-down of families and the ruination of society. Tracts against Bāuls or Sahajiyās are still being published in strongholds of Vaishnava orthodoxy such as Santipur, and form part of a long history of persecution of these unconventional traditions. Another accusation perhaps less often voiced these days, due partly to the increasing prominence of humanistic and egalitarian ideologies in Bengal, is that Bāuls worship human beings (*mānuṣ*) rather than images (*murti*).[5] (This issue will be discussed in chapter 8). Here suffice it to point out the connection between worship of images, Brahmins and caste hierarchies in general. Other related criticisms of Bāuls are that they maintain no distinction of birth group, and as atheists (*nāstik*) are outside *dharma*. A common grievance (also linked to that of worshipping human beings) is that Bāuls worship women, or, as their critics would have it, are addicted to women, this being the view of orthodox Muslims both in Rarh and Bagri, and of householders of all kinds in Bagri. This attitude reveals itself in various ways. One initiated (Vaishnava) woman, whose husband allows her greater autonomy than usual, is taunted as a Bāul by her in-laws and parents when she goes out by herself. A common complaint concerning Bāuls is that they do not want children. A Muslim initiate, with only one child after many years of marriage, told me that whenever a married couple fail to produce progeny with appropriate frequency, it is condemned as 'Bāul business' (*bāuler byāpār*). Moreover, it is commonly said that Bāuls consume faeces and urine (*gu-mut*), a characteristic also attributed significantly to children and to the mad. Such practices were condemned by the saint Rāmakṛṣṇa as 'extremely filthy' and likened by him to 'entering the house through the lavatory'.[6]

Finally, we come to views of Bāuls held by initiates of orthodox kinds of Vaishnavism (those who would not be considered *bāul*). In this connection it is significant that certain crucial Vaishnava texts inhibit any blanket condemnation of Bāuls. For example, in the *Caitanya Caritāmṛta*, Caitanya himself is referred to as *bāul*.[7] Nevertheless, such initiates are anxious not to be associated with Bāuls, and their attitude to Bāuls resembles those of non-initiates quoted above. This dilemma is resolved by the anti-Bāul Vaishnava Brahmin referred to above, in a way unacceptable to most Bengalis – he himself is not of Bengali descent – by doubting the authenticity of the *Bhāgabat* and the *Caitanya Caritāmṛta,* the most esteemed Vaishnava texts in Bengal.

5 The saint Rāmakṛṣṇa also remarked on the preference for living human beings rather than images: '*Orā ṭhākur pūjā, pratimā pūjā* "like" *kare nā. Jībanta mānuṣ cāy.*' (Śrī 'Ma' 1388 BS (vol. I):181). A self-proclaimed Bāul defined *bāul* as the worship of human being(s) (*mānuṣ bhajan*), which he associated with being mad (*khyāpā*).

6 '*E sādhan baṛa noṅrā sādhan, yeman pāykhānār madhya diyā bāṛir bhitar ḍhokā*' (Śrī 'Ma' 1388 BS (vol. I):181).

7 In the *Caitanya Caritāmṛta* (*antyalīlā*), we read how the attractive power of Krishna induced Caitanya to give up *bed-dharma* and become a *yogī*, a *bhikhārī* (almsman). He describes how, leaving house, wealth and possessions, he went to Bṛndāban, taking the name *mahābāul* (Sukumār Sen 1983a: 572–3). In another oft-quoted verse, Caitanya describes both himself and Rāmānanda Rāy as 'mad' (Sen 1983a:193). In the *Caitanya Caritāmṛta,* the original Bengali, here translated 'mad', is *bātul*. Most initiates who quote the verse substitute the word *bāul* for *bātul*. Even those faithful to the original take *bātul* to mean *bāul*, and thus that Caitanya referred to himself as *bāul*. There are also negative uses of the word *bāul* (and *bātul*) in the *Caitanya Caritāmṛta*, where, for example, it is associated with being unstable (*asthīr*), and with being a fake renouncer (Sen 1983a:312–13, 605, 379).

In considering the wide disparity of attitudes towards Bāuls in Santiniketan (Bolpur) and Krishnapur, it should again be emphasised that the discrepancy is not absolute, but rather a matter of predominance. While the variety of people whose views on Bāuls were solicited[8] was approximately the same in both Krishnapur and the Santiniketan area, it should be noted that, from the inception of Tagore's educational institution, the latter had attracted large numbers of *bhadralok* from outside the locality. Indeed Tagore's father Debendranāth, who founded the Santiniketan ashram, Rabindranath himself and K. Sen all fall into this category. The fact that Santiniketanites have remained largely aloof from their rural surroundings, despite Tagore's intentions to the contrary, has been mentioned earlier. In Krishnapur, interestingly, the very few people to express the Tagorean view of Bāuls were *bhadralok* from outside the area, for example college teachers or doctors employed by the state government.

It is also appropriate to compare those identified as Bāul in each case. In striking contrast to Bolpur PS, in Krishnapur PS there were no more than two Bāuls who earned their living from singing Bāul-songs, and that too only partially. While others called *bāul* may know or even compose songs, this is not the source of their livelihood. Those identified as Bāul in Krishnapur PS have a wide variety of occupations: they may be farmers, landless labourers, petty traders, barbers, blacksmiths, conch-makers, shop-keepers, deed-writers, schoolmasters, technicians, and renouncers who live from alms. A few of those called Bāul are wealthy, many are comfortably off by Bengali standards, but my impression is that the majority are poor. While many identified by others as Bāul are technically renouncers, they are supported by their disciples, from ashram land or from alms-taking without reference to singing. As the range of occupations listed above indicates, many Hindus called Bāul in Bagri, and almost all Muslims, are householders rather than renouncers.

In matters of appearance, it will be recalled that in Rarh, Bāuls draw on images of the renouncer, while distinguishing themselves, as a rule, from renouncers who are not *bāul*. This generalisation does not apply either to Fakirs of Rarh, or to Bāuls (Hindu or Muslim) of Bagri. In these cases, those who are householders, which includes virtually all of Muslim origin, are normally indistinguishable in appearance from other householders, while those who are renouncers almost always adopt one or other sartorial style of orthodox Vaishnavas.[9] In Bagri, this attempt of unorthodox initiates to maintain a low profile is understandable in view of prevailing attitudes of hostility. In this area, therefore, two attitudes to appearance prevail: first, a notion of disjunction between the inner (*antaraṅga*) and outer (*bahiraṅga*); second, a utilitarian idea of availing oneself of sectarian marks for social purposes. Some of those called Bāul say that they wear the Vaishnava wooden bead necklace (a sign of *mantra* initiation) in order to ensure that others will take water

[8] This was a question I asked of almost everyone I met, amounting to hundreds in each area. There are more *bhadralok* in the Santiniketan area, and more were asked the question there than in Krishnapur.

[9] Even if their appearance is distinctive, as in the case of some of Rāj's people, it will still not generally be considered *bāul*, since *bāul* tends not to be defined in relation to appearance.

(and food) from them. Others half-jokingly liken the necklace to the collar on a house dog – unlike a stray, it signifies that one belongs to someone!

In connection with the greater prevalence of householder patterns[10] among Hindu Bāuls of Bagri than among Hindu Bāuls of Rarh, a brief consideration of different patterns of initiation (discussed in more detail below) is pertinent. Among those called Bāul in Bagri, renunciation tends either to be presented as the culmination of esoteric practice, or to be denounced as in some way irrelevant to esoteric practice. One way or another, it is thus quite common for initiates to spend most or all of their lives technically as householders. In many areas of Rarh, on the other hand, the ideal of taking renunciation at the commencement of esoteric practice prevails. Interestingly early renunciation is the practice with Jat Vaishnavas in both areas,[11] and the prevalence of Jat Vaishnavas among Bāuls of Rarh should be recalled here, as well as the degree of Hinduisation of the Bāul phenomenon in Rarh. As mentioned above, there is virtually no tradition of renunciation within Islam.

Finally, these different characteristics can be placed in the context of differing patterns of settlement. Just as the renouncer, debarred from productive labour, lives from alms, so the Bāul singer (following a Vaishnava pattern) traditionally receives alms from singing. The logic of living off surplus restricts the numbers of Bāuls in any one area, and, especially nowadays when landed ashrams are in short supply, normally necessitates a pattern of semi-itinerancy over a wide area. Urban or semi-urban centres like Calcutta and Santiniketan, with their greater density of population and relative independence from the land, constitute only a partial exception to this generalisation, for in such centres self-proclaimed Bāuls compete for the attentions of the *bhadralok* and others. In Bagri, on the other hand, we have seen that many of those called Bāul are householders who earn their living in diverse ways, and who therefore may be found in large clusters, even whole localities and villages. This settlement pattern marks the spread of initiation into esoteric practice among neighbours, especially of the same caste-group. It also provides, especially for Muslims, a source of solidarity in the face of persecution from the orthodox.

In both Rarh and Bagri, Fakirs or Bāuls of Muslim origin tend to follow a pattern consonant with the absence of an ideal of renunciation in Islam.[12] As householders, most follow professions other than music and tend to live in clusters rather than isolated families. In West Bengal, as opposed to Bangladesh, the patrons of Bāul-songs are overwhelmingly found among Hindu rather than Muslim educated classes. This means in turn that the *bhadralok* appropriation of Bāuls and Bāul-songs has been overwhelmingly Hindu. It is probably for this reason that, in areas where this culture predominates (e.g. Santiniketan and Calcutta), Muslims who might be referred to in Bagri as *bāul* or *fakir* are exclusively referred to as Fakir.

[10] By householder patterns, I refer either to the technical status of householdership, or to the appearance of being a householder, irrespective of that status. The matter of status is not always clear.

[11] In their case, *bhek* (Vaishnava renunciation) is taken before or at the time of marriage.

[12] Whereas I know hundreds of Vaishnava renouncers, I know only two Muslims who have taken what is sometimes regarded as the Muslim equivalent of *bhek*: the *khelkā*.

One may trace to the same source the relative lack of professionalisation among Muslim Bāul singers.

It is clear from the above that those considered by others to be Bāul in Rarh and Bagri are by no means the same. The following section focuses on the views of those in Bagri (Vaishnava or Muslim) who are seen as *bāul* by others. (It should be borne in mind that who is or is not *bāul* is no more a matter of agreement in Bagri than it is in Rarh. This section is concerned with those who were sometimes thus identified.)

Some people I had been told were Bāul were consistent in their denial of this identity. While echoing general views of the locality (that Bāuls are addicted to women, to marijuana and so forth), they were also forced, as practitioners (*sādhak*) themselves, to develop more refined points of distinction between themselves and Bāuls. One initiate defined the difference between himself and Bāuls as follows: 'We do *ātmātattva*, but Bāuls do *dehatattva*', which roughly translated means, 'while we investigate and cultivate the self [Self], Bāuls focus on the body'.[13] The association of Bāuls with a focus on the body is often heard, and a related criticism is that Bāuls cultivate the organs of action (*karmendriya*), rather than the sense-organs (*jñānendriya*). Yet there is evidence that many of those who make these assertions – that Bāuls focus on material, gross realities rather than subtle ones – are themselves involved in some kind of body-centred practices (*sādhanā*) with a female partner, and this is certainly true of the initiates quoted. In a variation of the above arguments, some initiates maintain that while they only do the esoteric practice with their wives, Bāuls are indiscriminate in sexual matters. 'They bathe wherever they like, in any landing place (*ghāṭ*)', as it was put. And R.N. (one of Rāj's people) characterised Bāuls as 'those who marry informally by exchanging garlands', as opposed to formal marriage according to *smārta* rites. She also touched on another oft-repeated theme when she identified such Bāuls as mad men and women (*khyāpā-khyāpī*). A particularly creative individual, for whom *bāul* figured at that time as one of his less ostensible identities, summed up the basic association of *bāul* and the male–female relationship in the following etymology. 'Bāul', he said, 'means *ba* plus *hul*'. (The triangular shape of the Bengali letter *ba* suggests the female genitals, while *hul*, meaning 'antenna' or 'sting', refers to the penis.)

Many initiates claimed that while they practise retention of semen (being *aṭal*) during esoteric practice, Bāuls are not able or willing to do this. Yet, paradoxically, one also hears Bāuls being accused precisely on the grounds of being *aṭal* (retaining their semen). A wealthy business man and guru, R.B., told me: 'Bāuls practise absolute retention and are *aṭal*, for example Rāj Khyāpā.'[14] This comment was

[13] The terms *ātmātattva* and *dehatattva* have wide and varied connotations. Knowledge of this particular initiate leads me to infer an opposition between *deha* as body, and *ātmā* as a less apparent, more internal reality.

[14] Although R.B.'s *mantra* guru was a disciple of Rāj, he is not, for all that, in Rāj's lineage. He was initiated into esoteric practice by a guru of another 'line'. These complexities will be discussed in relation to the guru.

no doubt related to the almost total lack of progeny of Rāj and his immediate followers. R.B. was here criticising the pursuit of one's own interests and pleasure (*ātmāsukh*) allegedly involved in retention, as opposed to the practice of giving substance to one's partner. He went on to compare Bāuls to Candrābalī, Rādhā's sister, with whom Kṛṣṇa also makes love, because she too is a devotee (*bhakta*), albeit inferior to Rādhā. 'Candrābalī binds and forces Kṛṣṇa ... Bāuls are like that, they forcibly bind Kṛṣṇa with the four moons. But Vaishnavas are like Rādhā: through devotion (*bhakti*) they attract and keep him.'[15] The 'four moons' refer to practices using sexual and menstrual fluids, urine and faeces. Volumes might be written on such analogies. Here I confine myself to the following points: first, the aim is the same for both types of practitioner, that is, to bind Kṛṣṇa, however that is interpreted; second, the mechanical efficacy of the method attributed to Bāuls is not at all in doubt; finally, the opposition drawn between the more controlled and coercive method involving material substances attributed to Bāuls, and the more acceptable (and feudal) pattern of devotion to a superior in the hope of receiving favours is noteworthy. The association of Bāuls with *four* moons (as opposed to a lesser number) is common. Another guru, not of Rāj's lineage or 'line', told me: 'We all do *ras-rati*, but Bāuls also use faeces (*māṭi*).' (*Ras-rati* may refer to the male and female sexual and menstrual fluids (two moons), to these fluids and urine (three moons), or to bodily fluids in general.) Rāj Khyāpā people are sometimes accused of practising all four moons.

A leading male (householder) guru of the Kartābhajā group[16] (centred on Ghoshpara, near Kalyani, in south Nadia) criticised Bāuls for teaching the 'four moons' right from the beginning. He would not confirm the implication that the Kartābhajās might teach this at a more advanced stage, at least to some, remarking instead that their (not inconsiderable) organisation would be ruined if they taught such practices. Here it is worth noting that even the most strident critics of Bāuls, like the guru quoted, would not usually deny all validity to the four moons practices. Even Rāmakṛṣṇa, quoted above, admitted that it is possible to enter the house through the lavatory. A female guru of the Kartābhajās told me that their esoteric practice and that of Bāuls is basically the same. Leaning forward, she added in an awed whisper: 'but Bāuls have no limit, no fixity, no boundaries (*bāul-der kono māpā nei, kūl-kinārā nei, ṭhikānā nei* ...). They give fire to the fluid all their lives [a reference to sexual practices] ... They are endless, single-tracked. They don't look to right or left, or consider who is waiting for them at home. They want to go to the very end. They have no family attachment to impede them (*pichu ṭān nei*). But we have to consider our families. We are not single tracked, we are involved in this world and society (*saṅsārī*).' A similar idea was expressed by another (renouncer) guru, who, in the context of agreeing that Caitanya was a Bāul, explained that *bāul* means one whose awareness of externals is suspended. And

15 Again Bāuls are accused of seeking their own pleasure, as did Candrābalī, whereas Rādhā was concerned only for the pleasure of Kṛṣṇa.

16 On the Kartābhajās, see R. Chakravarti (1985:346ff.); Sanat Kumār Mitra (ed.) (1382 BS); Manulāl Miśra (1318 BS, 1332 BS), etc.

one of Rāj's living disciples defined *bāul* as one who casts aside the outside of the coconut, only consuming the kernel. Related to this perception are ideas that Bāuls have no group or tradition (*sampradāy*), and that they are mad (*bātul*, *pāgal*). These ideas are expressed by many initiates, including Rāj's people, who are themselves called Bāul by others.

One of the more common complaints made against Bāuls by those who themselves do similar practices is that they are lacking in circumspection and reveal the practices in inappropriate contexts. This, it is said, not only provokes social condemnation but enables people to practise at levels for which they are not fitted or prepared, and who thus may even become mad. There is a saying current among initiates in various forms, one version of which is: 'even if you have crossed [become released from] this world, do not abandon custom' (*yadi habe bhabapār, tabu-o nā chāṙibe lokācār*). D. D., mentioned above, explained his position thus: 'the whole of society is in the thrall of scriptural edicts (*bidhi*) and custom (*lokācār*). If one rejects these entirely one has no shelter (*āśray*), no place (*sthān*).' The theme of being without shelter, place, or refuge (*kul*), which figures in many Bāul songs, will be discussed in chapter 5. It is interesting to note the contrary charge made against 'orthodox' Gauṙīya Vaiṣṇavas, namely that they are gross hypocrites. For example, those who are convinced that women are indispensable in esoteric practice accuse the Gauṙīya Vaiṣṇavas of pretending to shun the opposite sex, while covertly having relations with them. In similar vein, they are accused of keeping cats to provide an excuse for buying fish, which they secretly eat themselves.[17]

P.G.B., a Scheduled Caste (Namaśūdra) guru originally from East Bengal, told me: 'the difference between us and Bāuls is that what we do secretly, they do openly . . . We conceal for fear of social criticism (*sāmājik nindā*) and persecution (*atyācār*). Also, these things are not for the unfit . . . Bāuls proceed in an unrefined (*amārjita*) way, without following a system. In our ashram, discipline is required. Bāuls have nothing like this. For example, in the case of Bāuls, guru and disciple may eat together. We don't do that here.' (Yet in other contexts, P.G.B. did call himself Bāul.) A related criticism of Bāuls was subsequently voiced by P.G.B., namely that they recruit from all birth groups, including Muslim. Even when admitting to the identity Bāul in private, P.G.B. was adamant that members of the Muslim Bāul lineages of the area were 'different'. He was very aware of his Hindu identity (a common feature of Namaśūdras), and with great labour (for he had little formal education) had written a book on Vaishnava theory. Another very well-endowed, established lineage, nicknamed 'Talitpur' after the location of their head ashram, is widely dubbed Bāul by initiates and non-initiates alike.[18] They were reluctant to own to this identity, however, except with many qualifications. Their main objection to Bāuls (and those called Āul, Darbeś and Sā̃i) was that they

[17] Cf. the theme of Kalighat paintings of the cat, sometimes bearing Vaishnava sectarian marks, with a fish in its mouth (Archer 1971:74).

[18] Talitpur is a pseudonym.

do not follow the guru. 'If we say that we are of the line of Caitanya, and do not follow the guru, our own disciples will not respect us.'[19]

It is interesting to compare the above criticism (that the Bāul guru and disciple eat together) with another, voiced by one of the Rāj Khyāpā people, D. G., who preferred in this discussion to call himself Vaishnava rather than Bāul. D. G. complained of Bāuls that even the disciples of the same guru often do not accept food from one another: 'we have a boundary (*gaṇḍī*); they don't'. I was later to conclude that D. G. himself takes food selectively from his brothers through initiation (*guru-bhāi*), or to put it another way, he avoids situations where he would have to eat with and especially from certain of them. In essence, of course, this accusation of lack of solidarity between *guru-bhāi* is identical to the first criticism, that is, not respecting the structures of identity and hierarchy established through the guru–disciple relationship.

A common thread runs through these perceptions of Bāuls. Non-initiated householders tend to see in Bāuls a threat to society, both because of their alleged disregard for social structure and morality, and because of their practices. Householder initiates, such as the Kartābhajās, dislike Bāul disregard for secrecy, but have a grudging admiration for their dedication to the goal. As with householder initiates, so renouncers (such as the Talitpur people) criticise the tendency to mock structures and not to differentiate between contexts, that is, to reveal secrets inappropriately. Structures in the society of renouncers, which are established through the basic guru–disciple relationship, are ignored by Bāuls, it is alleged. This is connected to another trait attributed to Bāuls – that they are divided and 'not on the path of the great ones (*mahājan*)'.

The meaning of *bāul* was discussed on one of my early visits to the house of R. S., a Muslim-born guru in the Rāj Khyāpā lineage. Despite having the same guru, Maṇi Gõsāi, and living only a few miles apart, D. G. and R. S. see little of each other.[20] Also sitting on the verandah of his tiny hut that evening were a few of R. S.'s disciples, Hindu and Muslim, and one or two surprisingly conventional looking (Muslim) associates. R. S., they told me, is disliked by both Hindus and Muslims, and especially by the latter since he abandoned any semblance of following Islamic practices. Called *bāul, mārphatī* or *fakir* by others, R. S. accepted the appellation Bāul with hesitation, saying that Bāuls are unpopular because they do not respect *jāt* (birth group, including Hindu–Muslim differences). He added that they neglect religion (*dharma*), ritual (*anuṣṭhān*), and precept (*niyam*). In fact, they knowingly deviate from the norm. In a more negative vein, he joked about (male) Bāuls being of four kinds: those driven by hunger, those driven by lust, those whose wives have died, and those who fear death, although in fact the proverb he quoted

[19] When I reported to a disciple of Maṇi Gõsāi what the Talitpur people had said about maintaining hierarchy and solidarity, he laughed and embarked on an array of stories illustrating how divided they are.

[20] I suspect that this is because R. S. has a Muslim rather than a Hindu identity. For various reasons, Maṇi's disciples have not maintained his total disregard of communal religious identity.

to illustrate this featured Vaishnava renouncers (*bairāgīs*).[21] More seriously R. S. complained that Bāuls are disorderly (*elomelo*) in their behaviour and comportment, and that their male gurus have sexual relations with female disciples. The Talitpur people, he alleged, are Bāul, since the women wear no vermilion in the parting of their hair (that is, they do not observe formal marriage rituals), and since they practise self-surrender (*ātma-samarpaṇ*), the implication of this being that they offer their female partners to the guru. In this connection it may be noted that while the Rāj Khyāpā 'line' is widely considered to be Bāul, many of Rāj's people disapprove of this practice, on the grounds that the guru is like one's father (or mother).

Another guru, originally from East Bengal and not of Rāj's line, expressed the usual ambivalence towards claiming Bāul identity, despite being widely known as a Bāul. He characterised Bāuls as *ādhyātmik*, a word usually rendered 'spiritual' in English translation (see Glossary), but explained by this guru with reference to *prakṛti tattva* (loosely, 'knowledge of (a) woman').[22] Contrasting Bāuls with Āuls, he said that whereas for the latter *yugal-sādhanā* (practices of a male and female pair) involves each of the pair separately worshipping the guru, for the former it entails the man and woman worshipping each other. The theme of the man–woman relationship sabotaging, or even replacing, that between the guru and disciple will be explored in chapter 6.

So, whichever way it is expressed, there is a tendency to see Bāuls as Other, and usually as inferior. Thus (technical) renouncers often say that Bāuls are householders, while initiated householders say they are renouncers. Bāuls may be seen as the lowest of Vaishnavas (of mainly Scheduled Caste provenance), by Vaishnavas of loftier origin; as exploiters of women in esoteric practice, by Sufis who say they eschew such practices; as practitioners of four moons practices, by those who use fewer or none; as being addicted to hashish, by those who don't take it, and to women, by those who claim to do esoteric practice with only one woman; as not able to retain their semen, by those who claim to have this control, and, as having many children, by those who have fewer; also, as retaining their semen, by those who advocate another practice; as being restless (*cañcal*) and wandering, by those who claim that to do esoteric practices properly one must stay in one place. In this last connection, the following words attributed to Caitanya, and quoted by practitioners are of interest: 'Be calm and return home, don't be (a) *bāul*. Don't (try to) make an impression by becoming a fake [literally 'monkey'] renouncer.' Here the tendency to leave home under impulse in the guise of a renouncer, that is, not in the spirit of renunciation, but in an imitative fashion, in order to impress

21 1. *Peṭ bairāgī* ('renouncers for the stomach', that is, in order to keep and feed themselves). 2. *Ceṭ bairāgī* ('renouncers for lust' – *ceṭ* being a slang word for penis). 3. *Māge poṙā*. *Poṙā* literally means 'to burn', and probably this means '(from) the death (cremation) of one's wife'. Alternatively it could mean '(from) being inflamed (afflicted) by his wife'. 4. *Yame khẽcā* ('from fear of death', literally 'pulled by death').

22 *Prakṛti* means 'nature', 'female energy' or, especially in this context, 'woman/women'; *tattva* means essence, truth, knowledge.

people, is criticised.[23] In such contexts, being calm and stable (*sthīr*) is opposed to being *bāul/bātul*. All these allegations must, of course, be seen in relation to another mentioned previously – that Bāuls do not keep esoteric practices secret.

All such perceptions tend to share a view of *bāul* as anti-structural. Householders see them as destructive of householder (*saṅsārik*) structures – and this of course is part of the attraction for the *bhadralok*. On the other hand, those belonging to the society of adepts (*sādhu-samāj*), including those such as Talitpur people who wear their renouncers' robes cynically, see Bāuls as disdaining structures established through the guru–disciple nexus. Even those who, while remaining householders, consider their true allegiance to be with the guru and relations established by the guru, criticise Bāuls for not maintaining hierarchy between guru and disciple. Thus Bāul is a term connoting 'others', those who are different from oneself, who are breaking down the structures which inform one's life, whether one is a householder or a renouncer. And, as we have seen, being Bāul is considered anti-structural in the further sense of being unstable and in flux. Similarly the consonance between the idealised *bhadralok* view of being Bāul and one *moving out* of householder society may be recalled. In this connection it is notable that the two contrary life-styles most associated with Bāuls, that is, a life of wandering and a life of seclusion, both constitute decontextualising options (cf. Kailasapathy 1987:398). So Bāul is almost invariably described in negative terms, as in the song by Rāj's disciple Hem Khyāpā, where *bāul* is being without lineage (*kul*), prestige (*mān*) and birth group (*jāt*). (This will be discussed below.)

This perceived anti-structural tendency means that Bāuls may be evaluated not only as the lowest, but also as the highest, these poles tending to look the same from within structure. The association of lack of structure with lowly status has been seen in the analogy of Bāuls or low castes being like mud, as opposed to bricks. On the other hand, the state of freedom from structure, or from 'awareness of externals' (*bāhyik jñān*) as adepts might put it, is envied (and feared) by householders, and aspired to by practitioners for whom such a state transcends discrimination, and is characterised as non-dual (*advaita*). As might be expected, the mad share this ambiguous status of the Bāuls. All this accords with the well-known anthropological principle that classificatory anomalies are either sacred or taboo.

This may be compared with a more structural approach to the term 'Bāul'. A few of those claiming Bāul identity in Rarh may attempt to present *bāul* as the goal of a specific path, with those who tread this path also being called *bāul* in another sense. Here *bāul*, as the goal, is of unambiguously high value. Just as those called Vaishnava may at times refute this identity with the modest statement 'I haven't been able to become Vaishnava' (such humility being itself a sign of being Vaishnava), so those called *bāul* (and they may be the same as those called Vaishnava) may say: 'I haven't been able to become *bāul*.' These self-deprecatory

[23] The version usually heard is '*sthīr haye ghare yāo, nā haio bāul. Markaṭ bairāgya nā kara lok dekhāiyā. . . .*' The original version in the *Caitanya Caritāmṛta* (Sukumār Sen 1983a:312) uses the word *bātul*, not *bāul*. *Bātul* is almost invariably replaced by *bāul* in the oral tradition.

statements should be understood, at least in part, in the light of ideas that Rādhā, or women in general, are the only true Vaishnavas, that Caitanya was *bāul* etc. It was noted (on p. 86), in connection with the value placed on esoteric practice, that the greater the association with a system of esoteric practice (with lineages, paths, stages etc.), the more other identities tend to over-ride Bāul identity. Even in Rarh, the attempt to fashion 'Bāul' on the pattern of 'Vaiṣṇava', that is, as a path relating to a particular goal, and by extension to a particular *sampradāy*, has had little success, for this model no more fits the prevailing Tagorean ideal of the mystic, mad Bāul, than it does the perceptions of those in Krishnapur.

So far the discussion has centred around predominantly Hindu, or mixed Hindu-Muslim lineages. My work has not focused on predominantly Muslim lineages, but the research of other scholars (e.g. S. N. Jhā, Carol Salomon) has led me to suspect that the word *bāul* may have more analytical utility in the Muslim context, at least nowadays. (Problems associated with the historical evolution of the category *bāul* were discussed earlier and will be considered again below.) To the extent that this is the case, I would relate it to two other factors. First, because the (largely Hindu) *bhadralok* seem not to have entertained the possibility of the existence of Muslim Bāuls, we do not find among them the kaleidoscopic pattern of mutual appropriations so striking in the case of non-Muslim Bāuls. Second, it is possible that a more unified orthodoxy precipitates a more uniform heterodoxy, and it is interesting to note that in nineteenth-century popular Bengali Islam, orthodox and heterodox forces apparently reached the peak of their activities about the same time (Ray 1995:21). In this connection it should be borne in mind that such habits of Muslim Bāuls as not eating beef, making music (often considered by the orthodox to be unlawful (*hārām*)), not doing *namāj*, observing Thursday (the day of the guru)[24] rather than the conventional Friday, and so on, stand out, in a Muslim context, in a way that dietary regulation, music-making, and avoidance of the temple and image worship do not in a Hindu context.[25] Perhaps connected with this, and with the status of Muslims as a minority, is the greater degree of organised oppression of Muslim Bāuls from orthodox Muslims than that experienced by non-Muslim Bāuls from conventional Hindus. From the orthodox Muslim point of view, Muslim Bāuls tend to look Hindu and more specifically Vaishnava, another way in which Bāuls are 'other'. Interesting in this connection are the remarks of R.S. (quoted above), to the effect that people like him are called Bāul by way of abuse, since Bāuls are thought to deviate wilfully from the norm, in their neglect of formal religion. On being asked the difference between *bāul* and *vaiṣṇava*, he said: 'Those of us who are Muslim call themselves *bāul*. Those who are not, take no name and fall within (the category of) Vaishnavas.' The more overtly confrontational attitude of Muslim Bāuls to orthodoxy, and vice versa, is perhaps discernible here.

In the light of the above discussion, it is appropriate to turn to a question I am constantly asked – that of Bāul numbers. Since there is no agreement on who is to

[24] *Gurubār* (the day of the *guru*) is another name for Thursday.

[25] For example, the home rather than the temple is the centre of Hindu worship.

be judged Bāul, the criteria for this being not infrequently contradictory, and since the category itself is largely constructed through an anachronistic projection, the idea of counting Bāuls would seem to be absurd. Nevertheless some authorities have suggested figures, the basis of which is rarely explicit. Sources generally envisage an expansion in numbers of Bāuls and similar communities, culminating in the nineteenth century and followed by a decline.[26] Upendranāth Bhāṭṭācārya estimated that in 1942 there were 250,000 Bāuls in undivided Bengal, a number in rapid decline (*BBBG*:*ṭa*). Āhamad Śarīph attributes this decline to Islamic reform movements and British education, and estimates numbers in the 1960s at 300,000 (1370 BS:29). Quoting the anti-Bāul tract *Bāul dhvaṅsa phatoyā* to the effect that there were over 6–7 million at the beginning of the last century, A. A. Caudhurī opts for a figure of 500,000 to 600,000 Bāuls at present (1992:30). In contrast to this picture of general recent decline, in Birbhum, Bāul and non-Bāul alike are wont to complain that there are too many Bāuls these days, although the assumption here is often that these multitudes of new recruits are not authentic Bāuls. It is ironical, yet entirely predictable, that the only people to wholeheartedly embrace Bāul identity are increasingly denied legitimacy by the same authorities who brought them into prominence.[27] In Krishnapur not only are non-Bāuls of the opinion that Bāul numbers are on the increase, those they call Bāul (such as Rāj's people) are of the firm view that there are far more initiates like themselves these days.

It is not my intention to attempt to account for these discrepancies. Here suffice it to say, in connection with Bagri, that one possible reason for the decline in Bāuls in the *bhadralok* view might be an increasing unwillingness on the part of a certain kind of initiate to admit to this identity, a phenomenon less likely to be misunderstood by local people than outside investigators attached to categories such as 'Bāul'. The greater number of Vaishnava initiates reported these days is probably also connected with the reported decline in Bāuls. At least until recently, and with the crucial exception of attitudes towards Muslims, Hindu conservatism was on the decline. This arguably allows more people to follow less orthodox, but specifically Hindu paths, or to do so more visibly. 'Bāul', on the other hand, has dangerously liminal connotations in a border locality where there has been considerable communal tension between Hindu and Muslim. Where Muslims are concerned, orthodox persecution of those seen as Muslim Bāuls and Fakirs is generally on the increase, as is resistance to this in some quarters (Isherwood 1990, Jhā and Ghaṭak 1997). Recent trends and specific events have arguably effected a clearer and more thorough cleavage between Hindu and Muslim, and the tradition of mixed

[26] Haq 1975:299; Ray 1995:21. Even ignoring problems connected with the word 'Bāul', where the initial 'expansion' of like communities is concerned, it is almost impossible to assess whether an actual growth in numbers is at issue, or simply an increase in awareness or concern among those whose opinions directly or indirectly entered the historical record. While there clearly was a growth in orthodox Islamic reform movements in the nineteenth century, the apparently parallel growth of heterodox forces is not so certain.

[27] The elderly convenor of the Bāul and Fakir sections of the festival of Pauṣ at Santiniketan, himself an associate of Tagore, was often heard lamenting that 'there are no real Bāuls these days'. Those who attend the festival, he maintained, are only interested in money and fame.

Vaishnava and Muslim Bāul lineages is generally under siege.[28] In these areas the label Bāul is often associated with flagrant disregard of communal boundaries.

The situation is different in areas such as Rarh, where the word Bāul has almost exclusively Hindu connotations, and where self-proclaimed Bāuls are mushrooming. Apart from Rarh, those embracing a Bāul identity are primarily found in the Calcutta hinterland, especially Howrah, Hooghly and the southern part of Nadia District. We may well see a spread of the phenomenon of the 'Hindu Bāul', especially with the growth of Hindu chauvinism, Muslim orthodoxy and the gradual spread through West Bengal of television and its '*filmi*' Bāuls – often debased descendants of the Tagorean ideal.[29] The supplanting of the non-sectarian Bāul by the Hindu Bāul (who incorporates at a lower level other 'paths', in the fashion of Rāmakṛṣṇa) is consonant with the rise of Hindu chauvinism, based specifically on enmity towards Islam.

Before attempting to relate the contemporary material discussed here to changing *bhadralok* perceptions of Bāuls, it is appropriate to quote a song by a self-proclaimed Bāul on the meaning of that term. Duddu Śā was a highly educated Muslim disciple of the famous Lālan, who died in 1890 CE, and whose own origins were a matter of total irrelevance to Lālan himself. As remarked earlier, Lālan, the most well-known and gifted composer of Bāul songs, never actually called himself Bāul. He usually signed himself in songs 'Lālan Fakir'. Similarly Duddu refers to himself in his idiographs in terms such as 'wretched Duddu', and to his guru Lālan as 'Sā̃i', as did Lālan to his own guru. In common with many Duddu songs, the unusual degree of transparency (even to a non-initiate) suggests apologetic intent.

> The religion (*dharma*) of Bāul and Vaishnava are not the same, brother,
> There is no relation between them.
>
> Vaishnavas are a particular tradition (*sampradāy*),
> They perform religious austerities and invoke the five authorities [of Bengali Vaishnavism].
> They are always counting their sacred basil beads and performing rituals.
>
> Bāuls worship the human being (*mānuṣ*),[30]
> Where the ultimate resides,
> They are absorbed in the nectar of matter (*bastu*),
> So their companion is always a woman.[31]

[28] Certain recently formed groups, such as the *Bāul-Fakir Saṅgha* of Murshidabad District, are attempting to reverse this trend.

[29] This of course is a very complex matter. The increase of anti-Muslim feeling among Hindus might effect a move away from Bāuls of any kind, or at least their further 'Hinduisation'. On the other hand, the image of the Bāul as the meeting-place of Hindu and Muslim furnishes an attractive symbol for those endorsing secularism.

[30] As opposed to the authorities mentioned above.

[31] The connection between *bastu* (matter) and women will be discussed in the following chapters. In another song (*BBBG*:808), Duddu calls Bāuls '*bastubādī*' (loosely 'materialist'), and in yet another, maintains that 'the *ātmā* (self, soul) can be called matter (*bastu*). The *ātmā* is nothing supernatural' (*BBBG*:810).

Nityānanda[32] had two sons,
Known as Bīrbhadra and Bīr Cūṙāmaṇi,
They were leaders (*gõsāi*) of two [different] schools,
We hear.

Bīrbhadra knew the traditional
Practices of *darbeśī bāuls*,[33]
Duddu here relates the words of Darbeś Lālan Sā̃i.[34]

Duddu is clearly concerned, in this song, to establish a certain notion of what it is to be *bāul*, while refuting another. His insistence on the difference between Bāuls and Vaiṣṇavas (although an ultimate lineal connection is conceded) is probably chiefly directed against orthodox Muslims, who typically condemn Muslim Bāuls on the grounds of being Vaishnava, or Hindu, and hence un-Islamic. It may also indicate the reaction of a non-Hindu scholar to Hindu *bhadralok* appropriation of the category Bāul.

The field material discussed in this chapter has demonstrated that the vast majority of rural Bengalis, especially in Bagri, share the view of the Bengali gentry that Bāuls are outsiders, transcending or opposing the structures which inform their lives. But whereas Bāuls are extolled by the gentry for these qualities, they are treated with ambivalence and even condemned by rural Bengalis, including, in Bagri, initiates and adepts called Bāul by others. As has been shown, the Bāul as outsider constituted a recurrent theme in the history of shifting *bhadralok* perceptions. Situated outside specific contexts, or beyond structure as such, this Bāul formed part of a far older and more widespread tradition of wise renouncers, holy fools and wandering madmen. What changed in the late nineteenth century was that a doubly alienated *bhadralok* – for they were both excluded, and no longer wished to be included – began to idealise and in various ways identify themselves with Bāuls, the iconic outsiders. By the end of the nineteenth century, outsider connotations are clear in the sub-classification – almost certainly of rural provenance – of (Vaishnava) Bairāgīs into *gauṙe* (householders) and *bāule* (mendicants) (Wali 1898:206 n. 5).[35] There may have been the added implication that those called *bāul* were beyond identity, not only in the sense of beyond structure (as in this case), but also as beyond the comprehension of others, and therefore mad. Such connotations are even more explicit in the word *bātul* (mad), which is commonly equated with *bāul*. As has been shown, these usages persist in Bagri to this day.

Unlike some of his guru Lālan's songs, Duddu's compositions are conspicuously free of any sense of loss or alienation. On the contrary, the song quoted

32 One of the authorities of Bengali Vaishnavism.

33 While *darbeś* (dervish) has Muslim connotations, many of those calling themselves *darbeś* nowadays are Hindu. Some Vaishnava manuscripts attempt to establish a connection between Bīrbhadra and Islamic tradition (Jhā 1995:6).

34 For the Bengali original, see *BBBG*:811.

35 There is some confusion here, in that Bairāgī usually denotes a Vaishnava renouncer and cannot therefore be a householder. The alternative referent (to Jat-Vaishnavas) is for various reasons unconvincing. At any rate, '*gauṙe*' suggests standard Caitanyite Bengali ('Gauṙīya') Vaishnavism, which would leave *bāule* as less established marginal groups.

virtually constitutes a Bāul manifesto. As will be shown in following chapters, many rural adepts and practitioners called Bāul eschew the bitter-sweet sentiment of the outsider for a positive rejection of the whole ethos of insider–outsider, we–they differentiation. For Duddu, Bāuls revere human beings, rather than deities or religious authorities. They affirm the value of material substance, as opposed to inferred, invisible, realities. They also value female companionship and reject celibacy. In modern Bagri (possibly Duddu's home area), Bāuls are also said to privilege the human being (thus violating or transcending conventional boundaries), and value material substance and female company – all characteristics viewed with considerable ambivalence. Another song, by a disciple of Rāj Khyāpā, deals more explicitly with the theme of the Bāul as outsider and madman. While many condemn Rāj as *bāul*, his disciples occasionally glorify him as such. Hem Khyāpā (Hṛdānanda) (1889/90–1947 CE), born of middle-ranking (Śaṅkhabaṇik) caste in Bagri, describes him in the following song (no. 157) as a 'perfect *bāul*':

> This time I shall be *bāul*, I shall lose birth-group (*jāt)* and lineage.
> People will call me mad and laugh, (but) I shall (merely) watch and listen (without reacting).
> When a person becomes *bāul*, some show him affection, some ill-will.
> I mean to enjoy the fun of it all.
> Welcoming joy and sorrow I shall reach a state of non-discrimination.
> As a destroyer of caste, ordinary people won't wish to touch me.
> I shall prance around happily, clapping my hands and singing 'don't touch me, don't touch me!'
> . . .
> My guru is named Rāj-Kṛṣṇa Paramahaṅsa.
> He is a perfect *bāul*, and [?]god to me.[36]
> I have realised these truths through his grace.
> Hṛdānanda says, I shall become *bāul* and accompany him.[37]

[36] The word for god or lord is *bhagabān* not *bhagamān*, which is written here. This suggests another meaning: namely one who has respect (*mān*), for a woman or women, literally 'vagina' (*bhaga*).

[37] This song may have been written before Hem and his wife took *bhek* (Vaishnava renunciation) from Rāj and Rājeśvar (his partner) in 1915 CE. Owing to shortage of time and the volume of material, most of Hem's songs were transcribed indirectly, that is, one person reading out the song and another writing it down. For this reason the absolute conformity of the copy used here to Hem's original text, especially in spelling, cannot be vouchsafed.

> *Ebār āmi bāul haba, jāt kul khoyāba,*
> *Loke pāgal balbe hāsbe āmi tāi dekhba śunba.*
> *Bāul haile pare keu ādar keu ghṛṇā kare;*
> *Āmār bāsanā tāi re se majā bujhba.*
> *Tāte duḥkha sukh bodhan kare advaita bhāb labhiba.*
> *Jāt nāsā baliye more jībe chute cābe nāre.*
> *Āmi ānande nācba re ār gīt gāhiba.*
> *Chusne chusne torā bale karetāli diba.*
> . . .
> *Rāj Kṛṣṇa paramahaṅsa nām*
> *Pūrṇa bāul sei bhagamān,*
> *Tār kṛpāy āmār e jñān.*
> *Se gurudeb.*
> *Hṛdānanda kay bāul haye tār saṅga laba.*

This song is unusual in that, although Rāj Khyāpā and his followers are often called Bāul by others, they rarely use the name of themselves. (This, as has been shown, is common in Bagri.) A term they do frequently use with reference to themselves is '*bartamān*', and for this and other reasons outlined below, the word *bāul* will shortly be abandoned in favour of *bartamān*. However, before leaving the term *bāul*, it is appropriate to draw some tentative conclusions from the material discussed so far.

As argued earlier, many of the problems in Bāul studies derive from uncritical acceptance of the essentialisation and reification of the word *bāul*. This tends to obscure the fact that at issue is not one essence or thing called Bāul, but several different phenomena which require separate consideration: a word (*bāul*), a category of person, a kind of esoteric practice, a type of song – and text and music are again not inextricable. Tracing any of these threads in time (through historical research) or space (in contemporary fieldwork) leads to fragmentation and, ultimately, dissolution of the category itelf.

Such was the immense significance attached to the substantialised category Bāul from the beginning of the twentieth century that otherwise clear-sighted scholars, for example S. B. Dasgupta, M. E. Haq and Dimock, were reluctant to accept or admit that the emperor had no clothes, or rather – to suit the analogy to the context – was clad only in patchwork tatters. This is not to say that where we say 'Bāul' some kind of void should be presumed. To turn to a wider, sub-continental analogy, as with the rope wrongly perceived to be a snake, something was there, but not what was thought.

Clearly the use of the word *bāul* – or related words, such as *bātul* – to denote certain qualities and loosely, by extension, persons possessing such qualities, has a long history in rural as well as urban Bengal. However, my argument would be that its transformation into a proper noun probably does not predate the middle of the nineteenth century, and that its substantialised use to denote specific groups or communities occurred even later than this.[38] As was shown in chapter 1, an initial crystallisation of a category Bāul comprising despised 'others' was succeeded by different but invariably positive evaluations of Bāuls by urban educated Bengalis. Along with transformations in *bhadralok* perception of Bāuls, and especially in the wake of the 'discovery' of Lālan in rural Bengal, the category Bāul underwent increasing if variable substantialisation. This manifests itself in the assumption that particular individuals or groups unambiguously are or are not Bāul, and that if they are Bāul, they are so exclusively – both in the sense that they are only Bāul and that they are not anything else at the same level of classification. Moreover, the scope of this substantialised category gradually extended to cover, often

[38] A possible implication of Sudhīr Cakrabartī's discussion of this issue is that the name *bāul* figures in lists of names emerging from the Vaishnava community from around the end of the eighteenth century (Sudhīr Cakrabartī 1989:17; and see p. 24). However, no date is given for the specific text quoted. Moreover, it seems unlikely that such exuberant compilations were intended to indicate separate groups in any mutually exclusive way, and there is evidence from other quarters that such names were often used as synonyms (Jhā 1999:58, n.12). H.B. Urban argues for the late nineteenth- to twentieth-century origin of the category Bāul (1999:15). This article only came to my notice when the present book was going to press, and therefore cannot be considered in detail here.

inconsistently, a whole range of composers, singers, rural adepts and practitioners not previously so classified. Some of these are identifiable with the pan-Indian array of Yogīs and Fakirs reported in significant numbers especially from colonial times. Others belong to less visible, fluctuating and sometimes named groupings or 'lines' of practitioners, whose history is obscure, not least because they regard it as irrelevant. Doubtless they include many of the 'Vaiṣṇava Sahajiyās' who apparently 'disappeared' during the late nineteenth century (Hayes 1995:335). The most recent research on antecedents of such Bāuls has been carried out by S. N. Jhā (1999). As suggested earlier, it was Western-educated *bhadralok* – aided and abetted by imperial officials and scholars – who substantialised 'Bāul' into a fixed and exclusive identity for certain kinds of rural practitioner, and even into a *sampradāy*. To say that the 'amateur' or other *bhadralok* Bāuls precipitated the 'real' Bāuls, rather than the other way round, constitutes only a slight distortion. Even the pioneering work of U. Bhaṭṭācārya (*BBBG*), invaluable though it has been for subsequent researchers, may be seen as contributing to this substantialising tendency, in which Bāul not only becomes a *sampradāy,* but also subsumes other named categories, such as Āul, Sā̃i etc. Parallels may be drawn here with an earlier process whereby a whole array of differently named categories came to be popularly known as 'Tantra' (Jhā 1999:58). Once 'Bāul' as a substantialised category was established, scholars and writers joined combat over what it means and who 'the Bāuls' are. Their expectations precipitated a variety of responses, and not only from many so-called Bāuls themselves. As positive qualities began to outweigh negative ones in some circles, being Bāul came to be seen as a source of prestige and even livelihood by an ever-widening circle of musicians, usually, but by no means always, of poor rural origins.

However, 'on the ground', substantialisation of Bāul identity was a partial and by no means unilinear process. Its lack of penetration in rural areas relatively untouched by *bhadralok* influence is clearly demonstrated by the fieldwork material from Bagri described in this chapter. On the other hand, Duddu's 'Bāul manifesto' indicates unambiguous substantialisation of the category Bāul, partly due, no doubt, to *bhadralok* interest. The same has been true of many predominantly Muslim lineages of Bagri, perhaps, in their case, as a precipitate of reformist Islamic opposition. As mentioned above, substantialisation of a Muslim Bāul category probably occurred later than the Hindu equivalent. This is reflected in the opinion expressed by several sources that Muslims only became associated with Bāuls in the latter part of the nineteenth century (e.g. Wali 1898:207). Moreover this phenomenon is confined to certain areas: for example, a 'Muslim Bāul' would be considered an oxymoron in the parts of Rarh I worked in. The name Bāul also came to function as a residual category. A charismatic guru with large numbers of disciples or a well-endowed and continuing tradition may crystallise into a named group (for example, Talitpur, discussed earlier), if only from the outsider perspective. Those who are not so defined are by default called Bāul.

One context in which the word *bāul* may be used as a noun, rather than an adjective (or ambiguously as both) in contemporary Bagri is in the identity (*paricay*) lists, written or memorised, which act as a kind of passport, especially in renunciatory circles. In these, each initiate's profile is shaped in response to a series of putative enquiries about his/her *sampradāy,* family (*paribār*), branch (*śākhā*), clan (*gotra*), group (*gaṇ*), doctrine (*mat*) and so on. On the rare occasion that the term 'Bāul' figures, it is usually categorised as a doctrine. So here too, 'Bāul', if it appears at all, is invariably one of a whole raft of identities. Arbitrariness and inconsistency in the elaboration of such systems indicate their irrelevance to most of those I worked with in rural Bengal, and the few with access to such lists rarely invoked them. Nor could they generally recall what was in them. What in a highly structured Vaishnava context is a means of pinning down identity becomes in the hands of many so-called Bāuls a way of sabotaging the notion of identity itself. The same is true of the oft-quoted series 'Āul, Bāul, Darbeś, Sā̃i', which many commentators regard as denoting different *sampradāy*. Yet those to whom these labels are said to apply show little interest in their plausibility, and often heap on them a surfeit of differing, often contradictory, accounts. Thus the notion that Āul, Bāul etc. are separate groups (sometimes alongside a host of others) is counterposed to the idea that they are stages of development; and the final blow is dispensed by 'deconstruction' of these names through various etymologising strategies. As we have seen in Duddu's song, the last three of these four names are all associated with Lālan and his followers. As one who finds herself perplexed or resistant when asked her identity, it came as no surprise that this is even more the case with many of those called Bāul. After all, they tend to elevate 'material substance' (*bastu*) above 'name' (*nām*), and regard the relationship between the two as contingent. They prefer identity-denying identities, such as 'human being' (*mānuṣ*), and occasionally *bāul*. More often they would say they are 'in *bartamān*', and it is this term I propose to use in preference to the word Bāul, for reasons given below.

Bartamān and *anumān*

My argument is not that the academic use of the term Bāul is always invalid, only that it should be used with awareness of its limitations. Problems arise when the word is used to confer a spurious unity or 'essence' on a vast array of disparate phenomena, and when the resultant contradictions lead to sterile debates about 'real' and 'fake' Bāuls, and what Bāul 'really' means. In my view, scholars should be listening to such debates, rather than taking sides in them. Moreover, when the isolation of Bāul as a unified and separate phenomenon is coupled with spiritualisation and masculinisation of the category, the result has been not only an impoverishment of an immensely complex array of theories and practices, but also the masking of a continuing tradition of indigenous radicalism. One reason for centring the rest of this book around the term *bartamān* as opposed to *bāul* is to highlight these neglected aspects.[39]

[39] Some recent scholars, especially S. N. Jhā (1985, 1985/6, 1999), but also Sudhīr Cakrabartī (1992b), have written in Bengali on these aspects.

Other reasons are as follows. As has been shown above, in areas such as Rarh, the word Bāul is appropriated by the *bhadralok* and overextended, while in other areas, such as Krishnapur, it is avoided and amounts to a fugitive category. While there may be some argument for using the word in the case of self-proclaimed Bāuls, it is obviously inappropriate to apply the label to those, such as the majority of adepts and practitioners in the Krishnapur area, who, for whatever reason, prefer to avoid this identity. Nevertheless some term with a broader referent than that of small groupings, such as Rāj and his followers, is desirable for the purposes of analysis, not least because such wider identities are called on by practitioners in some contexts. I suggest that an important pair of opposites on which one such identity may be built are *bartamān* and *anumān*. Rāj and his followers (along with many others) may be called '*bartamān-panthī*' (see below). The term *bartamān* recommends itself not only because it is an actor's category, but also because it is relatively unknown, and therefore freer of the kaleidoscopic projections and mutual appropriations that bedevil the label Bāul.

As stated earlier, Rāj, and many others called *bāul* in the Krishnapur area, would identify themselves as being 'in *bartamān*' as opposed to those they consider to be 'in *anumān*'. While *anumān* is translated as 'inference' in philosophical contexts, in popular Bengali usage it means hearsay or conjecture. For *bartamān-panthīs* it loosely connotes 'orthodoxy' and 'orthopraxy',[40] and is used to discredit both, whether Hindu or Muslim. It therefore covers a wide variety of practices legitimised with reference to authorised scripture: caste and other social and religious divisions, *smārta* and *śariyati* rituals, and so on. Whereas *bartamān-panthīs* base themselves on the 'existent' (*bartamān*), by which they mean, among other things, what can be ascertained through one's senses, and what is based on one's own judgement, they reject as hearsay or 'inference' (*anumān*) more 'orthodox' positions based on authorised scripture, or in fact any other knowledge which is not one's own. *Bartamān* has important associations with practices using a female partner and various bodily substances. The name *bāul* is often explicated in terms of *bartamān*, although, perhaps significantly, far less frequently vice versa. As one of Rāj's disciple's disciples asserted, '*bāul* **is** *bartamān*'. Another initiate, not of Rāj's line, told me in confidence: 'Yes, I am *bāul*. *Bartamān* **is** *bāul*. There is nothing in this which I haven't seen with my own eyes.'

This pair of terms was perhaps first mentioned in literature on Bāuls by U. Bhaṭṭācārya. He equates *bartamān* with esoteric practice based on the human body and *anumān* with a focus on deities (*BBBG*:323). *Anumān* and *bartamān* are also explicated as two 'streams' (*dhārā*) deriving from Caitanya's teaching (i.e. within Bengali Vaishnavism) by an initiate interviewed by the author. Broadly speaking, those in the *anumān* stream reject female companions as a part of

40 There are persuasive arguments for Hinduism being considered an orthopraxis, rather than an orthodoxy. The term 'orthodoxy' is more acceptable in the Muslim context, and indeed the word *bāul* itself has a more precise referent in the Muslim context. In using these terms, my aim is to reflect *bartamān-panthī* perceptions of a dominant and unified *anumān*, where Hindu and Muslim are not distinguished, let alone differences within either of these.

esoteric practice, whereas those following *bartamān* do not (*BBBG*:476). The terms *bartamān* and *anumān* have also been discussed from the historical and philosophical point of view by S. N. Jhā, especially in connection with Muslim Bāuls. This author does not propose '*bartamān-panthī*' as an alternative to the word '*bāul*', but confines himself to the statement that Bāuls call themselves *bartamān-panthī* (Jhā 1985–86(2):23).

In this book, the term *bartamān-panthī* is used to denote those who affirm themselves to be 'in *bartamān*', and *anumān-panthī* to refer to those whom the *bartamān-panthī* consider to be 'in *anumān*'. *Bartamān*, in other words, is an actor's category, not one applied to others. (Those dubbed 'orthodox' – *anumān-panthī* – by Rāj and others, use these terms less frequently, and in a very different sense.) In proposing the use of the term *bartamān-panthī*, it is not my intention to replace one 'essence' (*bāul*) with another (*bartamān-panthī*). It should be clarified that those who say they are 'in *bartamān*' would not as a rule call themselves *bartamān-panthīs*, and it is regrettable that this short-hand term conveys an inappropriate impression of uniformity. In common with more restrictive categories, *bartamān-panthīs* often identify others in *bartamān* by saying they are in 'our line' (*āmāder lāin*), or some similar term. However, closer enquiry would bring an elucidation such as the following: 'No, not the Rāj Khyāpā line, but one of us. S/he is in *bartamān*.' References to the '*bartamān* path' or 'line' are often heard, as well as statements such as 'We follow *bartamān*.' Being *bartamān-panthī* (or rather describing one's path and practices as *bartamān*, as against others called *anumān*) is often itself an anti-identity identity, on the pattern of 'human being' (*mānuṣ*). Even when the category assumes a positive content, it has no clear boundaries from the analyst's point of view. It comprises 'a complicated network of similarities overlapping and criss-crossing' (Wittgenstein 1958). It is important to bear in mind that both *bartamān-panthīs* and *anumān-panthīs* may be Hindu or Muslim, householder or renouncer. The further complication that various degrees of accommodation to the dominant culture may be considered inevitable, if only as a protective cover, will be considered later.

So from the researcher's point of view, there is no clear ideological or social boundary to the *bartamān* path. To take the social aspect – ideological aspects will be considered in chapter 8 – one can construct an approximate spectrum of initiates in whom generally agreed *bartamān* characteristics range from being predominant to minor, in relation to 'orthodox' (*anumānik*) characteristics. However, the spectrum may vary according to the criteria used at the time. Moreover, each initiate varies in her or his emphasis on *bartamān* versus *anumān* features according to context. Those in *bartamān,* however, often have a more definite sense of this boundary, especially where those of their own locality are concerned, and will include within the category *bartamān* a wide variety of people to whom (or to some of whose practices and ideas) they might be opposed in other contexts. Such ready assessments are facilitated by the assumption that familiarity has penetrated the various 'covers' of the 'line' in question, or because some fairly ostensible criteria are being brought to bear at the time. Thus a *bartamān-panthī* attending an assembly of adepts (*sādhu-sabhā*), where there are practitioners unknown to her or him, will rapidly assume that, for example, a fish-eating Vaishnava renouncer with a female partner, or a Muslim with a guru who avoids prayers and fasting, are 'in *bartamān*'. In most cases, however, s/he will have to depend on reliable hearsay, or develop some degree of personal acquaintance with the person in question, to arrive at a conclusion. Thus any difficulties in assessing who is or is not in *bartamān* are thought to arise from inadequate knowledge, rather than from any problems in the category itself. Just as a few cases lend themselves to rapid inclusion as *bartamān-panthīs*, so others may be summarily excluded. Thus a male renouncer with no female associate, or a (Hindu or Muslim) householder in overly 'orthodox' garb would generally be dismissed out of hand.

An interesting case is that of (Shakta) Tantrics. The indigenous category 'Tantric' is primarily based on the criterion of the necessity of a female partner in esoteric practice. This may then be sub-divided into Shaktas and Vaishnavas (the latter being loosely equivalent to non-Muslim *bartamān-panthīs*). However, those in *bartamān* almost invariably dissociate themselves from Tantrics, citing as reasons such *ānumānik* traits as image worship, the cultivation of deities and paranormal powers (*siddhis*), and a greater tolerance of (and acquiescence in) hierarchies. One adept told me: 'There is no *bartamān* among Tantrics. They worship images. They draw pictures of the female genitals (*yoni*) and worship that [rather than worshipping, in various senses, the actual *yoni* of a woman]. They are in *anumān*.' If it is pointed out that, on the 'folk Tantric' level at least, their practices with a female partner and use of bodily substances often resemble those of the *bartamān* path, some other way of drawing a distinction is introduced. For example, doubt may be cast on whether such practices are in fact performed. Alternatively their manner of practising, or their allegedly exploitative attitude to female partners may be cited. *Bartamān-panthīs* similarly distance themselves from *yogīs*, who are dismissed as practising without a partner (*ekak sādhanā*). If one points out that practices with a woman feature in the well-known manual *Haṭhayog pradīpikā,* some other distinguishing feature is adduced, for example that *yogīs* treat women simply as a source of valuable substance. Being 'in *bartamān*' is thus not a fugitive category as *bāul* tends to be in Bagri. Moreover, unlike *bāul*, there is fairly widespread agreement on who is or is not in *bartamān*, not least because this terminology is primarily used by those who would admit to this identity.

The various characteristics associated with being in *bartamān* tend to emerge more clearly in certain social and literary contexts than in others. Those in *bartamān* are often exceptionally and necessarily sensitive to social context, and one of the functions of 'intentional' language is to withhold knowledge from non-initiates or initiates at lower levels. For example, the allusive and complex rhetoric of a guru conversing with a group of initiates and non-initiates is in total contrast to the unambiguous and purely denotative language used in the private instruction of a disciple in esoteric practice. It is interesting to note, however, that antinomian content (for example, challenges to authorised scripture – Vedas or Koran – or to discrimination based on birth group or religion) tends not to be encoded. A *bartamān-panthī* may at different times present the identities *bartamān*, Vaiṣṇava (or Muslim), a caste identity (or a sectarian identity, if a renouncer), or even *bāul* etc. The approach to such multiplicity varies. Thus all such identities may be invalidated, often with reference to the concept *mānuṣ* (human being) – and this is one interesting referent of the word *bāul*. Alternatively, some of these identities may be retained together, in a mutually relativising strategy, to be thrown over, or discounted at any moment. Finally, especially if encouraged by the researcher, there may be an attempt to force oneself into the mould of one identity. It is of interest in this connection that the category *anumān*, in opposition to which *bartamān* is constructed, is associated with the divisive identities of caste, religion and sect etc. Just as *bāul* may denote an abandonment of all such identities, so, in a more confrontational way, may *bartamān*. In keeping with their aversion to such social identities, many of those in *bartamān* are inclined to identify themselves only as human being (*manuṣ*).

Rāj Khyāpā and his followers

As pointed out earlier, studies of those called Bāul have usually been vitiated by overgeneralisation and lack of detailed contextualisation. Partly in order to remedy this situation, the rest of this book will focus mainly on an individual commonly known as 'Rāj Khyāpā' (1869 to 1946/7), and those who see themselves (or are seen by others) as his descendants by initiation. Whereas most studies on Bāuls support their arguments with opportunistic quotation from the vast and heterogeneous collection of so-called Bāul songs, emphasis in the rest of this book will be on the songs (and other materials) of Rāj and his followers, songs of other lineages being generally confined to the notes. Occasionally, however, material relating to predominantly Muslim *bartamān-panthī* 'lines' has been included in the text. This was not so much an attempt to compensate for a general bias in India-based studies on Bāuls, but rather to forestall the emergence of a purely 'Hindu' background to this study, a not unlikely possibility in view of my own academic background in Hindu rather than Muslim traditions.

Before turning to Rāj Khyāpā and his followers, a few remarks on terminology are required. In what follows, Rāj's disciples, their disciples and so on (collectively *śiṣya-praśiṣya*) are generally referred to as 'Rāj's people' in order to distinguish them from other similar small, fluctuating and sometimes named groupings, usually called *ghar* (family, lineage) or *lāin* (line) – a word often without lineal connotatations in Bengali. For any one person, the phrase 'our line' may refer to a variety of concentric or cross-cutting identities, and its denotation only becomes more specific, if at all, in context. Thus 'our line' may refer to almost any perceived group with whom one wishes to express solidarity, for example the disciples of one of Rāj's disciples, the followers of Rāj in general, the followers of the Vaiṣṇava saint Caitanya, or the followers of *bartamān*, and so forth. It means, in short, something approximating to 'one of us'. The phrase 'Rāj's people' is not unproblematic owing to its erroneous connotations of primary identity and unity.

In fact, in most contexts, Rāj's descendants through initiation are not at all united, and not all would choose to identify themselves in this way.

As will be shown, words such as 'guru', 'disciple', 'initiation' and 'line' give a misleadingly simple and overstructured impression of what is in fact a very complex and fluid situation. Nevertheless I have found their usage unavoidable on occasion, partly because such terms are used by Rāj and his 'people' with varying degrees of literalness. Sometimes they are thrown into the discourse only to be subverted. Initiation (*dīkṣā*) of various kinds, as well as the statuses 'disciple' and 'guru' precipitated by this process, were at times subject to fierce critique by Rāj and his followers.

Studies of those called Bāul are typically based on so-called Bāul songs, which indeed are often the only source of information available. Rāj Kṛṣṇa, known as Rāj Khyāpā, (1869–1946 CE) was a prolific songwriter, as were several of his disciples. His songs are still heard in central Bengal, usually 'signed' 'Rāj', 'Rāj-Kṛṣṇa' or 'Rāj-Rājeśvar'.[41] This 'signing' suggests that it is through his songs that Rāj would have liked to be judged, for this was the face he showed to others, initiated and non-initiated. Apart from an iconoclastic Rāj, they reveal a Rāj intent on esoteric practice and the pursuit of love and wisdom. But Rāj wrote more than songs. His loose-leaved, verse manuscript, carefully preserved by the grandson and grand-daughter of Rāj's lover in a dilapidated rural cottage, comprises a variety of texts. Apart from nearly 200 songs, it contains treatises on theory and esoteric practice, an autobiography, medical remedies, riddles and miscellaneous writings, almost all in verse, dating at least from the early years of the twentieth century. Also preserved was a book of Rāj's accounts. Several of Rāj's immediate followers were also prolific songwriters. Of these, the songs of Hem or Hṛdānanda (1889/90–1947 CE), Maṇi or Mādhabānanda (*c.* 1882–1976 CE), and Satīś or Saccidānanda (born 1885, died between 1965 to 1969 CE) – who also wrote verse treatises on a variety of topics – have been used in this book. When I began my research, all these composers were dead, as were all but two of Rāj's immediate disciples. Apart from the latter, my fieldwork focused on three further generations of the 'lineage'. Oral histories were also collected, to supplement the textual materials described above. In addition to Rāj's followers, I also worked with other *bartamān-panthīs* in the same areas. Less systematic research was also conducted in five districts of central Bengal.

The wealth of different kinds of material concerning Rāj and his followers – unique in Bāul studies – may help us to place in perspective other Bāuls for whom we only have songs as a source. It should also help counteract the normal unidimensional and stereotypical views of so-called Bāuls. The fact that Rāj and his followers are relatively unknown, and that many of their songs (especially those of the disciples) are fairly pedestrian from the literary point of view, is also advantageous. Their intent, and the mechanics of their recycling of traditional

[41] Rāj-Rājeśvar is the combined names of Rāj and his lover. Two of Rāj's songs have found their way into U. Bhaṭṭācārya's collection of Bāul songs (*BBBG*: 844, 869 – although the former is in the idiograph 'Rām-kṛṣṇa'), as have at least two of his disciples' songs.

contents from various sources, are more transparent than in the case of a poetic genius such as Lālan.

For reasons of space, these textual materials and other sources relating to the lives of Rāj and his followers will be discussed in detail in future publications. However, in order to contextualise what follows, especially the songs, a brief outline of Rāj's life based largely on his own autobiography follows.[42]

Rāj tells us that he was born in 1869 CE in Sylhet (now Bangladesh) of Vedic Brahmin (Miśra) family. His paternal grandfather was an accountant who had retired to Benaras, and his father a pleader. Rāj's mother died on an expedition of many months duration undertaken to show the newborn child (Rāj) to his grandfather. This disaster, dealt with at length in the autobiography, is the first of a series of losses in Rāj's life. The stark reality of impermanence is voiced by Rāj's grandfather, the first of several renouncer figures in the work: 'Impermanent indeed is this worldly life (*saṅsār*), no one is anyone else's. Once one has taken birth no one can escape death.' The householder–renouncer opposition, presented as two opposing worlds, informs the entire autobiography. After returning home, Rāj lived with his father, his paternal uncles (one of whom was only a few years older than him) and, from when he was four, a step-mother. The maidservant charged with looking after Rāj died at about this time. Rāj's life was dominated by Western-style education, an orderly world increasingly threatened by a terrible quarrel between his father and his older uncle, to which Rāj devotes over one quarter of the autobiography. Division of the property and a protracted law-suit was followed by the financial ruin of Rāj's elder uncle and his departure from the family home. Even the peaceable younger uncle, loved by all, insisted on leaving his English-style education for a traditional Sanskrit school in Nadia. From there he fled in the guise of a renouncer, pursued in vain by Rāj's father through the sacred crossing places of India.

At the age of seventeen, Rāj's father married him to the daughter of a friend in fulfilment of a vow. This and his father's death a year later curtailed Rāj's education. Householder life – specifically the burden of possessions, and responsibility for his wife and step-mother – weighed heavily on Rāj. He made great efforts to persuade his alienated older uncle to return to the family home. Another death – that of his step-mother – was followed by the birth of Rāj's son. The event transformed his life: 'I could not contain my joy . . . it was as if an ocean of love had welled up in me.' This did not alter Rāj's feelings of failure as a householder, and he was relieved when he found a post as a railway storekeeper, albeit far from home. But soon his young wife died, and Rāj eventually insisted on bringing his four-year-old son to live with him and pursue his studies. The child died at the age of eight. For Rāj it was the end. He comments: 'Day and night my heart burned in the fire of this terrible grief. How shall I bear such agony?' He continues: 'Unable to endure the burning fire of worldly life (*saṅsār*), I left the place of my birth as a renouncer,

[42] For a translation of Rāj's autobiography and a commentary on the text see Openshaw 1994. For a longer summary of the autobiography, see Openshaw 1995. Both sources give the Bengali original of some key passages quoted in this book.

and wandered for a long time around the sacred crossing places . . .'. Several years later, aged about thirty-seven, he reached Icchāpur in Nadia and met the woman who was to change his life. 'Seeing the beauty of Rājeśvar – oh what incomparable beauty – I dedicated my life and youth to her.' (Rājeśvar, which significantly means 'Lord of Rāj', is usually feminised as Rājeśvarī by others.)

Rāj describes the development of this great passion in a manner reminiscent of Vaishnava narratives of the love of Rādhā and Kṛṣṇa: how each came to know of the other's love, how the villagers first suspected their relationship, and then had their suspicions confirmed, how most were against the lovers, but three, Rādhe, Hem and Satīś, were on his side, or 'mine' (*āmār*), as Rāj puts it. In parenthesis, it is worth noting that although these three are commonly known as Rāj's most intimate disciples, Rāj never mentions the words guru or disciple in his autobiography. Rādhe was an eccentric and wealthy Mahishya landowner, and friend of Rājeśvar. Hem was a Śaṅkhabaṇik Pāl, of whom more later, and Satīś, later to become a primary schoolmaster, was classified as Jat Vaisnava, being born of a Brahmin father (a widower) and a Mahishya mother. What Rāj omits to tell us directly is that the love between himself and Rājeśvar was in complete violation of social norms, for she was not only married but had a six-month-old daughter. Although there is some confusion about Rājeśvar's caste, her husband (and therefore she herself after marriage) was Jat Vaishnava. There are suggestions that Rājeśvar and her husband were Rāj's disciples, a fact which would make the relationship culpable in the eyes of the society of renouncers, as well as from the point of view of householder society.

Rāj was forced out of Icchāpur, but eventually returned to elope with Rājeśvar, with the help of Hem and Rādhe, one night in 1912 CE. As usual in the autobiography, Rāj is concerned to emphasise his emotional reaction to events, in this case, extreme elation. In a letter in song form, Hem was later to remind Rāj how he had wrung cooperation out of them, by threatening never to return to the area if they didn't bring him Rājeśvar. This is something of an irony, since a powerful caste-fellow of the local zamindar was in any case to ban Rāj from Icchāpur because of the elopement. The lovers fled far away, living in a series of ashrams in western Bengal, although Rāj always wished to return to his base in Nadia. Eventually they built an ashram on donated land in Birbhum, where they remained, apart from trips to Bagri when they stayed with disciples. Their new environment, Shakta and conservative, was to prove alien, and they seem to have made no disciples there. Rāj describes the *hiṅsā* (envy, hatred) he had to face, and his own proud policy of isolation in the face of this. Apart from the particular unsuitability of his new environment, it is usual for renouncers to characterise householder society in terms of *hiṅsā*. At this point the narrative peters out.

Material for the remainder of Rāj's life comes from his disciples and associates, and his book of accounts. These tell us that Rāj and Rājeśvar lived from the ashram land and by supplying various services, especially medical and other remedies. Rājeśvar's services were particularly in demand from Muslim women in purdah, and they were both on good terms with the local Muslim community. A local deed-writer (P.K.C.), not unsympathetic to Rāj, reported that the local people did not appreciate his iconoclasm or general philosophy. 'He didn't respect images and deities. He would challenge people: "show me where your deity is!" His philosophy was "I am everything" (*āmi sab*). He would call himself *brahma*. People here are of the opposite path. We didn't agree with him.' Rājeśvar does not usually emerge in the sources as the strong personality she undoubtedly was. Eventually she brought her young grandson, N.S.D.B., to the ashram. This caused some resentment among Rāj's disciples, who cite the principle that an ashram is not for householders. Rāj died at the end of 1946, and Rājeśvar more than ten years later. At the time of my research, a rough mound and a few unrecognizable pieces of a cement tomb protruding from a sea of paddy was all that remained of Rāj and Rājeśvar and their ashram.

III
Received classifications

5

Two shores, two refuges: householder and renouncer

I now propose to consider the path of *bartamān* in relation to the scholarly and indigenous categories of householder versus renouncer. First a brief outline of the householder-renouncer dichotomy as viewed by social anthropologists and historians is given. I then turn to renunciation in a Bengali context, and specifically among *bartamān-panthīs*. *Bartamān-panthī* attitudes to renunciation (*sannyās* or *bhek*), the guru, lineages and other structures which inform the world of renouncers are also considered. It should be borne in mind that the categories *anumān* versus *bartamān* in no way duplicate those of householder versus renouncer. Householders and renouncers alike may be categorised as *anumān-panthī*, and *bartamān-panthīs* may be judged technically to be of either status.

Whereas householder life is the norm and ideal of South Asian Muslims, non-Islamic traditions in the sub-continent are distinguished by their prestigious alternative to householder life, at least for males, namely the possibility of becoming a renouncer. Dumont even proposed that the key to Hinduism lay in the dialogue between the renouncer and the man-in-the-world, an opposition he considered to operate on both the ideal and institutional level (Dumont 1957:16–17; 1960:38). One difficulty with Dumont's seminal work on this topic was that he and other anthropologists tended to view renunciation from the point of view of the Brahmin householder, a view which is both partial and external to the object of study (Burghart 1983b:361). This bias may be attributed to the focus on village or caste-based studies in fieldwork in South Asia at the time, as well as to the emphasis on prescriptive texts, usually compiled by Brahmin householders (Burghart 1983a:636). In Dumont's case, one result of this is the presentation of the renouncer as an 'individual' (Dumont 1960:46). By contrast, Thapar emphasises the evolution of an institution which required not only internal reciprocity but also, because of its social and political role, reciprocal relations with the wider society (Thapar 1982:290). In his anthropological work on the Rāmānandī ascetics, Burghart also drew attention to the high degree of structure in the society of renouncers (1976), as well as to the hierarchical model of Hindu society held by the ascetic, one which differs both from that of the Brahmin householder and that of the king (1978).

The notion of the renouncer as individual also reflects the reality that it is often as individuals that people leave householder life, as in the case of Rāj's younger uncle and Rāj himself. (The fact that, where *bartamān-panthīs* are concerned, it is most usual for a man and woman to take renunciation together will be discussed below.) As an extension of Burghart's consideration of the ascetic from the point of view of his own conceptual universe, it is interesting to examine views on householder life and its alternatives held by individuals such as Rāj and his disciples at various stages of their lives, as they pass through various statuses. For example, while renunciation often attracts the disillusioned householder or lone wanderer as a possible refuge (*kūl*), it may subsequently be rejected, especially after renunciation, as replicating the structures and hierarchies of householder life. These issues will be considered below.

Thapar sees the Brahminical emphasis on individual renunciation rather than renunciate orders in terms of attempts to diffuse the renouncer's political potential (1982:294). She connects the power of dissenting renouncers to their 'non-orthodox understanding of knowledge' and their general rationalism and reliance on perception and experience rather than revealed knowledge. In the field of practice she cites an initial absence of deities, and a break from sacrificial religion (1982:294, 279; 1978:65; 1979:177ff.). As we shall see, these traits are all characteristic of the *bartamān* path, and, in some cases, may encourage an abandonment of householder life. Even 'orthodox' renouncers in Bengal use appeals to perception, experience and rationality to relativise and subvert the ideologies of householder life (*saṅsār*). What is striking about many *bartamān-panthīs* is that these same weapons are used to assail the structures and hierarchies of the society of renouncers also. Disillusionment with the world of renunciation is seen clearly in the songs of Rāj and Hem. Yet, as Thapar points out, if ostracism and low status are to be avoided, breaking away from caste entails association with religious sects (1979:193). On the other hand, joining a sect or order could modify or even negate the social aspect of the protest (1982:279). These dilemmas characterise the lives of many *bartamān-panthīs*.

It is worth mentioning at this point that scholars, as well as *bartamān-panthīs* and indeed Bengalis in general, place far more emphasis on the binary householder-renouncer model than the classical four stages of life (*āśrama*), that is, student, householder, forest hermit and renouncer (Olivelle 1993; Das 1982:36; Thapar 1982:281). It is the categories of worldly life and renunciation, rather than those of the *āśramas,* which inform the writings, songs and conversations of Rāj and his descendants by initiation. The four *āśrama* theory may be viewed as a Brahminical rearguard action to contain and incorporate the world of the renouncer, or alternatively as an attempt to mediate the opposition between two value systems (Olivelle 1993). Dumont has drawn attention to the artificiality of the model, pointing out, for example, that while two stages are obligatory, two are optional; and that stage three is redundant (Dumont 1960:45. Also Burghart 1978:525–6). Thapar too has opined that the third stage (forest hermit) was a 'transition' between householder and renouncer proper, and that its vagueness indicates a wide variety of 'opters-out' in society at the time the texts were written (1982:286). She also suggests that the relegation of renunciation (*sannyās*) to the end of the life-cycle after the fulfilment of householder duties constitutes an attempt to diffuse the authority of renouncers (1982:294). The bypassing of the householder stage could involve the reduction of gifts to the Brahmins, and an erosion of their power and status (1982:281).

Scholars have debated the relation of these two categories, one of which (renunciation) recruits from and thus encompasses the other (householder life), the two subsisting in a relation of complex mutual dependence (Burghart 1983a: 639–40). Burghart has questioned Dumont's characterisation of the relation between householder and renouncer of twice-born status[1] as one of opposition: 'the term itself cannot account for the specific character of each elementary distinction – negation, interiorisation, encompassment, sequence'. Following Wilden, Burghart also argues for a distinction to be drawn between logical and ideological opposition. By logical opposition he means 'oppositions composed of two symmetrical terms mediated by a third term which subsumes the opposition at a higher level of inclusiveness', the mediating term in this case being Brahmin (or twice-born) (Burghart 1983a:640; Wilden 1980:414, 509–11). Das also rejects the idea that the opposition between renouncer and man-in-the-world is unmediated. It is the Brahmin who mediates between the social and the asocial, a role confirmed by the fact that this category is sometimes opposed to that of renouncer and at other times resembles it (1982:46–7). In ideological opposition, on the other hand, the opposing terms need not be symmetrical, nor mediated by a third term (Burghart 1983a:640). Thapar points out that 'in the counterposing of the householder to the renouncer, the major obligations and characteristics of the one were deliberately and systematically negated by the other'. For example, entry to the householder stage was marked by marriage, whereas renunciation was characterised by celibacy. Similarly, the perpetuation of life, a prime duty of the householder, was negated in the ritual of renunciation, which is in effect a death rite. Moreover, the householder concern with property was counterposed by the ideal of the wandering renouncer (Thapar 1982:287; see also Thapar 1978).

I now propose to turn to renunciation in Bengal in general and among *bartamān-panthīs* in particular. The traditional view in Bengal, as elsewhere, is that a renouncer renounces householder life (*saṅsār*) effecting the death of his social identity through renunciation (*sannyās*), conferred on him by a guru.[2] The hierarchical structures of both worlds (householder and renouncer) are logically generated from a parallel vertical nexus, that of father–son or guru–disciple. However, while replicating the basic householder structure, the society of renouncers does not propagate its kind through birth from the womb (cf. Burghart 1983a:644). In Bengal it is said that disciples are created through another kind of seed, the *bīj* (seed) *mantra*.

[1] According to the Brahminical sources used by Dumont and Burghart, only males of twice-born birth (or only Brahmin males) are entitled to become renouncers (see Olivelle 1993:193–4).

[2] See Kane (1941:958; 1963:113, 231, 518–19) for classical Brahminical references to the act of renunciation. The ritual of renunciation requires no guru according to Manu, but this is not an idea shared by *sannyāsīs* (Burghart 1983a:652, n. 8). The term *saṅsār* refers to both the householder life and the transient world. Dictionary meanings of *saṅsār* in Bengali include 'the world; a region; earthly life; domestic life; earthly attachments and interests; (of men only) marriage; a wife . . .' (*SBED*).

The tongue of the guru is likened to a *liṅga* (penis), and the ear of the disciple to a *yoni* (vagina).[3] Here a conflation of two analogies for the guru-disciple relationship is discernible: father-son and husband-wife, both hierarchical (cf. Gold 1987:312).

In the all-India renunciate 'sects' (*sampradāy*), women are typically excluded from the ranks of renouncers, whereas, as will be shown, for *bartamān-panthīs*, not a step can be taken on the path without a woman. While the hierarchical relationship between guru and disciple may be assimilated to that between husband and wife in householder society, in the case of the *bartamān-panthīs* a more egalitarian model often predominates: that of the extramarital love of Rādhā and Kṛṣṇa, or the Brahmin Caṇḍidās and the Washerwoman Rāmī (one of nine pairs of similar lovers – the *naba-rasik*), who knew no guru other than each other, a model which is in tension with the hierarchical structures of the classical society of renouncers (*sādhu-samāj*).[4]

In the great orders of *sannyāsīs* such as Rāmānandīs and Daśanāmīs, clearly articulated hierarchical structures are most elaborate and visible (Sinha and Saraswati 1978). None of these traditional all-India *sampradāy* has its centre in Bengal, which in this and other respects is peripheral to the all-India society of renouncers,[5] as indeed it is from the point of view of traditional Brahminical householder ideology. Just as, in the case of householder society in Bengal, the theory of the four 'classes' (*varṇas*) is reflected in an incomplete way on the level of social structure,[6] so too the hierarchical structures of the society of renouncers are present in embryonic or fragmented form, and are elaborated if anything on the terminological rather than the organisational level. At the same time, these structures are implicitly subverted even at the level of local renouncer ideology, and explicitly, as we shall see, in the case of *bartamān-panthīs*, many of whom are technically renouncers. Moreover, despite the presence in Bengal of the classical schematic opposition between householder and renouncer society as an exclusive and exhaustive map of the social universe, this is to some extent undermined by the manifestly ambiguous status of particular groups, especially the Jat Vaishnavas, and of particular individuals at certain times.

The term 'renunciation' covers two phenomena: the renunciation of householder life, and the assumption of formal *sannyās* through a guru. Although these are often considered inseparable, in practice the former does not necessarily lead to the latter. Moreover, *sannyās* may be taken without leaving householder life, an option

3 This analogy is frequently heard among the *bartamān-panthīs*. For a written source see *Bibartta Bilās Granthaḥ* where it is said: '*Guru jihbā liṅga hay yoni karṇa nij*' (the tongue of the guru is the penis, one's own ear is the vagina). (K. Bhaṭṭācāryya n.d.:114).

4 The Rādhā Kṛṣṇa theme is constructed in various ways. Along with the quasi-feudal promiscuous and indifferent Kṛṣṇa is found a model of Kṛṣṇa and Rādhā as a non-hierarchical, equal pair, sometimes rationalised in terms of all the Gopīs being different forms of Rādhā (see also Marglin 1982:300).

5 Although routes for *sannyāsīs* and Fakirs did pass through Bengal, Bengal lies outside the circumference of Bhārat (India), as marked by the four classical pilgrimage centres (*tīrthasthān*), the easternmost one of which is Purī.

6 Apart from the Brahmins, all castes in Bengal are classified as Śūdra (N. Rāy 1980:18). Claims of the powerful Kāyastha and Vaidya castes to be placed higher in the four *varṇa* scheme were largely unsuccessful.

which itself covers a variety of phenomena, from *yugal bhek*, the practice whereby renouncing *bartamān-panthīs* take Vaishnava *sannyās* (*bhek*) with a female partner, to the formation and perpetuation of a 'caste' of Vaishnavas, the 'Jat Vaishnavas' (cf. Burghart 1983a:652 n. 8). Even when the renunciation of householder life leads on to formal *sannyās*, there may be a period of transition. As with all transitions, the crossing between the two worlds is hazardous. Many are not able, or perhaps do not wish to reach the other shore. Some even return to the shore from which they set out, but, as a song sung at a Bāul renunciation ceremony makes clear (quoted by A. A. Caudhurī 1992:27), this is not approved:

> You have donned the robes [of renunciation/of the dead].
> Make a good crossing.
> See if, having died, you can live.
> Lālan says, if you return,
> Both sides [*kūl*: householder and renouncer] will be dishonoured.

Here *kūl* meaning 'shore, bank of the river, refuge' has overtones of *kul* meaning '(one's own) family, lineage, society, class, species' etc. In Bengali these have the same pronunciation, and *bartamān-panthīs* often use one or other spelling to cover all these meanings, either separately or together. The meaning of *kul/kūl* as the refuge provided by a group (of whatever kind) should especially be borne in mind.[7]

For some *bartamān-panthīs*, unlike Lālan, the desire for a refuge (*kūl*) on one or other shore (*kūl*), with a group (*kul*) generated by blood or initiation, vies with the determination not to fall from the frying pan into the fire. Rāj's disciple Hem Khyāpā, otherwise known as Hṛdānanda, addresses himself at the end of a song (no. 156):

> Hṛdānanda, if you want to be a fakir [one who has nothing, i.e. a renouncer], you must first lose your caste and society (*kul*),
> But take care that you don't destroy your caste only to become a renouncer by caste!
>
> *Hṛdānanda tui yadi phakir habi re, āge jāt kul khoyāre,*
> *Tāi bale yena hasne punaḥ jāt bairāgī jāt māri.*[8]

Maṇi, another of Rāj's disciples, who spent the last part of his life in successive houses of his disciples, expresses few regrets that 'this refuge, that refuge, both are gone' (*e kul o kul du kul gela* – song no. 49). He comments:

> I shall no longer live on any shore [or 'in any society – generated by blood or initiation'].
> I have plumbed the mystery of shores [society].
> I built my house on the bank of the river, the bank crumbled and it fell into the water.

[7] The transcriber is forced to make a decision as to which is the closer in meaning, as is no doubt the case in the verse quoted.

[8] Most probably Hem is referring to lineages of Vaishnava renouncers which replicate caste characteristics (for example, concern with purity, restricted commensality, and so on). Another possibility is that the reference is to the Jat Vaishnavas – Hem took renunciation with his wife and any accidental progeny would have cast them into the Jat Vaishnava fold. Either way the sense is the same.

This shore, that shore, both have collapsed. I have lost all hope in shores . . .
One longs for the shore where there is no ill-will and condemnation . . .

Āmi thākba nā ār kono kule, kuler sandhān peyechi
Ghar bẽdhechi nadīr kule, kul bheṅge paṙiche jale
Ekul okul dukul bheṅgeche kuler āśā cheṙechi. . .
Ye kule nāi hiṁsā nindā sei kuler upare bāñchā . . .[9]

The motives for embarking on the voyage across the river, and the manner of doing so, are various. Contrary to hagiographical reconstruction of the lives of renouncers, an earlier investigation I carried out with Tantric renouncers (often of low-caste origin) suggested that the 'push' factors away from householder life far outweigh any 'pull' factors towards the society of renouncers. In a well-known Tantric centre in Bengal, none of the adepts (*sādhus*) had actually taken formal renunciation (Audrey Cantlie: personal communication). A whole range of factors may be operative here. The relative absence in Bengal of powerful and prestigious orders of renouncers, attractive to potential incomers, is doubtless of importance. Many, probably most, Bengali renouncers of householder life are of low-caste origin, which in any case debars or deters them from entry into established orders. The result is a more flexible, loosely structured and even improvised society of renouncers, one moreover which is increasingly marginalised due to pressure on the land, and the consequent paucity of viable ashrams. Interestingly, in Bengal the hoary concept of the fake *sādhu* covers not only those who dress up as a *sādhu* without taking renunciation, but also those who take formal renunciation for the worldly benefits this may bring them. It goes without saying that, just as what constitutes the householder state differs according to factors such as region, milieu, caste, class and so forth, so it is with the society of renouncers. While the latter is construed from the householder point of view in terms of a uniform, generalised status, or alternatively as isolated individuals who occasionally make incursions into conventional society, in practice it varies greatly and is experienced in vastly different ways.

Bengali Vaishnava renunciation is generally called *bhek* (referring specifically to the dress of a Vaishnava renouncer), rather than *sannyās*. In some contexts, this amounts to more than terminology. *Bhek* may be differentiated from *sannyās* on the grounds that the latter is only for Brahmins, or that it is inappropriate in this last degenerate age (*kaliyuga*). In contrast *bhek* may be seen as a democratisation of *sannyās* to include Śūdras and (according to some) women.[10] After *bhek,* no caste distinctions are supposed to remain. The ambiguity concerning the institution of

[9] Maṇi song no. 133. Outwardly the reference is to the two 'societies' (householder and renouncer). In Maṇi's case there may be an additional reference to a failed love-affair – the woman concerned may have constituted the refuge which collapsed. *Bartamān-panthīs* are often exhorted to take refuge (*āśray*) in a woman, who thus becomes their *kūl*. (The association of rivers and women should be borne in mind here.)

[10] 'Everyone who takes refuge in *bhek* will be liberated, whether they be a woman, a *śūdra*, an untouchable, or one of the twice born . . .' (*Bhekāśrame thāki sabe haibe mukta; strī, śūdra, anttaja* [*antyaja*], *dvija* . . .). Hārādhan 1391 BS:47.

renunciation in Bengali (Gauṙīya) Vaishnava circles, which is connected in turn to a problematic relationship with the four all-India Vaishnava 'sects' (*sampradāy*), is too complex a matter to be dealt with here. However it is pertinent to recall that although Caitanya (commonly, if somewhat erroneously, regarded as the founder of Bengali Vaishnavism) and some of his chief followers were renouncers, his movement is overwhelmingly headed by householder gurus. The oft-heard notion that there is no *sannyās* in Vaishnava *dharma* should be linked to the fact that the famous fathers of Gauṙīya Vaishnavism, Mādhabendra Purī, Īśvar Pūrī and Caitanya himself were almost certainly *sannyāsīs* of the non-Vaishnava Daśanāmī order founded by Saṅkara (De 1961:19–20). Moreover, until he reverted to householder life, the famous Nityānanda was an *avadhūt*, which most commentators take to indicate Tantric affiliation (R. Chakravarti 1985:62–3).

While the solitary flight from householder life, in favour of a companionless semi-itinerant life of indeterminate status, or initiation into a male renunciate order, is far from uncommon in Bengal, it is rarely found among male *bartamān-panthīs*, for whom life without a woman is considered fruitless. For a variety of reasons, far more (Vaishnava) *bartamān-panthīs* than Tantrics take formal renunciation of some kind, but this is almost always the highly unorthodox *yugal bhek* (renunciation taken by a man and woman together). The model of Caitanya leaving his home, his native place (Bengal) and his (second) wife to take formal renunciation is cited by orthodox Vaishnavas to condemn such couples, and by some *bartamān-panthīs* (such as Rāj's followers) to demonstrate the irrelevance of *bhek* to the path of *bartamān*.

In theory, only a 'wearer of renouncer's apparel' (*bhek-dhārī*) is qualified to give it.[11] For Vaishnava *bartamān-panthīs* the *bhek-guru* should be a different person from his or her other gurus (see below), whereas Muslim *bartamān-panthīs* tend to have only one guru (Caudhurī 1992:26). In the Vaishnava joint renunciation ceremonies I have seen, both the man and the woman being initiated had their faces completely covered with a loin-cloth (*ḍor-kaupīn*), in addition to the loin-cloth worn in the usual place by the man. These and their outer garments were (temporarily) dyed earth-pink (*geruyā*). (After the ceremony, the woman is generally supposed to dress like a widow, in white saris, and without ornaments or vermilion in her parting.) The couple fast for the ceremony, *mantras* are uttered, and their bodies are decorated with white sectarian marks (*tilak*). In most cases, the man's hair was shaved, except for the small tuft called the *ṭiki*. Both are given a stick (*daṇḍa*), a water pot (*ghaṭi*) and a earth-pink cloth bag for alms (*jholā*) (cf. Hārādhan 1391 BS:7). Grains of uncooked rice are placed on their hands and then scattered forcibly by the guru striking the hand from underneath. Thus their food, that is their wealth and power (*aiśvarya*), has been dispersed to the four corners of the earth, through which they must for ever wander to beg for alms (cf. A. A. Caudhurī 1992:27–8). The couple are then led through the locality, still blindfold,

[11] The fact that Brahmins sometimes confer *bhek* on disciples is connected to an equivalence sometimes drawn between *bhek* and the sacred thread (Hārādhan 1391 BS:62).

to solicit alms. At one ceremony I attended, the group surrounding the pair chanted continuously on their behalf: 'Give me alms, dwellers of the town; I shall go to fetch the black moon [a reference to Kṛṣṇa]' (*Bhīkṣā dāo go, nagar bāsī. Ānte yāba kāla śaśī*).[12] On the way, the couple received respectful greetings (*praṇām*), along with uncooked rice and coins. On returning to the ashram, the face cover was thrown back, and sugar and water was put in their mouths. Everyone, even their new *bhek-gurus* (male and female) touched their feet in respectful greeting. Celebratory singing followed, on one occasion people rolled in the dust, and *bhog* (food which can be taken by everyone) was distributed. '*Bhek* means we all join one clan (*gotra*)', I was told. And someone else summed up Vaishnava *dharma* as 'giving honour to those without honour' (*yār mān nei, tāke mān deoyā*). This contrasts with more conventional Vaishnava ideas of humility. As a standard text on *bhek* has it: 'Know yourself to be lower than the grass, and learn the quality of endurance, like a tree. Being without honour (*amānī*) give honour to others ...' (Hārādhan 1391 BS:7).

The fact that renunciation entails the death of one's social identity is well known. In the ceremonies described above, *bhek* was also likened to a new birth. For example, I was told that 'the face is covered during *bhek*, because one is still in the womb and cannot see'. The earth-pink cloth worn at the *bhek* ceremony (which afterwards washes off white) was said by some to signify the blood on the baby's body at birth. So Vaishnava *bartamān-panthī* renouncers of the locality generally revert to wearing white, worn in various non-householder styles, once the original *geruyā* has washed out. Unusually, followers of Rāj Khyāpā who don renouncer dress (usually without taking formal *sannyās*) wear *geruyā* all the time. In a geographical and cultural context where white is associated with renunciation even more than *geruyā*, this might suggest an attempt to identify more closely with the wider Vaishnava renouncer community. However, Rāj's people see contradiction and hypocrisy in the man and woman wearing the white colour of renunciation while living together, and argue for a combination of the white (male) and the red (female), that is earth-pink. As B.G. remarked: 'the cloth which was white has become red'. This relates to *bartamān-panthī* ideas about a man becoming a woman (in various senses and to various degrees) through a woman.

Among *bartamān-panthīs* at least, *bhek* itself is associated with women. Thus the cloth and waist-band worn by women during their menstruation is identified with the *ḍor-kaupīn* (loin-cloth). The analogy is heightened by the binding up and apparent disappearance of the male genitals when the loin-cloth is worn. Male egotism (*puruṣer abhimān*) and actions are said to be forbidden after *bhek*. In particular, sexual intercourse is absolutely forbidden by the more orthodox (who are said to remove the loin-cloth only at the time of urinating, defæcating and bathing), while *bartamān-panthī* renouncers adhere to less stringent restrictions, in theory confining themselves to the time of the woman's menstruation, and/or permitting

[12] I was told that this could mean either: 'I shall bring Kṛṣṇa back from Mathurā to Bṛndāban – money is necessary'; or 'give me the alms (*bhikṣā*) of your blessings (*āśīrbād*), that Kṛṣṇa will come into my body'.

intercourse with seminal retention. A *bhek-dhārī* also resembles a woman getting married, in that s/he moves from one (householder) lineage to another (within the society of renouncers), from which there is no return.

As remarked earlier, the renunciation of householder life has a far less prominent place in Muslim society, but it is interesting to note in passing the prevalence of death imagery in the Muslim equivalent of renunciation, called the *khilāphat*, holders of which wear the seamless clothes of the dead. This imagery is especially marked in Caudhurī's description (1992:27–8) of a clearly hybrid ceremony conferring *bhek-khilāphat* (*khilāphat* in the Vaishnava pattern) on a man and woman. During this the following song was sung:

> Tell us who put this dress on you, let us hear,
> The clothes of the dead on a living body, the [Muslim] shroud and the [Hindu] loin-cloth (*khirkā-tāj ār ḍor-kopinī*).
> Wearing the clothes of the living dead,
> Completing your own funeral rites [*churāt*],
> Destroying this earthly life –
> Let us see these impossible feats.
> Death will not touch
> The one who dies before death . . .

Consonant with the fact that renunciation constitutes the death of one's householder identity, dislocation in space is a precondition and a symbol of the social trauma involved. One of the many proverbs on this subject runs: 'When you take renunciation go to a far-off land, where there is no sign of kith or kin' (*bairāgya laiyā yāio dūra deś, yathā nāi ātmīya kuṭumber leś*) (cf. Hārādhan 1391 BS:8–9). In theory, *bhek-dhārīs* should never speak of their former life. In addition to a change of residence, a change of name, usually retaining the first letter of the old one, is emphasised by Bengali Vaishnavas. One effect of this is to obliterate caste identity. A *bhek-dhārī bartamān-panthī* with the usual propensity for word-play and a little English, told me:

> *Bhek* means 'break'! When you take *bhek*, you must live in an unknown place where you have no connections for twelve years. No progress on the path is possible if you keep returning home. Nor can you solicit alms in your old environment. Your mother and father should not even know if you are alive or dead. Your name must be changed, for the old name will keep pulling you back [to your former identity]. You move from your father's lineage (*pitṛ-kul*) to your guru's lineage (*guru-kul*). You must renounce everything – it is immensely difficult.

His derivation of the word *sannyās* was as follows: 'it means the destruction of the ten ['Hindu' householder] rites[13] – of all rites' (*daśa-bidha saṅskār nāś – sab saṅskār nāś*), of which more below.

[13] Vedic purification rites, generally beginning with a rite prior to conception and ending with marriage (Haridās Dās 501 (vol. I):812; Jñānendra Mohan Dās 1979). While *śrāddha* (death ceremonies) are normally excluded from such lists, they too figure in the householder rituals to be avoided by *bartamān-panthīs*, along with the practitioners of such rites.

Like other renouncers, *bhek-dhārīs* are debarred from productive labour, at least in theory, and are exhorted to live from alms. A song of Hem's (no. 40) speaks of leaving the plough or rudder (*hāl*) for poverty (*behāl*), the *behāl* also being a patchwork coat stitched over many years, a practice (*sādhanā*) with Islamic associations, and one followed by several of the Rāj Khyāpā people (see p. 11 and Glossary). Many derive the word *bhek* from *bhīkṣā* (alms). According to a proverb 'one receives no alms if one hasn't taken *bhek*' (*bhek nā hale bhikh mele nā*). The rules surrounding this status are complex and variable, one constant feature being the strenuous dissociation from the ten rites of passage (*daśakarma*, or *daśasaṅskār*) and their practitioners, mentioned above. According to B.G., who follows some of these regulations although he has not taken formal renunciation, it is forbidden to take alms from the house of a *yājak, ācārya, agradānī* (all various kinds of Brahmin priest), barber, midwife and washerman. It will be seen from this list that purity is not an issue here. 'No one is impure', B.G. would remark, and Muslim *bartamān-panthīs* often say 'there is nothing impure on this earth' (*e duniyāte kichui nāpāk nei*).[14] Alms should not be solicited on the nights of the full moon, new moon, or the eleventh lunar day of the dark and bright lunar fortnights, or on Thursdays (the day of the guru). 'Nor', added R.N., his wife, for good measure, 'should one collect alms from a house where people are quarrelling, the door is bolted, or a child is crying.' B.G. emphasised that weddings, funerals and all such householder rites are to be scrupulously avoided, as is (in theory) eating from one's uninitiated or non-renouncer relatives. Such lists reveal an interesting mixture of social positioning, religiosity (conventional and unconventional) and pure pragmatism (e.g. avoiding houses where one is unlikely to receive alms).

As in B.G.'s case, many *bartamān-panthī* initiates who have not taken formal renunciation attempt to separate themselves from the uninitiated through the observance of some or all of these prohibitions. However, withdrawal from one's kin, affines and friends in these ways is often extremely difficult to effect. Thus one of the reasons frequently given by *bartamān-panthīs* for taking formal renunciation is to escape the tasks and duties of householder life – to get society (*samāj*) off one's back, as it was put to me. This is a particularly effective strategy when initiates wish to remain in their own locality. An ex-Brahmin *bartamān-panthī* told me that he took *bhek* with his wife because of the constant pressure on him to be involved in householder affairs and rituals, such as marriages and funerals. 'I simply wanted to be left alone. Once you take *bhek*, society has no more power over you' (... *samāj ār ṭānbe nā*). This couple obviously had some savings from their former householder life (*purbāśram*), and now live a few miles from his family home in a locality populated largely by renouncer *bartamān-panthīs* of their lineage. An ex-Mahishya farmer and his wife continued to live for many years after taking *bhek* in a section of the family house, a situation rendered easier by the fact that his son and daughter-in-law are householder initiates. The father told me: 'We wear these robes in order to escape from the expectations of family members.

[14] For a significantly different list of prohibited categories, where considerations of caste (and religion) are merged with the avoidance of officiants of the ten rites, see Hārādhan 1391 BS:71.

They can't draw us back into it all.' An elderly *bartamān-panthī* renouncer couple of Rarh, who live from alms in a pilgrimage town and retain no connection with their former life, also said, 'many householders cannot do esoteric practices (*sādhanā*) because of the hassles of householder life (*saṅsār*). If you take *bhek*, no one bothers you anymore.'

While many householder initiates do nevertheless manage to effect some separation from household affairs, *bhikṣā* (alms-gathering) is only viable for those who are classifiable as renouncers, whether or not they have taken formal *sannyās*.[15] Several people told me that they took *bhek* because they were no longer able to work, and *bhek* would give them a licence for *bhikṣā*. (Unlike some other parts of Bengal, it is still feasible to live with some honour from alms in Krishnapur and surrounding areas.) A man of blacksmith caste, who has several children, took *bhek* with his wife in an elaborate ceremony which I attended. When I asked him about this afterwards, he cited the decline in his caste trade and persistent ill health as reasons for wanting to live from *bhikṣā*, an option which is feasible only if one takes *bhek*. Several people related how, when they came over from East Bengal as landless refugees, they took *bhek* in order to live from alms. (All the cases cited were already householder *bartamān-panthīs* before taking *bhek*. No doubt this is a fairly common motive for non-*bartamān-panthīs* also, although I suspect they would be less open about it.) It is worth pointing out that taking *bhek* not only provides access to alms, it also releases one from considerable household expenditure, especially that involved in rites of passage.

Having little expenditure and more time, *bhek-dhārīs* are able to devote themselves full-time to esoteric practices (*sādhanā*); this in fact is one of the implications of 'getting society off one's back'. Householder initiates, separated by their attitudes and practices from their society, may also be tempted to take *bhek* as a refuge (*kūl*), or from a desire to belong and be accepted by those one sees as specialists in esoteric practice. J.B., a householder disciple of Maṇi, complained: 'one is only respected as a Vaishnava by (householder and renouncer) society if one takes *bhek*'. Several *bhek-dhārīs* commented that '*bhek* is taken for show' (*jagat dekhāte bhek neoyā hay*). 'Someone who take *bhek* receives devotion (*bhakti*) and respect (*sammān*).'

Related to this is the common *bartamān-panthī* notion of *bhek* as a cover, or a way of legitimising practices disapproved of by society. One *bhek-dhārī* of a large and well-established 'line' spoke of the general antipathy evoked by esoteric practice with a female partner. 'To retain people's respect we have to take *bhek*', he said. Adulterous couples may take *bhek* as a way of living together legitimately. At least in the past, and even now if the disparity is great, widowed and single people with inter-caste sexual relationships are forced to take *bhek* in order to live together. In these cases, moving to a distant place is often necessary also, and this is conveniently in conformity with the rules of *bhek*. A case in point is one of Rāj's

[15] Thus B.G. qualifies for *bhikṣā* from strangers on grounds of his (unusual) renouncer garb, and from acquaintances, who know he has not taken formal *sannyās*, by his demeanour, his accomplishments in *sādhanā* etc.

Brahmin disciples, who formed a relationship with a widow of fisherman caste after his own wife had died. They now live far from their native place, and present themselves as *bhek-dhārīs*. Initiated and non-initiated householders alike often joked about *bhek* being a good cover for burglars, smugglers and lechers, since people trust *bhek-dhārīs* and grant them access to their houses. We saw earlier that R.S., a Muslim disciple of Maṇi, denigrated Bāuls by quoting a sarcastic quip about Bairāgīs (Vaishnava renouncers). A similar saying from Rarh runs:

> For one's balls, for one's belly, [because] the old lady has died, or one has no roof over one's head – these are the origins of Vaishnavas!
>
> *Eṭṭātme, peṭātme, māg marā, jhubaṙi-marā,*
> *Ei hacche vaiṣṇaber gõṙā.*[16]

The practice of joint renunciation is fiercely condemned by anti-*bartamān-panthī* tracts. One author attacks Bāuls and others (Sahajiyās, Buddhists and many 'small groups') for 'applying the colours of Caitanya's religion of love', only to take *bhek* with a woman. 'The aim of this renunciation is to have intercourse with women using some device to stop having children.' He asserts that this kind of renunciation is a perversion of the theory of non-dual knowledge (*advaita jñān-bād*) – the author does not even favour the 'unperverted' variety! (Dās Brahmacārī 1389 BS (vol. I):55).

Some *bartamān-panthī* renouncers told me that they had taken *bhek* simply in order to avoid cremation. A wealthy *bhek-dhārī*, whose trade and business interests are now managed by nephews (he has no children), baffled by the obtuseness of my enquiry as to why he took *bhek*, exclaimed: 'Have I spent all this time cultivating the body and mixing with adepts just to be burned by these bastards?', gesticulating in the direction of his relatives who were having tea with us. 'After all this effort, let this earth [indicating his body] be placed in that earth [indicating the ground].[17] . . . There is no escape from the fire until you take *bhek* . . . Of course it is best if you have disciples who maintain your tomb (*samādhi*) each day, or at least if you are buried by a river bank and there is an annual feast, but any hole in the ground is better than burning!'[18] This, of course, is reminiscent of Parry's account of cremation as a sacrificial act of violence perpetrated on a sentient being (1989:506, 509).

Finally, *bhek* may be taken (and given) to evade or cheat society, that is, to elevate those of depressed status in the eyes of society. Rāj's disciple Maṇi used this strategem widely. One of his householder disciples told me with a laugh: 'Maṇi never usually gave *bhek*, but he did occasionally, loin-cloth and all, to Scheduled Castes (*taphasilī*), to raise them up in society. He used to say, "Be a Vaishnava!" (*Baiṣṇab hao!*). He gave *bhek* to cheat society' (*samāj-ṭāke phā̃ki deoyār janya*). In the areas of Nadia and Murshidabad near Krishnapur, it is mostly Dāis (Dhātris

[16] I am indebted to Sushil Mandal, an authority on the dialects of Rarh for this interpretation. He derives *eṭṭātme* from *aṇḍa* (testicles), where *aṇḍa* > *eṇḍa* > *ẽṙ*. *Jhubaṙi* (in Puruliya) means a part of the roof, and thence the house.

[17] The word here translated 'earth' is *māṭi*, which has many connotations, including that of *mā* (mother).

[18] It is said that if a *samādhi* is made in an ashram it requires daily worship (*pūjā*). If it is placed by a river bank, an annual feast in honour of the dead suffices.

or Hāṛis), those of 'midwife' caste, who have availed themselves of this mechanism. B.G., another disciple of Maṇi, described this as 'emancipation from *jāti*'. One *bhek-dhārī*, who had formerly been Dāi, and had been given *bhek* by another guru, was very strident in his views. 'Don't think', he said forcefully, almost before I'd finished asking why he took *bhek*, 'don't think for a moment that I took *bhek* to get Krishna or anything like that. I took *bhek* because of this society', and he went on to describe in detail the hardships and indignities of life as an Untouchable. Rāj also conferred *bhek* on those disciples whom he felt might benefit from it, and in his manuscript there is a '*bhek-mantra*'. Several of his disciples were given another name, with the traditional suffix '*-ānanda*' (thus obliterating caste identity) and symbols of *bhek* also, such as the loin cloth and the outer garment of a renouncer. Perhaps it is a reflection of changing times that while Maṇi seems to have thought that only Scheduled Castes required *bhek*, Rāj thought fit to confer it (in some sense) on disciples of a wider range of castes. Those in *bartamān* have theoretical reasons for regarding renunciation with cynicism. However I suspect that research on other renouncers might reveal the role of similarly practical concerns in their decisions to leave householder life. Such material provides a useful counter-balance to Dumontian models of renunciation (1960) and a supplement to text-based research (e.g. Olivelle 1992).

It goes without saying that, even were there a will to do so, the local societies of Vaishnava renouncers are neither sufficiently united nor authoritative enough to control entry to the ranks of *bhek-dhārīs*. If a man and woman wish to take joint renunciation in order to live together, there is always someone somewhere willing to 'give them the robes'. Similarly, if someone openly wishes to take *bhek* in order to escape caste prejudice, there will always be someone, like Maṇi, who is ready to oblige. Moreover, such *bhek-dhārīs* will almost always find sufficient numbers of initiates in a similar category to themselves for support, even though their genuineness as *bhek-dhārīs* may be disputed by others. Apart from the original motives for taking *bhek*, reasons for discounting others as authentic *bhek-dhārīs* may include their guru's alleged unfitness to give *bhek* (this is where lineages become pertinent), and any subsequent conduct judged inappropriate for *bhek-dhārīs*, such as having a child (who will then be Jat Vaishnava), continuing to eat with their previous kith and kin, resuming their former occupation, and so on.

Songs expressing cynicism about the institution of *bhek* as well as other trappings of formal religion are widespread among those on the path of *bartamān*. For example, a song collected in Rarh asserts:

> That love cannot be attained through sectarian marks and chaplets, loin-cloth and alms-bag.
> It cannot be gained through tongs, matted hair, blanket, water-pot, or by dragging on a chilum of hashish.
> Nor by shaving the head, or retaining a tuft of hair, or by smearing the whole body with ash . . .[19]

[19] These are all features or accessories of various kinds of renouncer.

What is the result of wandering around the four pilgrimage centres and the eighty-four stations?
You walk on water, rise up in the air, turn fire into water [acts attributed to Yogis].
These meaningless effects lead to the deepest hell
And desire (simply) grows . . .

Tilak, mālāy, kaupīn, jholāy se prem nā mile.
Mile nā cimṭe jaṭā kambal loṭā, gā̃jāy dam dile.
Milenā māthā muṙāle, ṭiki rākhle, mākhle bhasma sārā gāy.
. . .
Catur dhām curāśi mokām ghure kibā phal?
Jale hāṭa, śūnye-i uṭha, āgun kara jal,
E sab anarther phal yāy rasātal
Bāṙe lālsā . . .

With the usual *bartamān-panthī* emphasis on the body, Maṇi (song no. 44) argues for the artificiality (and therefore uselessness) of all the appurtenances of *bhek*, and indeed formal religion in general:

. . . Where did you get your sectarian marks and chaplet, your loin-cloth and alms-bag?
Fasting on the eleventh [lunar] day will be your body's downfall.
Where did you get your scriptures, sacred-texts, Veda, and Purana?
Seduced by hearsay and inference (*anumān*), you keep worshipping and meditating
While the Great One (*mahājan*)[20] revels in the upturn in his business.
Listen, my mind, be straightforward. Use the touch-stone and see now (for yourself):
Did you bring all this stuff with you when you emerged from the womb?
[Did you come out with] drum, cymbals and your store of divine names tucked under your arm?
Can you tell me which of you has done so? Let me touch his feet in reverence![21]

Most *bartamān-panthīs* treat *bhek* at best as a mere formality, and quote the well-known saying: 'There is no renunciation in *bhek* without instruction . . .' (*Bheker bairāgya nahe binā upadeśe . . .*). B.G., who has not taken formal *sannyās*, but calls his a 'renunciation of [conventional] society' (*samāj-tyāg*) explained: 'If one becomes perfected (*siddha*) in esoteric practice,[22] then *tyāg* [an attitude of renunciation] comes by itself [that is, there is no need to take *bhek*], and if one cannot achieve that stage, then *tyāg* will not come and taking *bhek* will not help.' Another quip was: 'Be a *sādhu*, don't imitate [literally 'dress up as'] a *sādhu*!'

[20] *Mahājan* literally means 'a great or virtuous person'. Maṇi here probably intends a double reference, to great merchants, wholesalers, creditors or money lenders, and also, in the *bartamān-panthī* context, to revered gurus and composers, perfected in esoteric practice.
[21] For the original (transliterated) Bengali, see Openshaw 1997b:303–4.
[22] Esoteric practice is taught by the *śikṣā-guru* (see chapter 6). There is common agreement that the *bhek-guru* teaches nothing. His task is simply to give one the robes of *bhek*.

(*Sādhu hao, sādhu sājo nā*). In an oft-quoted incident, the sixteenth-century saint Caitanya is represented as upbraiding a follower who wished to become a renouncer, his criticism being of those who take *sannyās* in an imitative fashion, in order to impress people.

Bartamān-panthīs often point out that *bhek*, as the path of passionlessness (*bairāgya*), is opposed to their own path of passion (*rāg*).[23] Lone male renouncers are therefore considered to be completely on the wrong track. A disciple of Maṇi was keen to dissociate his guru from the path of renunciation (*tyāg*) on the grounds that the latter is the dry (*śuṣka)* path of lone practice (*ekak sādhanā*), that is, without a woman; whereas theirs is the path of fluid or emotion (*ras)* associated with practice with a partner of the opposite sex (*yugal sādhanā*). Here various oppositions are implied: dry knowledge (*jñān*) versus the emotion (*ras*) of *bhakti*; formality versus informality (*śuṣka* also means formal); the dryness of the male as opposed to the female who is full of fluid, etc.

As mentioned above, some *bartamān-panthīs* are tempted, despite these objections, by the vision of *bhek* as a refuge, an alternative to the ill-will (*hiṅsā*) and divisiveness of householder society. Hem, a disciple of Rāj whose life trajectory will be considered in more detail in chapter 6, also nurtured these hopes, but like so many others he was rapidly disillusioned. J.B., a householder disciple of Maṇi, complained: '*Bhek-dhārīs* also soon form groups (*dal*) and don't eat or mix with each other, let alone with householders.' Other *bartamān-panthīs* relate this to a general lapse into *anumān*, such as following (orthodox) scripture, making offerings to Caitanya, whom no one living has seen, rather than to one's own guru or other living human beings. It is living beings, especially the guru, who may help the initiate steer a middle path between the two shores, householder and renouncer.

[23] *Bairāgī* is normally synonymous with *bhek-dhārī*. See *BBBG*:86.

6
Evading the two shores: the guru

One of the defining attributes of Bāuls as constructed in various ways by scholars is their devotion to the preceptor, that is, the *guru* or *murśid* (a Sufi term). This characteristic has been used to bolster arguments that Bāul is a continuing essence or entity of some kind. It is crucial for those who argue that Bāuls are a *sampradāy*, because the continuity of tradition depends upon gurus and fidelity to their teachings. There are indeed many Bāul songs which extol the *guru/murśid*,[1] although it cannot be assumed that these terms always refer to the institutional male preceptor. My argument is that the search for continuities has privileged uniformity over diversity, and conformity over creativity and dissent. These latter aspects are particularly prominent in the case of Rāj Khyāpā and his followers, especially in connection with the institutional guru. However, even the most fervent espousal of the doctrine of the primacy of the guru (*guru-bād*) tends to be undermined by contrary tendencies: including the multiplicity of gurus, the internalisation of the guru, and the fact that esoteric practice of necessity involves a male–female pair. The theoretical and practical importance conferred on women by *bartamān-panthīs* tends to subvert the predominantly male guru lineages (Hindu, Muslim or mixed), as does a readiness to divinise human beings as such, rather than only perfected human beings, such as the guru.

The human guru is clearly preferred to the conventional worship of god or gods. In contrast to the worship of transcendent deities or icons, which are classified by *bartamān-panthīs* as *anumān*, that is, based on imagination or hearsay, respect for the (human) guru is presented as *bartamān* (in that he is present in the flesh, known by one's own experience etc.). One guru (not of Rāj's line) quoted the following verse: 'Those who abandon the guru and worship Gobinda [God] are sinners and will suffer in hell' (*Guru chāṛi Gobinda bhaje, Se pāpī narake maje*).[2] However there is tremendous variation in this matter, between 'lines', between individual *bartamān-panthī* initiates, and the statements made by any one initiate at different times. For example, not a few *bartamān-panthīs* affirm that they revere human beings rather than the guru (*mānuṣ pūjā* as opposed to *guru pūjā*), thus rejecting the institutional guru and his lineage, and the we–they (*āpan–par*) distinctions

[1] As this aspect has been adequately dealt with in other sources, I shall not dwell on it here. For songs emphasising the vital importance of the guru, see those embedded in the text in *BBBG*:304–10ff.

[2] Gobinda is a name of Kṛṣṇa or Viṣṇu.

thus generated. Here the hierarchy generated by initiation represents *anumān* and undifferentiated human beings *bartamān*.

The ideal number of preceptors tends to differ for 'Hindu' and 'Muslim' *bartamān-panthīs*.[3] For reasons which will be considered below, Muslim *bartamān-panthīs* expect to take only one guru. Vaishnava *bartamān-panthīs* typically speak of three gurus for three initiations or stages, and this is the model considered here. The three gurus are the *dīkṣā-guru* (*dīkṣā* means simply initiation, or the preliminary initiation), the *śikṣā-guru* (*śikṣā* means learning or training), and the *bhek-guru* or *sannyās-guru* (*bhek* denotes the robe of a Vaishnava renouncer and this guru initiates the adept into a life of renunciation, *sannyās*). Similarly, four births are sometimes cited: birth from the mother, *dīkṣā, śikṣā,* and *bhek*.

Dīkṣā-guru

The word *dīkṣā* itself means 'initiation'. It often refers to the initiation taken by many Bengali householders from an hereditary family preceptor (*kul-guru*), a system whereby a line of householder gurus is associated with a householder lineage down the generations. Most people hold that, whether or not the *dīkṣā-guru* is also the *kul-guru*, he should technically be a Brahmin. Others, especially those who regard *bhek* as equivalent to the sacred thread, assert that a *bhek-dhārī* Vaishnava may also give *dīkṣā*. The conferral of *dīkṣā* by a *bhek-dhārī* may be viewed as a strategy to appropriate Brahminical functions by, or on behalf of, those who would be rejected by conservative Brahmin *dīkṣā-gurus* because of their low-caste origin. Such is not the case with Brahmin *dīkṣā-gurus* like Rāj's disciple, Maṇi, who initiated Untouchables and Muslims. '*Adhikārī*' (meaning one who has competence or authority) is a common title for such Brahmin householder gurus, and another of Rāj's disciples (S.A.) has this title. He has hundreds, perhaps thousands, of disciples to whom he has given *dīkṣā*, that is, a *mantra*, for which he receives a fee (*dakṣiṇā*), and occasional gifts and hospitality. In addition to being an hereditary family priest to the locally dominant, middle-ranking Māhiṣya caste, Maṇi also functioned as a *dīkṣā-guru* and gave many hundreds of disciples this preliminary initiation. Although there is an economic aspect to being a guru of any kind, it is *dīkṣā,* of the three, which is most often deprecated by *bartamān-panthīs* as a merely economic enterprise, especially on the grounds of its scale, and because the right (*adhikār*) to earn one's living in this way is technically acquired by birth. In a song (no. 44), Maṇi reproaches himself: 'Maṇi, you have become a priest-tout of Bṛndāban with your (guru) business!' *Dīkṣā* is also denigrated by *bartamān-panthīs* on other grounds. *Nām* (which includes *mantra*) is contrasted unfavourably (as *anumān*) with *bastu* (substance), the concern of those in *bartamān* (see chapter 8).

[3] As stated earlier, these are short-hand terms for *bartamān-panthīs* whose background is Hindu or Muslim, identities which are subsequently invoked, inflected and denied in varying ways and degrees.

Bhek-guru

Although *bhek* (Vaishnava *sannyās*) is often thought to follow on from (or represent a culmination of) *śikṣā*, it is appropriate to deal with the *bhek-guru* before the *śikṣā-guru*. This is not only because *bhek* has been already discussed, but because, along with *dīkṣā*, this is an initiation by no means confined to *bartamān-panthīs*. As pointed out, in taking *bhek* one leaves one's householder lineage (*kul*), and enters – or is born into – another *kul* in the society of *sādhus*. The *bhek-guru* is also known as the *bhārati-guru*,[4] or, more rarely in Vaishnava circles, as the *sannyās-guru*. The tension between the classical model of the lone renouncer, epitomised for Bengali Vaishnavas by Caitanya, and the *bartamān-panthī* pattern of *yugal-bhek* taken with a woman has already been outlined. Just as *bartamān-panthīs* tend to deprecate the *dīkṣā-guru* for various reasons, the *bhek-guru* is generally dismissed on the grounds that he does nothing except confer the robes on the initiate,[5] a formality subject to classification as *anumān*.

Śikṣā-guru

The *śikṣā-guru* is the *bartamān-panthī* guru par excellence. Even if a *bartamān-panthī* has three gurus, she or he will almost invariably value this guru most highly, and if s/he has a guru-lineage, it will be that of the *śikṣā-guru*. Moreover, when *bartamān-panthīs* speak of one guru (with reference to a male institutional guru), it is the *śikṣā* guru to whom they refer. Even when the *bhek-guru* is apparently given primary importance by *bartamān-panthīs*, this is because he has taken on the role of *śikṣā-guru*. For example, those calling themselves Sā̃i in western Rarh tend to see *bhek* as marking the beginning rather than the culmination of *śikṣā*, in which case the *bhārati-guru* functions as a *śikṣā-guru*. Consonant with this is the prevalent notion in those areas that only a *bhek-dhārī* is entitled to give *śikṣā*. However, this appropriation of the path of *bartamān* by renouncers (or vice versa) is in contrast to the situation in Bagri, where there is a robust non-Brahmin, non-renouncer tradition of gurus, and where even renouncers on the *bartamān* path are often dismissive of the institution of renunciation.

Śikṣā means 'learning, instruction, training', and advocacy of the (separate) institution of the *śikṣā-guru* implies the denigration of *dīkṣā* to the status of a mere formality, and the futility of *mantra* (the speciality of the *dīkṣā-guru*) in contrast to the esoteric practice taught by the *śikṣā-guru*. It is the *śikṣā-guru* who teaches one to 'plough' (*śikṣā-guru cāś sekhān*). As Rāj puts it (song no. 73), 'the *śikṣā* guru comes and teaches you agriculture . . . ' (*śikṣā-guru ese kṛṣi karmma śikhāila* . . .). This analogy, along with another taken from everyday rural life in Bengal – that of steering the boat through the waves (Rāj: song no. 40) – indicates the sexual nature of the practice as well as the labour and skill involved.

[4] 'Bhārati' is one of the Daśanāmī titles. A *bhek-dhārī* told me that the *bhek-guru* is called the *bhārati-guru*, because Keśab Bhārati gave *bhek* to Caitanya.

[5] In practice this is not always the case, especially where the mechanism of *bhek* is a respectable way of changing one's guru or one's 'line'.

Rāj also likens *śikṣā* to school education (Text B:26). One *bartamān-panthī* renouncer told me that 'the guru is the person who helps you understand your body'. One common reason for taking *śikṣā* is to stop having children; and others who cannot have children will go for a remedy to the same gurus, knowledge of conception and contraception being two aspects of a subject in which *bartamān-panthī* gurus generally have considerable expertise. Sometimes the male guru shows the esoteric practice to the female disciple, who then shows her partner; sometimes the *guru-mā* (the guru's female partner) shows the male disciple (*śiṣya*) and the guru the female disciple (*śiṣyā*). This is said to turn base metal – the disciples – into gold (Jhā 1985:476). Other *bartamān-panthīs*, including Rāj's people, dissociate themselves from these methods. Whatever methods are used, the instruction involved in *śikṣā* entails the necessity for prolonged and intimate contact with the *śikṣā-guru*, as he (sometimes she) teaches stage after stage of practice. This enhances his importance, in contrast to the brevity of the *dīkṣā-guru*'s task (in *bartamān-panthī* eyes), which is virtually complete once the *mantra* has been given. As pointed out above, *śikṣā* is sometimes thought to culminate in an attitude of renunciation. Although, as was shown earlier, an endorsement of renunciation as an institution does not necessarily follow from this, this notion does reveal a degree of conformity with the attitudes of the society of renouncers.

I would argue that, where *bartamān-panthīs* are concerned, the *dīkṣā-guru* is the guru of the householder realm, and the *bhek-guru* of the renouncer realm. It is against this background that the positing of a separate *śiksā* guru (by Vaishnava *bartamān-panthīs* of Bagri) should be seen. The single guru of Muslim *bartamān-panthīs* is plausibly related to the fact that, in general, the institution of the preceptor has not been appropriated by more conventional religious elements in this way. Whereas renouncer lineages with *bartamān-panthī* practices provide a more-or-less respectable refuge for *bartamān-panthīs* (albeit less so than a lineage of ascetics without female partners would be), householder life is virtually the only option available to Muslims, in theory and in practice.[6] Within householder life, the very act of taking a preceptor represents a move away from orthodox Islam.

Whether they be householder or renouncer, Vaishnava adversaries of the path of *bartamān* are particularly vehement in their denunciation of the institution of the *śikṣā-guru*, their argument generally being that instruction (*śiksā*) is part of the duty of the *dīkṣā-guru*.[7] A recent example of this, dating from the early 1980s, is

[6] The *khilāphat* (which in this context may be seen as the Muslim equivalent of *bhek*) is an extremely rare occurrence, especially in the Krishnapur area. In contrast to hundreds of Vaishnava *bhek-dhārī bartamān-panthīs*, I know of only two cases of Muslims who have taken *khilāphat* (and one of these cases was in fact *bhek*, given by a Hindu guru. The recipient has subsequently reverted to householder life). Moreover, reports from Bangladesh suggests that the *khilāphat* is conferred on the disciple by his original *dīkṣā* guru, or his widow (Ābul Āhasān Caudhurī 1992:26, 28).

[7] In the *Caitanya Caritāmṛta* of Kṛṣṇadās Kabirāj, a text held in great respect by both orthodox Vaishnavas and (Vaishnava) *bartamān-panthīs*, the concept of three gurus, called *dīkṣā, śikṣā* and *caittya*, is found. However, the role of this *śikṣā-guru* differs significantly from that of a *bartamān-panthī śikṣā-guru*. In the *Caitanya Caritāmṛta*, the *dīkṣā-guru* gives the *mantra*, while the *śikṣā-guru* gives instructions in how to hear and chant the divine name, and worship the divine image (cf. Bharati 1970:122). The *caittya-guru* teaches the esoteric significance of the teachings of the first two gurus to a sincere disciple (S. C. Chakravarti 1969:206, 208).

a non-Brahminical Vaishnava tract against Bāuls, allegedly based on older texts, entitled: *Chastisement of the Sahajiyās: a judgement on the matter of the dīkṣā and śikṣā gurus of the religion of love of Śrīśrīcaitanya* (Dās Brahmacārī 1389 BS). Sahajiyā is identified with Bāul on the first page of the volume, and is subsequently denounced as a 'heretical, atheist and demonic tradition' (*nāstik, pāṣaṇḍa, āsurik sampradāy*). It is asserted that: 'He who gives *dīkṣā* will give *śikṣā* on that subject.' The argument is that the authoritative lineage is the *dīkṣā* guru lineage, and that nowhere in scripture has a separate *śikṣā mantra,* and therefore guru, been mentioned (Dās Brahmacārī 1389 (I):10, 14; (II):59ff.). The author goes on to allege that Bāuls and others have introduced, as a *śikṣā mantra,* what was originally a *dīkṣā mantra* ('*haṅsa*') of Shaivas, Shaktas, Nāths and so on, in order to corrupt and destroy Vaishnava *dharma*. In turn, practices he alleges are taught by this *śikṣā* guru, that is, sexual practices without seminal emission (*aṭal sādhan*) and 'four moons' practices, are said to derive from 'ghoulish Aghorapanthīs' (an extreme form of Tantric). The tract cited relates the *mantra 'haṅsa'* to the title Paramahaṅsa, which in turn is identified with Bāuls (Dās Brahmacārī 1389 (II):21).

Such attacks may help to account for the refusal of those called Bāul and *bartamān-panthīs* to be identified as Tantric. Where Rāj is concerned, he was indeed called Paramahaṅsa by his disciples, and *haṅsa* is the only mantra to find favourable mention in his songs (e.g. nos. 95, 98), and those of his followers. (They normally adhere to a more typical *bartamān-panthī* view: that all *mantras* are classifiable as mere name (*nām*), as opposed to the more highly valued substance (*bastu*) – see pp. 193ff.). However, for *bartamān-panthīs*, these usages indicate a position beyond tradition and sectarianism, not allegiance to a non-Vaishnava tradition or sect. The *haṅsa mantra* is also known by them as the *ajapā mantra,* so called because it consists of the natural breath and therefore requires no active recitation (*jap*).[8] The ever-flowing breath (. . . *haṅsa haṅsa* . . .) gradually becomes '*sohaṅ sohaṅ* . . . ' ('I am that . . . ', a phrase associated with conservative Advaitin philosophy). But in the hands of *bartamān-panthīs* such as Rāj, this philosophy of non-discrimination is used against the distinctions and hierarchies of both householder and renouncer societies. Mani (song no. 23) contrasts *nām jap* (recitation of divine names), which is artificially imposed and therefore *anumān*, with the naturally present breath of the body, *ajapā*. For *bartamān-panthīs* the identification of the two syllables of *haṅ-sa* as male and female respectively is also significant (cf. Gupta *et al.* 1979:110, 180).

The isolation of a separate *śikṣā-guru* role allows Vaishnava *bartamān-panthīs* of Bagri to take gurus who are neither Brahmin (as is the *dīkṣā-guru*) nor renouncer (as is the *sannyās-guru*), and thus to preserve some independence from the hierarchies of both worlds. Their concern to differentiate *śikṣā* from *dīkṣā* is clear. For example, *dīkṣā* may be categorised as *anumān*, in that it consists of the transfer of an

[8] The '*a*' syllable of '*a-japā*' is a privative. *Haṅsa* and *ajapā* both mean the breath, in addition to other meanings. Rāj (text A:246) says that the outbreath is the 'ha' syllable, the inbreath the 'sa' syllable, but this is often reversed. *Haṅsa* has a wide variety of meanings. From the root meaning, 'swan', its other meanings include *paramātmā*, *parabrahma*, Śiva, guru.

invisible and magically efficacious *mantra* from the guru, while *śikṣā* is much more a matter of systematic instruction of skills (classified as *bartamān*). As mentioned above, in the giving of a *mantra*, the tongue of the guru is likened to a penis, and the ear of the disciple to a vagina. This analogy undergoes further inflection with the *bartamān-panthī* concept of 'sowing the seed of the guru' (*guru-bīj ropan*), which in the *bartamān-panthī* context normally refers to incorporation of the guru's semen. Whereas in *dīkṣā, mantra* (*bīj*) is given, in *śikṣā* the actual seed (*bīj*) may be given. In such cases, the guru 'dies', transferring his potent, life-giving substance to the disciple (cf. Kakar 1981:137; O'Flaherty 1973:96ff.).[9] The fact that the 'death' or 'slaying' of the guru is involved here casts doubt on the universality of Kakar's statement that the 'incorporation of the potent seed of authority figures' is related to the 'consolidation of the homo hierarchicus element in Indian identity' (1981:133; see Openshaw 1998 for a fuller discussion of the 'killing' of the guru).

As one might expect from the ambivalence regarding the formal initiations given by the *dīkṣā* (and *bhek*) gurus, there is at times a tendency to collapse the two roles (or three if one includes *bhek*) into one guru, primarily the *śikṣā* guru. A disciple of Maṇi (D.G., of Hindu birth) asserted that the idea of three gurus is *bidhi* (based on scriptural injunction, that is, external). In *rāg* (a reference to the 'path of passion' – *rāg-mārg*) there are no rules. Another of Maṇi's disciples (R.S., of Muslim birth) remarked that for them, *dīkṣā* and *śikṣā* are not different, *dīkṣā* meaning to show, and *śikṣā* to proceed to the end of the path. The Talitpur people, technically renouncers, give all three initiations themselves. The emphasis on one guru relates not only to the disdain of *bartamān-panthīs* for both *bhek* and *dikṣā*, but also to the tendency to devalue any formal initiation as such. Thus *śikṣā* is often said to have no separate *mantra*. The absorption of all roles into one guru (primarily the *śikṣā-guru*) may also foster the formation of separate groups, as is the case of the Talitpur people. A Talitpur *bhek-dhārī* guru said that if a would-be disciple had not even taken *dīkṣā*, he would give him/her *dīkṣā* and *śikṣā* (just *dīkṣā* would be considered useless). If s/he has already taken *dīkṣā*, *śikṣā* would be given, and if *śikṣā* had been taken from another *bartamān-panthī* 'family' (*ghar*) he would formally give her/him *bhek*. In cases like this, *bhek* functions as a mechanism for incorporating disciples from other 'lines'.

Even where the importance of one guru is strongly emphasised, as in the case of Talitpur, this male institutional guru is undermined in various ways. First, the critique of the formal *dikṣā* and *bhek* gurus tends to cast a shadow over the *śikṣā* guru also, especially to the degree that he absorbs their qualities and functions. Moreover the guru, and *a fortiori* the lineage, is undermined by the universally accepted necessity for self-cultivation and arduous practice on the part of the disciple. As will be seen below, even as devoted a disciple as Hem was forced to realise that his guru (Rāj) could not 'take him across'. The guru typically shows the

[9] One analogy used is that the guru's semen is like the starter of curd (thickened or transformed – *pakka* – milk), which gradually turns into curd the ordinary milk (of the bodies of the male and female disciples) with which it is mixed (Jhā 1985:532 n. 7). For a similar initiatory practice among the Aghoris, see Parry 1994:259.

way, but the disciple must do the work. A householder initiate of the middle-ranking locally dominant caste (Mahishya), who has taken *śikṣā* from the same Brahmin (not of Rāj's 'line') who gave him *dīkṣā*, told me that his guru is completely different in these two different roles. In his role as *dīkṣā-guru*, he observes all the conventions and 'displays overlordship' (*aiśvarya dekhācche*), whereas as the *śikṣā-guru* he observes no formalities (including commensality restrictions), and acts towards his disciple as a friend. He elaborated these two roles in terms of 'the path of conventional prescriptions and observances' (*bidhi mārg*), as opposed to 'the path of passion' (*rāg mārg*). He also brought in the common *bartamān-panthī* idea of the *dīkṣā-guru* as father (who simply sows the seed) and the *śikṣā-guru* as mother (who gives birth, nurses, and generally brings up the child). Gold discusses the tension between the idea of all gurus in a lineage being equal, and that of the *ādi-guru* as a quasi-divine figure whose teachings it is the function of all subsequent gurus to propagate (1987:324). Among the *bartamān-panthīs*, for whom guru lineages, being in the category of *anumān*, are of relatively less importance, this tension is less overt than another: that between the guru as the source of authority and knowledge, and the emphasis on one's own work, achievement and realisation, this latter being given particular emphasis by Rāj and his followers.

Women as gurus

The *śikṣā-guru* also has a rival in the partner of the disciple. An initiate from Rarh remarked that, in addition to the *śikṣā-guru*, the wife is guru to the husband and the husband to the wife. While the idea that a woman's guru is her husband is conventional, the contrary is related to the notion that a man's success in esoteric practice depends largely (some would say wholly) on his female partner. I was told by male initiates that the two rows of the Vaishnava sectarian necklace signify the *śikṣā-guru* and the 'guru of passion' or 'guru of the esoteric path' (*rāger-guru*), that is, their female partner. One of Rāj's living disciples explicated the word 'guru' as follows: '*gu*' means '*guhākār*' (the shape of a cave – that is, the vagina), and '*ru*' means '*rudrākār*' (the shape of Rudra [Śiva], that is, the phallus). Thus 'guru' may be woman and man together in union. According to a song of Rāj (no. 93), *ātma-tattva* (essence of oneself – that is the man) plus *paratattva* (essence of the 'other', that is, woman) equals *guru-tattva* (essence of the two together). In this sense *gurutattva* is called Caitanya, for Caitanya is said to have combined Kṛṣṇa and Rādhā in himself (*BBBG*:311–12; Jhā 1985:471). Connected with this is the notion that the (external) guru is like Caitanya himself.

In so far as the *śikṣā* guru offers an alternative vertical line of authority to the traditional *dīkṣā* and *bhek* gurus, this itself is under threat from the horizontal bond between the male and female practitioners. Since esoteric practice is more for men than for women (both in theory and practice), seeing woman as the guru is only a short step from each partner seeing the other as the guru. Maṇi states: 'Woman is man's guru' (*nāri puruṣer guru*) (song no. 31). In private, many *bartamān-panthīs* will give primacy to their female partner over other gurus (cf. Sudhīr Cakrabartī 1989:150–1). She may be called *rāger-guru* (see above), the *cetan-guru* or *caitanya-guru*, the *śrīguru* or simply *strī-guru*.[10] It is common to liken the *dīkṣā-guru* to the father, and the *śikṣā-guru* to the mother.[11] While women are normally said to be competent to be *śikṣā-gurus*, it is usually held that they cannot be *dīkṣā* or *bhek* gurus (gurus, that is, of the structured worlds of householder and renouncer).[12]

It will be seen in chapter 7 that women are considered to be without *jāt* (birth-group) or *bidhān* (rules and prescriptions, such as the sacred thread ceremony or circumcision), conventions which, in *bartamān-panthī* eyes, create artificial divisions within humankind. This relates interestingly to the idea that women either have no seed (*bīj* – the source of lineages), or have seed which produces no plant (progeny), this being a sign of perfection in *bartamān-panthī* terms. In connection with this rejection of institutionalised authority, it is of note that women are often said to be *svayaṇ-siddhā* (perfected of themselves), that is, they are naturally perfected without having to undergo esoteric practice, and therefore need no guru. What a woman is and does naturally, a man must achieve through cultivation and practice.

Rāj's people are very clear about the status of women, and call them the principal (*mūl*) or true (*āsal*) gurus. At times Rāj's people append the title Gosvāmī or Gõsāi (titles of gurus) to the first names of their female partners. For Rāj she is 'the boat to take one across', 'the helmsman' or 'the illustrious one of the crossing' (*pārer taraṇī/kāṇḍārī/mahājan*) (song nos. 8, 56, 91). Hem agrees that no one can get anywhere without a woman (song no. 73). He argues that one should worship Hari, not in *anumān* (that is as Viṣṇu), but in *bartamān* (that is as a woman) (song no. 74). ('Hari' is a common *bartamān-panthī* term for 'woman', a meaning derived from '*haraṇ*' (plunder, stealing), for it is women who have the power to steal the seminal essence from men.) At times, especially in Rāj's case, the partner becomes the sole guru, and all reference to the formal male *śikṣā* guru is dropped. He precedes a long text on theory (*tattva*) with a dedication in Sanskrit, not to any male guru, but to Rājeśvar: 'Praise be to Rājeśvar, most kind, ocean of compassion. At the mere remembrance of her name, the ocean of love overflows and so many emotions awake. There is no guru like her, I make obeisance to Rājeśvar.'[13] This is then followed by a whole series of praise songs (*bandanā*) to Rājeśvar. Raj's conferring

[10] The external meaning of *cetan-* and *caitanya-guru* is 'the guru of (i.e. who awakens) consciousness or knowledge'. The term *śrī-guru* plays on several meanings: *śrī* as an honorific, as a name of the goddesses of wealth and learning, and as 'beauty, grace' etc. *Strī-guru* means 'woman guru'.

[11] The *Bibartta-bilās* identifies the *dīkṣā-guru* with Kṛṣṇa (male), and the *śikṣā-guru* with Rādhā (female) (K. Bhaṭṭācāryya n.d.:51).

[12] On the generally high status of women in Bengali Vaishnavism, and the Vaishnava Sahajiyā notion that women are gurus by nature and may be institutional gurus also, see Dimock 1966:96ff.; Hayes 2000. Women were permitted to become disciples and gurus according to one Tantric text, and this practice is fairly common nowadays (Gupta *et al.* 1979:79–80. On the woman as guru in Tantra, see Gupta 1991:208, Silburn 1988:158). Among the Lālan-panthī *fakirs*, the *guru-mā* (guru's female partner) may give *khilāphat* (Islamic renunciation) to disciples after his death (Carol Salomon: personal communication).

[13] *'Bandehaṅ karuṇā sindhuṇ, Rājeśvar dayānidhin . . . Stasya tūlya guru nāhi, pranamāmi Rājeśvaraṅ.'*

on his lover the masculine name 'Rājeśvar' (Lord of Rāj), usually feminised as 'Rājeśvarī' by his disciples, should be seen partly in the light of the fact that he regarded her as his guru.[14] Recalling the first day he met Rājeśvar, Rāj writes:

> On the first day I saw you, mother, I knew you to be my guru,
> How long I travelled the three worlds, yet I never felt this way before.
> I saw many divine men and women with my own eyes; yet I never knew anyone in this world to be the guru.[15]

The following *mantra* in Rāj's manuscript is cited as 'my own *mantra*': '*Oṅ driṅ triṅ klīṅ śrī-guru Rājeśvar – oṅ svāhā*' (Text A:275). There are numerous other references in the manuscript to Rājeśvar as the guru, in one of which Rāj refers to her as 'the great *śikṣā-guru*' (*śikṣā mahājan*) (Text A:218, 231–2). In one of his texts, Rāj writes that the One (Hari, who is woman) gives *dīkṣā* in the form of the Brahmin guru, *śikṣā* in the form of the *sādhu*, and tests everyone in the form of *śakti* (the female partner) (Text B:26). While it is conventional to take refuge in the guru, the writings of Rāj and his disciples are replete with injunctions to take refuge in a woman (Text A: 223ff.). Nor is this unique to Rāj's people. Consider, for example, the following song by Duddu (*BBBG*:816):

> Place the feet of a woman on your head.
> There is no salvation in this world except through her.
> Abandoning women and dwelling in the forest
> You have become a fake renouncer.
> In the feet of a woman are all the sacred places,
> But you never cared to see.

Many gurus

The importance of any one formal guru is clearly undermined by the prescription of two or three gurus. An extension of this process is seen in the further increase in the number of formal and informal gurus. There is general agreement that there can be only one *dīkṣā* and one *bhek* guru, and for *bartamān-panthīs* there is little reason to change a guru whose role (giving a *mantra,* or conferring the robes of renunciation) is transient and of little importance in any case. Where the *śikṣā-guru* is concerned, a wide variety of views is held. Some maintain that the *śikṣā-guru* can never be replaced or added to. Others agree but allow for the possibility of one or more advisory (*upadeś*) gurus in addition to the original *śikṣā-guru*. On the other hand, the term *upadeś-guru* is sometimes used as a synonym for the *śikṣā-guru*, and indeed '*upadeś*' (like *śikṣā*) means 'instruction' or 'teaching'. Yet others, especially in Rarh, maintain that there may be many *śikṣā-gurus*. It should

[14] There are also possible implications here concerning the role reversal of man and woman at certain times of esoteric practice, which will be discussed in Part V. In one of the praise songs referred to, Rāj says: 'You are sometimes a man, sometimes a woman . . . you, mother, are Rāj-Rājeśvarī . . . (*Kakhana puruṣ tumi, kakhana ramanī . . . Tumi mā Rāj-Rājeśvarī . . .*)' (Text A:7). (Rāj-Rājeśvarī refers to one of the ten goddesses of great knowledge – *daśamahābidyā.*)

[15] Text B:8. For transliterated Bengali text, see Openshaw 1994:171.

be borne in mind that the task of the *śikṣā-guru*, who instructs in the various stages of *sādhanā*, is onerous; and the expectations of the disciple are correspondingly great. In practice it is quite common to change one's guru, perhaps because one is dissatisfied with the first, or perhaps to learn different practices.[16] Relations with a previous guru (and the kin created by that link) are not necessarily severed on taking a new guru. To amplify the number of gurus still further, there is the injunction to 'mix with adepts' (to do *sādhu-saṅga*). It is often said that the guru speaks the *mantra* in one ear, leaving the other free for *sādhu-saṅga*. This is a favourite maxim of Muslim *bartamān-panthīs*, and indicates, even in their case, a challenge to the monopoly of the single guru. In connection with rejection of the idea of one guru, *bartamān-panthīs* are fond of quoting the saying:

> Make hundreds of gurus, the *mantra* is essential.
> Quote whomever your heart desires as your guru.[17]

The guru may also be said to be (any) one who brings light or consciousness (*caitanya*) into the darkness. In one song (*BBBG*:792), *dīkṣā*, *śikṣā* and other gurus are differentiated from 'one's own guru' who is recognisable because s/he 'removes blindness'. The word '*guru*' may be derived from '*gu*' meaning 'excrement' or 'darkness', and '*ru*' meaning 'light' (Jhā 1985:467).

In many songs the gurus are said to be countless (*asaṅkhya, aganan*). Rāj places the *dīkṣā* and *śikṣā* gurus in the same category as one's father, mother, insects, trees and creepers (song no. 73):

> Tell me, in what form shall I revere the guru? . . .
> See, there are countless gurus. Which shall I call the original guru?
> Father and mother are gurus, so are *dīkṣā* and *śikṣā* gurus – and there are many more.
> If you consider the matter, the gurus are without number.
> See, everyone gives instruction (*upadeś*), even insects and flying things, trees and creepers.
> The *dīkṣā* guru purifies the body, he only gave the seed [*mantra*].
> The *śikṣā* guru came and taught agriculture.
> I cannot call them the original guru [or, as a double meaning: 'their principal guru is (a) woman']. They only show the way across this mundane world.
> Rāj Kṛṣṇa says,
> One needs to know that principle guru,
> Otherwise there is no possibility of transcending this earthly life.
> We hear that, without the guru, there is terrible danger in crossing the ocean of this world.

16 Bharati argues that the idea of many *dīkṣās* (for different purposes) is traditional (1970:197, n. 3). A few *bartamān-panthīs* of my acquaintance cite previous initiations into Shaktism, Shaivism etc., to demonstrate their omnicompetence.

17 In most contexts, as we have seen, it is *mantra* rather than the guru which would be rejected. Talented *bartamān-panthīs* would reinterpret '*mantra*' here. For transliterated Bengali text, see Openshaw 1998:15.

Here Rāj opposes the 'original (*mūl*)' guru to the formal *dīkṣā* and *śikṣā* gurus. The fact that the 'principal guru' is a woman is suggested by the pun on *nāri,* meaning 'I cannot (*nā pāri*)' and 'woman (*nārī*)'.[18]

In another song (no. 94), Rāj points out that all differences between person and person, even that between guru and disciple, are incompatible with 'knowledge of the self' (*ātmatattva/ahaṅtattva*):

> Father son, guru disciple, Brahmin Kṣatriya Vaisya,
> All are merged in the 'I'. The pure and the impure [literally: the cobbler] – all will be one.
> He who says the guru pervades the world is lost in delusion.
> Why does your guru speak of [refer to himself as] 'I', and you also?
> If truly there is no one in the three worlds apart from the guru,
> Then why do you wonder how to be delivered from this earthly life?
> 'Guru, guru' is forever on your lips, but tell me, who labours [in esoteric practice] for the guru? [The answer of course is no one.]
> The 'I' (*āmi*) predominates in everyone. We always thinks 'what will become of me?' . . .[19]

Initiation patterns in Rarh

Initiation patterns are somewhat unusual in those parts of Bengal where the commercialisation of Bāuls and Bāul songs predominates, in much of Rarh, for example. Nevertheless the tendency towards multiple initiations sometimes found in these areas, and especially among singers of Jat Vaishnava origin, illustrates certain general principles. As in Bagri, in Rarh also it was often pointed out to me that the purpose of initiation is to establish relationships. In theory at any rate, with each initiation one enters a ready-made and sometimes vast family, consisting of guru, *guru-mā*, brothers and sisters through initiation, and so on. '*Dīkṣā* means *dekhā-dekhi*' (mutual visits), 'the purpose of *mantra* is to establish a relationship', and '*dīkṣā* means "I am yours," ' I was informed. (In all these cases, *dīkṣā* means initiation in general, not simply the first initiation.) A guru from Rarh told me that while *dīkṣā* (the first initiation) is taken only once, *śikṣā-gurus* are endless. I once heard it said of a Birbhum Bāul[20] singer, who had taken so many initiations it exceeded even local Bāul tolerance, that his aim was to acquire many kin through his gurus, which in turn might lead to invitations (to sing or to stay in various homes and ashrams) and greater prestige (*sammān*). Kin networks are spread even wider when one considers that not a few of the local Bāuls were brought up or otherwise strongly influenced by one or more *dharma-mā* (loosely 'god-mother'), or various foster-mothers whose other kin (in 'blood' or *dharma* etc.) again

[18] For transliterated Bengali text, see Openshaw 1998:16. For songs on the same theme, see *BBBG*:866f. (song no. 458), *BBBG*:1048 (no. 679) translated in A. & M. A. Dasgupta 1977:65; *BBBG*:792 (no. 358), 600 (no. 88) translated in Dasgupta 1977:47.

[19] For transliterated Bengali text, see Openshaw 1998:16.

[20] In this section, the word Bāul is used for those (in Rarh), usually singers, who would call themselves this; the term *bartamān-panthī* is used more inclusively.

become one's own kin. (This may also happen if one's guru(s) maintain relationships with kin of these sorts.) In addition there are usually 'blood' kin of one's own. All this is yet further broadened by the emphasis on friendship. *Bartamān-panthīs* often insist that we are all *mānuṣ* (human beings), in contexts where they wish to negate bonds of family, *jāt, sampradāy* and so on: to make others (*par*) into one's own (*āpan*), as it is put. In their own localities and outside, at festivals, other ashrams and on the road, many opportunities for forming friendships with Bāul and non-Bāul alike present themselves. *Bartamān-panthīs* voice many ideals consonant with that of friendship: for example, that of not distinguishing between 'one's own people' (*āpan*) and 'strangers' (*par*), that of being spontaneous and easy (*sahaj*) in one's actions etc. Such friends often again become 'kin' (see Inden and Nicholas 1977:33), but many *bartamān-panthīs* value friendship in its own right, and do not attempt such a transformation. The dark side of this Rarh picture will be readily understood. Often motivated by economic insecurity and a desperate need to belong, there is a danger that the bonds of friendship will be vitiated by want and rivalry. Moreover, multiple initiations not only weaken the power of any one guru (which adversely affects would-be gurus), but also the bonds of kinship established through initiation with him.

Criticism of the guru

Although criticism of the guru is by no means unique to Rāj's people or even to *bartamān-panthīs*,[21] it is a special feature of Rāj's people, and appears in particularly uncompromising form in the songs and sayings of Rāj and Maṇi. A well-known *bartamān-panthī* saying runs: 'How can I worship [or "understand"] what I haven't seen with my own eyes?' (*Yeṭā dekhi-ni nayane, seṭā bhajiba [bujhiba] kemane*). Rāj's version of this is typically more forceful: 'What I haven't seen with my own eyes won't do, even if the guru tells me!' (*Yeṭā dekhi-ni nayane, seṭā guru balle-o calbe nā*). Rāj apparently always discouraged would-be disciples, but if they persisted he had a test for them: 'If you and I were to disagree', he would ask, 'whom would you believe?' If the other said 'I would believe you, as my guru', Rāj would retort: 'If you can't be my equal, how can you be my disciple?' Māṇi, a highly successful guru of *dīkṣā*, *śikṣā* and even *bhek*, condemns gurus, including himself, even more vehemently (song no. 44):

> Guru of initiation, guru of instruction – for business, all become
> wish-fulfilling trees!
> You never bothered to find out who is your real guru.
> Your guru is someone with whom you have a money relationship.
> Maṇi, you have become a priest-tout of Bṛndāban with this [guru] business![22]

[21] Hess and Singh (1986:152) cite the following song by Kabir:

> I've burned my own house down, the torch is in my hand.
> Now I'll burn down the house of anyone who wants to follow me.

[22] For original (transliterated) Bengali, see Openshaw 1998:17.

Here Maṇi compares himself as guru to the troublesome, grasping touts (*pāṇḍās*) familiar in pilgrimage centres. Bṛndāban, a Vaishnava pilgrimage centre in north India, was the alleged site of the *līlā* of Rādhā and Kṛṣṇa. There is also a heavenly Bṛndāban where that *līlā* eternally takes place. For *bartamān-panthīs* Bṛndāban also refers to the human body or a part of it.[23]

In a similar vein, another song (no. 47) ends: 'Maṇi says, who is whose guru is largely a matter of money!' (*Maṇi bale ke kār guru byābsā hala mūl kāraṇ*). A song was cited earlier in which Maṇi rejects the appurtenances of formal religion on the grounds of their artificiality (no one is born with them). A similar argument is used in another song (no. 39) against the guru–disciple relationship also:

> You entered the world naked, you will leave naked. The confusion comes in between.
> Some call you 'father', some call you 'uncle', some call you 'brother' and other such nonsense. . . .
> Some are devotees of the goddess, some are engaged in reciting the name of Hari,
> Some are Shakta, some are Vaishnava, (yet) all are born to the same lineage [i.e. from a woman] . . .
> . . .
> Being denuded Mad Maṇi sees only men and women.
> Everyone comes naked, only this guru disciple [business] creates confusion.

> *Esecha neṅṭā yāibā neṅṭā mājhkhāne kebal gaṇḍagol,*
> *Keu bale bābā keu bale kākā keu bale bhāi ābol-tābol . . .*
> *Keu hala māyer bhakta keu hala harināme rata,*
> *Keu śākta keu baiṣṇab eki kule sabār janam . . .*
> . . .
> *Pāgal Maṇi neṅṭā haye dekhe yata puruṣ meye*
> *Sabāy ela neṅṭā haye kebal guru śiṣya bā̃dhāla gol.*

The guru within

A tendency to discount the formal gurus in favour of one 'real' guru, a (male or female) *śikṣā-guru*, or the female partner, has been noted above. Alternatively, 'guru' may denote an inner reality of some kind. Since the word 'house' may refer to the body, the following song (no. 11) by Maṇi may refer to either of the last two possibilities:

> It is not easy to recognise the guru, why do you roam about (searching)?
> You'll be able to see fake gurus, (but) the real guru is in your house . . .[24]

[23] For a similar attitude towards the guru among the Matuyās see S. Bandyopadhyay (1995:166). What makes Maṇi distinctive is his self-criticism as a Brahmin *dīkṣā-guru*.

[24] For transliterated Bengali text, see Openshaw 1998:17.

The guru within is variously identified. One meaning is the semen, the sperm or something even within this. It is in this sense that the 'guru's wealth' (*guru-dhan*), and the 'guru [or guru's] substance' (*guru-bastu*) are spoken of. A standard meaning of *guru* is 'heavy', and, for *bartamān-panthīs*, the semen, which is likened to mercury, is the heaviest substance in the body. As mentioned earlier, 'guru' may also refer to the combined essences of male and female. Just as guru in an external sense may denote a man, a woman and man (who are guru to each other) and finally a woman alone, so the inner guru has three parallel referents: first, the male essence (that is, semen or something within this, which may be called the *kṛṣṇa-bindu*); secondly, the male and female essences together; and finally, the female essence alone (that is, menstruation or something within this – the *rādhā-bindu*). S. N. Jhā has suggested that the *rādhā-bindu* may correspond to the ovum, which is the guru who saves, gives shelter and consciousness to the sperm.[25] Familiar ideas of the (male) seed and the (female) field, or even the (typically) male embryo in the woman's womb may be at issue here. Also relevant here are parallels between sperm and ovum and male (*puruṣ*) and female (*prakṛti*) principles, inside and outside respectively, as Gaurāṅga (Caitanya) was Rādhā on the outside and Kṛṣṇa on the inside.

The institutional guru may therefore be undermined in many ways, of which the last two are in interesting contrast. On the one hand, the category is expanded to include various human and even other living beings; on the other, we find an opposite tendency towards interiorisation. The latter illustrates an interesting tension in *bartamān-panthī* ideology. While a focus on vision and common sense is crucial in the assault on various conventional religious positions categorised as *anumān*, progressive interiorisation (beyond the semen and menstrual blood) may lead to a reassertion of invisible, 'spiritualised' realities.

Hem Khyāpā (Hṛdānanda)

This discussion on the guru ends with an illustration of the contradictions which the doctrine of the primacy of the guru (*guru-bād*) may generate for *bartamān-panthīs*. In common with other *bartamān-panthīs*, Rāj, in his autobiography, constructs an opposition between the worlds of the Hindu householder and renouncer whereby the latter, negatively defined as 'not-*saṅsār*', is posited as an alternative to the former. It is instructive to compare Rāj's transition from householder life to that of a renouncer of a kind, with the trajectory of one of his main disciples, Hem Khyāpā (or Hṛdānanda – a name given him by Rāj), as read from his songs. While Rāj's lone flight from householder life is not typical of those on the path of *bartamān*, Hem followed the more usual pattern of taking joint renunciation with a woman, in this case his wife. This of course is hardly surprising, since Hem was already on the path of *bartamān* when he renounced householder life, whereas Rāj was not. An examination of Hem's songs reveals the difficulties of following the traditional male guru on the path of *bartamān*. It offers an insight

[25] S. N. Jhā personal communication. Cf. Jhā 1985:488–9, 503ff.; 1985/6 (II):17.

into the structural contradiction between the society of renouncers, based on the guru-disciple relationship, and the non-hierarchical logic of the *bartamān* path.

Hem, a close disciple of Rāj, was instrumental in his guru's elopement with Rājeśvar, wife of his neighbour, who had taken *bhek*. Hem and his wife had no children, and his brother's descendants now live in his house as an ashram. Apart from the information provided by them, by disciples of Hem's wife and by other village inhabitants, most of my knowledge of him comes from his own songs. There are no disciples of Hem in his home area. In the following brief analysis, my assumption is that the song numbers are a rough reflection of the order in which they were written.[26]

It seems that Hem began writing songs after he became Rāj's disciple, for Rāj is mentioned in the idiographs, along with Hem himself, from the first song. Hem's songs are characterised by traditional devotion to the guru. He exhorts himself not to leave Rāj's feet, and to worship Rāj Kṛṣṇa Svāmi. Rāj is addressed as Śiva, Param-iṣṭadeb, Kṛṣṇa, Gaur (Caitanya) come again to Nadia, and so forth. All this is in striking contrast with Rāj's songs, where the guru, scarcely mentioned other than in direct connection with Rājeśvar, is never unambiguously identifiable with a male institutional guru. Eventually, songs lauding Rāj and Rājeśvar, most usually as Rādhā and Kṛṣṇa but also as Caṇḍīdās and Rāmī, outnumber those to Rāj alone, or to Rājeśvar alone. Although the identification of Rāj and Rājeśvar with Caṇḍīdās and the washerwoman Rāmī is slightly less emphasised than that with Rādhā Kṛṣṇa, the former seems in many ways more apt a parallel, Caṇḍīdās and Rāj both being Brahmins in love with lower-caste women, and in both cases vanishing with their beloved to a distant land.[27] Indeed it is precisely in the context of the scandalous affair and elopement of Rāj and Rājeśvar that this analogy figures. One might tentatively attribute Hem's preference for the Kṛṣṇa Rādhā model, over the self-sufficient and isolated dyad suggested by the Caṇḍīdās and Rāmī legend, to the fact that the former allows the possibility of relationship with the divine pair as a Gopī, or a woman of Braja and so forth, which is how Hem specifically speaks of himself and the other disciples in these songs. (In Hem's songs, Kṛṣṇa is never anything but wholly devoted to Rādhā, unlike other characterisations of him as fickle and unfeeling, an image often used to demonstrate the superiority of women.) Hem's great devotion to Rāj, which enabled him to accept the elevation of a woman who was his neighbour, and probably his sister through initiation, as his (guru) mother, and to assist, at considerable personal cost, in an elopement which separated him from the one he loved most, Rāj himself, comes out clearly in many songs.

[26] Details of song numbers are given in Openshaw 1995:122–3. I am indebted to Dr S. N. Jha and his local students for their labour in copying out the songs from the original handwritten manuscript in difficult conditions. The song numbers quoted hereafter are Hem's original numbers.

[27] In the popular song, Caṇḍīdās sat with his fishing line at the pond where Rāmī washed her clothes, without ever catching anything. After twelve years of this, Rāmī finally spoke to him, Caṇḍīdās caught his fish, and said to her: 'We shall stay no more in this land (*e deśe ār raba nā, raba nā*).' The more esoteric meanings to be read here do not invalidate the overt story-line. There are, of course, other legends concerning Caṇḍīdās and Rāmī. See Dinescandra Sen (1928, 1932) for other tales of love between high-status men and lower-status women.

But the irony is that this tremendous devotion to the guru (and that of the other disciples) was part of a model undermined by that same guru's entire life and ideology. The highest aim of more conventional Bengali Vaishnavas is to witness the *līlā* (divine acts) of Rādhā and Kṛṣṇa. For *bartamān-panthīs*, however, the second-hand experience involved in merely witnessing the *līlā* of others, god, guru or whoever they may be, is typically categorised as *anumān*. Hem poignantly relates: 'When I was absorbed in the love (*prem*) of Rāj and Rājeśvar, I thought that they were the givers of love. Now s/he [Rāj or possibly Rājeśvar] tells me, "I am not the one to take you across (*pārer karttā*)" ' (no. 67). Rāj and Rājeśvar are thus no more than examples to be followed. In a song concerning the search for the *maner mānuṣ*, without whom one's life is fruitless, Hem remarks wistfully: 'Rājkṛṣṇa and Rājeśvar have each other, they are always in love, which is good. Hem hopes for such a boon, for everything is possible in this life!' (no. 68). Amidst the considerable disorientation discernible in Hem's songs at this point, we see an increasing emphasis on Woman, who is referred to as *śakti* (divinised female energy), *maner mānuṣ*, *prāṇeśvarī* (goddess of life), *pārer karttā* (ruler of the crossing) and indeed *guru*. It is interesting that this shift coincides with the greater prominence given to the theme of the contrary pulls between householder life and the life of renunciation. Hem had suffered great opprobrium because of his involvement in Rāj's elopement, and when Rāj and Rājeśvar finally gave Hem and his wife *bhek* in 1915 CE, it was in part to escape this censure (song no. 227). In taking *bhek* and renouncing caste, lineage and all social distinctions based on the we–they (*āpan–par*) dichotomy to become *fakir*, Hem's chief aim was the attainment of love. It is significant that at this point Hem begins to focus on a particular woman, his wife Suśīlā, as opposed to Woman in the abstract, praising her for renouncing everything and staying with him. A subsequent song is devoted entirely to her, and Hem even addresses her by name, possibly signifying her changed role from wife to partner in esoteric practice, *guru, maner mānuṣ* etc. However, such a transformation was perhaps difficult to effect, for we see Hem praising her in terms of her devotion to her husband, in other words as a wife![28] Moreover, having initially gloried in the appurtenances of a renouncer, Hem was soon to become disillusioned with his new status, remarking that love cannot be attained through a *geruyā* robe and a loin cloth (no. 256). It is not uncommon for expectations of the society of adepts as devoid of hatred and ill will[29] to be frustrated in this way. The predominant tone after this is one of failure. In one song extolling Rāj and Rājeśvar as the supreme *rasik* and *rasikā*, he remarks that only those living in Braja[30] (that is, Rāj's disciples) know of the great turmoil that lay behind their union. Hem concludes sadly (no. 261):

[28] It is perhaps significant that while Rāj unconventionally places his lover in a superior position, calling her 'Lord of Rāj', Hem (Hṛdānanda) follows a more conventional route, calling Suśīlā 'Hṛdānandinī' (defining her as a female version of himself).

[29] New *bhek-dhārīs* are exhorted to renounce ill-will and enmity (*para-hiṅsā, para-dveṣ*) towards others (Hārādhan 1391:13).

[30] Place of the divine love sports of Kṛṣṇa and Rādhā.

Once upon a time Hṛdānanda dwelt in Braj.
Due to some wrong-doing he fell from grace.
His whole being longs desperately for that joy,
But this time that hope is vain.[31]

Hem and Suśīlā went far away, like Rāj and Rājeśvar, partly because taking *bhek* had not rendered them immune from the scandal after all. They made disciples in other parts of Bengal and Assam, and returned home much later, and considerably wealthier, after the death of their main persecutor. Hem, ever devoted to Rāj, was to die prematurely only a few months after his guru. After his death, Suśīlā, a highly respected woman, made disciples in the locality, but seems to have confined herself to a more conventional role (teaching *mantra* and so forth), eschewing the *bartamān* practices involving man and woman.

In view of the contradiction between the ideal represented by Caṇḍīdās and Rāmī and that of guru and disciple (emphasising either the transmission of techniques or the grace of the guru), it is understandable that Hem, embracing the latter model, should feel himself a failure with respect to the former. In contrast to Lālan, Rāj was strident in his opposition to the institution of the guru. Those who were most devoted to him to the exclusion of other teachers, and therefore in one sense most clearly in his line, are in radical dissonance with him precisely on this matter. A disciple like Maṇi, on the other hand, is commonly said by Rāj's followers to have adopted Rāj's 'mood' (*bhāb*), while not being among his most intimate disciples. If there were disciples so influenced by Rāj's mood as to become like Rāj himself, we naturally would know nothing of them in relation to their guru, just as we know nothing about Rāj's own guru(s). Any attempt to perpetuate structurally or to routinise the Caṇḍīdās–Rāmī ideal is therefore futile. In the final analysis, love (*prem*) and its characteristic abode, the extramarital relationship, cannot subsist within the structures of either householder or renouncer society.

This account elucidates a point made earlier: that the more entrenched practitioners become in a lineage, the more other identities tend to override Bāul or *bartamān* identity. 'Real Bāuls' are as elusive as the Tagorean version, but for different reasons. This may be contrasted with the situation in Tantra, where *sampradāy* are formed from continued oral traditions (*paramparyā*) (Goudriaan and Gupta 1981:12). If the institutional guru is treated with ambiguity, how much more so a line of gurus (*guru-praṇāli* or *guru-tālikā*) tracing descent from a founder, often Caitanya or Mahammad, and therefore bifurcating the *bartamān* path into two sectarian identities? All *bartamān-panthīs* disparage lineages in some contexts, and some in all, for only one's guru is of any import. One only sees and knows one's own guru. All the rest are *anumān* (based on inference). However, a lineage may be useful as a way of establishing one's credentials, especially in renouncer circles. Even Rāj's manuscript contains a lineage – the only place in which a male guru is mentioned. It may be thought that lineages are related to the

[31] For transliterated Bengali text, see Openshaw 1995:146, n. 61.

'lines' which have figured periodically in this book. However, in *bartamān-panthī* parlance, 'lines' mean any grouping of living people who are considered to be related through initiation. This preference for horizontal over vertical loyalties may again be linked with the pre-eminence given to existent (*bartamān*) living beings rather than those classed as imaginary (*anumān*).

Between or beyond: evading the two shores

The preceding sections have dealt with *bartamān-panthī* attempts to evade or transcend the two shores or refuges, that is, the structured worlds of householder and renouncer. I have argued that even the specifically *bartamān-panthī śikṣā* guru may be undermined by the continued intent to avoid we–they divisions as such. I propose to end this chapter with a brief consideration of *bartamān-panthī* notions of anti-identity identities, specifically being human (*mānuṣ*), and being mad. As with the *śikṣā* guru, the aspiration is for a space which, although it may arise from or in reaction to established classifications, evades determination by them.

In general the domain of *bartamān-panthīs* (*śikṣā*) is considered to be situated between the realms of householder (*dīkṣā*) and renouncer (*bhek*). Indeed the triad is commonly enunciated in this order: *dīkṣā, śikṣā, bhek*. Being in-between, or following the 'middle path', is a common motif in *bartamān-panthī* discourse, and steering a mid-stream course in the river is a popular theme in Bāul songs. In apparent conformity with the Bengali Vaishnava community, some *bartamān-panthīs* invoke links with Madhva (or Madhvācārya), founder of one of the four classical all-India Vaishnava *sampradāy*. However, these and similar names are almost invariably derived from the word for 'middle' (*madhya*) – which has the same pronunciation in Bengali, and indeed is written by Rāj as Madhya (Madhyācārya). The notion of the middle path (familiar from Buddhism) has a multitude of nuances for *bartamān-panthīs,* each with different connotations. These include balance and wholeness, as well as negation. The middle path may be said to be between Hindu and Muslim, or between the Hindu Veda and Muslim Koran;[32] it may signify being both male and female (rather than neither in this case). In the context of yogic physiology, it may refer to the diversion of energy to the middle channel of the body (*suṣumnā*) from those of left and right; alternatively, it may refer to having sexual intercourse but no seminal emission (or at least no progeny).

As we have seen, in the case of *śikṣā* and the *śikṣā-guru*, the middle path can amount to a somewhat hazardous strategy for evading the two shores (in this case the householder and renouncer worlds), while cannibalising from both in opportunistic fashion. But *śikṣā* is also susceptible to a more conventional renouncer interpretation: for it chronologically leads on to and appears to culminate in renunciation, which thus represents the highest value.

[32] '*Hindur bed musulmāner korāṇ, tār mājhkhān diye eder sarāṇ* [path].' '*Bāme hindu, dakṣiṇe yaban, madhye madhye eder sarāṇ.*'

Jīb, īśvar, mānuṣ

Three corresponding terms which follow a different order are *jīb, īśvar, mānuṣ*, literally 'living beings, gods and human beings'.[33] *Jīb* usually applies to animals, but in a wider sense means sentient beings. As explicated by *bartamān-panthīs*, it means those who live, that is, are born from the womb, and therefore die. Death here refers to both emission of semen and, intimately connected with it, the physical death of the body. In other words, this is the realm of the uninitiated householder, caught up in worldly life (*saṅsār*) and its pattern of death and rebirth, whether this be conceived of in terms of an individual self (*ātmā*), or in the lineal sense of death as seminal emission resulting in rebirth as one's own child. This ideology denies the effectiveness of complex transformations and transactions associated with caste. All that matters is whether one lives or dies. The nature of an uninitiated householder is to die (that is, to lose his substance). A *bartamān-panthī* renouncer told me in a vivid phrase: '. . . the characteristic mode of householder society is putting ornaments on a dead body' (. . . *mṛta dehe alaṅkār deoyā*).

Īśvar (god) refers to a state of being subject to neither birth nor death. Here again birth and death may be read with respect to the individual or the blood lineage. This is the realm of the classical renouncer who does esoteric practice without a female partner, and whose aim is to completely arrest seminal emission, and thus the flow of life and death on both an individual and lineal level. Like his namesake (god) he is characterised as being without desire. *Bartamān-panthīs* deride such adepts as interested merely in their own welfare or happiness (*ātma-sukh*), in the sense that their sole pursuit is their own liberation.[34] The category *īśvar* may also be applied (by those who advocate a different practice) to those who do practise *sādhanā* with a female partner, but with total retention of semen and in an exploitative fashion, again for their own welfare or happiness. The *jīb–īśvar* opposition is also spoken of as *ṭal–aṭal* (that which falls, as against that which is unwavering – referring to the seminal fluid) (*BBBG*:421).

Certainly in contexts where this triad is evoked, *bartamān-panthīs* prefer a more relational model than that of *īśvar*, and this final stage is referred to as *mānuṣ* (human being). *Mānuṣ* is superior to *īśvar*, and, needless to say, *jīb* – a new reading of a conventional Hindu position. In this connection the well-known Bengali Vaishnava verse is often quoted (Sukumār Sen 1983a:374):

> Of all the sports of Kṛṣṇa
> That as a human being (*nara*) is supreme.
> The human body is the essence of Kṛṣṇa.

33 This may parallel the three dispositions (*bhāva*) in Hindu Tantra, *paśu* (animal), *divya* (divine) and *vīra* (hero), this last being primary (Bharati 1970:231, 236).

34 This statement is not usually connected, as it might be in a Buddhist context, with the desirability of remaining in worldly life for the purpose of liberating others, but rather with the notion of serving others, especially one's female partner.

There is also the famous verse ascribed to the poet Caṇḍīdās:

> Listen my fellow humans –
> The human being is the truth above all truths
> There is nothing higher.
>
> *Śuna he mānuṣ bhāi*
> *Sabār upare mānuṣ satya*
> *Tāhār upare nāi.*

I once heard a Muslim *bartamān-panthī* relate how all the angels (*ferеśtā*) except Ājājīl (Azāzīl) had bowed down to Ādam. For his hubris, Ājājīl became Satan (*śaitān*). He concluded, 'So all those who do not worship human beings (*mānuṣ*) as supreme are *śaitān.*' This glorification of humanity is not confined to *bartamān-panthīs* within the Muslim community (Bandopadhyay 1995:161).

It is often thought that the stage of *īśvar* must be attained and transcended in order to reach *mānuṣ*. Thus, in the context of sexual esoteric practice, it is held that seminal retention (*īśvar*) is a sine qua non of subsequent practices, where mingling and exchange of substances, that is *mānuṣ*, is the aim. The order of this triad is therefore generally different from that of *dīkṣā*, *śikṣā* and *bhek*. *Jīb* and *īśvar* are often equally rejected as being *baidik* (literally 'Vedic', which here means 'orthodox'). Yet in a reversion to the middle position of the third term, one also hears that there is no welfare in either *bhog* (enjoyment, the characteristic of householder life), or *tyāg* (renunciation – the characteristic of the *sannyāsī*). 'In between there is a path which is ours.' And indeed, the kind of limited exchange envisaged above lies in between the extreme loss of the (male) householder and extreme retention of the (male) renouncer.

Larson argues, against Marriott, for the importance of dyads, and asserts that in any case triads are sometimes reconceived in terms of dyads mediated by a third term.[35] As shown above, in the case of *dīkṣā*, *śikṣā* and *bhek*, a third term mediates a basic dyad. In one sense it is also the case that *mānuṣ* mediates, or perhaps encompasses, the absolute loss of *jīb* and the absolute retention of *īśvar*. However, in another sense these and other similar triads consist of two sets of dyads. Thus one moves from being *jīb* (householder) whose pursuit of his own selfish happiness (*ātmasukh*) is rewarded by death (seminal and bodily), to being *īśvar* (renouncer), which is conducive to life (in both senses) and is not concerned with the pleasures of orgasm and progeny. In the next stage, however, it is *īśvar* (the renouncer) who represents *ātmasukh* (retaining all for himself) as against *mānuṣ* who prefers the (controlled) flow of exchange (*len-den, kenā-becā*), mingling or simply giving (*dān*). Thus it may be said that it is *īśvar* who dies, for he is immovable (*aṭal*), and resides in the thousand-petelled lotus (*sahasrār*) at the crown of the head.

[35] Larson 1990:244. On dyads, triads and pentads, see also Larson and Bhattacharya 1987:86–8. Marriott remarks that 'it appears to be Western dualistic structuralism, rather than indigenous thinking, that leads to reconceiving Hindu triads as dichotomies mediated by a third term' (1990:8 n. 6).

Mānuṣ (also called *suṭal*) resides in the two-petalled lotus (*ājñā-cakra*), the point of creation (*BBBG*:422).

The *jīb, īśvar, mānuṣ* triad is at times revealingly assimilated to another: *yonija, ayonija* and *saṅskār* (or again *mānuṣ*). *Yonija* means 'born of a vagina' and is parallel to *jīb*. *Ayonija*, meaning 'not born of a vagina' and thus parallel to *īśvar*, can refer to the 'birth' after initiation, or to those who have no sexual desire. *Saṅskār* means 'purified', 'transformed', 'refined' or 'perfected'. However, for *bartamān-panthīs*, *saṅskār* refers to the esoteric practices which forge *mānuṣ* (the human being), whereas for householders it is the conventional rites of householder life (*saṅskār*) which construct a human being (Madan 1987:42–3).

The fact that an alternative third term of this triad is *svataḥ-siddha* (automatically or spontaneously perfected) is of interest, for this is an epithet commonly used by *bartamān-panthīs* for women. As mentioned earlier, women are commonly regarded as having no *jāt* – the defining feature of householder life. Nor have they any place in the classical society of renouncers. Moreover, women attract rather than lose substance in sexual intercourse, and do not therefore follow the pattern of householders. On the other hand, unlike *īśvar*, an isolated monad absorbed in his selfish happiness, a woman overflows with valuable fluids (especially menstrual fluid and breast milk) which she freely gives for the nourishment of others. She incurs no loss through this gift for, like the moon which reaches fullness, her fluid spills over through excess; she only wanes to wax again.[36] Indeed in one sense it is she who is *mānuṣ*. It is often said that only *mānuṣ* can create another *mānuṣ*, *īśvar* being powerless in this respect, a notion which, in the present context, may be taken to refer to a woman's ability both to create a child, and to produce a *mānuṣ* like herself of (or within) her male partner in esoteric practice (see chapter 9). The *Bṛhat-nigam* identifies *mānuṣ* with woman and *īśvar* with man ('*Iśvar purus haen pikiti mānus*') (*BBBG*:384). As mentioned earlier, the *śikṣā* guru may be likened to the mother, and indeed may be a woman. Thus what women are spontaneously and 'naturally' (that is, they are *mānuṣ*), men must strive to attain through esoteric practice (*saṅskār*). The *Bṛhat-nigam* identifies woman as the 'natural person' (*sahaj-mānuṣ*), and man as the 'cultivated person' (*siddha-mānuṣ*).[37]

It is clear that there is a tension between the notion of *mānuṣ* as the realised or perfected human being (who may be woman) and *mānuṣ* as human beings in general. In the present context, the former is most prominent in the sense that *mānuṣ* is one who has transcended the stages of *jīb* (householder) and *īśvar* (renouncer) to reach this final stage. However, there are also echoes of the more general denotation, in the sense that *mānuṣ* is a concept destructive of the hierarchies of both householder and renouncer realms, or for that matter discrimination of any

[36] In contrast, male loss of semen is considered, by and large, irrecoverable. For an elaborate discussion of the moon symbolism, see Jhā 1985:501ff. See Shaw 1994:45 for a similar concept of woman in Buddhist Tantra. This material suggests that there are gender dimensions to the various transactional strategies outlined by ethnosociologists (Marriott 1976, 1990).

[37] '*Āmi sahaj mānuṣ hai kisuri svarūp. Tumi siddha mānuṣ hao kṛṣṇer anurūp*' (quoted in *BBBG*:384).

kind. This position of non-discrimination or non-dualism (*advaita*) is one where all are classified as *mānuṣ*.[38] It might even be said that *mānuṣ* in the former sense (perfected, realised) is characterised by the non-dual vision of *mānuṣ* in the latter sense. Such a realisation is conceived in various ways. I was told that *mānuṣ* is one who clothes the naked, feeds the hungry and gives water to the thirsty; and the word *mānuṣ* is sometimes glossed as '*mān-huṣ*', where '*mān*' means self-respect, and '*huṣ*' means awareness or consciousness. The tension between these two senses of *mānuṣ* is also seen in the use of the term *sahaj-mānuṣ* for the realised, perfected human being. As we have seen, *sahaj* means (among other things) 'innate' or 'natural', and Dimock renders *sahaj mānuṣ* as 'one who has realised his own nature' (1966:117). As mentioned earlier, women are also referred to as *sahaj-mānuṣ*. It should be clear from the preceding discussion that no opposition of nature and culture is tenable here. As Ramanujan says in relation to Tamil poems: 'culture is enclosed in nature, nature is reworked in culture, so that we cannot tell the difference' (1990:50).

In one sense, therefore, the essence of being *mānuṣ* consists in a rejection of all distinctions between *mānuṣ* and *mānuṣ*. Here it is important to bear in mind not only that *bartamān-panthīs* frequently suffer discrimination themselves (as in the case of Rāj and Hem), but that all *bartamān-panthīs*, by virtue of being initiated into a world of esoteric practice, are, in varying degrees, set apart from householder life (*saṅsār*). This conduces to a reassessment and relativisation of the structures of *saṅsār*. The fact that many *bartamān-panthīs* have realised the arbitrariness of such distinctions through their transcendence of householder and (in some cases) renouncer life lends an added force to the generalised rejection of all we–they (*āpan–par*) divisions crucial to the *bartamān-panthī* interpretation of *advaita* (non-dualism). The following couplet is attributed to Caṇḍīdās, a Brahmin who, like Rāj, suffered opprobrium for his love of a lower-caste woman:

> I have made my home into the outside [world] and the world into my home.
> I have made 'others' into my own people, and my own people into 'others'.[39]

Thus in abandoning one's home, all those who were *āpan* (kin) become *par* (other) and those who were *par* (other) become *āpan* (through kinship created by initiation). Another connotation (whether or not one leaves householder life) is the elevation of one's sexual partner to the status of *āpan* (conventionally, a wife is commonly referred to as *parer meye* – the daughter of 'others'), and the concomitant demotion of one's patrilineage from being *āpan* into *par*. Thus even non-renouncing *bartamān-panthīs* may refuse to eat from their (uninitiated) kin, while accepting food from their partner in esoteric practice and their kin by the guru.[40]

[38] See Dimock 1966:108 for the idea of 'equality' or 'sameness' among the 'Sahajiyās'.

[39] Harekṛṣṇa Mukhopādhyāy 1961:56. See p. vi for transliterated Bengali text.

[40] There are further connotations of *āpan* and *par*, particularly where '*par*' is glossed as '*paramātma*' (and as such frequently equated with women), which cannot be dealt with here.

The experience of *āpan* becoming *par* and vice versa confers immediacy and authenticity on the doctrine of *advaita* (non-discrimination), which in *bartamān-panthī* terms involves a generalised rejection of we–they (*āpan–par*) categories. Thus Hem writes (song no. 166):

> When anyone has non-discriminatory (*advaita*) knowledge, do the illusory attachments (*māyā*) of father, mother, wife and son remain?
> The world is deluded with discriminatory (*dvaita*) knowledge; its own mysterious activity (*līlā*) is not revealed.
> Drowning in the waters of *māyā*, (we) constantly suffer agony . . .
> S/he who opens the eye of pure knowledge will see that the one 'I' (*āmi*) moves and plays in different forms in this universe.
> Can s/he ever think in terms of various castes, or 'us' and 'them' (*āpan* and *par*)?
>
> You listen (to others) and make these distinctions.
> Which of you can practically demonstrate [the validity of these judgements]? . . .[41]

In another of his songs (no. 160), Hem describes a passionate devotee (*anurāgī*):

> S/he always wanders this world with non-dual knowledge (*advaita jñāne*), knowing the truth that *brahma* is in every container [body].[42]
> S/he no longer makes distinctions between castes, or judges in terms of 'us' and 'them' (*āpan* and *par*) . . .

Madness

From the point of view of structure (whether it pertains to householder or renouncer worlds or even to the *bartamān-panthī* path), such transcendence of structure may look like madness or death. *Bartamān-panthīs* commonly characterise their aim as being 'dead while living' – *jiyanta marā*. An uninitiated and well-to-do caste fellow of Hem told me: 'Everyone used to call Rāj and his disciples "*khyāpā*" (mad). The *khyāpās* don't wear sectarian marks. They say that the "I" is everything.' As mentioned earlier, *khyāpā-khyāpī* (male and female *khyāpā*) are said not to bother with social marriage – they simply exchange garlands. Nor do they belong to any *sampradāy* or group. The attribution of madness is partly an attempt to marginalise critics such as Rāj and neutralise the impact of their statements. However, this attribution is appropriated and subtly subverted by *bartamān-panthīs* such as Rāj. Thus disciples of Satīś (Rāj's disciple) told me that their *bāul* method is that of the mad (*pāgaler mat*): 'our actions, (religious) path and our values (literally "worship") are all oriented to human beings' ('ours is *mānuṣer karma, mānuṣer*

[41] For transliterated Bengali text, see Openshaw 1994:190.

[42] 'Body' here translates '*ghaṭ*', literally 'container'. One of the important meanings of *brahma* for *bartamān-panthīs* is the male and female essence (*rajaḥ-bīj*, that is, menstrual and sexual fluids). This will be discussed later. For the transliterated Bengali text of this verse, see Openshaw 1994:190.

dharma, mānuṣer pūjā.'). According to another (Muslim) initiate: 'We are called mad (*pāgal*) for not distinguishing 'us' and 'them' (*āpan par*). We care nothing for worldly and family life (*saṅsār*). But whereas ordinary mad people are incapable of thinking about *saṅsār*, we simply don't wish to.' In the words of Rāj (song no. 32):

> You won't understand the words of a mad person (*pāgal*),
> (Only) the mad can understand everything the mad say.
> They run on the reverse path (*ulṭā path*),
> They eat whatever they get,
> They don't abide by Veda, scripture, conventional prescriptions (*bidhi*) or whatever others say.
> Yet what ordinary mortals (*jīb*) cannot do, all mad people can do.
> They do not judge according to birth-group, but treat everyone alike. They ignore considerations of purity and impurity (*śuddhāśuddha*). (To them) the world is one (*ekākār*).
> They have despatched aversion (*ghṛṇā*), shame (*lajjā*), lineage (*kul*) and honour (*mān*).
> The mad do not observe correct behaviour, nor practise *mantra, pūjā* and so on.
> Intoxicated with love, there is eternal bliss in their hearts.
> In great joy they dance about clapping their hands.
> It's a funny business being mad. The mad suffer four times as much punishment (as others), (but) suffer it in devotion, and do not deviate (from their path).
> Rāj Kṛṣṇa has reflected on this and says, you will understand when your bud blooms.[43]

Hem writes that wise scholars (*jñānī paṇḍit*) have lost their own knowledge in following that of others. Only the mad person (*pāgal*) realises peace (song no. 161):

> In this world only one who has become mad has gained peace.
> . . .
> S/he who knows the truth (*tattva*) has seen the whole world as one in the knowledge of *brahma*.[44]
> S/he makes no distinctions of birth-group (*jāti*), s/he does not heed the observances of society, s/he always proceeds with non-dual knowledge (*advaita jñān*). S/he has abandoned hatred, aversion (*hiṅsā*), shame, condemnation, deceit.
> When s/he is hungry and thirsty, s/he eats whatever anyone gives.
> This certainly maddens ordinary mortals (*jīb*).
> Hṛdānanda gradually understands how wonderful is this kind of madness.[45]

Similarly Hem writes (no. 50):

[43] For transliterated Bengali text, see Openshaw 1994:191.

[44] For *bartamān-panthīs*, the (non-dual) ground of all being (Brahma) is identified with the creative source and essence of the whole universe (*bīj* or *rajaḥ-bīj*).

[45] For transliterated Bengali text, see Openshaw 1994:191–2.

> The mad person has no code of conduct, nothing is pure or impure to him/her, the world is all one to her/him, s/he does not discriminate according to birth-group.
> S/he says: my play pervades the world, there is nothing apart from me ('I') . . .
>
> . . . *Pāgaler nā āche ācār, śuddhāśuddha kichui nāi tār, jagat ekākār, nāi jātir bicār.*
> *Bale jagat-may khelā āmār, kichui nāi āmi bine . . .*

Both Rāj and Maṇi embrace the role of madman as a defence against social condemnation. Rāj writes (song no. 75):

> Am I still in any *kul* (class, family etc.)? I have left this *kul*.
> The system of *kuls* is illusory, so now I have destroyed *kul*.
> So many people are speaking against me for abandoning *kul* and *mān* (honour).
> All ordinary people (*jīb*) are condemning me, (so) I am pretending to be a madman . . . [46]

In song no. 168, Hem notes that everyone is advising him not to mix with 'Khyāpā Rāj' (Mad Rāj), otherwise he too will become mad (*khyāpā*) and lose caste, society, honour and be driven from his house. In the following song (no. 19), he refers to his 'mad father and mother' (Rāj and Rājeśvar):

> . . . Our father and mother are mad (*pāgal*) and we are the children of those madmen.
> If I say that in these three worlds there is only one 'I' (*āmi*), everyone will laugh and be convinced I am just crazy (*pāgal*),
> Without being mad how can one say that this fellow pervades the three worlds . . . [47]

Finally one may recall that being mad, with all the above connotations, is associated with being *bāul*. As Hem promises himself (song no. 157) 'This time I shall be *bāul*. I shall lose birth-group (*jāt*) and lineage. People will call me mad and laugh . . . ' (see p. 110).

The theme of madness features more prominently in the repertoire of Rāj and his immediate followers than that of many *bartamān-panthīs*. Its salience is probably connected with the social opprobrium they suffered after Rāj's love affair and elopement. In such songs, the assimilation to actual human beings of pan-Hindu mythical themes and imagery (Shaivite, Shakta and Vaishnava)[48] casts unconventional individual lives in a potentially more favourable light. The overt critique of conventional social structures of those in *bartamān*, a characteristic by no means confined to this theme or to Rāj's line, intentionally resonates with elements of

[46] For transliterated Bengali text, see Openshaw 1994:192. Similar sentiments are expressed by Maṇi (song no. 49).

[47] 'This fellow' denotes Hem himself, this being the reference when he says 'I'. Those like Rāj, who were wont to assert 'I am everything' (*āmi sab*), were often accused of megalomania. For the transliterated Bengali text of this song, see Openshaw 1994:192.

[48] Although not featuring in the above example, Islamic equivalents are also common. A tendency to humanise rather than divinise mythical characters has a long history in popular Bengali culture.

the prestigious discourse of classical Hindu and Islamic philosophy, for example, 'non-dualism', and the assertion of the equality of human beings respectively. The relationship between these two levels may be interpreted in variety of ways. It may be construed in terms of a popularisation and potentially radical reinterpretation of 'high' Hindu and Islamic thought. Alternatively, these latter may be regarded as a refinement and reworking of more or less continuing popular forms. All this helps legitimise a particular ideological stance, which may be characterised as *bartamān* or even *bāul*.

IV

Reworking the classifications

7

Affect: love and women

In many contexts, all distinctions between person and person are conflated by *bartamān-panthīs* into a fundamental we–they (*āpan–par*) dichotomy. In this section, the affective base of such divisions as judged by *bartamān-panthīs* will be considered. Those in *bartamān* tend to oppose the ill-will or discrimination (*hiṅsā*) which generates we–they divisions, to the love (*prem*) characteristic of the path of *bartamān*. In connection with affect, it should be borne in mind that for *bartamān-panthīs* all emotion is the subtle form of a physical reality (substance or event). For example, an adept once told me: 'Even the finest joy has a material base.'[1]

In Bengal, renouncers and householders often characterise householder society in terms of *hiṅsā*, the former viewing it as an inevitable concomitant of householder society (*saṅsār*), irrespective of time and place, the latter more often seeing it as a malfunction of a basically sound system.[2] However, an important divergence of view should be borne in mind in the case of Hindu householders. Whereas members of upper castes frequently account for caste in terms of ideas such as division of labour and cooperation,[3] lower castes tend to experience the system as one of unjustified discrimination (*hiṅsā*). Classical models of the social system as a cosmically based and hierarchically ordered organism (Doniger and Smith 1991:6–7) are also current among upper-caste householders, and this too is countered by the lower-caste alternative, reinforced by *bartamān-panthīs*, according to which they see themselves as victims of discrimination and ill-will (*hiṅsā*).[4] In this connection, it

[1] This is reflected in the use of the word *ras*, which combines physical, sensual, aesthetic and affective referents (see Glossary).

[2] According to Inden and Nicholas, 'love is the independent variable in the Bengali kinship system; property, control of resources, duties, and so on, are "dependent variables". If kinsmen have the proper love for one another then they will enjoy well-being and they will not be divided by greed, selfishness, or envy' (1977:88).

[3] This is a view one hears continually from well-educated upper-caste people. Similar views were expressed in the nineteenth century, for example by Bhudev Mukhopadhyay (T. Raychaudhuri 1988:70).

[4] Bengal has witnessed a long history of challenges to Brahminical models of birth group (*jāt*), Budddhist, Vaishnava and Islamic. As Derné remarks, 'Dumont's argument that Hindu society is based on the principle of hierarchy wrongly implies that those at the bottom of the hierarchy consent to it' (1990:259). See also Berreman 1971, Appadurai 1986, Beteille 1983, and Mencher 1974 on this point.

should be recalled that most *bartamān-panthīs* recruit from the lower castes and classes.

The classical model of the Hindu social system as natural and therefore inevitable is challenged by *bartamān-panthīs* such as Rāj and the famous Bāul Lālan, who instead maintain that caste is contingent and artificial in common with other divisions within the only true *jāt* (birth group) which is humankind. (*Jāt* has many referents: caste, religious community, species, nation and race.) For example, the enduringly popular song by Lālan,[5] who died at the end of the nineteenth century, begins:

> Everyone asks what *jāt* has Lālan in this world (*saṅsār*).
> Fakir Lālan says, what form has *jāt*? I have never seen it with my eyes . . .

The argument that what cannot be seen, or otherwise experienced by the senses, is a matter of supposition (*anumān*), and thus invalid, is characteristic of *bartamān-panthīs*, and is a subject with which Rāj deals extensively in his writings. Lālan's song proceeds with a refutation of the classical model and the idea of the division between Hindu and Muslim in the following terms:

> . . . If circumcision makes [a male] a Muslim.
> What is the ruling for a female?
> I can tell a Brahmin on the evidence of his sacred thread,
> But how am I to identify a Brahmin woman? . . .
> Where are the marks of *jāt* at the time of coming and going (to and from this world)? . . .

Here Lālan demonstrates that *jāt* (birth group) is in fact not *jāt* (that is, it is not inborn), since at birth (and death), and throughout life for women, such distinctions are not present. (A common *bartamān-panthī* notion is that women have no *jāt*.) Similarly, Maṇi writes (song no. 39):

> You entered the world naked, you will leave naked. The confusion all comes in between.
> Some call you father, some call you uncle, some call you brother, and other such nonsense.
> . . .
> Some are devotees of the goddess, some are engaged in reciting the name of Hari,
> Some are Shakta, some are Vaishnava, (yet) all are born in the same lineage [i.e. to a woman]. Everyone goes crazy when they hear this.
> Everyone has eyes yet cannot see. No one has a grasp of the true knowledge,
> And brother is set against brother.
> From one seed come Hindu and Muslim – a mere cut on the penis [circumcision] causes the trouble.

[5] '*Sab loke kay Lālan kī jāt saṅsāre*. . .'. This song is found, in slightly different versions, in most collections of Lālan songs, and to my knowledge was first brought out in 1895 CE by Saralā Debī and Akṣay Kumār Maitreya in the same article but in two different versions, the former being severely truncated (Saralā Debī 1302:278, 280). For a strikingly similar song attributed to Kabir, see Hess 1987:150.

Being denuded Mad Maṇi sees only men and women.
Everyone comes naked, it's only this guru-disciple (business) which causes difficulties.[6]

In another song, Lālan says fiercely: 'If I could take *jāt* in my hands, I would incinerate it with fire' (*BBBG*:620 no. 122). It is not uncommon for even conventional Bengali Vaishnavas to counterpose the orthodox idea of many *jāts* (or *varṇa* – the classical four estates) with the idea that there are only two *jāts*: the Vaishnava and the non-Vaishnava, where the former may be classified as Brahmin and the latter as Śūdra.[7] More radically, *bartamān-panthīs* may hold that there is only one *jāt* – human beings. They also often speak of two *jāts*, but for those in *bartamān* these are male and female, a distinction which is considered to be inborn. A similar song of Maṇi's was quoted earlier (p. 138): 'Where did you get your sectarian marks and chaplet, your loin-cloth and alms-bag? . . . Did you bring all this stuff with you when you emerged from the womb? Did you come out with drum, cymbals and your store of divine names tucked under your arm? . . . '. For *bartamān-panthīs,* on the other hand, the human body is everything.[8] Echoing the above sentiments, an adept once told me 'One comes into the world naked, one goes out naked and one practises naked.' Rāj writes pages ridiculing *jāt*. He agrees that there are certainly *jāt* among so many birds, beasts and insects, of which human beings are one. Within each of these, male and female may be called *jāt* also, since the distinction is discernible, but all human men and women are visibly of the same form. Caste is simply a matter of name. One doesn't lose caste if flies or a cat have touched the food – only when one's own human *jāt* has done so! All this nonsense comes down to aversion (*ghṛṇā, hiṅsā*); and so on (Text B:48ff.). Satīś also devotes a chapter to an attack on caste in his bound manuscript. Related subjects, such as pollution (*aśuc*) and the pure and impure (*śuddhāśuddha*) are also held up to ridicule (e.g. Rāj Text B:61ff.).

Throughout his autobiography, Rāj characterises householder life in terms of *hiṅsā*, particularly in connection with the terrible quarrel between his father and uncle. Recounting that dreadful time, Rāj laments that those who are 'one', of the same seed and womb, have become so divided, separate (*bhinna*), and different (*anya*). Subtly transformed, these conventional sentiments play a potentially subversive role in *bartamān-panthī* theories of non-discrimination, or *advaita*, a term more usually associated with Vedantic idealism. From the nineteenth century, *advaita* had increasingly come to function as the apex of a conservative high-Brahminical system where philosophies, rituals, social groups and ultimately gender were ordered in a fixed hierarchy, a process associated with an increasingly

6 For transliterated Bengali text, see p. 152, and Openshaw 1997b:302–3.

7 Thus even a Brahmin who has not taken *dīkṣā* is regarded as a Śūdra, while members of any caste are Brahmins once initiated (Dās Brahmacārī 1389 BS (vol. II):6, 38). On Vaishnavism as a neo-Brahmin order, see R. Chakravarti (1985:322–3).

8 In common with Tantra, an equivalence between the macrocosm (*brahmāṇḍa*) and the microcosm (*bhāṇḍa*, that is, the body) is often expressed by *bartamān-panthīs* (see *BBBG*:323ff.). Moreover, there is the notion that there is even something in the body which is not found in the universe: '*yeṭā brahmāṇḍe nāi, seṭā ei bhāṇḍe āche*'.

bounded 'Hinduism' and ultimately a chauvinist Hindutva (Sumit Sarkar 1998:326, 368–9). However, since non-dualism denies the ultimate validity of all differentiation, it could equally plausibly be mobilised against such distinctions by *bartamān-panthīs* and the Kartābhajās (R. Chakravarti 1985:379) among others. Fieldwork in Nadia and Murshidabad revealed a general and highly radical consensus, not confined to those in *bartamān*, that *advaita* amounted to 'not saying anything is mine', especially in connection with land and other possessions. For Rāj and others, the conventional idea of being born of the same father and mother, and thus indivisible, is modified into the notion that it is *bīj* in general which is the father, and *rajaḥ* in general which is the mother (terms denoting male and female generative fluids respectively, or some finer essence within these), these basic substances being classified as *bastu*. (The polyvalence of the word *bastu*, as 'substance' and 'truth' as well as 'matter', is deliberately exploited by *bartamān-panthīs*.) The corollary of this is that all human beings have the same father and mother and all are therefore one. In the words of R.S., a Muslim disciple of Maṇi, 'in each of us is the same mother and father, *rajaḥ* and *bīj*'. This interpretation of non-dualism entails the rejection of the basic we–they dichotomy (*āpan–par* in *bartamān-panthī* phraseology), so characteristic of social life everywhere; and *a fortiori* its derivative forms such as caste, religious community, sect and even, in some contexts, gender. In the view of *bartamān-panthīs*, all these expressions of the *āpan–par* dichotomy are a manifestation of, or are generated by, *hiṅsā*, the defining affective base of householder society. Maṇi sees all such divisions as forms of *hiṅsā* (song no. 47):

> Hindu, Muslim, Buddhist and Christian,
> All are from the same lineage, the same seed and walk the same path.
> You and I, female and male – these are not different;
> So why do you judge according to birth-group, my brother? The problem comes with *dharma* . . .
> Human beings are one and the same, [so their] *dharma* is one and the same.
> What is the reason for all this enmity (*hiṅsā-hiṅsī*)? . . .[9]

In another song (no. 146), Maṇi raises the rhetorical question 'Why are Hindu and Muslim divided?', and concludes that 'the root cause of this is *hiṅsā-hiṅsī*'. Another song (no. 34) finds him lamenting that 'this worldly life is full of *hiṅsā* and condemnation' (*hiṅsā nindā pūrṇa hayeche saṅsār*). Maṇi's disciple, B.G., told me flatly: 'Discrimination according to birth group (*jāti-bhed*) is just a matter of *hiṅsā*, and *hiṅsā* is one's downfall.' Similarly, Satīś writes that discrimination based on birth group and factionalism arise from *hiṅsā* ('*Jāti bhed dalā dali hiṅsāy sṛjan*').[10] Reversing the logic, D.G., another disciple of Maṇi, remarked: 'In the realm of human beings, there are only human beings (*mānuṣ jagate mānuṣ*). There is no place here for discrimination according to birth group. If one makes distinctions of *jāti* and *sampradāy*, then aversion (*ghṛṇā*) and envy (*hiṅsā*) are awakened.' So

[9] For transliterated Bengali text, see Openshaw 1997b:304.
[10] Chapter on 'Jāti' in unpublished manuscript by Satīś, p. 137.

although in Bengal '*hiṅsā*' is the colloquial equivalent of 'jealousy' and 'envy', in the *bartamān-panthī* context it may be identified with the discrimination which divides human beings, whereas love, with which the *bartamān-panthīs* seek to oppose *hiṅsā*, oils the path of relatedness between all. *Bartamān-panthīs* often say that in their path there is no room for aversion, shame and fear, all forms of *hiṅsā* in their tendency to non-relation rather than relation.[11]

Such attitudes are not only held in theory. Once I arrived unexpectedly at an ashram of renouncer *bartamān-panthīs* in a completely new area with no introduction. A long-haired, bearded adept dressed in white was engaged in making a bamboo and rope ladder by the well in the large compound. On seeing me he immediately laid down his work, spread a mat on the verandah for me, and solicitously enquired if I wanted water, if I had eaten, whether I wanted to rest or to talk etc. In the case of ordinary householders, an unknown woman would have been greeted with polite suspicion. Enquiries would have been made at some stage concerning my place of origin, my marital status, whether I have children, how it is that my husband let me come on my own and so on. *Bartamān-panthīs* were concerned with my immediate needs as a human being, rather than my identity and status. When I came to know the people of this ashram better and commented on the contrast, I was told: 'We simply think "A human being (*mānuṣ*) has come." We don't have the aversion (*ghṛṇā*) and fear (*bhay*) of worldly life (*saṅsār*).'

In projecting such negative traits on to worldly (householder) life in general, *bartamān-panthīs* display little concern with models of chronological degeneration within it, such as the notion of the present *kali-yug*, last and darkest of the four ages. Despite the importance conferred on this model by some sections of the population (see S. Sarkar 1989c, 1992), it rarely figures in *bartamān-panthī* discourse. Where it does appear it tends to be inverted, and applied to the 'four ages' of individuals (particularly women), so that *kali* (which also means 'bud') may apply to a young girl and *satya* (conventionally the first and best age) to an older, sometimes post-menopausal woman.

A striking characteristic of Rāj's autobiography is that his reaction to events is given more weight than events themselves. The emphasis on affectivity (feelings, sensations, desire) is part of a general *bartamān-panthī* repertoire. In the mode of a renouncer, Rāj portrays the householder world (*saṅsār*) as inimical to love. Love in that sphere is doomed to be vanquished by divisiveness, separation and envy, by *hiṅsā* in short. It is also inevitably transient, and a persistent theme in the autobiography is the loss of loved ones. Rāj's emphasis on affectivity may be related to the Vaishnava culture of emotion, radically modified of course by the *bartamān* path and its emphasis on the physical body. (This is seen, for example, in the *bartamān-panthī* tendency to espouse notions of the identity, or coterminousness, of the self and the body.) Relevant here, too, is the distinction between *bahiraṅga* and *antaraṅga*, the former implying mere externals (such as clothes and religious marks), as well as acting, triviality and even hypocrisy, in short *anumān*; the latter

[11] '*Ghṛṇā lajjā bhay tin thākte nay.*' The many different ramifications of this phrase cannot be dealt with here.

connoting the naked body, or the core, the essence (*sār*), the 'real' world of experience, in short *bartamān*. As will be discussed (in chapter 8), this cathexis on inner realities is consonant with the *bartamān-panthī* emphasis on '*āmi*' ('I'), which is especially marked in Rāj's writings.

Rāj follows typically Vaishnava patterns in his concern to trace the development of his love with Rājeśvar. All this is reminiscent of romantic stories of illicit love, especially of Rādhā and Kṛṣṇa, current at the time.[12] In his songs, Rāj mentions Caṇḍīdās and other legendary lovers, such as Vidyāpati; we have seen how Hem compares Rāj and Rājeśvarī to Caṇḍīdās and Rāmī, to Kṛṣṇa and Rādhā. Whereas, in householder society, egalitarian love is thought to be potentially divisive and is thus subordinated to hierarchical love (Inden and Nicholas 1977: 87–8), for *bartamān-panthīs* the hierarchical love of husband and wife (*svakīya*) is logically subordinated to the more egalitarian extramarital (*parakīya*) model.[13] As Kakar and Ross remark, 'the love story is the prime subverter of . . . official mores, especially those relating to authority and the relations between the sexes' (1986:9).

In this connection, it is important to differentiate the concepts of *kām* (desire) and *prem* (love), the latter being the word used in the autobiography to describe Rāj's feelings for his son and subsequently for Rājeśvar. From this usage it is clear that the connotations of the word *prem,* unlike *kām,* are not confined to the erotic.[14] While the arena of *kām* is often taken to be narrowly genital, that of *prem* is most usually wider, and includes emotions (*bhāb*), including the idea of caring for the other, rather than simply for one's own pleasure.[15] As one might expect, more orthodox Vaishnavas emphasise the opposition between *kām* and *prem,* the latter only arising when, or to the extent that, *kām* is subdued. Alternatively, the erotic dimension is distanced, through an emphasis on separation (*viraha*), or through its displacement on to some heavenly sphere in which '*līlā*' takes place. On the other hand, *bartamān-panthīs* lay more stress on the continuity or close connection between the two, consonant with their high valuation of women and intimate relationship with them (cf. Dasgupta 1969:135).

Bartamān-panthīs often differentiate *prem* from *kām* by the criterion that the former does not involve emission of semen, which is associated with concern for one's own pleasure (*ātmasukh*).[16] As in some other cultures, seminal emission is referred to by practitioners as 'death', and apart from other deleterious effects,

[12] See Banerjee 1989:78ff., 93. On the long history of such a tradition on both the learned and the popular level, see R. Chakravarti 1985:7–13, 20–8.

[13] In practice, the majority of *bartamān-panthīs* do esoteric practice with their wives, but in these cases the relationship, at least in private, is said to be transformed.

[14] Rāj makes this point in one of his works on theory (Text B:45). See also Marglin 1982:306.

[15] *Bartamān-panthīs* often quote the following passage from the *Caitanya Caritāmṛta* in this connection: 'The wish to satisfy one's own senses is called lust (*kām*). The wish to satisfy Kṛṣṇa's senses is called love (*prem*)' (S. Sen 1983a:17).

[16] Acyutānanda, a name of Kṛṣṇa, is often glossed as 'one whose seed does not fall' (Marglin 1982:306). Van der Veer informs us that in the case of Rāmānandī ascetic initiates, the patrilineal clan name is replaced by the 'achut-gotra' (the clan of the One whose seed does not fall) (1987: 684). As has been noted, in other contexts total seminal retention is also condemned as *ātma-sukh*, this logic operating within a different context (one where seminal retention is transcended in favour of controlled and limited emission).

this death is linked in various ways with the final death of the physical body. For example, seminal emission is thought to decrease one's life-span. When asked his reasons for beginning esoteric practice, an elderly adept told me; 'Everyone dies. I started on this path in the hope that I wouldn't die.' In this typical response, both senses of the word 'die' (*marā*) are implied. The link between seminal death and procreation marks *kām* as the kind of relationship a man has with his wife (*svakīya*) in the transient householder realm (*saṅsār*). This realm is one of possessiveness and overlordship (*aiśvarya*), which is contrasted with the sweetness (*mādhurya*) which characterises *prem* (Marglin 1982:303ff.). Of note here is the correspondence between the wider meaning of *saṅsār* as an endless cycle of death and rebirth (of the individual), and the 'death' which is seminal emission resulting in (re-)birth (in the womb of the wife), and which provides the basis of the continuity of householder life (*saṅsār*).[17] By contrast, *prem* implies retention of semen (at least in most circumstances), and therefore no procreation. *Prem* then is the realm of extramarital or extra-social relationships (*parakīya*),[18] and Rāj, of course, never mentions *prem* in connection with his wife. This non-*saṅsārik* realm of deathlessness (in the sense of seminal retention) is connected with a wider realm where there is no death or rebirth. Thus, as we have seen in the case of Hem, this realm of *prem* outside *saṅsār* may be identified with the society of renouncers, but many *bartamān-panthīs* who seek it there become disillusioned with the *hiṅsā* and hierarchies there also.

Whereas an ordinary householder would associate *kām* (one of the four valid aims of a human being) with continuity (of the lineage), for *bartamān-panthīs* (who identify the *ātmā* with seminal essence etc.), it is *kām* which is divisive. In this connection one sometimes hears the following: 'While the love which is *kām* leads to separation, the love which is *prem* binds' (*Kāmer piriti hay chīrā-chīri. Premer piriti hay mākhā-mākhi/jorā-jori*). Here *kām* separates one from oneself, splitting off and creating children. There is also the notion of a lack of unity and intimacy with one's partner. *Prem* however not only does not disrupt the self (*ātma*), it unites male and female who were, or so it seemed, separate. In this context, the relationship of *kām* to *prem* replicates that of *hiṅsā* to *prem* noted above. *Bartamān-panthīs* are often distinctly ambivalent towards any children they might have, referring to them as 'mistakes' (*bhul*). D.G., Maṇi's disciple, referred to his grandchild as 'an amplification of *māyā* ... Due to a fundamental error I had children and had to spend time other than in joy (*ānanda*) and mixing with adepts.'

[17] The equation of a man's seed with his offspring is by no means new (O'Flaherty 1980b:26). This analogy may be further extended: after death, it is necessary to cross Baitarinī, a river of pus and blood, which Parry equates with the womb (Parry 1982:85; 1989:508). Where *bartamān-panthīs* are concerned, another gloss on Baitarinī – typically more body-centred – is found. 'Tarinī' is the word 'boat' (*tarī*) with a feminine suffix, referring to the (boat-shaped) genitals of the woman. This boat carries the male practitioners to heaven, here meaning that with this aid the semen rises to the area above the navel of the man (Jhā 1985:499).

[18] For the distinction between intra-social and extra-social sexuality in connection with folk-tales, see Bahl 1981.

Contrary to Chakravarti's view that all 'deviant' orders are anti-intellectual (1985:324), the *bartamān-panthī* emphasis on affectivity does not entail an anti-rational stance. Whereas main-stream Gauṛīya Vaishnavas tend to focus exclusively on devotion (*bhakti*), *bartamān-panthīs* reject neither knowledge (*jñān*) nor, as will be seen in relation to esoteric practice, action (*karma*) (cf. P. Das 1988:108ff.). In fact, *bartamān-panthīs* would seem to be firmly situated within the tradition of *tarkavidyā* (the 'science of disputation'), characterised by its assault on *anumān*, that is ideology and prescriptions legitimised by reference to the authorised scripture.[19]

It is in this spirit that Rāj's disciple Satīś argues against the conventional notion of woman as the gateway to hell (*nārī naraker dvār*). Satīś's chapter on women contains a whole host of rebuttals, among which the following may be briefly mentioned.[20] Woman is the creator of all, without her, and intercourse with her, nothing would exist. If anything, man is the woman's gateway to hell, he argues. Because of his lust, she suffers the pain and dangers of child-birth. Sometimes he even abandons her when she gets pregnant. She takes enormous trouble to rear her child, feeding him, cleaning up his urine and faeces etc. That very son whom she tended with such loving care grows up and proclaims 'Woman is the gateway to hell'! Men wrote the scriptures opportunistically, which is why men have all the freedom and women all the bondage. They dominate women and make them subordinate. If women had written the scriptures, they would similarly have framed the rules for their own convenience. He contradicts many renouncers in maintaining that if a man loses his semen, it is his own fault, not that of the woman. Women are not tigresses (as some renouncers affirm) but givers of joy. Mocking the celibate, he points out that all the gods and seers had at least one wife as well as children. For them, having children is divine sport (*līlā*), but for human beings it is a sin (*pāp*). He even combats the standard Hindu view of life in the womb as confinement amidst a host of noxious substances, with the idea that life in the womb is very comfortable.

Deep suspicion of women seems to have been a constant feature in Bengali culture, one shared, moreover, by such widely disparate sections of society as Hindus and Muslims, upper and lower castes, renouncers as well as householders (S. Banerjee 1989:200–1; S. B. Dasgupta, 1969:244–9). As might be expected, general misogyny has often been overtly directed at those powerful women who are perceived as threatening hierarchical structures, for example the educated woman or the stereotypical 'disorderly wife' (Sarkar 1989c:39f.). The counterposed 'good woman', the virtuous (and firmly chaste) wife or mother, is portrayed as restoring the hierarchical norms, through what Sumit Sarkar terms 'assertion-within-deference' (1989c:6, 41). It is interesting to note that Satīś, a village primary schoolmaster, appears to echo in his writings the popular satire, often of the lower orders, against religious hypocrites, be they gurus, Vaishnavas or Brahmins,

[19] For details of this tradition, see Chattopadhyaya 1959, 1990. See also S. Sarkar 1989c:33–6.

[20] These points are from a long chapter entitled 'Woman' (*Nārī*), in a handwritten text by Satīś, pp. 108, 122, 127.

prevalent since at least the nineteenth century (S. Banerjee 1989:132). When it comes to women, however, Satīś shares with many other *bartamān-panthīs* a view of women and female sexuality which is at variance with prevailing attitudes.[21] This is all the more interesting from a man whose *guru-mā* threw over her role as wife and mother for the love of Rāj Kṛṣṇa, in other words the 'disorderly wife' par excellence.

So the vilification of women is yet another manifestation of the *hiṅsā* of householder society combated by Rāj, his disciples and other *bartamān-panthīs*. Rāj's autobiography reveals a profound transformation in his attitudes towards women. At first he displays conventional attitudes: mistrust of women (except as mothers), the omission of female names (for every woman is the daughter or the wife of one or other patrilineage) etc. Along with the author, we enter another world when he encounters Rājeśvar. To Rāj she becomes everything: not only lover and guru, as shown earlier, but also overlord, deity and mother. Rāj's stress on the personal name (albeit one probably conferred by him) of his lover, Rājeśvar, is a striking indicator of his unconventional attitude. Rāj never once uses the *bartamān-panthī* convention of referring to the (male) guru at the end of a song, as Lālan does to Sirāj Sā̃i, for example. Instead, Rājeśvar's name appears either alone or coupled with Rāj's in many contexts in the manuscript, especially in the signature (*bhaṇitā*) of a large number of songs, in the form Rāj–Rājeśvar. A similar joint *bhaṇitā* is that of Yādubindu (occasionally Yādabindu) referring to the composer Yādab whose female partner was Bindu (*BBBG*:688). However, it is unusual even for *bartamān-panthīs* to overtly name a particular woman, even in disguised form, in such public contexts.[22] More commonly she is extolled in generalised form as woman (*nārī*) or girl (*meye*). Alternatively, she may be called *śakti*, *prakṛti* or *mā* (mother), which may be glossed by the unwary as a unilinear reference to the traditional goddess. Rāj also, perhaps increasingly, called Rājeśvar *śakti* and *bhairabī*, terms referring to the goddess Śakti as well as to the female partner in Tantra.

Women are also typically cast in the role of 'gateway to hell' by renouncers, for whom the crucial element is the preoccupation with retention of semen.[23] Extreme orthodox injunctions against even looking at a woman or her image are mercilessly derided by the *bartamān-panthī* as absurd and useless. Even a goddess-worshipping *sādhu* with a Tantric background such as Rāmakṛṣṇa was deeply suspicious of women (S. Sarkar 1985:95, 99ff.). While many elements in Rāmakṛṣṇa's ideological and affective repertoire are also drawn on by those on the

[21] Not that these attitudes were entirely confined to those in *bartamān*. Romantic poets of the nineteenth century such as Biharilal Cakrabarti (who also, perhaps significantly, wrote songs in the pattern and by the name of Bāul songs) placed great stress on love, especially womanly love, and were strong supporters of the cause of women (S. B. Dasgupta 1969:162; S. Sen 1971:238–9). Such attitudes are also to be found in Tantra.

[22] Hem writes one song mentioning his wife (and partner in esoteric practice) by name. He also addresses several of his songs to Rājeśvarī. It should be noted that, because of their form, outsiders might not even be aware that the latter half of the idiographs 'Rāj–Rājeśvar' and 'Yādubindu' refer to women.

[23] Not that householders are free of this preoccupation, at least among some high castes in some parts of India (Carstairs 1970:83–8). For Gandhi's views on this, see Kakar 1989:105–6. See also O'Flaherty 1980b:44ff.

path of *bartamān*, a comparison of Rāmakṛṣṇa and Rāj reveals a different emphasis on women as mothers and women as (sexual) partners, although the *bartamān-panthī* position is better represented as a conflation of these two roles (see below). Thus while both would agree on the general desirability of retaining semen,[24] the *bartamān-panthī* approach is one of either bearding the lion in her den (otherwise known as *vīrācār*), or, in a different and more typical mood, treating the woman as guru, especially within the sexual relationship.

Rāmakṛṣṇa's emphasis on the mother–son dyad contrasts with Rāj's emphasis on the more equal relationship between man and woman as sexual and life partners. For while Rāj extols Rājeśvar and her grace (*kṛpā*) towards him, this attitude would have been reciprocated, thus creating a more symmetrical relationship. For example, Rāj asserts that if man and woman do not take refuge in each other, there is no way that they can find the path. Whatever esoteric practice they do is doomed to failure.[25] What Sumit Sarkar terms Rāmakṛṣṇa's 'reversion to childhood' is related to this emphasis on the mother–son dyad, while being replicated in an attitude of general subordination to superiors and acquiescence in prevailing hierarchies. While the sexless child (usually Gopāl) constitutes an ideal for orthodox Vaishnavas, this is rarely the case for *bartamān-panthīs*.

In a parallel way to child-reversion, Rāmakṛṣṇa took refuge in femininity. While transvestism and the idea of transformation into a woman in various senses are by no means excluded for male *bartamān-panthīs*, such leanings are combined with and often subsumed by the reality of being male in sexual relation with a female partner. This is one difference between orthodox Vaishnavism in which all are encouraged to identify with a confidante (*sakhī*), who merely assists or witnesses the love-play of Rādhā and Kṛṣṇa, and *bartamān-panthīs* for whom every man is Kṛṣṇa and every woman Rādhā (cf. P. Das 1988:167ff.). Thus the *bartamān-panthī* gloss on the famous *mantra* '*hare kṛṣṇa*', as an exhortation to 'be Kṛṣṇa!' (*ha re kṛṣṇa*). The idea that all women are Rādhā is often expressed by Rāj and his disciples (e.g. Rāj Text A:223, Maṇi song no. 172), and Rāj also equates all men with Śiva and all women with Gaurī (Text A:227). In another context, he argues that the one body was divided for the sake of *līlā*, in order to experience itself, and that Rādhā came down to Nadia as Rāj–Rājeśvarī, the wife of Prāṇ-kṛṣṇa (and formerly as Sitā in Janakpur, etc.). He then praises the qualities of Rājeśvar's mother, without which Rājesvar would not have been born in that lineage. Thus Rāj Kṛṣṇa (Kṛṣṇa to her Rādhā) has been bound in devotion to her through the ages (Text B:42–3).

As pointed out above, *bartamān-panthīs* do not exclude the idea of women as mothers; rather they combine it with that of women as lovers. Bengalis of all kinds use the word '*mā*' (mother) of certain classes of women, to express an attitude of lust-free reverence or affection. The female partner of a Vaishnava renouncer is often called 'Mātājī' (revered mother), and *bartamān-panthīs* are sometimes

[24] For *bartamān-panthīs*, absolute retention may be superseded at subsequent stages of esoteric practice.

[25] Song no. 8. See Openshaw 1995:148 n. 83 for transliterated Bengali original.

mocked by others for calling the woman with whom they cohabit '*mā*'. However, *bartamān-panthīs* would also maintain that theirs is not an attitude of lust (*kām*) but of love (*prem*). In his writings Rāj often spoke of Rājeśvar as mother (*mā*) as well as lover. At one point in Text B, probably written in the period when Rāj had been persuaded to leave Icchāpur before his elopement, Rāj has crossed out 'mother I love you' and replaced it with 'I love Rājeśvar' (Text B:12). Of the praise songs (*bandanā*) to Rājeśvar which begin Text B, one is to Rājeśvar as mother. In this context Rāj is the 'insignificant child' while she is 'full of compassion' (Text B:5–6). While the loss of a father matters little, Rāj argues, a child can scarcely survive without its mother. It is tempting to see a conflation of the loss of his own mother and that of Rājeśvar (through exile from Icchāpur) in this passage.[26]

Of interest in this context is a *bartamān-panthī* interpretation of the aphorism, *yathāy janma tathāy karma, tathāy dharma adharma*, of which a literal rendering is: 'the place of birth is the place of work(s), and the place of righteousness and unrighteousness'. This is generally taken to advocate acceptance of one's station in life, according to the principle that birth group determines occupation and moral code. However *bartamān-panthīs* prefer to interpret this maxim along the following lines: everyone is born from the vagina (the place of birth), and it is here that the man must do esoteric practice. (Esoteric practice and indeed any sexual activity is called *karma*.) Esoteric practice correctly performed constitutes right action, whereas losing one's vital seminal essence is immoral. The suggestion of returning to the place of one's birth is part of a general ethos of reversion, whereby the semen reverts upwards towards the crown of the head from where it is considered to descend, and the process of creation and multiplication is arrested and reversed, so that instead of the two (man and woman) becoming three (with the birth of a child), they become one. So for *bartamān-panthīs* all women are in one sense equated, rather than being divided into the usual two groups: mothers and wives. A friend once told me: 'Your *yoni* (vagina) is my *yoni* – all *yonis* are one.' And perhaps because she is a woman she added: 'and all penises are one'. Ideas of woman and earth (both called *prakṛti*) are closely related, and *māṭi* (earth) and *mā* (mother) are equated in many contexts. Looking at it from the male point of view, the place where one takes birth, lives, experiences joy and dies is both the earth (*māṭi*) and the vagina (*mā*). (It will be recalled that seminal retention is identified with life, and seminal emission with death.) As we have seen at the end of the last chapter, women may also be identified with *sahaj* (the innate, inborn, natural).

Another of Rāj's praise-songs to Rājeśvar (no. 2) extols her as the overlord (*rājā*) who, through the ages, from birth to birth, has reigned supreme and unchallenged in Rāj's heart. Here Rāj himself is her subject (*prajā*). As such he also calls her lord of the gods (*debeśvar*), lord of life (*prāṇeśvar*) (Text B:3), and we have seen that the name Rājeśvar means 'Lord of Rāj'. In one of his songs (no. 8), Rāj calls

[26] Also Text B:11. This combination of mother and lover is also found in Tantra, but predominantly in relation to the goddess. Such worship would be classified as *anumān* by *bartamān-panthīs* who instead regard their living female partner in this way.

Rājeśvarī (*sic*) the proprietor of love (*premer adhikārī*) and primordial female energy (*ādya śakti*).

Bengali Vaishnavas classify the relationship between Kṛṣṇa and the devotee according to (usually) five main modes, each with its particular emotional quality (*bhāb*). In the peaceful mood (*śānta bhāb*), Kṛṣṇa is seen as Supreme God in contrast to the insignificant worshipper. *Dāsya bhāb* is where the devotee considers Kṛṣṇa as master and himself as servant (*dās*). In *sākhya bhāb* Kṛṣṇa is seen as a friend, while in *bātsālya bhāb* the worshipper considers himself a parent to the child Kṛṣṇa. Finally, and most important, in *mādhurya bhāb* the devotee relates to Kṛṣṇa as a lover, as did Rādhā and her companions, the *gopīs*. This last erotic mode is of supreme importance to *bartamān-panthīs* also. However, for Rāj and other male *bartamān-panthīs,* whose emotions and energies are focused on their female partner, rather than on a supreme male deity, the direction of two of these *bhābs* is reversed. Instead of being parent to the child Kṛṣṇa, the male initiate is himself a child in relation to the female partner as mother. Similarly, as we have seen, he assumes the role of Kṛṣṇa in relation to the female partner as Rādhā.

To Rāj, as we have seen, Rājeśvar is supreme deity, overlord, mother and lover. The elaboration and cultivation of this kind of emotional repertoire clearly relates to the traditional classification of *bhābs* outlined above. Rāj's adoration is undisguised:

> I don't want a divine body. I cannot be satisfied with wealth.
> My desire is not for happiness but for Rājeśvar . . .
> Rāj prays that he may never forget your feet . . .
> I want nothing else . . . I have no other *mantra*, *pūjā* or song of praise . . .

As mentioned above, Rāj's focus on a particular named woman is unusual even by *bartamān-panthī* standards. In his writings we also frequently find the more common pattern of extolling woman in general (and/or womanhood as represented by the *yoni*). The notion of the female partner as the guru has been discussed earlier, and Rāj writes (in song no. 8) that without her there is no *sādhan-bhajan* (cultivation of oneself and the other). Moreover, as will be shown (in chapter 8) worship of images and deities is rejected in favour of that of the living woman. There is more than one passage in Rāj's writings where rituals for the worship of the female partner are given. In one of these, the male partner invests life (*jibānyās* (*sic*)) into the female partner as one would an image, following which he worships her. The word *caraṇāmṛta* (literally 'nectar of the feet'), normally applied to the water in which the feet of images, or worshipful human beings, are washed and which is sprinkled on the head, drunk and so on, here refers to the water with which the man washes the *yoni* of his partner (Text A:270). It is sometimes said that one who is in *bartamān* 'respects' (*mān*) the path (*bartma* – pronounced the same as *barta*), where 'path' may be taken to mean the vagina.

Songs of Rāj's disciples express similar sentiments. Maṇi (song no. 28) remarks that it is futile to lord it over woman, who is after all 'lord of the world' (*jagater rājā*). He asserts that if you worship 'woman', who is 'bestower of liberation' (*mukti-dātā*), you will get everything (song no. 25). Women may be called Nityānanda and Caitanya, and are often called Allah and *nabī* (prophet) by Muslim *bartamān-panthīs*. As a common saying has it: 'The one whom you call prophet is not the prophet but the woman of the house' (*Yāre bala nabī nabī, nabī nay se gharer bibi*).[27] One might perhaps read contradictions with prevailing attitudes in the following saying: 'By night he calls her the prophet, by day he calls her whore and bitch' (*Rāte bale nabī nabī, dine bale śālī māgī*).

For those in *bartamān*, women represent the love of relatedness rather than divisive malevolence. As noted earlier, it is commonly said, by men and women, that women have no *jāt*. When asked whether she called herself Bāul or Vaishnava, a female adept and guru (and singer of Bāul and Vaishnava devotional songs) told me, 'I am a woman and women have no *jāt*. Only men have *jāt*.' For non-initiated male householders, women share with the mad and renouncers the qualities of being 'other' (*par*) and 'soft', and thus the potential for evading and even threatening *jāt* and other social boundaries.[28] Women are also thought to be more vulnerable to madness and allied states, a condition related to their penetrability (D. P. Bhattacharyya 1981:38; 1986:150ff.). Interestingly, many male practitioners aspire not only to womanhood, but also, in some sense, to madness. Rāj calls the woman of his songs 'love's merchant' or 'love's guru' (*premer mahājan*). I was once told by a male initiate: 'All the good qualities are in woman: *sneha, bhakti, prem, bhālabāsā, yatna, sebā, dayā* [all different kinds of love and service to others[29]], but in man there is nothing but ego (*ahamikār*)!' As such, women are to be emulated, and many male practitioners aspire to womanhood (in various senses), or claim it with pride. In one of his songs (no. 15), Rāj exhorts his listeners to become women ('*meye ha-nā*!'). According to one of many common aphorisms on this theme, one should become a woman before uniting with a woman (*prakṛti haiyā, kara prakṛti-saṅga*).[30] The idea of becoming woman with a woman is in contrast to the Bengali Vaishnava notion of becoming a woman (or realising one's womanhood) in relation to Kṛṣṇa, or becoming a female companion of Rādhā who observes or assists in the love-making of Rādhā and Kṛṣṇa. In addition to the

[27] Alternatively, Allah may be identified with *bīj* (semen or sperm), and *nabī* with *rajaḥ* (menstrual and other female sexual fluids), the essence of man and woman respectively. Thus 'the prophet comes each month, floating intoxicated on the ebb-tide' (*Āsche nabī māse māse, unmatta āśe bheṭel bhāse*) (Jhā 1985:597–8).

[28] My impression is that these statements are more likely to apply in the case of upper castes and Hindus. *Bartamān-panthīs* sometimes present themselves as being 'soft'. A Muslim initiate opposed the *śariyat* (exoteric Islam) to the (esoteric) *mārphat*: 'The *śariyati* do not like us (the *mārphati*) . . . We do not fast, or do *namāj* or any of these external (*bāhyik*) acts. That is why they dislike us. They are hard (*śakta*), like iron. With iron one can do much, construct buildings and so forth. But we are soft (*naram*) like the cotton filling of a pillow. Our method is very subtle (*sūkṣma*).'

[29] *Sneha* is love of superiors (such as parents) towards inferiors. *Bhakti* is the loving respect of inferiors for superiors. *Prem* has been discussed above. *Bhālabāsā* also means love. *Yatna* is tending others. *Sebā* is serving others. *Dayā* is compassion, mercy.

[30] The idea that gender divisions are not immutable is a common theme in South Asia (O'Flaherty 1980b, Ramanujan 1973:27, 29).

assumption of womanly qualities, there are different ways in which a man may 'become' a woman. For *bartamān-panthīs* this injunction is likely to involve coition without emission of semen, or erotic play without actual coition. Those in *bartamān* differ on these matters. For example, the prescription that the woman should become a (male) transvestite (i.e. without a vagina), and the man a eunuch (i.e. without a penis), associated especially with the Kartābhajās,[31] is dismissed by many *bartamān-panthīs* as only suitable for those too old to do otherwise. As an adept asked rhetorically: 'Why should one use the foot to do the work of the hand?'[32]

Of note here is the difference between the attitude towards women described above and that of the *sampradāy* called Balāhāṙi or Balarāmī, often placed in the same category as Bāuls. The Balāhāṙi associate women with activity and change (*pravṛtti*), which 'tempts, subjugates and destroys the male body' (P. Chatterjee 1989:206 n. 59, based on S. Cakrabartī 1986). As has been shown, this view of women is not predominant in the case of *bartamān-panthīs*. The *pravṛtti–nivṛtti* (activity–cessation) opposition may be assimilated to others previously mentioned, such as the path of nature (*jīb*) versus the path of god (*īśvar*), or worldly life (*saṅsār*) versus renunciation. As will be apparent from the previous discussion, women are generally associated by those in *bartamān* with both these realms, or with neither, in that they transcend both and are perfected by nature (*svayaṅ siddhā*). As an aphorism has it: 'She who robs you will also make you whole' (*yini haraṇ karen, tini pūraṇ karen*). So the woman has the power of life and death over the man. The menstrual flow, often seen by more orthodox practitioners as disqualifying a woman from esoteric practice (that of retention), is here viewed as the gift of one who is replete and overflowing, a gift which in no way depletes the giver. This is in conformity with the position outlined by O'Flaherty that 'women are meant to give, men to keep' (1980:44), with the *bartamān-panthī* ramification that the menstruation is placed in the same category as the breast milk, as something which is given for the life of others, without harming oneself, as opposed to semen which is to be preserved (on the whole) to enhance one's life.

Finally it should be pointed out that attitudes of (especially male) *bartamān-panthīs* to women are far from consistent. Just as men and women are sometimes said to be of the same human *jāt*, and sometimes to belong to two different *jāts*, so women are sometimes identified with the self by male initiates and sometimes cast in the role of other.[33] This oscillation is seen in many different ways: for example, in the former role, women are enjoined to do esoteric practice in the latter not, and so on.

[31] The following maxim offers one version of this: '(When the) woman is a transvestite and the man a eunuch, then they will be *kartābhajā*' (*nāri hijṙe puruṣ khojā, tabe habe kartābhajā*). The Kartābhajās (literally 'those who revere the master or guru') are an established *sampradāy* with, in many cases, a *bartamān-panthī* core.

[32] I am indebted to Dr S. N. Jhā for this quote.

[33] The *āpan–par* opposition is not necessarily implied here. Man and woman may be seen as complementary, as together forming one body and one self, with the woman often being valued more highly than the man.

8

Theory: images, the 'I' and *bartamān*

In this chapter, I turn to the more theoretical aspects of being in *bartamān*. Emphasis is placed on topics important to Rāj and his followers, such as the rejection of image worship in favour of that of human beings, especially women; and the 'I' as a device for invalidating distinctions between person and person. Finally, the distinction between *anumān* and *bartamān* is elaborated.

In *bartamān-panthī* discourse, the subjects of women and image worship (*mūrti-pūjā*), decried as 'worshipping dolls' (*putuler pūjā*), are often linked. Maṇi writes (song no. 171):

> Brother, everyone worships the mother, but no one recognises her.
> If they did, would anyone in this world pay respects to a mother of clay [an image]?
>
> What business can be done from image worship in Bengal!
> No other place has worship [on this scale]. It's a sheer waste of money...
> How much is squandered at all these pilgrimage centres in India.
> How cunningly the priest-touts come like gurus with (their lists of) names and places.[1]
>
> So many people in the country are starving,
> But in their [the priests'/gurus'] case, money is forked out.
> Maṇi says, listen all you who serve the feet of a mother of clay.
> You haven't recognised the one who bore you in her womb.
> Although she kept you alive with her milk, you never revered her.
> [Instead] everyone reviles her. Worship the mother of the house![2]

Rāj contrasts the worship of inanimate images representing Hindu goddesses, the wives of others (the gods), with the neglect of one's own wife 'who moves and talks' (song no. 24). The more usual forms of reverence for womanhood – as the embodiment of a/the goddess (Shaw 1994:39–47), as an abstract notion, as an 'essence' such as the menstrual blood, or as that emblem of creativity, the vagina – all this becomes something far more extraordinary in the hands of Rāj and his

[1] A reference to the records kept by pilgrimage priests of clients from various places. See A. G. Gold 1989: 206–7, 220–1 on the pilgrimage priests.
[2] For transliterated Bengali text of this song and the next (no. 29), see Openshaw 1997b:306–7.

followers. In a characterically forthright song (no. 29), Maṇi asserts:

> . . . Deluded people worship images of clay, metal and stone. . .
> Maṇi relates the words of Rāj – do not worship an unknown treasure.
> First comes the worship of the one who eats, sleeps, shits, and speaks with me.

This unusual song points to the distinctiveness of the *bartamān-panthī* position. In contrast to the more conventional Bengali idealisation of woman as goddess and mother,[3] *bartamān-panthīs* emphasise female sexuality. However, it is their occasional divinisation of the flesh and blood woman who is also an agent (in that she speaks) which is unique.

The notion of conflict between image worship and reverence for one's female partner is not confined to Rāj's people. In similar vein Duddu writes (*BBBG*:816):

> You haven't seen the living Kālī in your house
> Blind (even) in the day, you wear yourself out worshipping dolls!

A group of initiates told me: 'We don't worship images. We serve the human being (*mānuṣ bhajanā*), we worship (in) *bartamān*.' The saint Rāmakṛṣṇa, passionate worshipper of an icon of the goddess, condemned those such as Bāuls for this: 'They don't like to worship deities or images. They want a living human being (*jībanta mānuṣ*).'[4] The idea that image-worship is *anumān* is common. Rāj, Maṇi and Satīś all emphasise this. An adept of another line said to me: 'Image worship is *anumān*. If I do worship (*pūjā*) to you and you to me, that is *bartamān*.' A Muslim *bartamān-panthī* told me that *bāul* means the worship of the human being (*mānuṣ bhajan*). Reverence of women is thus associated with *bartamān*, and, as mentioned earlier, in one important sense, they are *mānuṣ*.

In connection with the *bartamān-panthī* stance against image worship, it is important to bear in mind the association of such practices with hierarchy. It is in the context of the lavish, annual festivals of icons established by landholding families, and performed by Brahmins, with subsidiary roles for Garland-makers (Mālākār), Barbers (Nāpit), and so on, that the caste hierarchy is most clearly revealed and reaffirmed.[5] Renouncers of the Ramanandi order emphasise Ram without form (*nirguṇa*), whereas image worship (of Ram with form – *saguṇa*) is generally viewed as a concession to the laity, who are considered unable to worship except through images. There is general agreement that caste distinctions are a prerequisite of image worship, since the images of Ram and Sita can only be attended by high status priests. This does not apply to aniconic forms, which in turn are associated with the itinerant life-style of the ideal renouncer, a way of life entailing the neglect of caste (Van der Veer 1987:689).

[3] Such attitudes were prevalent among middle-class and nationalist Bengalis. In 1882 CE, Bhūdeb Mukhopadhyāy identified the feminine sphere with the spiritual and god-like, as opposed to the masculine sphere, associated with the material and the animal-like (Chatterjee 1994:125).

[4] Śrī 'Ma' 1388 (vol. V):181. Rāmakṛṣṇa actually refers to the Kartābhajās here.

[5] Hierarchy is not absent even where *bhek-dhārīs* are allowed to do *pūjā* to Kṛṣṇa and Rādhā. See also S. Sarkar 1989b:314.

In his treatment of Untouchable reformist ideology in Lucknow, Khare associates an anti-idolatry stance with denial of temple entry to Untouchables by caste Hindus (1984:47). This connection is not so clear in the case of *bartamān-panthīs* in contemporary Bengal, where temple entry is, for various reasons, not such an issue. While most *bartamān-panthīs* are of low-caste or low-class origin, it is often those of Brahmin or Muslim origin who are most strident in their opposition to image worship. Khare somewhat regrets the approval of the idol of Ravidas by Jigyasu, the Chamar ideologue (1984:48). While such reinstatement of images is rarely found in the *bartamān-panthī* context, their position on similar issues is not without contradictions, as will be outlined below. I would argue that attitudes against image worship may be reinforced for Hindu *bartamān-panthīs* by real intimacy (of a kind not encountered in conventional society) of people acculturated into some form of Islam and thus finding such practices absurd. Hindu *bartamān-panthīs* arm themselves against image-worship using Muslim perceptions of idols as involving the worship of mere clay, metal and wood. On the other hand, Muslim *bartamān-panthīs* use Hindu notions of the embodied (incarnate) god, or of the human being as superior to god, to combat notions of the bodiless, transcendent Allah. Both arrive by different routes at the idea of the supremacy of the living human being. By contrast, the Untouchable ideologue privileges the Absolute, or the Void (Khare 1984:31). I would argue that the greater radicalism of many *bartamān-panthīs* on a variety of issues, and especially in comparison with other so-called deviant orders in Bengal, is related to the association of Hindus and Muslims in the world of *bartamān*, an intimacy which conduces to the reinforcement and perhaps even generation of anti-orthodox positions.

There are many stories about Rāj's attitudes to image worship, some of which draw on traditional themes. As a child he apparently used to perform *pūjā* to the household deity, Kālī, who was said to be so 'powerfully present' (*jāgrata*) that she would physically consume the offerings presented to her. One day, curious to see the Goddess eat the food, he kept watch, only to see a big black cat enter and devour the offerings. Thereafter he refused to do the *pūjā*, saying that he wouldn't worship a cat. Rāj's blatant mockery of image worship has been remarked on earlier. He would make provocative statements such as 'Who is your Kālī? Who is your Śiva?, I am Brahma! I am everything!' [or 'the "I" is Brahma/everything']. These apparently led to at least one of his ashrams being razed to the ground, and contributed to his lack of acceptance in the Birbhum village he settled in with Rājeśvar. What would be regarded by Rāj and other *bartamān-panthīs* as self-dependence, that is dependence on one's own knowledge and judgement, amounted, in the eyes of the more conventional, to 'having no respect for anything' or even to megalomania. After all, it was only two years before Rāj's arrival in Nadia District that another anti-caste, ganja-smoking and music-loving, wandering Brahmin *sādhu* had been the centre of a great scandal in Bikrampur (S. Sarkar 1989c).

Towards the end of the nineteenth century, the onslaught of Christian missionaries and Brahmo reform had provoked a debate in certain *bhadralok* circles concerning the relative worth of worship of deity 'with form' (*sākār*) or 'without form' (*nirākār*). Ironically, some Brahmos lauded the Bāuls as *nirākār*, a position they took to be in conformity with their own, and which they used to demonstrate an indigenous source for their ideas (see p. 36). Yet while the opposition of Brahmos to image-worship (*sākār*) involved an emphasis on a formless high God (*nirākār*), *bartamān-panthīs*, as we have seen, tend rather to oppose the mystification involved in wood, clay or metal masquerading as a living being to actual living human beings (*mānuṣ*). So Rāj, being in *bartamān,* is said by his disciples to be an advocate of *sākār*, the form in this case being a living human being. According to this logic, *nirākār* is reduced to the imaginary, or a mystification, and therefore *anumān*. Muslim *bartamān-panthīs* are often strident in their opposition to the formless Allah of classical Islam. As mentioned earlier, Lālan was at pains to dissociate himself from Brahmos, whom he was thought to resemble. However, the *bartamān-panthī* approach to this and many other topics is characterised by a creative fluidity rarely found in élite debates. Thus *sākār* (*sa* + *ākār* = with shape) is sometimes construed as *svākār* (*sva* + *ākār* = one's own shape – which has the same pronunciation), in conformity with the position that even the worshipful 'you' (*tumi*) is ultimately 'I' (*āmi*) (see below). On occasions when a *nirākār* position appears to be endorsed by *bartamān-panthīs*, they tend to gloss the negative '*nir*' as '*nīr*', which means water or liquid, something, in other words, which is on the verge of form. One guru told me '*nirākār* means the shape of water. There is nothing without form.'

As usual in *bartamān-panthī* circles, the shifting nature of the terms of the discussion is notable. For example, there are debates concerning the validity of such practices as doing *pūjā* to the entombed body of the guru, or a photograph of the guru. Thus the worship of entombed gurus is considered by some *bartamān-panthīs* to be as *anumānik* as image-worship. Maṇi Gõsāi is said to have instructed his disciples to leave his body on the bank of a river for the vultures to devour. One of his disciples, D.G., confessed that, when it came to it, they did not feel able to accede to this unconventional request, and instead entombed him in the room of the house where he had died. The attempt by the woman disciple whose house contains the tomb to use it as a focus for the disciples has on the whole proved futile. One important reason for this, apart from the usual fissionary tendencies of such lines, is the readiness with which such practices are categorised as *anumān*, and their consequent lack of conviction. In one *bartamān-panthī* ashram the entombed guru is honoured with elaborate service (*sebā*). A mosquito net is hung over the tomb every evening, food and marijuana is served the deceased guru as they used to be in life, and so on. Opinion is divided in the ashram as to whether the guru really consumes the offerings or whether the disciples are performing these rites for their own benefit. Other *bartamān-panthīs* attending the festival for the entombed guru's death day (a day of celebration) were less circumspect. One of Rāj's people muttered subversively: 'Let's dig him up and see him eat a plate of food!' And someone else opined that *bartamān* practice was to feed living beings, not the dead (who are *anumān*). In fairness to the ashram there was a great deal of that going on also.

The *bartamān-panthīs* of this ashram justify these practices in terms of the same *anumān-bartamān* categories by which others contest them. Thus they point out that they only make offerings to their immediate (deceased) guru whom they knew in *bartamān*, not to the guru's guru, nor to Kṛṣṇa. The argument here is that one knew the living guru (but not the guru's guru or Kṛṣṇa), and so the source of the representation is ultimately one's own experience. A similar justification is given for the more common practice, especially among non-Muslim *bartamān-panthīs*, of keeping a framed photograph of their guru (and often performing rudimentary *pūjā* to it), a practice clearly only as old as the penetration of photography into local towns. In common with most of Rāj's people, inhabitants of the above-mentioned ashram also reject the practice of making offerings to Caitanya, the six Gosvāmīs, and so on, which are to be performed by renunciate Vaishnavas only, just as image worship should technically be performed only by a Brahmin.

I now propose to turn to another aspect of *bartamān-panthī* theory: the 'I' (*āmi*). The contrast between the more orthodox Vaishnava traits of modesty (*dainya*) and total subservience to the guru on the one hand, and the more assertive anti-idolatry, anti-hierarchy, *āmi sab* ('I' am everything) stance of Rāj on the other, was discussed earlier. Similarly, the *bartamān-panthī* orientation towards oneself and one's experience, where every man is Kṛṣṇa and every woman Rādhā (or every person is both together) was contrasted with another perspective: where the whole focus is on the (male) guru and the power of his grace, or where the highest possible achievement of a human being is merely to *witness* the *līlā* of Rādhā and Kṛṣṇa. Rāj's attitudes also contrast with the general acceptance of subordination and hierarchy of sages such as Rāmakṛṣṇa (S. Sarkar 1985:34–5). While Rāmakṛṣna followed the well-worn route of devaluing householder values in relation to the world of renunciation, Rāj's main thrust was to discredit the hierarchies of both worlds. A clear desire not to reject one set of structures (those of *saṅsār*) only to be enslaved by another (those of renouncer society) is apparent in the attitudes of Rāj and his disciples. As will be shown, Rāj uses his deceptively *advaita* 'I' concept to demolish differences between guru and disciple, as well as between father and son. It will be recalled that Hem too was keenly aware of the tendency of the hierarchical structures of householder society to replicate themselves in the society of renouncers. Rāj and his disciples differ from many *bartamān-panthīs* in the greater consistency and sharpness of their critique of renouncer as well as householder society, a feature partly, but by no means wholly, connected to Rāj's distance from these two worlds. Lālan, who apparently took the Muslim equivalent of renunciation, and was merciless in his attitudes towards the structures of householder life, was not concerned to challenge the idea of the guru.[6]

Rāmakṛṣṇa's conformity with what Dumont (1960) called the characteristic stance of Hinduism, namely a tendency to inclusion and hierarchy, is in contrast with Rāj's predominant drive towards rejection and equalising, that is, rejecting all paths classified as *anumān*, and equalising all human beings in terms of their humanity, that is, as *mānuṣ*. As Rāj puts it (song no. 10):

[6] S. N. Jhā 1995. As mentioned earlier, the word 'guru' does not always denote the institutional guru. Even so, the absence of such a critique in Lālan is of interest. Similarly, the very presence of this is significant in Rāj's tradition, even though it persists along with apparently contradictory contents.

> ... As long as you judge in terms of high and low you are deluded.
> All are the same to one who knows reality ... [7]

In contrast to Rāmakṛṣṇa, Rāj abandoned his home and relatives, and, on the whole, subsequently maintained a critical distance from the hierarchies of renouncer society also. While zamindari patronage was succeeded by that of wealthy householders in the case of Rāmakṛṣṇa, Rāj's challenge to Hindu hierarchies in word and deed exacted its own price – the alienation of many who might otherwise have been his patrons. The fact that he was bereft of this kind of support in Birbhum is less surprising than the amount he managed to retain in Nadia, the scene of the crime, so to speak. The support he received from one or two zamindars and wealthy landowners (*jotdārs*), while not being sufficient to enable him to stay in Nadia, points nevertheless to strong elements of non-conformity, even among the wealthier sections of rural society, at least in some parts of Bengal. It is interesting to note in this connection that while songs concerning *yugal sādhanā* (practices of a male and female couple) typically use intentional language to conceal insider meanings from outsiders, songs lampooning caste, sect, gurus and gender discrimination are totally transparent (see S. N. Jhā, 1991, for examples). Aimed primarily at the uninitiated, they provide an indicator of the fascinating frontier between *bartamān-panthīs* and the world of householders from whom they largely recruit, and to whom they offer a constant critique of their universe.

The concept of 'I' (*āmi*) is one of the arguments used by Rāj and others to dissolve distinctions between person and person, be they those of householder or renouncer society, and even, in the final analysis, between man and woman ('I' and 'thou'). Rāj opens a song (no. 94) concerning 'knowledge of the self' (*ātmatattva*) with the traditional question 'Who am I?' (*Ke āmi*).[8] He argues that whichever different personal pronouns we use, the same 'I' (*paramātmā*) is in all. Whomever I address replies as 'I'. Distinctions of religious community, class (*varṇa*), generation and even (as was shown earlier) that between guru and disciple are obliterated using the 'I' concept:

> ... You, s/he, this person, that person, we hear many names [terms of address and reference];
> We know it is the same supreme Self which has taken many forms.
> Everyone whom I approach and ask says 'I', 'I'.
> There is nothing else apart from 'I', the one 'I' is everywhere.
> Go and ask Hindu, Muslim and Christian one by one,
> In reply you will get nothing but 'I'.
> Father son, guru disciple, Brahmin Kṣatriya Vaiśya,
> All are merged in the 'I'. The pure and the impure, all will be one.[9]

[7] See p. vi for transliterated Bengali text.

[8] Songs on this and other related subjects, including the *maner mānuṣ*, but in a more idealistic and pessimistic vein, were written by Īśvar-candra Gupta (1812–59 CE), in a period before links between the *bhadralok* and Bengali folk poetry had been severed.

[9] For transliterated Bengali text, see Openshaw 1997a:24.

In a section of one of his texts called 'I' (*āmi*), Rāj equates man and woman, guru and disciple, overlord and subject, you and me (*āmi*), and devotes a good deal of space to the refutation of a contrary argument that the guru is everything (Text B:57ff.). In the following section called 'You' (*tumi*), Rāj argues:

> Whomever I address as 'you' will never admit to being 'you'.
> Consider this my mind, s/he also calls her/himself 'I', s/he is not different from me, that person **is** 'I' [or '**I** am that person'].
> For the sake of *līlā* the 'you' comes from the 'I'.
> In eternity you and I are together, as one 'I'.[10]

Maṇi also affirms (song no. 151) that 'you and I are not different'. Another male practitioner, not of Rāj's line, remarked that 'I must first get to know myself (*ātmatattva*). Then I can get to know the other (*apar*, here the female partner). I shall then understand that we are all the same "I" (*āmi*).' Associated with the philosophy of *āmi* is that of *sohaṅ* ('I am that', see p. 144). As was argued earlier, the *bartamān-panthī* interpretation of non-dualism (*advaita*) is almost diametrically opposed to that of its more conventional idealist adherents. Similarly, any superficial resemblances of Rāj's *āmi* to more orthodox interpretations are misleading, for Rāj's *āmi* is ultimately identifiable with (or closely associated with) *bastu*, in the sense of the female and male generative essences (*rajaḥ-bīj*).[11] Maṇi says 'I am *bīj*, I am *rajaḥ*' [or 'the "I" is *bīj*, the "I" is *rajaḥ*']; and with the same progressive interiorisation observed in the context of the guru (see p. 152), he continues: 'I am within *bīj* . . .' (song no. 50). Duddu writes: 'The self [*ātmā*] can be called matter [*bastu*]. The *ātmā* is nothing supernatural' (*BBBG*:810). *Bartamān-panthī* espousal of the theory that self or soul (*ātmā*) and body are coterminous, called *dehātmabād* (colloquially, *deha-i āmi*), attracts severe censure from their opponents (e.g. Dās Brahmacārī 1389 BS[I]:46). This suggests parallels between the role of *bartamān-panthī* concepts of the 'I' (*āmi*) and the human being (*mānuṣ*) on the one hand, and, on the other, that of the individual of Lucknow Untouchable ideologues, in counteracting caste order and its collectivism (Khare 1984:62). This apparent appropriation of orthodox philosophical terminology must have constituted a particular irritant to the adherents of the schools concerned.[12] The very different use to which Rabindranath put the 'I' concept was noted in chapter 1 (see p. 32).

The *āmi* concept invokes a cathexis on inner realities, on *antaraṅga*. In another version of the notion of there being only two birth groups (*jāt*), a guru told me that these two are not man and woman, but those who face outwards (*bahir-mukhī*)

[10] For transliterated Bengali text, see Openshaw 1997a:24. One of Rāj's sources here was probably the *Caitanya Caritāmṛta*: 'Rādhā and Kṛṣṇa are thus eternally one in essence. They become two forms in order to taste the flavour of their *līlā*' (S. Sen 1983a:14).

[11] Not that such notions are without textual precedence. For the Upanisadic notion of the deceased passing through a natural cycle and eventually ending up as semen prior to a new birth, see Halbfass 1980:297.

[12] An equivalence between *ātmā* and *bastu* is drawn in orthodox philosophy, where it is glossed in a very different sense from that of *bartamān-panthīs*.

and who are concerned with externals, and those who face inwards (*antar-mukhī*). (In a typical *bartamān-panthī* elaboration of this, he added that the former cannot preserve their semen, while the latter can.) The value of such inwardness was clarified by another guru: 'All the different traditions (*sampradāy*) are only for the outside world. Here there is no birth group (*jāt*), nor even renunciation (*bhek*). Nor is there any special dress, sectarian decoration or any outward signs.' Yet while in one sense this assimilation of everything to oneself is consonant with the Vaishnava culture of interiority, the affective tone of the *āmi* concept is not at all typically Vaishnava, as has been seen above. The orthodox Vaishnava devotee is recommended to be 'humble as grass' and 'patient as a tree' (see Dimock 1966:111), qualities diametrically opposite to those implied by the *āmi* concept as popularly interpreted. The common rendering of this philosophical position as 'I am *brahma*', 'I am everything' often comes in for criticism. H.R.H., one of Rāj's disciples clearly in the habit of defending his guru on this and other issues, told me that rather than 'I am *brahma*,' it is wiser to say 'I am imbued with [or full of] *brahma*' (*āmi brahmamay*), a phrase also used by Rāj at times. Lālan was fully aware of the ambiguities of the 'I' concept (see song nos. 146, 147, 156 in Jhā 1995:47ff.). Rāj obviously played on these in some of the phrases he used, such as *āmi sab*, which in Bengali means either '(the) "I" is everything' or 'I am everything.' A modern tract attacks Bāuls, Sahajiyās and so on, for asserting 'I am god' and 'I am Kṛṣṇa-Caitanya' and so forth, notions which are obviously thought to detract from the uniqueness and importance of Caitanya. Similarly, the concept of *sohaṅ* ('I am that') is fiercely criticised in the same tract, and even the renowned Vaishnava guru, Bijay Kṛṣṇa Gosvāmī, felt moved to upbraid its advocates (B. G. Ray 1965:76–7). Such attitudes result, the tract's author continues, not only in indulgence of sensuality, but in the formation of many different small groups (*dal*) (Dās Brahmacārī 1389 BS[II]:59).

Allegations of fissiparous tendencies are sometimes confirmed by *bartamān-panthīs* and especially those who call themselves Bāul, although not normally in connection with the *āmi/sohaṅ* philosophy. An initiated Jat Vaishnava singer of the Santiniketan area, who describes himself as Bāul or Vaishnava, as do his father and brothers, was lamenting a family situation characterised by extreme dissension and general chaos: 'Because we are *bāul*, each of us goes where he wills. We all pull in different directions.' Whenever I asked the reasons for initiates and even *guru-bhāi* not mixing with each other, such factionalism was often accounted for in terms of 'the allurement of leadership'. One initiate said that there are so many different opinions (*mat*) and groups (*goṣṭhī*) because each person says 'this is the right way for humankind (*mānuṣ*)' and every other person says 'no it isn't'! However, in these cases, *bartamān-panthīs* do not see themselves as unique, and frequently draw parallels with progressive fissions within the communist parties of West Bengal.

It is apparent from his writings that even Rāj was sometimes on the defensive about the *āmi* concept. In one song (no. 95) he writes:

> Why does everyone get angry when the 'I' is talked of?
> Nobody notices that the 'I' is in every container (body/person).
> However much you think (in terms of) 'you' and 'him', it all becomes 'I'. . .
> Where shall I seek and find one who is not here? . . .[13]

Of course, it was largely this very denial of established boundaries, hierarchy and authority which exercised conventional opponents. This is seen in the fact that *bartamān-panthīs* could receive as much flak for losing their individuality (inappropriately, that is, to the guru), as for exaggerating it (Jhā 1997:103 n.18, quoting anti-Bāul tracts).

The affective tone of the *bartamān-panthī* concept of the 'I' can be appreciated in contrast to another mode of demolishing we–they (*āpan–par*) categories, in which everyone is thought of as *par* (Other).[14] One initiate told me: 'We talk of mother, father, aunts and, so on. But this is worldly talk. Actually all are Other (*par*).' According to another practitioner, 'the adept (*sādhu*) has no one, apart from the guru. He is everyone's affine (*kuṭumba*), no one is his kin (*āpan*). He is always at peace. When anyone comes he is content, when anyone goes he is content.' At times, what may be a device for cutting bonds of duty and affection for one's family takes the form of isolation and even alienation. Such sentiments are especially prevalent in the songs of Lālan.[15]

The *āmi* philosophy is not confined to *bartamān-panthīs* of Hindu origin. Indeed Haq traces it to a Sūfi source, as well as to 'Hindu pantheism'. However that may be, the following song by a Bāul of Muslim origin reveals that the reaction of orthodox Muslims and Hindus to such ideas tended to be similar (Haq 1975:315):

> After due deliberation I see 'all is I'.
> I am He! O, I am He:
> Ah me! people speak ill of me.
> From 'I' Allāh and his apostle come, and everything comes from 'I' . . .
> Sure I shall be killed if my countrymen take my words as they are;
> Remember! whoever knows the self knows God.

This chapter ends with a reconsideration of the basic dichotomy: *anumān* and *bartamān*. *Bartamān-panthīs* are not highly trained or professional philosophers. Theirs is more a kind of folk philosophy. Here brief consideration is given to possible parallels and antecedents in Indian philosophical thought for the concepts of *anumān* and *bartamān*. Finally, a more detailed exploration of *bartamān-panthī* usage of these terms is undertaken.

13 For transliterated Bengali text, see Openshaw 1997a:25.

14 Thinking of everyone as *āpan* (we, one's own people) is not identical with the *āmi* concept, although it is closer in mood.

15 S. N. Jhā 1995. In keeping with the tradition of modesty, Lālan's treatment of the *āmi* theme is somewhat different. Thus he ends one song: 'Had I known who I am [the 'I'], this confusion would disappear' (*BBBG*:621).

As stated earlier, in popular usage the word *anumān* means supposition, a guess, a conjecture. *Anumān* as 'inference' also constitutes one of the 'essential means of arriving at valid knowledge' (*pramāṇa*) in Indian philosophical traditions. As such, it became one of the main preoccupations of a school of philosophy called neo-Nyāya, which specialised in logic, and had its centre from the fifteenth to the seventeenth centuries in Nadia district, where many 'obscure religious cults' including Bāuls are thought to have originated. This contiguity may in part account for the familiarity of those in *bartamān* with notions such as *anumān*, as well as their identification of *anumān* with orthodoxy, in the sense of the legitimisation of social structures and rituals by reference to authorised scripture. For another *pramāṇa* recognised by the school of Neo-Nyāya is 'testimony' (*śabda*), which includes the idea of the validity of all knowledge derived from the Vedas (S. N. Dasgupta 1975 [1]:308, 335). Interestingly a third *pramāṇa* accepted by the Nyāya school is *pratyakṣa* (perception, or sense-object contact), which is of primary importance to those in *bartamān.* However, despite its contributions to empirical epistemology and logic and its opposition to idealism, the 'orthodox' (*āstik*) slant of Nyāya is indicated here too by its inclusion within the *pratyakṣa* category of 'extraordinary' (*alaukik*) as well as 'ordinary' (*laukik*) perception (Chattopadhyaya 1972:179–80).

Parallels may be discerned between the *bartamān-panthī* counterposition of *bartamān* and *anumān* and the two valid *pramāṇas* of the Buddhist logicians, Dig-nāga and Dharmakīrti (fifth and seventh centuries CE respectively). These are *pratyakṣa* (direct experience) and *anumān* (inferential reason) – authorised scripture being subsumed under the latter category, just as it is for *bartamān-panthīs.* Of these two, *pratyakṣa* was thought most effective, and in any case the other(s) were considered to ultimately derive from it (Thurman 1988:120). *Pratyakṣa* and *bartamān* are often identified by *bartamān-panthīs*. The term *bartamān*, unlike *anumān*, has not acquired the status of a classical philosophical term, and in Bengali it means 'the present (time), present (as opposed to absent), current, modern', and, most relevant in the present context, 'now existing or living or alive' (*SBED*).

A persuasive argument has been made for relating *bartamān-panthīs* to the school(s) of Indian materialism, called the Lokāyata or Cārvāka (Jhā 1985/86, 1999; on the Lokāyata, see Chattopadhaya 1959, 1990). Little can be said for certain about this tradition, since it is known only through the writings of its opponents, who denigrated it as sceptic and hedonist. Nevertheless, the generally presumed central tenets of this 'heterodox' (*nāstik*) school include: the primacy of sense perception (*pratyakṣa*) as a source of valid knowledge, the idea that ultimate reality consists of four material elements, the theory that there is no self without the body (*dehātmabād*), and the refutation of classical notions of *karma* and rebirth. All these ideas figure prominently in the *bartamān-panthī* repertoire. The emphasis on sense perception is of course related to the heterodoxy of the Lokāyata, that is their denial of the absolute validity of the Vedas. It is significant that 'Lokāyata', as well as meaning the 'materialist philosophy' also means the 'philosophy of the people', leading at least one scholar to doubt the common assumption that the Indian philosophical tradition was one of continuing idealism or spiritualism (Chattopadhyaya 1959:1–4). Other scholars have also joined combat with notions of the 'spiritual East' by emphasising the general 'materialism' of sub-continental culture (Ramanujan 1990; Nicholas 1982; Marriott 1976). Certainly where *bartamān-panthīs* are concerned, the label 'materialist' is more appropriate than 'idealist' or 'spiritualist'. However the distinction between matter and spirit presupposed by such labels is not made by them. In common with Chinese philosophers, *bartamān-panthīs* can also be said to turn 'matter into spirit by making it thin', and Taoist continuities between 'solidity' and 'emptiness', 'matter' and 'spirit' undoubtedly apply to them also (Needham 1974:85–6).

As mentioned earlier, the similarity of terms used by neo-Nyāya (among other philosophies) and those used by *bartamān-panthīs* (such as the equivalence of *ātmā* and *bastu*, the use of terms such as *anumān*, *nām* and so on) belies the different meanings attributed to these terms by *bartamān-panthīs*. The conventional approach is to think in terms of appropriation from such orthodox schools, but the true picture may be the reverse, or at least one of continuous mutual influences. The origin of Nyāya philosophy has been associated with the methodology of public debate, one reason given for this emphasis being the necessity of silencing arrogant disputants (S. N. Dasgupta 1975 [I]:360ff.). In more recent Bengali history, orthodox Brahmanism was wont to denounce those who used the 'science of disputation' (*tarkavidyā*) to challenge the authority of the Vedas and to establish empiricism (*pratyakṣabād*), positions associated with current identifiable heterodoxies, such as Lokāyata, Tantra and Buddhism (S. Sarkar 1989a:12, 17–18 n. 57). The role of debate and disputation in the *bartamān-panthī* attack on *anumān* has been described by S. N. Jhā (1985/86 [I]:25). Rāj shared with sages like Rāmakṛṣṇa a dislike of scripture (a trait which was scrupulously elided in subsequent accounts of that prestigious saint). However, unlike Rāmakṛṣṇa, Rāj was obviously not opposed to scholarship as such, simply to the conventional and discriminatory attitudes of orthodoxy in support of which it was all too often marshalled. Rāj and at least three of his disciples all wrote prolifically, cannibalising the very weapons of orthodoxy in their attack on it: using reason, analogy, puns and even scriptural precedent, with varying degrees of success.

Futher consideration of the relationship between those on the path of *bartamān* and neo-Nyāya, Materialist and Buddhist traditions lies outside the scope of this work. I now propose to turn to *bartamān-panthī* perspectives on *anumān* and *bartamān*. The contrasting *bartamān-panthī* categories of *anumān* and *bartamān* may usefully be introduced via a parallel contrast, that of *nām* (name) and *bastu* (substance, matter). One of Rāj's disciples, H.R.H., an elderly man of Fisherman caste (now dead), told me of a continuing dispute he had with some *bartamān-panthī* relatives before his own initiation. The disagreement concerned the relative importance of the name and the thing (or matter) (*Nām baṛa nā bastu baṛa*?). At that stage he was a conventional Vaishnava and put the name (*nām*) above the thing (*bastu*), only to reverse his position after his initiation with Rāj Khyāpā. He told me: 'You can't get the thing from the name (*nāme bastu mele nā*) . . . You can recite *mantras* for scores of births; nothing will be gained!' Maṇi, his brother through initiation, enquires (song no. 24):

> What's the significance of a name? Can the eight fetters and three fires be destroyed by name? Explain it to me.
> I shall understand when I come to a conclusion based on direct experience (*pratyakṣa*).
> Without such a conclusion, does anyone anywhere heed mere words?
> Without examples I shan't listen to any conclusion.
> Tell me, who has ever become wealthy from the word 'wealth'?
> Whose stomach has ever been filled by the word 'food'?
> Is one's thirst slaked by the word 'water'?
> In the absence of cloth, can one cover nakedness with the word 'cloth'?
> Do crops grow at the words 'seed and field'?
> If words are useless in the case of all these external matters
> Can they protect you in that most arduous task [esoteric practice]?
> Mad Maṇi here speaks the words of Rāj-kṛṣṇa
> With words you will never gain wealth,
> If you preserve the jewel (*maṇi*), you will be the richest of the rich. No one ever came to this world with names.[16]

This affirmation that the qualities of matter do not inhere in the name, contradicts the orthodox Gauṛīya Vaishnava doctrine of the essential identity of the name and the named.[17] At times, such Vaishnavas even assert that the name is of greater importance, since the name of God leads the devotee to God. As will be shown, the more conventional assumption of consonance (between name and named), where *bartamān-panthīs* assume dissonance, also applies in the case of the categories *anumān* and *bartamān* themselves. Also to be noted in the song quoted is the emphasis on sense perception (*pratyakṣa*). A song by Bhabānanda, another disciple of Rāj, similarly emphasises the contrast between the (ineffective) *bīj mantra* and the *bīj* (seed) from which the body arises and which is the basis of esoteric practice (song no. 105 of Maṇi's manuscript). *Nām* thus has clear connotations of *mantra*, Vaishnava *saṅkīrtan*, scripture and so forth. One guru identified himself as *bastubādi* (usually, but a little misleadingly, translated as 'materialist'), as opposed to *ādhyātmik* (usually translated as 'spiritual', even more misleadingly).[18] 'Only *bastubād* matters', he said.

Bastu is of course connected with *pratyakṣa* (perception), as *nām* is with *anumān* (inference). Thus the relationship between *nām* and *bastu* is echoed in a further

[16] For transliterated Bengali text, see Openshaw 1997b:299. In the penultimate line, 'jewel' (*maṇi*), a pun on the composer's name, refers to the body's essential substance, semen.

[17] *Nāma-nāminor abhedaḥ* (see Paritosh Dās 1988:90). There are many songs illustrating the same point as Maṇi's song (see Jhā 1985/86 pt. 1:26). These opposing views echo those of the Nyāya and Mīmāṅsā schools of philosophy respectively (Matilal 1990:35). (I am indebted to Dr C. Pinney for drawing my attention to this parallel.) Of course, as folk philosophers and gurus, *bartamān-panthīs* are more concerned with getting their message across than with consistency.

[18] Many of those on the *bartamān* path would equate these two rather than oppose them. For them *ādhyātmik* is equivalent to *dehatattva* (the theory, or truth of the body).

pair of contrasting categories: 'what is heard' (*śonā kathā*) and 'what is seen' (*dekhā kathā*). One guru told me: '*Bartamān* is what can be and is shown directly.' 'What is seen' has the wider implication of 'one's own experience, one's own knowledge '(*nij bicār, nij jñān*), as against 'what is heard' which is dismissed as 'the knowledge or judgement of others' (*parer jñān*). Thus 'what is heard' also means 'hearsay' (*anumān*) (Rāj song no. 64). A song I heard sung by Muslim Bāuls begins: 'I shall no longer listen to hearsay. I want to see and judge for myself...' (*Āmi śunba nā ār āndāji kathā, dekhe bicār karte cāi* ...). As mentioned above (on p. 151), *bartamān-panthīs* often say: 'How can I worship what I haven't seen with my own eyes?', or alternatively, 'How can I understand what I haven't seen with my own eyes?' As modified by Rāj, this runs: 'What I haven't seen with my own eyes won't do, even if the guru tells me.' Rāj also put a similar idea like this (song no. 93): 'Who can see with another's eyes, if one's own are ruined?' (*Parer dekhāy ke dekhte pāy, yadi naṣṭa hay ā̃khi*?) In a passage dealing with the *anumān-bartamān* opposition, Rāj asserts: '*Anumān* is just a blind man's mirror' (*Anumān hay śudhu andher darpan*) and '(those in) *anumān* don't worship what they see with their own eyes' (*pratyakṣa darśane bhaje nāi anumān*). At issue here is not an exclusive reliance on sense perception (*pratyakṣa*) to the exclusion of *anumān* in all contexts, as sometimes alleged by the opponents of those in *bartamān*. Thus, according to Rāj, it is possible to move from *bartamān* to *anumān* but not vice versa. He writes:

> You can imagine something which you have experienced, but not something you have never known in reality (*bartamān*).
> You (try to) imagine without knowing in reality [but] how can you imagine what you have never seen? ...
>
> *Barttamān jiniser anumān hay, barttamān nā jānile anumān nay.*
> *Barttamān nāi jāne anumān bhābe, adṛśyer anumān kemane bhābibe* ...[19]

What one needs, concludes Rāj, is 'knowledge of the thing' (*bastur jñān*), as opposed to the name (Text A, 19ff.).

'Orthodoxy' (*asti*) legitimises itself with reference to scripture, that is, *śruti* (literally 'what has been heard', the Vedas) and *smṛti* (literally 'what has been remembered'). While, in the final analysis, these are predicated on the vision of the seers (and indeed the word for philosophy, *darśan,* also means 'vision' or 'perception'), such a source would be rejected by *bartamān-panthīs* as 'another's vision' and therefore useless. Vision has typically been associated with power and control, by Foucault, for example. It is therefore interesting to find this sense marshalled against prevailing power structures by the declassed and dispossessed as a way of establishing autonomy. Whereas Fabian finds in the primacy of vision, for anthropologists and others, a distancing device (1983:105ff.), it is notable that

[19] This provides a rationalisation for practices such as reverence of the photograph of the guru, and also the creation of a mental image (*naksā, murti*), usually of the guru or one's partner (see S. N. Jhā 1985:500–1). Chattopadhyaya has argued that inference from *pratyakṣā*, but not, of course, vice versa, was allowed by followers of Lokāyata (1972:188ff.).

for *bartamān-panthīs* vision is characterised by immediacy. 'What is heard' is experienced as at best at one remove and usually much further than this, whereas 'what is seen', as one's own immediate experience, is a way of cutting through mystification. For example, a significant contrast is drawn between the orthodox presentation of inaccessible realities such as Self or Soul (*ātma*) or the Ground of all Being (*brahma*) with the *bartamān-panthī* gloss on these same words in terms of bodily substance, visible to the eye. (For example, *brahma* is often glossed as seminal essence, the 'Ground of all Being' in another sense.) [20]

For Rāj and others, the path of *bartamān* (the present, the living) is opposed to the path of *anumān* (inference). *Anumān*, the world of name and 'what is heard' is often identifiable with scripture and orthodoxy, especially in the sense of conformity with *smārta* prescriptions. *Bartamān* is the world of matter (*bastu*), of direct knowledge from the senses (though not in any crude, reductionist interpretation of *pratyakṣabād*). One of the many ramifications of this is the affirmation of this-worldliness (*ihabād*), and in many cases the rejection of transmigration and/or other after-life concepts. One initiate, technically a renouncer and formerly Scheduled Caste, defined *bartamān* as follows: 'I shall eat and enjoy myself. I shall serve others so that they do the same. We shall live in joy (*ānanda*).' This may in turn be related to a cathexis on the living human being (*mānuṣ*) and her/his needs and experience, rather than on deities, for example. A well-known singer of Rarh told me: '*bartamān* is serving the human being'. Duddu writes (*BBBG*:831):

> The one who seeks god in the human being is *bāul*,
> S/he seeks and finds god in matter.
> S/he doesn't believe in previous or future lives,
> S/he doesn't pay attention to *anumān*,
> S/he serves the human being in *bartamān*,
> To this s/he is bound. . . .

It is important to note that for *bartamān-panthīs*, *anumān* is generally not merely a provisional acceptance on trust, eventually to be verified (made *bartamān*). This, with its implication of different ways of apprehending the same reality, would be a more orthodox gloss on this dyad. The conventional argument would run as follows: what one assumes or accepts on (someone else's) authority is *anumān*; when one realises those same truths through one's own experience, they become *bartamān*; that is, they are directly experienced. Reflecting their opposition to religious and social authority, *bartamān-panthī* usage of these terms generally implies a radical dissonance. In their discourse, *anumān* often carries connotations

[20] It should be added here that there are contexts where 'what is seen' is demoted in favour of even more immediate modes of experience, such as touch sensation or feeling. A woman guru told me: 'From sight (*darśan*) one gets twelve annas, from touch (*sparśa*) fourteen, and some even get sixteen [that is, everything].' Thus esoteric practice must be experienced, not witnessed. 'What is seen' may itself be considered misleading in some contexts. For example, the appurtenances of conventional religiosity (sectarian dress, decorations etc.) are all visible, whereas the 'path of passion' has no signs (*baidhik dekhā yāy; rāg dekhā yāy nā*).

not only of error, but of a web of deception. Rāj refers (song no. 93) to 'Vedic deceit' (*baidik phāki*),[21] and Hem Khyāpā, one of his disciples, writes: 'They tell you without seeing for themselves, and establish their views through deception' (*Nā dekhe sunāy, phā̃ki kare bhāb sthāpite*) (song no. 58a). Identifying substance or thing (*bastu*) with truth, and 'name' with falsehood, he writes (song no. 88b):

> You maintain no connection with truth, you're besotted with falsehood.
> You keep no relation with 'matter' (*bastu*), all of you are intoxicated with 'name' (*nām*)...

Similarly, Maṇi speaks of 'lies' of the Veda ('*Bede kay yā mithyā kathā*' – song no. 166).

Anumān is therefore most characteristically expressed in what is called '*bed-bidhi*' (Sanskrit: *veda-vidhi*). Veda means, in addition to its restricted sense, any orthodox text (for example, in this sense the Koran is Veda), while *vidhi* means 'conventional rites and precepts'. *Bed-bidhi* therefore amounts to orthodox ideology and prescriptions legitimised by reference to authorised scripture, be they Hindu or Muslim. The famous Bāul Lālan asserts: 'The Vedic cloud casts a fearful darkness and the day's jewel cannot rise...' and 'As much as you read the Vedas and Vedānta, so much will your delusion grow...' (see Dimock 1966:262). A guru of Rarh contrasted the householder and renouncer orthodox worlds (*baidik-saṅsār*), which are characterised by ill-will (*hiṅsā*), vilification, complexities and deceit, with that of the world of the 'perfected ones' (*sādhu-saṅsār*), where it is realised that everyone is made from and of [the same] male and female essence (*rajaḥ-bīj*). A verse goes: '*Mānuṣ* is within *mānuṣ* but is difficult to find. As long as one is dazzled by *bed-bidhi*, the gateway to *mānuṣ* will remain closed.'[22]

While *bed-bidhi* legitimises the hierarchies and inequalities of society, its mystifications disguise their nature as false constructs. It is, of course, the prime example of *parer-jñān* (the knowledge of others, as opposed to one's own). In one of his songs (no. 10), Rāj says:

> ... Whoever remains within the confines of society has to go according to the judgement of others ...
> You will not be liberated by the knowledge of others; your own knowledge will (only) be eroded.
> ...
> Rāj says, cast off the bonds of society, (and) the bonds of this world will (also) be severed.[23]

[21] In the version of this song in Bhaṭṭācārya's collection (*BBBG*:844 no. 430), not only is the idiograph 'Rām-kṛṣṇa' rather than 'Rāj-kṛṣṇa', but '*baidik thāki*' ('remaining in the Veda') has replaced the opposite '*baidik phāki*'. The latter is clearly written in Rāj's version – albeit without the usual nasalisation – and is a phrase of his well known to his followers.

[22] It should be noted here that while *bed-bidhi* is almost invariably rejected, another word for scripture, *śāstra*, is sometimes allowed, in contexts where *bartamān-panthīs* wish to appeal to a tradition of their own. Here *śāstra* tends to refer to the songs of the great gurus (*mahat* or *mahājan*).

[23] For transliterated Bengali text, see Openshaw 1997b:301.

In connection with *bed-bidhi*, it is interesting to look at S. N. Jhā's survey of Bāuls of Murshidabad, a Muslim majority district of West Bengal.[24] Respondents (all of Muslim birth) were asked to identify the 'people who follow the Veda' (*baidik lok*), that is, orthodox people. (It will be recalled that Veda and Vedic refer respectively to authorised scripture in general and those who are orthodox with reference to it.) The answers included the following: Vedic (orthodox) people are: those who don't acknowledge the authority of human beings (*mānuṣ*), but of scripture (*śāstra*), the *śariyat* [Islamic scripture] and their injunctions; those who respect the Koran and the Hadith rather than the guru; those who adhere to texts (*grantha*) rather than the guru or the human being; those who proceed by guesswork (*āndāje*) and are on the path of *anumān*; those who are not on our path, who don't follow our view (*mat*); ordinary Hindus or Muslims; and so on. Respondents were also asked what it means to be against Veda, a position with which they identified themselves. Here the answers emphasised having no scripture, going in the opposite direction from scripture, or being actively opposed to scripture. Opposition to *anumān*, and to 'ordinary *ānumānik* religion' (*dharma*) is also emphasised, as well as the non-observance of *namāj* and *rojā* (Muslim prayers and fasting). 'Veda is *anumān*, our theory is *bartamān*.' There is also the idea that ordinary, conventional religion is false, worthless (*asār*) or external (*bāhyik*), whereas their own view represents the real essence (*sār*), which is internal, and secret (*gopan*). The hidden meanings (*gūṙha artha*) of the Koran and Hadith tend to be emphasised, rather than the literal meanings (*ākṣarik artha*) or the explicit meanings (*prakāśya artha*). Other remarks of interest include: 'One should know the Veda which is the body, not the written Veda.' 'We are against customary, conventional religion [*dharma*].' 'We respect the human guru [*mānab guru*] rather than written scripture.' 'We are against *śariyat*.' 'First [come] human beings', and so forth.

Thus the Muslim *bartamān-panthīs* of this survey reveal the same attitudes as those of Hindu origin: the rejection of texts (and *anumān* in general) in favour of the guru or human being(s) or the human body (all classified as *bartamān*); the consciousness of being in the minority with an esoteric culture; as well as the combination of an oppositional tendency with a necessity to adapt to some extent to the dominant culture (for example, by the use of conventional religious terminology). In another part of the questionnaire, of over 200 (Muslim) respondents, whereas more than 180+ people each said they respect Mahammad, Caitanya, Āli, Fatemā, Rādhā, Kālī and Śiva, only one respondent reported respect for Maulvīs and five for Hindu priests. (The fact that, in the case of Mahammad, Caitanya and so forth, the least likely referent is to historical or mythical figures, all these names being frequently subject to reinterpretion on *bartamān* lines, does not detract from the interest of this response.)

The oppositional tendency of those in *bartamān* is discernible in the use of the terms 'reverse', 'contrary' or 'opposite' (*ujān, biparit, ulṭa*) to characterise

[24] Unpublished survey, partly incorporated into Jhā 1985. Over 200 respondents were interviewed. The answers are not placed in order of preponderance (S. N. Jhā: personal communication).

the *bartamān-panthī* path or practice. Such terms apply to esoteric practice, not only in connection with attempts to counteract the normal outward or downward seminal flow, but also in the advocation of sexual intercourse at precisely the time when it is normally forbidden (during the menstruation), the unconventional 'woman astride' position, and the 'four moons' practices, one aspect of which is to confer value on what is regarded as dirt or excreta by others. Apart from attempts to reverse the flow of life (at least up to a point), there is another aspect to this oppositional tendency. Ramakanta Chakravarti cites the following passage from a so-called 'Sahajiyā' work:[25]

> The whole world regards something as a sin. I regard it as something holy.
> The whole world considers something to be good. To me it is bad. The whole world regards something as absolute truth. To me it is absolutely false. . . .
> Those whom the whole world adores are exceedingly dishonourable to me.
> What is generally considered reprehensible is, in my estimation, very good.
> The whole world lays down rules. I consider these rules bad. Those whom the world ignores on the ground of poverty are, to me, very rich.

In an echo of this tendency, B. G., Maṇi's disciple, told me that Vaishnavas (by which he obviously meant unorthodox Vaishnavas) avoid the four traditional aims of life. He elaborated: '*dharma* [the ten ritual acts], *kām* [begetting progeny], *artha* [the concern with property] and *mokṣa* [which he equated with heaven (*svarga*)] – none of these are Vaishnava'.

Finally, it should not be thought that the pairs of terms (*anumān-bartamān, nām-bastu, nām-nāmī,* etc.) discussed in this section are invariably construed in terms of opposition. The relation between the two terms of each pair is drawn in various ways, not infrequently by the same person in different contexts. Thus, to take the example of the relationship between name (*nām*) and the named (*nāmī*), what is called 'opposition' would imply different incompatible paths, most usually the assumption being that 'name' is plainly useless and a waste of time (see Maṇi's song quoted on p. 194). Alternatively, *nām* may be redefined so as to exclude it from consideration. For example, one initiate opined that *nām* means *nāmā* (to descend), by which he meant that the energies must be brought down in order to do *sādhanā* in the first place. Or the relationship may be hierarchical, in which case 'name' is incorporated at a preliminary, or inferior level. The relationship of *anumān* as exoteric (*bahiraṅga*) and *bartamān* as esoteric (*antaraṅga*) may take this form. I have even heard a *bartamān-panthī* voice the orthodox idea that name and named (*nām* and *nāmī*) are one, thus collapsing the categories. As folk intellectuals and teachers, the arguments of *bartamān-panthīs* are more sensitive to context (Ramanujan 1990, cf. S. B. Daniel 1983), than those of trained classical philosophers. Despite these fluctuations, however, *bartamān* and 'matter' invariably retain their superiority over *anumān* and 'name'. As will be argued in chapter 9, this is not the case with other hierarchies of value, where reversal is a

[25] *Svarūpakalpataru*, attributed to Narottam Dās (R. Chakravarti 1985:340). Nowadays, *sahajiyā* is largely, if not wholly, a scholarly category.

possibility. Thus the identification of *bartamān* in some contexts with the gross (*sthūl*), in the sense of the visible and material, is at times in tension with that of *bartamān* as esoteric, inner and subtle. It is probably not incorrect to surmise that all *bartamān-panthīs* avail themselves of all these varying positions at one time or another. Just as they appropriate the contents of the dominant culture, so they do also the various structural arrangements of those contents, marrying them with contents and structures (for example, rejection and equalising) unstated or uncathected in the dominant cultures.

V

Practice (*sādhanā*) and talking about practice (*hari-kathā*)

9

Practice (*sādhanā*)

Volumes could be written on the subject of *bartamān-panthī* esoteric practice (*sādhanā*), but consideration of this complex subject will necessarily be brief in this context. The subject of esoteric practice cannot be omitted, in view of its centrality to *bartamān-panthīs* themselves. While I have found it necessary to provide an outline of the practices, in view of the paucity of reliable accounts, especially in English,[1] one of the aims of the following presentation is to suggest that much of the confusion surrounding this subject derives from inappropriate generalisation and systematisation. For reasons discussed earlier, such problems are particularly acute when attempts are made to consider the material under the rubric 'Bāul' (R. P. Das 1992).

Even when considered from the perspective of *bartamān*, generalisation and systematisation are hazardous, often for different reasons. It is all too easy to distort the practices of those in *bartamān* through oversystematisation, thus ignoring or underestimating the licence given to eclecticism (for example, through experimenting with practices learned through 'mixing with adepts' – *sādhu-saṅga*) and the ultimate autonomy of the practitioner. It is not my aim to attempt an account of the great variety of related practices of those in *bartamān*. Moreover, the presentation of this material is in part determined by considerations of confidentiality and privacy. In the widest terms, it may be said that *bartamān-panthī sādhanā* concerns the psychophysical organism and, more specifically, the human body, especially in relationship with a person of the opposite sex. Alternatively, since the esoteric practice is basically oriented to the development of men (even according to women), it may be said to be centred around women. For this and other reasons, esoteric practice is typically described from the male perspective, and to some extent the following presentation reflects this bias.

Esoteric practice with a woman may not be considered necessary for a male practitioner at all stages, but a *bartamān-panthī* must have done esoteric practice with a woman at some time, and generally an initiate without a female partner has no credibility in *bartamān-panthī* circles. The vital role of women has been

[1] Main sources on *bartamān-panthī sādhanā* are *BBBG*:369–437, and Jhā 1985, 1995, 1999, all in Bengali. For an English language source, see Jha 1995.

pointed out earlier. The saying 'The one who steals also makes whole' asserts that just as a woman is capable of robbing a man of his vital essence, so she alone is capable of restoring him to fullness. The idea of 'woman', specifically the vagina (*yoni*), as the place of birth, death (emission of semen) and esoteric practice has already been mentioned. As Rāj puts it, this is the highway (*rāj-path*) by which we all enter life, to which all paths lead, and which is the only path for esoteric practice (song no. 54). As mentioned earlier, the triangular shape of the Bengali syllable '*ba*' is used to gloss '*bartamān*' – and '*bāul*' for that matter – in terms of womanhood.[2]

It is sometimes said that there are three types of esoteric practice: of *bāyu* (air), *bastu* (substance) and *bākya* (speech). The term *bartamān* may also be related by practitioners to these three, which begin with the same consonant 'b'. However, those on the *bartamān* path often give priority to *bastu*, not only over *bākya,* that is name and mantra, but also over *bāyu,* associated by *bartamān-panthīs* with Yogis. The main emphasis in practice tends therefore to be on substance, often visible substance, rather than breath. The breath is used as a general guide to the condition of the body. It is often used at an elementary level to distract the mind and prevent 'death' during intercourse, as also may mantras ('name' as opposed to 'substance'). It may be used as a way of manipulating and moving substance, at elementary and even at more advanced levels of esoteric practice. Bhaṭṭācārya states that retention of air (*kumbhak*) is the basis of Bāul esoteric practice, and, in general, emphasises the role of breath (*damer-kāj*). He asserts that practitioners established in retention of breath are the 'real' Bāuls, others being 'fake' and interested only in sensual enjoyment (*BBBG*:409–18). No doubt for many practitioners it does play a central role – it is important for some of Rāj's people – but this is by no means the case for all *bartamān-panthīs* at all times, as Bhaṭṭācārya seems to suggest. Even in the context of Rāj's line, B.G. maintains that practices using the breath are only appropriate at an early age and in a preliminary way, and Hem Khyāpā is sometimes alleged to have died prematurely through the inappropriate use of such practices.[3] Crucial here are notions concerning the effective level of intervention in the psychophysical organism. That the movement (or lack of movement) of substance (*bastu*) and air (*bāyu*) – and mind for that matter – are intimately related would generally be agreed. Differences of opinion would arise rather concerning the effectiveness, necessity or wisdom of attempting to manipulate substance through intervention at the level of the breath. Bhaṭṭācārya's emphasis on the primacy of breath is most questionable in connection with the more alchemical aspects of *bartamān-panthī* practices, especially those involving bodily substances, which are classified under the rubric 'four moons' (see chapter 10). In this connection it should be noted that esoteric practice involves not only the movement and relocation of substances, it also entails their transmutation

[2] The inverted triangle is a widely known Tantric symbol of *prakṛti* (the female aspect).

[3] At issue here is a range of practices and an equal range of terms apart from *damer-kāj*, such as *nyās*, *bāyur-kāj, śvāser-kāj* and *prāṇāyām*. *Bartamān-panthīs* often use these terms interchangeably.

according to principles of physiological alchemy.[4] My impression is that, in certain contexts, *bartamān-panthīs* deliberately emphasise the role of prestigious 'yogic' practices such as *prāṇāyām* and total seminal retention. In others, they are more concerned to differentiate the path of *yoga* (associated for them with respiratory techniques and esoteric practice without a woman) from their own path – that of *ras* or *bastu* (fluids, substance).[5] A *bartamān-panthī* gloss in terms of sexual esoteric practice of a verse ostensibly about *prāṇāyāmik* practice is revealing in this connection (Jhā 1997:98). *Bartamān-panthīs* may also draw on the conventional Vaishnava rejection of *yoga* in favour of devotion (*bhakti*). Rāj asks (song 12): 'What's the point of doing *yoga*? What counts is *anurāg* (passionate devotion).' In the *bartamān-panthī* case, however, the object of that devotion would be a human being rather than a deity.

The predominant attitude of *bartamān-panthīs* towards esoteric practice may be highlighted in contrast to that of Rāmakṛṣṇa, a sage characterised by the somewhat random and inspired acts (*līlā*) of the *avatār*, or at least of one who need not labour in this life for realisation. While such notions as *kṛpā* (grace), involving submission to the will of a more developed being, be it god, guru or (in this case, most likely) a woman, do form part of the repertoire of *bartamān-panthīs*, a more dominant model for those on the path of *bartamān* (by no means confined to them) is that of working persistently and laboriously towards a particular goal (*sādhanā sādhte hay*). One sometimes hears gurus complaining of their disciples' laziness: 'one has to work, one has to make efforts' (*karma karte hay, pariśram karte hay*). The term *karma* is most often used by *bartamān-panthīs* to refer to effective action, which for them means esoteric practice. It thus comes to mean sexual practices,[6] or indeed sexual intercourse in general, for this is the arena in which the man lives or dies. One practitioner, when asked the identity of his 'house' (*ghar* – a rough equivalent to 'line') replied: 'Those who labour efficiently in esoteric practice (*karmer karmī*) are of my house.' Emphasis is frequently placed on practice (*abhyās yoga*) – this being one way practitioners demystify their achievements and devalue guru–disciple hierarchies. Similarly, the analogy whereby progress in esoteric practice is likened to that in school – one has to work to pass one's exams, and only then can one be promoted to the next class, and so on – may be relatively modern, but its great popularity betokens new clothing for an old concept. Here again the main emphasis is on persistence and diligence. In these contexts, the guru is cast

[4] This is a world of sublimation and fixation, of prevention and making up of loss (*kṣay*), of the production of elixirs, the thickening and refining of substance, and of the transmutation of the gross body into gold, thus rendering it free of disease, decay and death (D. G. White 1995). For example, in a process analogous to the transformation of base metal into gold, first menstrual fluids, or potent drop(s) therefrom, are thought capable of transforming the male practitioner's mortal body into a golden, that is deathless, body (see also Jhā 1985:511).

[5] In fact, as the *HYP* reveals, *yogīs* and *bartamān-panthīs* share many practices in common, especially the various *mudrās*: *mūlabandha, vajroli* and so on.

[6] 'Sexual *sādhanā*' refers to a variety of erotic practices, for example, sexo-yoga (usually involving the use of breath), ritualised intercourse (often entailing the 'divinisation' of the partner), etc.

in the Buddhist mould as one who simply shows the way. It is true that speaking of grace (*kṛpā*) often has the power to impress: it shows modesty, for one is giving credit to another rather than one's own efforts. It may also move others deeply, perhaps because of its connotations of the pure gift; and men usually conceive of women as giving grace. The notion of the pure gift, and the love from which it arises, contrasts with that of calculated exchange (*kenā-becā*, literally 'buying and selling' of substance). However, it is often said that without esoteric practice there is no grace – in one sense it has to be earned. Thus *kṛpā* may be equated with *k̲ar̲e p̲ā̲oyā* (to receive, having acted), and those who speak in terms of many lives may rationalise this life's *kṛpā* in terms of *karma* of a past life or lives. Here, as in other contexts, an emphasis on the comparative autonomy of the practitioner in contrast to the general tone of orthodox Vaishnavism and Islam is notable.

The tension between the notion of non-discrimination on the one hand, and that of differentiation according to degree of realisation on the other (discussed in relation to the *mānuṣ* concept, p. 160) is most acute in relation to *bartamān-panthī sādhanā*. In the initial stages of esoteric practice, dietary and other restrictions establish degrees of separation from others, and progress on the path is marked according to stages of accomplishment in esoteric practice. Yet, in a way parallel to the *mānuṣ* concept, the highest stage of esoteric practice, often called *siddha* (perfected), is characterised by an absence of all rules and regulations.

The path of *bartamān* is often said to be divided into four (or three) main stages: *sthūl, prabartak, sādhak* and *siddha*, a notion which is lambasted as un-Vaishnava in anti-Bāul tracts (e.g. Dās Brahmacārī 1389 [I]:3). *Sthūl*, which means 'gross', signifies either the stage before esoteric practice begins (in which case it is associated with the uninitiated – *jīb*), or the first stage of esoteric practice itself. In the former case, *sthūl* may be omitted from consideration leaving the other three stages (*BBBG*:111, 405; P. Das 1988:82ff.). An illustration of the great variety there is in practice is that some gurus initially prescribe (along with a period of celibacy) such practices as *prāṇāyām* and even *mantra*, while others may begin directly with the esoteric 'four moons' practice (see chapter 10), usually practised alone at this initial stage. Both of these may be conceived of in terms of purification of the body (*deha-śodhan*) in readiness for subsequent practices. *Prabartak* (which means 'beginning' or 'establishing') is followed by *sādhak* (literally 'endeavouring to achieve an end') and then *siddha* ('perfected', 'realised'). The class of practices known as *yugal sādhanā* (joint esoteric practice, with a partner of the opposite sex) usually begins in *prabartak* (the end of *prabartak*, in the case of there being only three stages) and continues through *sādhak* until one is *siddha*. There is great variety in the prescription of the 'four moons' practices. As stated above, they may be given at the initial stage, while, at the other extreme, some gurus reserve these practices (unless *rajaḥ sādhanā* is included in the four-moons) until the very end, if at all.[7] Like the popular analogy of classes at school, the initiate perfects

[7] *Rajaḥ* (menstrual and other female sexual fluids) is one of the four moons, and is included in four moons esoteric practice by Jha (1995). However, many Vaishnava *bartamān-panthīs* who concede the centrality of *rajaḥ-sādhanā* deny the necessity of 'four moons practice'.

one stage and thus leaves it behind for the next. Each of the four divisions of this classification is technically susceptible to subdivision into four identically named stages, for example, the gross part of the gross stage (*sthūler sthūl*), the beginning part of the gross stage (*sthūler prabartak*), and so on, although such elaboration tends to occur only when the original three or fourfold division is found wanting in subtlety, and especially in the context of establishing superiority over others in discussion. Thus I have never heard anyone capable of (in other words, interested in) an elaboration of all sixteen stages. Nor, as pointed out above, are the stages elaborated in the same way. The artificiality of the basic fourfold division is also apparent in many contexts, as is that of the 'Āul, Bāul, Darbeś, Sā̃i' series, which in some senses parallels it (see p. 113).[8]

A simpler classification of esoteric practice, popular with Rāj and his followers, is the threefold division: *ātmatattva*, *paratattva* and *gurutattva*. *Tattva* means 'theory', 'knowledge' or 'truth', *ātma* means 'self' (or 'Self'), and *par* means a 'stranger', 'another', 'woman' or 'God'. The conventionally devout would read this triad as 'knowledge of the Self', 'God' and 'the Guru' respectively. To (male) *bartamān-panthīs*, *ātmatattva* refers to knowledge of the self in the sense of the male body; this initial stage is followed by *paratattva*, that is, knowledge of the female body (of *par*). The final stage is that of *gurutattva* which, as mentioned earlier, refers to the combination of the two (male and female bodies, substances etc.). One of Rāj's most popular songs elaborates this theme: 'Bird of my mind, let me see you consider the theory of the self (*ātmatattva*) . . .'.[9] In this he likens *ātmatattva* to vowels, *paratattva* to consonants, and *gurutattva* to compound or conjunct letters, which in this context means consonant and vowel joined together (cf. Gupta *et al.* 1979:105). The primary point of this analogy is the inseparability of the two, which is indeed the case in Bengali orthography.

Initiation is taken for various reasons. Before the advent of contraception, at any rate, a primary motive seems to have been prevention of the birth of further children.[10] It is widely known that the gurus possess the secret of both the suppression and enhancement of fertility, for knowledge of conception is also knowledge of contraception. Many years ago, R.N., B.G.'s wife, persuaded her husband that they should take initiation with a suitable guru in order to stop having children. Even nowadays, opposition to the most easily available contraceptive method

[8] To quote a textual example, four out of the five chapters into which Dīn Śarat divides his Bāul songs are called *sthūl, prabarttak, sādhak* and *siddhi* respectively, but as the writer of the foreword asserts, this is clearly an imposition (Nath 1341 BS:ḍ).

[9] Rāj-kṛṣṇa (song no. 93): '*Ātmatattva bicār kara dekhi ore man pākhi* . . .', transcribed with some errors (including the replacement of the idiograph 'Rāj-kṛṣṇa' by 'Rām-kṛṣṇa') in *BBBG*:844.

[10] In the rural areas around Santiniketan, I was struck by the fact that well-educated householders and sometimes even doctors had no knowledge of fertility in relation to the menstrual cycle. Indeed, many thought that the menstruation was the fertile period. On the other hand, *bartamān-panthīs* normally have an extremely accurate grasp of such matters. For example, the method of assessing fertility from the viscosity of vaginal secretion (also favoured by the Roman Catholic hierarchy) is well known to *bartamān-panthīs*, whose coded phrase for it is '*nāl dekhā*' (inspection of the 'saliva'). This phrase conventionally refers to a similar test for the transformation of sugar-cane juice into molasses.

(sterilisation) is widespread, especially among initiates, largely on grounds of the undesirability of blocking the flow of substance in the channels *(nāṛis)* in the body. Other reasons for taking initiation include a desire to understand the meaning of the songs, or being impressed by a guru's ability to render comprehensible obscure or apparently meaningless scripture. Some wish to experience the bliss (*ānanda*) of which so many *bartamān-panthīs* speak. Other presumed benefits of the path of *bartamān* include the cultivation of a strong healthy body, long life or even immortality.

As remarked above, a significant characteristic of the *siddha* stage (or in the sixteenfold scheme, *siddher siddha*) is that of transcending all norms and contexts. *Siddha* has the same connotations in Tantra (Gupta *et al.* 1979:156). Before reaching that stage, rules are often prescribed to *bartamān-panthī* initiates. For example, if an initiate partakes of certain 'heating' foods (such as eggs, meat or alcohol) during the initial stages, it is thought that the semen is more likely to be spilled during esoteric practice.[11] Similarly, the conventional idea that the qualities of the giver[12] are transmitted to the recipient often precipitates different kinds and degrees of incipient hierarchy, as seen in practices such as only eating from renouncers, or only from one's own guru-kin. Not infrequently, practitioners who continue to live with their uninitiated relatives refuse to eat from and with them. (This is one way in which one's own people become 'other'.) However, in contrast to convention, the notion of the transfer of qualities is not elaborated in such a way as to demarcate distinctions of caste or religious community, but most often with regard to whether or not a person is 'dead' or 'alive'. As the saying goes: 'the touch of the dead increases the tendency to die' ('the dead' here referring to those whose tendency is to lose substance, that is, chiefly, semen). There are similar rules concerning whom one may do esoteric practice with, some advocating complete restriction to one partner (*ekaniṣṭhatā*), and others (male) recommending one, two or even three of the four types of women as suitable.[13] It is widely thought that all such rules become irrelevant once one has reached the final stage of *siddha*. With the achievement of *siddhi*, the esoteric practice is said to become part of one's 'nature' (*svabhāb*). The arduous path of esoteric practice has thus become *sahaj* (easy or natural), a state at times associated with womanhood (see p. 160).

[11] Fish, for a variety of reasons, is considered to be beneficial, and is classified by *bartamān-panthīs* as 'cooling'. While alcohol is considered 'heating' and, as a fluid, 'downward-moving' (*nimnagāmī*), ganja is seen as 'cooling' and, as smoked, 'upward-moving' (*ūrdhvagāmī*).

[12] For *bartamān-panthīs* 'giving' includes persons who cook or serve food, but also those with whom one has sexual intercourse, or whose bodily products one ingests or otherwise applies to the body.

[13] In descending order, these are *padminī* (lotus), *citrinī, saṅkhinī* (serpent) and *hastinī* (elephant), generally considered dangerous except for those who are *siddha*. The first two are usually considered best. Some say only the *aśva* (horse) male can do *sādhanā* with *saṅkhinī*. There are also four types of male, but less emphasis is placed on them, since, as one guru told me: 'The man wants to know about the woman, because it is the man who is in danger [of losing his (seminal) substance]. The woman doesn't have to ask such questions.' The idea of compatibility between types, rather than one (or two) types of woman being best for all kinds of man, is drawn on especially when those on the *bartamān* path are required, as experts in sexual matters, to advise on marriage partners for uninitiated householders. These types are also subject to glosses by those in *bartamān* which differ from those of the Kāmaśāstra, classical texts on the erotic arts.

Maṇi's disciples considered him to have achieved such a stage. Blatantly indiscriminate about both the food and the giver, he would exclaim: 'The stomach is a fire. It will consume whatever you give. The question is not whether I can eat your food, but whether you can feed me!' The combination of Maṇi's general advocacy of sexual restriction (to one partner) and total absence of food restrictions, compares interestingly with the habit of another *bartamān-panthī* acquaintance who claims to be indiscriminate about women (and their fluids), but refuses to accept water or cooked food from anyone but his wife. These two extremes – most initiates fall somewhere in between – illustrate the wide variety in *bartamān-panthī* practice.

It is not only at the stage of *siddha* that simplistic oppositions of nature and culture are inappropriate (cf. Ramanujan 1990:50). *Bartamān-panthī* gurus frequently exhort their disciples to imitate nature, and especially animals, in their cultivation of esoteric practice. A guru told me: 'One comes into the world naked, one goes naked and one does *sādhan-bhajan* naked.' Practices presented by *bartamān-panthīs* as natural are often those most repulsive, and least natural, by householder standards: for example, sexual intercourse during the woman's menstrual period, prolongation of sexual union, oral sex, consumption of urine, faeces and other fluids. It often seemed to me that this emphasis on the natural was a way of persuading initiates that such practices are deviant only by narrow conventional standards.

It is highly unlikely that any individual initiate or couple could ever accomplish the wide variety of practices which *bartamān-panthī sādhanā* comprises. As mentioned above, these tend to be classified into a few overlapping categories: sexual practices (*yugal sādhanā*) of which control over seminal emission is a vital component for the male, and where prolonged intercourse may be emphasised; practices associated with the three days' menstrual flow, especially that of 'catching' the 'uncatchable person' (*adhar-mānuṣ dharā*) or the 'natural person' (*sahaj mānuṣ*); practices associated with the ingestion, absorption and exchange of substances, especially exudations of the body, most notably the 'four moons' (*cāri-candra*), usually glossed as urine, faeces, menstrual fluids and semen (or other fluids generated in intercourse) – these four may be extended to include all exudations of the body. One or more spheres of experience may be cultivated: emphasis may be placed on transmutation of substance according to the principles of physiological alchemy, on manipulation and relocation of substance through the breath, on exploration of the sensuous (or sensual) aspects of substance, or its emotional or even aesthetic dimensions.

Yugal sādhanā

Yugal-sādhanā ('joint' practices involving a man and woman together, as opposed to a lone individual) is an essential component of *bartamān-panthī* practice. Within *yugal-sādhanā,* it is considered essential for the man to learn control over seminal emission. What Joseph Needham terms 'coitus reservatus', 'coitus convervatus' and 'coitus thesauratus' may all apply in the case of *bartamān-panthīs* (1983:199d). The term 'coitus reservatus' is used here as an inclusive term to cover these and other practices of seminal retention in sexual intercourse.[14] Genital intercourse, as opposed to other forms of eroticism, is advocated at and for varying periods. It is sometimes said that intercourse of this kind is permissible only during the woman's menstruation. Alternatively it may be allowed during the fourteen days which follow the three days of the menstruation (*BBBG*:405). In general, those times prescribed by scripture for the conception of children are scrupulously avoided. Sometimes restraint is advocated – excessively long practice being regarded as counter-productive or ultimately harmful. At other times, prolonged intercourse (without ejaculation of the male) at any time will be advocated. Those who recommend regular intercourse only during the menstruation usually advocate other kinds of erotic practice at other times, certainly in the initial stages of esoteric practice. In short, there are many variations. Attempts are sometimes made to accommodate these within the framework of three, four (or sixteen) stages, but my impression is that there is little uniformity in the way this is effected.

Especially in manuscripts, such practices may be framed by various rituals and mantras. For example, cultivation of the perception of the partner as Rādhā or Kṛṣṇa, Gaurī or Śiva, and so on, may be recommended. The attribution (or realisation) of 'divinity' to the partner is one meaning of the term *āropa*. Thus, as in Rāj's text, instructions may be given for bathing, dressing and decorating the various parts of the body of the female partner with different *mantras*, as well as worshipping her on the pattern of *pūjā* to an image (Text A:270, see p. 180 above). There is a clear relation to Tantric practices here (see Gupta *et al.* 1979:154–5, Shaw 1994:32, Bharati 1970:264–5). In Rāj's text, there are also *mantras* for embracing, for thrusting the *liṅga* into the *yoni*, for arresting the sudden descent of the semen and so forth (Text A:272). While texts vary considerably, it is significant that they tend to emphasise the aspects of ritual and mantra. Although a sequence of practices may be apparent from a text, if only because the mantras are prescribed as accompaniments of certain actions, these written accounts clearly form an optional supplement to essential oral instructions. While ritual techniques may be used to intensify and refine the erotic experience (primary *bartamān-panthī* aims), many gurus regard them simply as a way to distract the beginner's mind and save the (typically male) practitioner from seminal loss. Indeed, more often than not, gurus seemed to be unfamiliar with written material of this kind, even when presenting it to me themselves. This was in striking contrast with their confidence when it came to oral instruction concerning esoteric practice. Such textual material is variably viewed as providing a protective religious veneer for *bartamān-panthī* practices, as enhancing and transforming the sexual act for those conditioned in a particular way, and – the opposite view – as a

[14] Coitus interruptus (withdrawal and external ejaculation) is sometimes conceded to beginners as a damage-limitation exercise. The semen may then be consumed, singly or mixed with other fluids, or applied to the body.

means of distracting the unsteady mind and preventing the uncontrolled flight towards death (seminal emission), rudimentary respiratory techniques also being used for this purpose. It is clearly of little significance to many, probably most, *bartamān-panthīs*.

In contrast to often cavalier attitudes to rituals, mantras and respiratory techniques, the matter of preventing seminal loss is treated with the utmost seriousness. On one occasion, the assertion of a guru with whom I was working to the effect that all men realise the debilitating effects of seminal emission provoked me into the unwise remark that my husband enjoyed his! When the guru subsequently came to tea at our house, this normally reticent and courteous individual omitted even to say hello or sit down before accosting my bemused spouse (whom he was meeting for the first time) with urgent requests to reform his ways, to understand the relation between seminal loss and general decline, mental and physical ill-health and death of the body. This same guru reduced *mantra* (the *kām-gāyatrī*) and *prāṇāyām* to a means of distracting the mind and keeping the body cool (*ṭhāṇḍā*) during intercourse. Although he spoke of the importance of ensuring that the breath is passing through the left nostril (or, even better, both nostrils), for otherwise 'death' is inevitable, he also emphasised the consumption of the mixed urine after intercourse (thought to contain semen) and laid most stress on practice (*abhyās*). For the majority of gurus the man's ability to retain semen is a matter of practice (*abhyās-yog*), although the grace of the woman partner, who has the power to grant life or death, is often considered crucial. A Muslim *bartamān-panthī*, emphasising that practice is the most important factor in seminal retention (*bastu-rakṣā*), quoted: 'It can't be retained through *tantra* or *mantra*' (*tantre mantre yāy nā dharā*).

The identification of the semen (or generative fluids) with the 'I' (*āmi*) and the Self/self (*ātmā/ātma*) was discussed on p. 189. Maṇi's statement 'I am *bīj*, I am *rajaḥ*' alternates with 'I am within *bīj*.' Along the same lines as Duddu, N.G., a disciple of Maṇi who took *bhek* from another 'line', declared that the self (*ātma*) is substance (*bastu*), and that one's *dharma* is to preserve substance – he glossed *dharma* as *dhāraṇ karā* (to retain) – and the context made it clear that the reference was to retention of seminal fluid. The generative fluids are similarly identified or closely associated with the absolute (*brahma*) and the 'supreme being' (*paramātmā*). Of hundreds of similar statements the following song, quoted by a senior '*darbeś*' guru of Rarh, may be cited.

> The one who practises *brahmacarya*[15] will recognise *cintāmaṇi* [the philosopher's stone, God].
> If he doesn't lose his semen, he will be able to see (it) day and night.
> Rādhāpada Gõsāi [the guru] says: truly semen is *brahma*,
> Kṛṣṇa Dās [composer and disciple] your body is bursting open, you are losing your *brahma* substance.

[15] *Brahmacarya* (abstinence from generative intercourse), conventionally interpreted as the first (and celibate) stage of the four stages of life, is routinely glossed by *bartamān-panthīs* as the practice of retention of semen (*brahma*) within *yugal-sādhanā*.

Brahmacarya karen yini, tini-i cinben cintāmaṇi
Dekhte pāben din rajanī, nā hay yadi śukra kṣay.
Rādhāpada Gōsāi raṭe, ye śukra se brahma baṭe,
Kṛṣṇa Dās tor deha pheṭe, brahma bastu kṣay hacche.

Another established guru of the same area stated: 'The essence of life is semen. We are lustful (*kāmuk*) and don't understand this fact and so waste it. The *paramātma* is in the form of semen (*śukra*). This is the theory of substance (*bastu-tattva*).'

The non-dualistic ramifications of the assimilation of *bīj* (or generative fluids in general) with *ātmā, brahma* and/or *paramātmā* are drawn out in the following argument advanced by a guru of Rarh: 'From food one becomes full (*puraṇ*), and on the other side of the balance there is loss (*haraṇ*) [through losing one's *bastu* in various ways]. In this respect no one is rich or poor. Everyone has the same wealth (*sampatti*). One is rich or poor according to *karma*.' D.G., a disciple of Maṇi Gōsāi from Bagri and himself a guru, used a similar model to reach seemingly different conclusions:

It works like this – I am poor and eat little, so I must think of retaining and utilising my food as efficiently as possible. This is preservation of the body (*deha rakṣā*), preservation of the self (*ātma-rakṣā*). I must calculate my incomings and outgoings. If the body is in good condition, everything else will also be in good condition . . . It's a matter of income and expenditure (*āy-byāy*). Children are the main expenditure here [of semen],[16] and besides the cause of so much worry later. Retention leads to health and longevity, for disease arises from want of semen (*dhātur abhāb*). While ejaculation should gradually be decreased, at a certain stage intercourse without ejaculation should be increased as much as possible.

Despite the implication that seminal retention is a strategy of the poor and malnourished, in practice this guru emphasised the importance of seminal retention to all his disciples, rich and poor alike.

The idea that semen, and indeed other substances emerging from the body, are products of food, and may also be treated as food themselves, will be considered in chapter 10. Here two main ideas about the formation of vital essence are of note: first, that individuals are born with a certain amount of 'capital' from their parents which should not be frittered away, and secondly, that vital essence is the most refined product of food. *Bartamān-panthīs* also hold various opinions on matters such as the whereabouts of semen outside the act of sexual intercourse (usually thought to be at the top of the head, or dispersed throughout the body), its relation to *rajaḥ* and female sexual fluids, etc. Whatever their views on these matters, the general desirability of preserving, or at least controlling, seminal essence is assumed, in common with many non-*bartamān-panthīs* of South Asia (Carstairs 1970:83ff.). The assumption is, as Cantlie puts it, that 'using' is 'using up' (1977:255), and opinions differ as to whether the resulting deficit is irretrievable

[16] There is a general idea that the seminal loss which results in the creation of a child is far greater than the one ejaculation needed for conception. This relates to the idea that the foetus requires to be nourished with further seminal emissions.

or can be reclaimed or made up in other ways.[17] Where *bartamān-panthīs* differ from most others is in their conviction that retention of vital essence can only, or at least most effectively, be achieved with a female partner. (As pointed out earlier, there is also the idea that women can even make up the loss.) It is sometimes said that the seminal fluid must be induced to descend to be heated on the fire of sexual intercourse with the woman. Here *bartamān-panthīs* may use metaphors of churning or stirring, as in the processes of thickening sugar-cane juice or preparing sweetmeats (*raser bhiyān, raser pāk*) over a fire. Alternatively, an analogy may be drawn with the process of alchemical sublimation, in which heat applied to the vessel containing the fluid (semen) either refines the latter, or produces a vapour, which subsequently forms a solid on cooling – in the head. Another alchemical notion availed of is that of 'fixation' (or 'killing'), where mercury (*pārad* or *ras*), that is semen, is 'killed' (made solid and immovable) with sulphur (*gandhak*), that is, the woman (cf. Eliade 1962:133ff.). Śiva and Gaurī are associated with mercury and sulphur respectively.

Bartamān-panthīs are familiar with and avail themselves of the well-known and prestigious physiological model (associated with Yoga, Tantra and the Nāths) of the individual body as the microcosm, according to which the male aspect (Śiva or *puruṣ*) is located at the top of the head, and the female aspect (Śakti or *prakṛti*) in the genital region. Typically associated with this is the system of *cakras* (plexuses where the three main channels meet), the *nāṛis* (a network of channels, three of which are most significant), and the *kulakuṇḍalinī*, dormant energy visualised as a coiled serpent. The desired awakening and upward progress of the *kuṇḍalinī* through the central channel and each *cakra* may be conflated with the notion of a reverse or upward flow[18] of the seminal essence. (This assimilation of the female aspect (*śakti* and the *kuṇḍalinī*) with the *śukra* (semen), which, for *bartamān-panthīs*, represents primarily the male aspect, will be considered further below.) At any rate, both notions usually involve the regressive unification of male and female aspects, and a reversal of the normal downward flow of physiological creation. This is one meaning of the term *ulṭā-sādhanā* (reverse, or regressive *sādhanā*) or *ujān-sādhanā* (the practice of proceeding upstream, against the current). These matters will be considered further below. For the present, it should be noted that there are far more variations of this model than proponents of 'authorised' versions care to admit.[19] This is all the more the case if the matter is viewed from an historical perspective (S. B. Dasgupta 1969:91ff., 120–1, 229ff., 235ff.) and *a*

[17] This in turn relates to other issues, such as the inevitability or otherwise of the death of the physical body, and the loss of vital essence (*bastu*) through other excretions of the body. Whether or not a man can reclaim spent seminal fluid is a matter of disagreement among *bartamān-panthīs* (see below).

[18] These may be variations, rather than different ways of expressing the same concept. Thus the former suggests a model where the semen is originally stored in the head (see O'Flaherty 1980b:46), whereas the latter draws up semen produced in some other way.

[19] For an account of the more 'authorised' version, which does note variations within Tantric texts, see Gupta *et al.* 1979:168–9, 170ff.

fortiori from that of *bartamān-panthīs* (R. P. Das 1992:396ff.).[20] At this juncture too, the obvious point should be made here that seminal retention is not invariably associated with the upward flow of vital essence. Where it is, this is not necessarily on the pattern of the yogic model, as, for example, in the model of alchemical sublimation outlined above. *Bartamān-panthīs* often refer to the male and female partners as representing 'half' (*ādh*) each. While the ultimate aim is to unite these two, the first concern of the male partner is at least to retain – or reclaim – his half, that is, his seminal essence.

The question of loss or retention of substance was considered earlier in relation to the triad *jīb, īśvar* and *mānuṣ*, meaning literally (ordinary) living beings, gods and human beings (p. 158). These connotations emerge even more clearly in a parallel triad: *ṭal, aṭal* and *suṭal*. Here *ṭal* (representing the condition of uninitiated, typically male, householders) refers to the 'fall', 'dislocation' or loss of vital essence. *Aṭal* (meaning literally 'unmoved' or 'steady', and associated with god – *īśvar*) has two possible meanings, which in turn determine the definition of *suṭal*. This term may have been coined by *bartamān-panthīs* to mean 'movement (or emission) for a good purpose, or in a good way'. One connotation of *aṭal* is desirelessness (and thus practice without a partner – *ekak-sādhanā*), in which case *suṭal* tends to mean intercourse without ejaculation of semen (coitus reservatus). B.G., a disciple of Maṇi, followed his guru in the practice mentioned earlier called *behāl-sādhanā* (pp. 11, 134). B.G. remarked that he felt absolutely no desire during the twelve years of this practice. 'This is the *sādhanā* of *īśvar. Jīb, īśvar, mānuṣ* – in this last it (seminal fluid) comes down, and sometimes even mixes (with female fluids).' Alternatively, *aṭal* may itself refer to intercourse with retention – for *īśvar* does not lose substance. In this case *suṭal*, if advocated,[21] refers to emission of substance of some kind. Despite their tendency to publicly deplore any seminal emission, in fact many *bartamān-panthīs* secretly advocate the occasional practice of *suṭal* in this sense (see also *BBBG*:397–8). For male practitioners the goal is control over seminal emission rather than total retention. Emission of some kind is often required at some stage during the menstruation of the woman (the timing and type varies). Many reasons are given for this practice, for example, to obtain something in exchange from the woman, or simply to give for her benefit, or, indeed, one's own – it is sometimes said that total retention eventually renders a man impotent and unable to continue esoteric practice. However that may be, the capacity for total seminal retention seems to be considered an essential qualification for further practice. The tension between *aṭal* and *suṭal* is sometimes reflected in the relative importance attributed to the *sahasrār* and *ājñā cakras* respectively,[22] and indeed to a broader philosophical debate between non-dualism and various sorts of dualism.

20 The beauty of this model (or models) is that it lends itself to a multitude of glosses on different levels. Here I have deliberately excluded those glosses which *bartamān-panthīs* rarely use.

21 Some practitioners seem only to be familiar with a *ṭal–aṭal* dyad. Others add further terms (in addition to *suṭal*), such as *ṭalāṭal* (combining *ṭal* and *aṭal*). In general, I found the *jīb-īśvar-mānuṣ* triad less susceptible to atrophy, addition and variation than the corresponding *ṭal-aṭal-suṭal* triad.

22 The two highest plexuses of the yogic model discussed here, usually located at the crown of the head and at a point behind the centre of the forehead respectively. For problems concerning these two plexuses, see R. P. Das 1992:396–7.

Interesting though it is in the present context, Bharati's broad association of seminal retention with Buddhist Tantra on the one hand, and ultimate seminal emission (on the pattern of ritual oblations into the sacrificial fire) with Hindu Tantra on the other (1970:265–6), probably obscures the more likely possibility of a tension between these two practices in each tradition. (See Shaw 1994:159–62 for the Tantric Buddhist aspects of this matter.)

Lest it be thought that the male practitioner is only concerned with preserving his own substance, or even increasing or supplementing it through gifts or opportunistic theft from his partner, it should be pointed out that another reason for *coitus reservatus* is frequently expressed. This is the cultivation of extreme and limitless joy in union, an experience which would be arrested by ejaculation.[23] Indeed it is sometimes said that the aim of these practices is to establish the intense and refined joy (*ānanda*) of union in the body on a permanent basis, even outside the context of physical union itself.[24]

It will be recalled (see p. 171) that *bartamān-panthīs* postulate two alternatives to the multiplicity of conventional birth groups (*jāt*): either that there are only two, namely male and female (*puruṣ* and *prakṛti*), or that there is only one, that is the human being (*mānuṣ*). This ambiguity towards women – are they 'self' or 'other' – is reflected in the context of esoteric practice, where they may be cast in the same mould as men (all are *mānuṣ*), and/or as fundamentally different from men (*prakṛti* to *puruṣ*). In practice, *bartamān-panthīs* avail themselves of both these models as appropriate.

For example, women may occasionally be contrasted with men on the grounds that they do not possess seed (*bīrya*) to be lost in intercourse. More common is the notion that women are like men in that they do have seed (*bīrya*), which they too must endeavour to retain. This is a view held by many women practitioners. However, even here, *bartamān-panthīs* tend to consider either that women accomplish this more easily than men, or indeed that they are 'perfected' (*siddhā*) in this accomplishment. These notions may not be unrelated to similarities between female sexual secretions on the one hand and, on the other, those of the male after a prolonged period of *coitus reservatus*. The transparent fluid emitted by a man in such circumstances is sometimes seen as a sign of his being perfected (*siddha*). By contrast, the white colour of male orgasmic fluid is attributed to the presence of seed (*bīrya*) and indicates loss of vital essence. The fact that female secretions, orgasmic or otherwise, are transparent may be related either to the absence of female seed, or, perhaps more commonly, to a woman's ability to retain seed.[25] As

23 Ambivalence is expressed on the subject of female orgasm, because the loss of substance is not so visible, and also because this does not necessarily terminate intercourse.

24 S. B. Dasgupta identifies the search for *mahāsukh* (great happiness), associated with the Buddhist and Vaishnava Sahajiyās, not only with the practice of *yugal-sādhanā*, but also with a high valuation of women. On the other hand, the quest for physical immortality (also a strand in *bartamān-panthī* thought) is associated by Dasgupta with the Nāths, who, unlike most *bartamān-panthīs*, were misogynist in their general attitude, although prepared to use women for their own ends (1969:249–50).

25 White vaginal discharge is a source of great anxiety in rural Bengal. A whole variety of doctors, gurus and home remedies are resorted to in such cases.

seen earlier in connection with the concept of the human being (*mānuṣ*), women may be seen as 'perfected' by nature, whereas men must attain perfection through esoteric practice.

The model of women cast in the same mould as men may be elaborated into a virtual duplication of the Tantric model outlined above, where two separate individuals each have their male and female essence (albeit in different proportions). Even here, esoteric practice with a woman is advocated. Apart from the desirability of gaining the quality of being perfected (*siddha*), the male and female essences are often likened to two half-moons, which must be brought together to make the whole, that is *mānuṣ*. This model may occasionally approximate to the zero-sum game of war and theft of substance familiar from some Tantric and Taoist traditions.

Where the difference of women from men is emphasised, this revolves around the opposition (and complementarity) of seed (*bīj*) and substances associated with the menstruation (*rajaḥ*), that is, the male essence (*puruṣ sattā*) versus the female essence (*nārī sattā*). Different *bartamān-panthī* ways of accounting for the absence of seed in the transparent female orgasmic fluid have been noted above. An additional explanation is that the female seed (*bindu*) makes its appearance at the time of menstruation, rather than at orgasm. It could be argued that the common *bartamān-panthī* notion that women are more complete than men is related to a conflation of these two perspectives, so that women are conceived of as both like and different from men. For example, women may be thought both to retain their vital essence in orgasm (thus being *siddhā*), as well as having another kind of seed associated with menstruation. In relation to the 'four moons', it is usually said that women have all four (or three and a half) – that is, faeces, urine, menstrual fluids and semen (which may be half), while men have two and a half or three.

Finally, a more shadowy model should be mentioned. This inverts the first model mentioned, in that here the man is cast in the mould of the woman, rather than vice versa. For example, he too is said to possess (on some level) or to be able to develop a menstrual cycle (see R. P. Das 1992:413–14). This may be expressed in several different ways: for example, that a menstrual cycle develops along with the attainment of womanhood, or that the cycle is there in hidden form, and becomes evident with this acquisition.

Rajaḥ sādhanā

The first important point to note in the consideration of *rajaḥ sādhanā* is that *bartamān-panthī* evaluation of menstrual fluids (*rajaḥ*) is at total variance with conventional attitudes. The notion that these fluids are 'bad', polluting blood is well attested (e.g. Parry 1989:499). In Bengal, menstruating women are theoretically barred from the kitchen at this time, and sexual intercourse is strictly forbidden.[26]

[26] See Kakar (1981:93) on the horror experienced by men on 'approaching' a menstruating woman. He quotes Manu to the effect that 'the wisdom, the energy, the strength, the might and the vitality of a man who approaches a woman covered with menstrual excretions utterly perish'.

Negative attitudes towards menstruation are not confined to householders. Some orthodox renouncers construe the inevitable loss of substance each month as a sign of a woman's inferiority and incapacity to do esoteric practice, while the man is presumed to be able to arrest his seminal loss through abstinence from sexual intercourse. *Bartamān-panthīs* draw completely different readings from these biological events. Whereas the emission of male seminal fluid is considered to occur in response to the magnetic power of the woman, and is therefore a sign of weakness, the menstrual flow is construed as a manifestation of overflowing abundance. The difference between these two kinds of secretion is also seen in the regularity of the menstruation, which is said to occur naturally and of itself. The menstrual blood is thus a valuable gift and should be used appropriately. In an inversion of conventional attitudes, many *bartamān-panthīs* advocate intercourse only at the time of menstruation.[27] The author of one text cites animals as an example to be followed here, and condemns human beings as sinful for straying from this practice. He forbids the male practitioner to have intercourse with a woman (even his wife) except at this time, and specifically enjoins the couple to follow what is forbidden in scripture.[28]

The following incident is indicative of the general attitude towards menstruation. A male adept (M.D.) and I once caught sight of a woman's corpse floating down the Ganges in front of his home, which he had constructed around the tombs of other *sādhus*. Remarking on her youth and beauty, he added that she had no doubt died an untimely death because she had not given her menstrual blood to a (male) practitioner.[29] When subsequently I asked M.D. and an older adept what the woman gains from esoteric practice, the latter endorsed the common notion that the woman's role is to contribute to her male partner: 'There is nothing for the woman to gain. The woman enables the man to gain' (*Nārīr pāoyār kichu nei. Nārī puruṣ-ke pāoyāche*). M.D., however, demurred: 'Everyone is the same. Everyone gets the same thing. Love-making is the thing, and here *liṅga* and *yoni* are the same.' He proceeded to exhort me to consume my own menstrual fluids. When I enquired why women should take back in what comes out naturally, he replied, not a little impatient at my obtuseness: 'Ah! You are not feeding a child, so I am asking you to feed yourself. Eat the child's food yourself.[30] This is the very best food. From this, male and female bodies are made.' I also heard from women

[27] Shaw relates that this was a practice she found in Hindu, but not Buddhist Tantra (1994:249 n. 81).

[28] *Ṛtu binā paśu ādi gaman nā kare, Se niyam laṅghe pāpī mānab nikare.*
...
Ṛtukāl binā nahe svastrīya sparśan . . .
Ṛtukāl binā nārī saṅga nā karibe, Śāstrete niṣiddha yāhā abaśya pālibe . . . (Hārādhan n.d.:30).

[29] M.D., notorious among *bartamān-panthīs* and reviled by many ordinary householders, once confided in me that a guru needs a wide range of disciples to ensure a continual supply of substance from female disciples.

[30] Probably two ideas lie behind this statement: first, that the menstrual fluids nourish the foetus (*piṇḍa*) in the womb; secondly, the notion that breast-milk is converted menstrual blood (perhaps related to the fact that the former seems to replace the latter). This notion is not uncommon in South Asian thought (see O'Flaherty 1980b:40ff.).

practitioners that we should consume our own menstrual fluid if alone – with a partner we should share it.

The practices of the three (or four) days of the woman's menstruation are of great importance for *bartamān-panthīs*. Apart from prescribed, but not always followed, ritual accompaniments, including worship (*pūjā*) of the woman and especially her *yoni* (see above; also cf. Shaw 1994:155), this practice includes some (not necessarily all) of the following: intercourse (as pointed out above, some advocate intercourse only at this time); emission of some kind from the male (ranging from the alchemically significant few drops to full ejaculation); ingestion through the penis of the menstrual fluids or the combined fluids of male and female; the consumption of the menstrual fluids, or the combined male and female fluids, or these mixed with urine (faeces may be included to make up 'four moons'). Especially where ingestion through the man's 'lower mouth' (the penis) is concerned, the inverse position – woman above – is usually recommended. In drawing in the woman's fluids, practices using the breath (*bāyu*) may or may not be considered essential. Female fluids produced in intercourse are also highly valued, as well as menstrual fluids.[31]

A tendency to progressive interiorisation in search of essence has been noted earlier in connection with the concept of 'I' and the guru (pp. 189, 153). In the context of esoteric practice, this involves the movement from a consideration of semen as the essence of the body, to the seed within the seminal fluid, and perhaps something even within the seed. A similar tendency is found in the notion of further (progressively more refined) channels (*nāṙis*) within the *suṣumnā*, the central and most important of the bodily channels (*nāṙis*), that is, the *bajra-nāṙi, citriṇī-nāṙi,* and finally the *brahma-nāṙi* (*BBBG*:444). Where the female body is concerned, attention may shift from the menstrual fluids to the *bindu* (the vital drop), also called the 'natural' or 'uncatchable person' (*sahaj mānuṣ* or *adhar mānuṣ*), who comes floating or frolicking in the waters of the flood tide (the menstrual flow).

Here, as in the wider context of 'four moons' practices, contrary notions are found: first, transformation through absorption of as much as possible of a substance, and secondly, transformation through the ingestion of one (or a few) potent drops.[32] For example, as the essence of womanhood, as one of the 'four moons' and a nourishing food, the menstrual fluids themselves are to be ingested. Although the fluids of some kinds (or ages) of women are often thought to be more valuable that those of others, also found is the general notion that the more (of any kind) ingested the better. Alternatively, *rajaḥ-sādhanā* may be practised over a long period by a particular man and woman, one of the aims being the development of *samatā* (equilibrium or even identity) between the pair. At more advanced

---

[31] See Schoterman 1980:31–2 for similar attitudes expressed in the *Yonitantra*. Possible connections between female sexuality (and fluids) and both auspiciousness and lack of hierarchy have been explored by Marglin (1985).

[32] The latter is often compared to the action of a small amount of yoghurt starter on a much larger quantity of milk.

levels, the aim of the male practitioner may be to catch the 'uncatchable person' (*adhar mānuṣ*), the vital drop (*bindu*) which appears in the menstrual fluid at a particular time. Accounts of this process vary and timing is of the essence – although there is diversity of views concerning the appropriate time for catching the *bindu*, ranging generally from the end of the second to the fourth day.

B.G.'s account of this process, sometimes called *bindu-sādhanā,* is as follows: Women have the power of attraction, that is, the power to draw in substance. The nature of men, on the other hand, is to be attracted by women. Alternatively, it might be said that the *dharma* of the male is to lose substance, while the *dharma* of the more powerful female is to attract it into herself. This she does unfailingly except for the three days of her menstruation, during which she gives out substance rather than taking it in. This natural cycle of the woman provides the basic framework for esoteric practice. The woman has more power (*śakti*) and, as mentioned previously, is self-perfected (*svayaṅ siddhā*); and the task of the man is to become (in some sense) a woman, or at least more like a woman. For various reasons, this is only thought possible during the three days when normal bodily dynamics are reversed, and, as it is said, she becomes male. While statements by practitioners at times suggest that the male is impelled into a female mode by this volte-face of his more powerful partner, the notion generally predominates that this is rather an enabling factor, which requires control over seminal emission at the very least.[33] Indeed it is usually thought that the capacity to draw in substance from the woman is only present if equilibrium (*samatā, samaras*) has been cultivated by an individual couple, through lengthy esoteric practice together. If the equilibrium is finely tuned, he draws in precisely *because* she gives out. Rāj writes of Rājeśvar (Text A:7): 'Sometimes you are a man, sometimes a woman . . .'. Aphorisms concerning the goddess Kālī may be quoted in this connection, on the pattern of 'Kālī . . . is not only female. Sometimes she . . . emerges male',[34] an image which for *bartamān-panthīs* is associated with the 'reverse' (*biparit,* that is, woman above) posture, used especially at the time of the menstruation.[35] For *bartamān-panthīs*, the image of Śakti (or Kālī) in inverse intercourse with Śiva, as a corpse, is identified with the condition of *jiyantamarā* (the living dead), a state where no death (in both senses) is possible because one is already dead. Another often used expression is: 'Become a woman and then unite with a woman' (*prakṛti haiyā kara prakṛtir saṅga*). As

[33] On a popular level, yogic retention of semen is thought by itself to lead to feminisation, on the analogy between the phallus and the breast (*bartamān-panthīs* might be more inclined to draw an analogy between the fluids themselves). Just as the milk is produced by the female when her 'seed' (menstrual blood) is obstructed, so the yogi, in obstructing his seminal flow, develops breasts (O'Flaherty 1980b:44).

[34] '*Kālī śudhu meye nay . . . kakhono kakhono puruṣ hay.*' This version is from a devotional song by Kamalākānta Bhaṭṭācācarya (McDermott 1995:67). Similar sentiments feature in Rāmprasād's songs (e.g. Lupsa 1967:145, song no. 121).

[35] In his analysis of Indian romances (*premākhyān*), Bahl connects intrasocial sexuality (associated with the man astride posture) and the process of creation on the one hand, and, on the other, extrasocial sexuality (associated with the woman astride posture) and the reversal of the process of creation. Bahl in turn connects the latter with death and immortality, and the transformation of the participants into the state of non-duality (*advaita*) (1981:114 nn.9, 10).

Rāj exhorts in his characteristically more forceful fashion (song no. 15): 'Be a woman!' (*Meye ha nā*!).

Male Yogis and some *bartamān-panthīs* are renowned for their capacity to draw in fluid through the penis.[36] This ability, normally thought to depend on control of vital air (*bāyu*) is generally cultivated with a view to taking in female fluids and is potentially consonant with the idea of theft from the female. *Bartamān-panthīs* often accuse Tantrics and Yogis (and sometimes individual *bartamān-panthīs*) of stealing substance from reluctant women. Some *bartamān-panthīs* operate with another model, which is that the fluids will naturally flow from the female to the male. I was told: 'Just as the fluid from a full bottle will naturally run down into an empty bottle placed beneath it, so (with the inverse posture in intercourse) the fluid will naturally flow down from the woman into the man.' Whatever the precise mechanism is thought to be, the implications of this reverse (*biparit*) flow are of interest. Marglin (1982), O'Flaherty (1980b:78) and Shaw (1994:158) all infer a reversal of normal power relationships between the sexes from the reversal of the sexual fluids in 'normal' intercourse (from man to woman).

B.G. likens male and female to two half moons which together make the full moon. This full moon is *mānuṣ*, and *mānuṣ* is thus one (half plus half: man plus woman). Although *mānuṣ* is one, s/he becomes two for pleasure. In joining the two halves a new body is made, but whereas there is creation of a child (*sṛṣṭi*) if the substances unite in the woman's body, there is none if they unite in the man's.[37] An adept with a pot belly may be likened, only half in jest, to a pregnant woman. The foetus within the man represents his own immortality or that of the pair. There are clear parallels here with the so-called Vaiṣṇava Sahajiyās (Hayes 1995, 2000), as well as with Tantra, Yoga (Gupta *et al.* 1979:183) and even Taoism (J. Needham 1983:208–9).[38] As Ramanujan remarks in another context: '. . . the microcosm is both *within* and like the macrocosm, and paradoxically also contains it' (1990:51).

While the male and female essences are sometimes conceived of as half each (of the same basic substance), in the context of *bindu sādhanā* the disparity between the *bindus* of the man and woman may be stressed. Thus B.G. pointed out that, in contrast to the inextricable relationship of the male *bindu* (essential drop) and his *rati* (fluid produced in sexual intercourse), there is no such association in the case of the woman. 'On the contrary', he said, 'the menstrual fluid contains the (female) *bindu* as the white of an egg does the yolk.'[39] There are, in fact, several ways of construing the combination of the male and female parts. For example, while the

[36] See Eliade 1954:250ff.; J. Needham 1983:270, 274–5; *HYP* 3: 83–91 (Sarasvatī 1987:214ff.).

[37] For a variation on this idea, see S. N. Jhā, who reports from his field work that 'if the woman takes in the two (substances) through her mouth, or through her lower organ at the time of menstruation (when there is no conception) and draws them up into her body, she (also) can gain full life potency (*pūrṇa prāṇ śakti*)' (1985:491–2).

[38] See J. Needham (1983:84, 233) for some striking illustrations of this 'divine embryo', the 'baby boy' or, in Needham's coinage 'the enchymoma' (1983:27), in which the image of a Lohan draws aside the walls of his abdomen like a curtain, to reveal a small being or a face.

[39] This would appear to lend credence to Jhā's idea that the Rādhā-bindu is the ovum

uniting of the two half moons is often conceived in terms of the joining of two *ratis* (male and female sexual fluids), B.G., in the previous discussion, envisaged the uniting of two *bindus* differently related to *rati* in the male and female. Another important variant, included within the 'four moons' practice, is the ingestion of fluids through the (upper) mouth, rather than the lower (the *liṅga*). However, all these permutations involve, in some sense, the reversal of the creative flow of the transient world of householder life (*saṅsār*), and the recovery of wholeness.

It is of interest to compare B.G.'s version of *bindu sādhanā* as a kind of reverse conception, with that presented by the scholar and fieldworker, U. Bhaṭṭācārya. Unlike B.G.'s account, that of Bhaṭṭācārya is based on the yogic physiological model (outlined above). This typically involves a male practitioner engaged in practices without a female partner (*ekak-sādhanā*). Instead, the female aspect is incorporated and encompassed on a subordinate level, in a version of what is sometimes known as 'internal' (*marma* or *mukhya*) as opposed to the less valued 'external' (*bāhya* or *gauṇa*) intercourse.[40] In the case of Bāuls, Bhaṭṭācārya presents a duplication of this model, so that male and female practitioner are both considered to have their male aspect in the head, and their female aspect at the perineum. According to Bhaṭṭācārya's account of *bindu-sādhanā,* the male aspect (*bīj*) in the female practitioner's head is attracted each month to her female aspect (*rajaḥ*) when it reaches its acme, becomes full and overflows in the form of menstruation. The former thus descends and unites with the latter, playing in the menstrual flood tide, as the *sahaj mānuṣ* (natural person). There is some ambiguity as to whether *sahaj mānuṣ* refers to the male aspect, the male aspect during union with the female aspect, or the combined male and female aspects. At any rate, it is the *sahaj mānuṣ* which the male practitioner aims to isolate and draw within himself up to his head, where he experiences the blissful union of male and female aspects (*puruṣ* and *prakṛti*) (*BBBG*:387f., 398f.).

All this is highly problematic, as R. P. Das has pointed out (1992:408), in particular the probable overall equation of the *sahaj mānuṣ* with the woman's male aspect, which seems to entail the unlikely implication that the aim of *bindu-sādhanā* is to unite the male aspects of the man and woman (1992:408). Das's proposal that we assume that 'the Prakṛti is cranially situated in the woman just like the Puruṣa in the man . . . ' (1992:409), by no means amounts to a resolution of all difficulties, as Das himself is aware. One might mention, in particular, the implausibility of its corollary: the allocation of the woman's male aspect to her perineum. Das's statement that 'most tantrism seems to be concerned only with males' (*ibid.*) is

[40] See R. P. Das 1992:414, 403 n.103, and *BBBG*:481. Although, in this discussion, the word 'yogic' refers to those doing esoteric practice without a female partner (the normal *bartamān-panthī* usage), the identification of the model of vertical male/female polarity within one body as 'yogic' is at best an abstraction. As Briggs points out: 'In the accounts of the text-books of Haṭha Yoga, the two aspects of the discipline, that which deals wholly with matters within the physical frame, and that which involves two individuals, are so interwoven, and the shifting from one to the other is so frequent and abrupt, that it is sometimes difficult to separate them' (1938:324). In the context of Tantra, Flood remarks: 'the cosmic polarity between Śiva and . . . Śakti is reiterated both within the body and between male and female bodies' (1992:49–50).

unexceptionable. However, more probable corollaries of this focus on the male body than a fixed and elaborated reversal of the 'normal' *puruṣ-prakṛti* poles for the female, are vague, relatively undifferentiated and ultimately contradictory models of the female body. Thus the (undifferentiated) female may be seen as an adjunct to the (differentiated) male. (This is consonant with notions of women as soft, and without structures and hierarchies, particularly *jāt*.) Alternatively, it is tempting to speculate that, just as the presence of the female partner in esoteric practice undermines hierarchical guru–disciple relationships (see pp. 146–148), so it displaces the hierarchical polarity of male and female within the (male) individual on to two individual practitioners, man and woman. In other (Vaishnava) words, rather than visualising the eternal *līlā* of Rādhā and Kṛṣṇa within himself, the male practitioner becomes Kṛṣṇa to his partner's Rādhā. (Advocates of the former would cite this as confirmation that *bartamān-panthī sādhanā* operates at the gross (*sthūl*) level.) Hence the absence of the yogic model of vertical polarity in B.G.'s account, described above. Moreover, the *Bṛhat Nigam,* quoted by Bhaṭṭācārya, seems to be identifying the process of the division of the one 'self' (*ātmā*) into two male and female human beings, rather than two poles within one human being (see *BBBG*:382).

In connection with Bhaṭṭācārya's account, it should be mentioned that in some other contexts, B.G. does identify the *sahaj-mānuṣ* as the male aspect (*puruṣ*) within the woman, as Bhaṭṭācārya tends to do. Yet, as shown above, B.G.'s model of inverse conception differs fundamentally from the yogic model with its vertical *puruṣ-prakṛti* poles availed of by Bhaṭṭācārya. Moreover, in other contexts, B.G. is inclined to present the *mānuṣ* who appears on the menstrual flood-tide as female – Rādhā, or a goddess whose body or robes are of a certain hue, and so on. This provides a salutary warning not only against the assumption of clearly worked out invariant models, especially where the female body is concerned, but also, in a wider sense, against the presumption that *bartamān-panthī* terms have fixed meanings. Dyads such as *puruṣ-prakṛti* (loosely 'male-female')[41] are not only applied to different bodily dimensions, but are susceptible to various kinds of inflection, conflation and interchange. Thus the seminal essence (*bīj*) of the male is commonly known as his *śakti* (loosely, his powerful, female aspect) – parallel with its identification with the *kuṇḍalinī* (mentioned on p. 213). Significantly, a woman practitioner told me: 'The *śakti* of the man is the woman, and the *śakti* of the woman is her *śukra* (seed).' In B.G.'s account of inverse conception, the woman becomes male precisely when her female aspect, in *bartamān-panthī* terms, reaches its acme. This fluidity of reference is apparent in other contexts also. For example, alongside the classical association of moon with the male, and sun with the female is found another, where moon is identified with the ovum and sun with the seed (S. B. Dasgupta 1969:236–7). Where the application to various bodily dimensions is concerned, *puruṣ* and *prakṛti* may be identified with the top and

[41] It goes without saying that *puruṣ/prakṛti*, Śiva/Śakti and other dyads which overlap in some instances cannot be seen as identical in all contexts. However the analyst's problems are not diminished by the fact that *bartamān-panthī* practitioners themselves variously (and often variably) conflate these different dyads.

bottom of the spinal cord, and the right and left (or even left and right) of the body respectively. Relevant in the case of B.G.'s association of the *sahaj-mānuṣ* with the male aspect is the identification of *puruṣ–prakṛti* with inner–outer respectively. This is reminiscent of the *liṅga* within the *yoni*, the (typically) male child within a female womb/body, or perhaps the male sperm within the ovum (the seed and the field), etc. Thus Caitanya, and by extension all human beings, is said to be female outside and male inside, a notion related to the standard Vaishnava concept of there being only one male in the universe, that is Kṛṣṇa. Here it should be recalled that Kṛṣṇa is often used as a term for semen. Of course, in the process of their adaptation from more rigidly structured sources, the order of value of such dyads is subject to greater ambiguity. To take the case of the inner–outer dyad, at times supreme generative power is attributed to the seed (*bīj*), the drop (*bindu*) within. Here *bartamān-panthīs* are drawing not only on the conventional image of conception (the seed and the field[42]), but the presumably related alchemists' notion of the potent drop. However, according to another view, the encompassing substance has greater value: thus *bartamān-panthīs* may identify the (male) seed with *jībātmā* (the individual self), and the female essence which surrounds it with the *paramātmā* (the supreme Self; in conventional terms, God).

As discussed earlier in this volume, the presence of uniform usage would be more surprising than the lack of it. It is important not to confuse practice (*sādhanā*) and talk about practice (sometimes called *hari-kathā*), or to assume that either are uniform. Just as there may be several ways of talking about the same practice, so too the same term or metaphor may be applied to different practices.

Despite the problems inherent in Bhaṭṭācārya's account of *bindu-sādhanā*, it is significant in its attribution to women of the qualities of completeness and perhaps autonomy, which in turn are connected with their other characteristics. Thus, according to Bhaṭṭācārya's interpretation, the woman is able to unite the male and female aspects within herself, while the male is dependent on the female in this respect. As remarked in previous contexts, whereas he is doomed to uncontrolled and continual loss of his life essence, she is like the full moon, overflowing with plenty. While he is forced to calculate in terms of loss (*jīb*) and gain (*īśvar*), she simply gives, without detriment to herself and entirely outside the considerations of exchange which dominate worldly and householder life (*saṅsār*). Whereas the male suffers a state of self-alienation, which also dominates the wider body of *saṅsār*, the female represents the love of relatedness. As such, the man is forced to labour for an achievement which the woman possesses naturally. This is one possible interpretation of the following verse of the *Bṛhat Nigam* (*BBBG*:384):

> . . . I am the natural person, the essence of the adolescent girl [Rādhā];
> You are the cultivated (perfected) person, corresponding to Kṛṣṇa . . .
>
> *. . . Āmi sahaj mānuṣ hai kisuri svarūp,*
> *Tumi siddha mānuṣ hao kṛṣṇer anurūp. . .*

[42] See Inden and Nicholas 1977:52–3; O'Flaherty 1980b:29f.; Östör *et al.* 1983.

The completeness of women is emphasised in other contexts also. As mentioned earlier, it is sometimes said that they possess all 'four moons', that is, *ras* (urine), *māṭi* (faeces), *rati* (sexual/seminal fluids) and *rajaḥ* (menstrual fluids). Even alternative views, for example, that women possess three and a half moons (*rati* being counted as half plus half, according to this calculation) present them as more complete than men, who possess two and a half only. Thus the aim of the male practitioner may be construed in two different ways. He may wish to ingest either her femaleness (to unite with his maleness), or her completeness – that is, to become complete (*mānuṣ*) like her. In absorbing her female qualities, he attempts to gain not only the other half of his half-moon, but also her capacity for autonomy, for the creation of completeness (and complete life) within herself.

The model outlined by B.G. is far removed from a Freudian perspective, according to which only men are worthy of envy. Nevertheless, it could easily be argued that, through the processes described above, *bartamān-panthī* men are simply trying to appropriate the only value (powers and substances) conceded to women, for the purpose of fostering their own immortality. Indeed, in the case of certain male practitioners, I found this a compelling argument. More often, I was struck by the relatively high value, ranging from intimacy of unusual depths to reverence, displayed by male practitioners for their female partners. This emerges particularly clearly in Raj's case. The *bartamān-panthī* association of the female with power is of course shared with high Hindu culture, especially in Bengal. As argued earlier, what is significant in the *bartamān-panthī* case is that this association is often deflected from the divine sphere and applied to unidealised, human women.

10

'Four moons' practice and talking about practice

Since the class of esoteric practices known as 'four moons' *sādhanā* (*cāri-candra bhed*)[1] has been discussed in detail by S. N. Jha (1995), I propose to confine myself here to a general outline and a few specific points. Despite the endeavours of H. C. Paul (1973a) and others who have sought to spiritualise them, when *bartamān-panthīs* speak of the 'four moons' they generally mean: urine, faeces, menstrual fluids and fluids produced in sexual intercourse. The most commonly used code terms for these four are *ras, māṭi, rūp* and *rati* respectively (see Glossary). There are more variations in name than in substance. Where the latter is concerned, the idea that the four moons comprise the three days' menstrual flow and semen is sometimes found. This is susceptible to reclassification as *rajaḥ-bīj* (for other variations, see Jha 1995:88f.). Names of the 'moons' are far more varied;[2] and not all names have fixed meanings. For example, of the four mentioned above, only *māṭi* (literally 'earth') and *rūp* (literally 'form, colour, beauty') are relatively fixed, as faeces and menstrual fluids respectively. (For the remaining two terms, see *ras, rati,* and *ras-rati* in the Glossary.) The four moons are commonly identified with the four elements: earth, air, fire and water. One code word for faeces is *māṭi* (meaning earth).

The four moons are all substances which are secreted or excreted from the body, and the practices of the moons involve reassimilating these substances. This is a project manifestly in violation of conventional concerns,[3] and is not simply attributable to the commonly heard *bartamān-panthī* idea that there is nothing impure in this universe (*pṛthibite kichu-i nāpāk nei*), which itself is intimately connected with their interpretation of non-dualism (*advaita*). Apparent here are other aims encountered earlier: of reversal, reversion, regeneration and the reattainment of wholeness.

The case of Pāglī (the 'Mad Woman') illustrates some of the points at issue. A family of prosperous Muslim *bartamān-panthī* farmers of my acquaintance had

[1] *Bhed* literally means 'piercing', 'penetration', 'discrimination' etc. (see below).

[2] One of two lists in Rāj's manuscript mentions *ādya, āpta, unmat* and *garal* (Text A:276–7). In one of his songs (no. 175), Hem lists *sādhya, nij, unmād* and *garal* (see also Jha 1995:88–9). These probably refer to fluids produced in sexual intercourse, urine, faeces and menstrual fluids respectively.

[3] Parry reports that Brahmins of Benaras often represent the body as a 'sack of impurities'. He notes their preoccupation with the idea of food lying rotting in the stomach, and the need felt to eliminate this speedily (1989:500).

given refuge to a young woman of Muslim (but otherwise obscure) origin who had come across the border from Bangladesh. Pāglī, as she was known, had dishevelled hair and wore red clothes. She also carried a red trident and smoked quantities of hashish, usually in the name of Śiva. Particularly fascinating to her hosts and others was her alleged abstention from eating, drinking and (conversely) urinating and defaecating, claims which persisted even in the absence of any endorsement by Pāglī herself.[4] Other *bartamān-panthīs* to whom I presented these stories about Pāglī often reacted with scepticism or outright disbelief. Those inclined to entertain the possibility of this kind of body also tended to assume as a matter of course that Pāglī never bathed, because she would never need to. For some *bartamān-panthīs,* Pāglī seemed to embody the ideal of the autonomous body in stasis, losing none of her vital essence, even in perspiration, and therefore requiring no intake. Presumably an attempt was being made to cast her in the image of the 'living dead' (*jiyanta marā*), in one of the many senses of that term; one who, being dead (immobile, 'fixed' in the alchemical sense), is no longer subject to death.[5]

Four moons practices, in particular the use of *māṭi* (faeces), are often likened to the application of tar to a leaking boat. Yogic texts speak of the reduction in excretion from the body as a sign of an advanced practitioner (*HYP* 3: 65, Sarasvatī 1987:197). While claims to not eating, drinking, urinating or defaecating were made by (or of) no *bartamān-panthīs* of my acquaintance,[6] not a few practitioners do abstain from bathing, while apparently remaining as free from odour as those who do so daily. B.G., for example, has apparently not bathed for over twelve years and certainly did not smell. Not needing to bathe, especially in a hot country, is naturally viewed as a remarkable achievement. The issue is not necessarily that *nothing* is being secreted or excreted from the body (as alleged in Pāglī's case), but rather that what does emerge from the perfected (*siddha*) body is different from that of ordinary bodies in that it contains no vital essence. It was seen earlier (p. 215) that transparency is one of the qualities indicative of absence of 'seed' (*bīj*) in sexual secretions. Other such qualities may include lack of odour (or odour of certain kinds) and evaporation without residue. These criteria are not confined to sexual secretions; here, for example, they are applied to perspiration.

As pointed out previously, *bartamān-panthīs* may impose distinctions through interiorisation of 'essence' on arenas which in other contexts remain

4 When I came to know her, she shared tea with me on one occasion, on another a tangerine and on a third we both went off to the bushes to urinate.

5 Echoes of this basic repertoire of ideas may be discerned in male groups for whom total retention of semen and avoidance of women constitutes the ideal. The ideal celibate (*brahmacārī*) describes himself as follows:

> . . . My body smells like a lotus flower,
> My eyes glitter as the diamond-like stars;
> My body is light and *excretion scanty*.
> My voice is powerful and sweet.

From 'Song of a Brahmacārī' in *Practice of Brahmacarya*, by Svāmi Sivānanda, p. 207 (my emphasis).

6 Impossible to classify, Pāglī was not in *bartamān* by many criteria.

undifferentiated. The notion that any alienation of bodily substance entails a loss of vital essence coexists with another, which entails a gradation of substance, so that the inner essence is encompassed by derivative, secondary or more gross substance. In connection with *rajaḥ sādhanā* (p. 218), the notion of the desirability of ingesting substance in quantity (approximating to the principle of the more the better) was contrasted with that of the search for (or the sufficiency of) one or a few drops. This tension may be found in the context of the ingestion of other 'moons' also.

Contrasting notions were also noted concerning the concept of *mānuṣ* – as human beings in general or as realised human beings. In the case of the esoteric practice of the moons, a similar tension exists. Thus it is sometimes said that the four moons of human beings as such are pure and beneficial. On the other hand, categories of human being may be differentiated and graded according to various hierarchies of value. For example, the products (moons) of a woman's body may be thought more valuable than a man's, and in turn, those of a woman of a certain category (according to type or age) than those of other women; those of the guru (or *guru-mā*) or a perfected one (*siddha*) as opposed to an ordinary person, and so on (see also Jha 1995:71–2).

Not surprisingly, in view of the above, there are many variations in concept and practice. Thus the moons may be used individually or in various combinations; through internal ingestion or external application; in different orders and at various dates and times (dates normally being calculated according to the woman's menstrual cycle). One may use one's own moons, those of a particular partner, those of others, or various combinations of these. There are differences of opinion over the precise manner of usage: for example, whether the moons should be taken straight from the body (without the touch of air), whether they can or should be subjected to heat, whether they should be mixed with other (non-'moon') substances (for example, to make them more palatable), which portion is to be used, which kind of container is appropriate for their storage if any, and so on. Other variations concern accompanying dietary restrictions, and ritual, including mantra. The exact boundaries of four moons practices are difficult to determine. Jha, who takes the widest definition possible, includes within this rubric the use of one, two, three or four of the substances called 'moon', as well as their use by practitioners without partners (1995:69f.). By contrast, many initiates and non-initiates in Krishnapur understood four moons practices to refer to ingestion through the mouth of these substances, and the popular perception that Bāuls eat faeces and urine (*gu-mut*) was mentioned earlier. Many initiates do various esoteric practices concerning *rajaḥ-bīj* (that is, *rūp* and *rati*, or *ras-rati*), while strenuously denying that they practise the four-moons. Practitioners such as B.G., who tend to prescribe the use of urine and faeces only in the case of certain physical or psychological disorders, exclude this usage (and their own practice) from the category of four moons practices.[7]

[7] Evidence for the practice (or at least the prescription) of four moons esoteric practice is to be found in Rāj's writings. Hem also lists 'four moons' or rather 'four substances' (*cār bastu*) in a song, knowledge of which he evidently obtained from Rāj (see n. 2).

One might enquire why these substances should be referred to as 'moons'. Jha has quoted a passage from the *Haṭhayoga pradīpikā* in illustration of the connection between the moon (in this context, the brain) and secretion (1995:67). There is also a close relationship between the moon and water (representative of all fluid), and in turn between this element and the *bartamān-panthī* four moons as well as other substances issuing from the body, such as saliva (see Jha 1995:76, 94). As in many cultures, *bartamān-panthīs* draw a parallel between the monthly cycle of the moon and the woman's menstruation (*rajaḥ*). On the other hand, the moon is also associated with the male aspect, that is, with Śiva and his abode in the head, and with the *iṙā nāṙi* (channel) associated with the left of the body. In one sense, both semen (*śukra*) and menstrual fluids (*rajaḥ*) are thought to wax and wane like the moon (Jha 1995:74–5). Thus the moon is suggestive of themes already discussed in connection with *bartamān-panthī sādhanā,* namely the uniting of male and female, or the transcendence of such distinctions. *Bartamān-panthīs* attribute to women (and the moon) the enviable ability to regain fullness after loss (real or apparent), to wax once more after waning. Significantly, the full moon may be likened to the female *rajaḥ*, and the dark moon to the male *bīj* (Jha 1995:81–2).

Since many more than four substances issue from the body, the question arises as to why there are only four moons, and why these particular four. First, it should be noted that some practitioners do emphasise all issuents from the body. A certain guru advocated tasting the fluids (*ras*) from all the sense doors, before washing in the morning, including tears and saliva. 'This is the meaning of *rasik*', he said. 'S/he who has tasted everything is a *sādhu*.'[8] Some *bartamān-panthīs* emphasise the nectar (*amṛta*) of saliva, and some form of the associated *khecarī-mudrā*. This involves what Needham calls 'in-mission' of saliva, parallel to that of the seminal fluid,[9] in a process parallel to the interiorisation discussed above.

An important connotation of the number four, whether it be the four moons or the four elements, is that of fullness and completion. The association with completeness of women, who according to some calculations possess all four moons, was mentioned earlier. Jha relates the four moons, and their association with the four elements, with a materialist outlook, and, conversely, the tendency to extend the four elements to five (not normally called 'moon') to the influence of idealism. Thus 'ether' or 'the void' (*śūnya*) may be added to earth, air, fire and water. Among *bartamān-panthī* practitioners the fifth element may be *rajaḥ-bīj*, or *śūnya* (with reference to the female or combined male–female essence). Others derive the body and four elements from *rajaḥ-bīj*, or vice versa (Jha 1995:77–8).

Of the many exudations of the body, the four representing the totality are precisely those which naturally move downwards from the lower portion of the body. (As mentioned earlier they also move outwards from within.) Thus an important aim of four moons practices is to reverse the flow upwards and inwards. In other

[8] '*Ye sab kichu svād kareche se sādhu.*' The speaker is here punning on '*svād*' (taste) and the first syllable of '*sādhu*', indistinguishable in Bengali, as the '*v*' is not pronounced. Rasik is a term *bartamān-panthīs* sometimes use for themselves (see Glossary).

[9] J. Needham 1983:261–2, *HYP* 3: 32–54 in Sarasvatī 1987:167ff.

respects, however, these four substances are viewed as dissimilar. For example, different emphasis may be placed on their nutritional and medicinal qualities. Moreover, it is normally thought that only one substance is exclusive to women, and only one is produced in intercourse. However, in this connection, another important idea should be mentioned: namely, that the four moons (representing the four elements) become transmuted by sexual intercourse, also called the 'churning of the body' (*deha manthan*), parallel to the mythical churning of the ocean;[10] or, alternatively, that only substances thus created or transmuted constitute the four moons. Four moons practices are often referred to as *cāri-candra bhed*, literally, the 'penetrating, or discrimination' (*bhed*) of the four moons.[11] As Hess and Singh remark in connection with Kabir, in Hindi, the word *bhed* can mean 'mystery' or 'innermost secret' (1986:27). Jha has suggested that the word *bhed* may be derived, by a process of metathesis, from *bedh,* which in alchemy refers to the transmutation of base metal into gold (1995:76–7). Certainly one aim of this class of practices is to render the bodily substances immutable, and therefore immortal. Transformed and rendered immutable through esoteric practice, the four elements of the body can no longer mix with the macrocosmic four elements at death, as would happen with a 'normal' body.

There is a clear antinomian element in four moons practices (consonant with *bartamān-panthī* ideas noted earlier),[12] and indeed another shared characteristic of these four substances is the horror generally evoked, in Hindus and Muslims alike, by any suggestion of their ingestion or external application. However, this aspect should not be exaggerated. On the whole the four moons are regarded by those on the path of *bartamān* as supremely nourishing and/or medicinal, and evidence for the perceived value of these substances is frequently cited. Women initiates are well aware of the value of their bodily fluids for male practitioners. An elderly woman guru told me that the man takes menstrual fluid in his mouth and gives some to his partner: 'This is the exchange (*kenā-becā*) of the first stage (*sthūl deś*). If I have something valuable and I love someone, I want to give it to them. And if I give someone something to eat, I must take it myself too, so that he knows it is good, and not poison.' A. K. Datta noted the idea that the four moons come from the father's seed and the mother's womb and should not therefore be wasted, but taken back into the body (*BBUS*:112). In other words, they tend to be regarded as secretions (of essence), rather than excretions (of waste products) – the latter gloss would support the antinomianism of four moons practices, since it implies taking in what is meant to go out. Nor is the high valuation of the moons confined to *bartamān-panthīs*. The use of two moons (*rajaḥ* and *bīj*) is common among non-*bartamān-panthī* initiates, especially Tantrics, while the use of urine,

[10] In the mythical churning of the ocean both poison and nectar are produced. *Garal* or *biṣ*, both meaning 'poison', are found as names of one or more moon.

[11] The phrase, *ṣaṭ-cakra-bhed* (piercing of the six plexuses) is used in connection with raising the *kuṇḍalinī* through those plexuses.

[12] See p. 198–9. The emphasis on inversion is of note here: inversion of gender relations, the adoption of inverted postures in intercourse (woman astride position or oral sex), the prescription of intercourse at periods prohibited for non-initiated householders, etc.

for the enhancement of general health as well as for specific medical reasons, is not uncommon even among the uninitiated population.[13] The sight of animals and insects consuming their own moons as well as those of others of their own and different species is common in rural Bengal, and cited as justification for these practices by *bartamān-panthīs*.[14]

The perceived value of the moons is construed in different ways. As already mentioned, where one's own moons are concerned, the idea of recouping loss often predominates.[15] Another important model, especially in the case of a female partner's moons, is that of the foetus (or child) nourished by the menstrual fluids (or breast milk) of the mother. In this connection, the practitioner's identification with the essence within, the embryo of immortality created by reverse conception, should be recalled (p. 220). One mature practitioner of my acquaintance pointed out an image of the child Krishna, chubby, white and with tiny but perfectly formed genitals, as his ideal and aim in life. A child is seen as both male and female, or neither, and therefore complete,[16] and this practitioner, in the course of the same conversation, had boasted of his increasingly female body, specifically his swollen belly, somewhat pendulous breasts and decrease in body hair. Here again are ideas of the (re)attainment of balance, of wholeness, through an incorporation of female elements to balance the predominance of male elements. The notion of the incorporation of wholeness (rather than simply femaleness) was noted earlier. Yet another related idea is the development of 'equality' or 'identity' (*samatā, samaras*) between the two partners, ultimately forming one body out of the original two. The concept of nourishment (as of a child) has different parameters from the idea of the transfer of qualities. The latter, although not irrelevant in the mother–child relationship, is also applicable to the absorption of moons of any superior or possessor of desired qualities, for example the guru. Yet another rationale for the moons practices is the notion that recycling the moons ('returning' the fluid (*ras*)) leads to their thickening and refinement. As Jha observes: '*Sādhaks* sometimes remark that they have noticed from their own experience that in recycling their own *ras,* all bad smell and bitter and sour taste disappears, and instead they find a taste like the water of the young coconut.'[17] Here there are clear parallels with notions of the raising and/or revolving the vital essence

13 Mahatma Gandhi and Moraji Desai are two of the best-known practitioners. Urine and saliva are often used in rural Bengal for medicinal purposes.

14 For instance, the fairly common sight of a dog drinking the urine of a cow as it is produced may be cited as an example of the value to an inferior being of the moons of a superior being (for example, the guru, or a woman).

15 See O'Flaherty for an Upanisadic source on reclamation of spilled semen (1980b:30–1), and attitudes to the drinking of seminal fluid (1980b:51–2).

16 Urvashi Misri discusses similar ideas about children in Kashmir. A child is considered to be like God, she says. It is non-dualistic (*a-bed*), and does not discriminate between strangers and kin, self and other, male and female, right and wrong. The child is also characterised as sinless and immune to pollution (1986:128–9).

17 *Ras* here refers to urine. The following song is often cited in this connection: 'Taking the *ras* in again and again, the finest sugar will be made. The less one throws away, the thicker and finer the sugar will be' (Jha 1995:99).

within the practitioner's body, in a form increasingly dense, pure and refined, and indeed with various kinds of rotation – of air, substance and/or emotion, within one body or between two bodies (see *BBBG*:398–9, R. P. Das 1992:402–3).

The use of the moons for specific ailments, as well as for the more general 'disease of life' (*jīban byādhi* – that is, loss of vital essence) is many and varied. One often hears the view that these substances are 'cooling' (*śītal* or *su-śītal*). Even those *bartamān-panthīs*, such as B.G., who ostensibly confine themselves to the practices of menstrual fluids (*rūp*) and fluids produced in intercourse (*rati*), and reject four moons practices as such, would not deny the medical utility of urine and faeces.[18] The chief point of debate among *bartamān-panthīs* is whether or not four moons practices assist in retaining or restoring vital essence (*bastu*). While practitioners such as B.G. deny that such practices assist in retention, others, such as D.G., his brother through initiation, assert that, while retention can be learnt without four moons practices, this accomplishment is only secured (*siddha*) with it. This debate is intimately linked to another, that is, the futility or otherwise of attempting to reabsorb vital essence through the mouth once it has been lost. Hārādhan asserts that such practices are not for Vaishnavas by lineage, but for followers of Tantra. He asks rhetorically 'what sort of practice is ingesting semen (*bindu*)? If one feeds a cow with her own milk does it return to the udder? Does life return once one is dead? If the *bindu* is emitted through the four petals [the *mūlādhār cakra* at the genitals], it will not rise to the thousand petals [the *sahasrār* at the top of the head]' (Hārādhan n.d.:12–13). The author further opines that 'the practice of *rūp* (menstruation etc.) is formidable. What is the point of drinking it? Draw it up the channel of the penis by means of esoteric practice' (Hārādhan n.d.:33).

The four moons practices are rarely denied all validity even by their opponents. As mentioned earlier (p. 97), although the sage Rāmakṛṣṇa deplored the habit of 'entering the house through the lavatory', he did not dispute that it was possible to do so. Similarly R.B. had no doubt of the feasibility of 'binding Kṛṣṇa with the four moons' (p. 101). There is a widely held view that such practices preserve the body, even if the ultimate importance of such an achievement may be questioned. A few large and powerfully built men of the Krishnapur locality, one nicknamed 'The Elephant', were commonly said to have attained this enviable physique through the four moons practices, and especially the use of *māṭi*.

One explanation of the moons practices, rarely given by *bartamān-panthīs* themselves, is that they are a means to overcome aversion. Of course, this is a reason provided by those, such as Rāmakṛṣṇa, who see these substances as excreta rather than as nourishing essences. Not that like ideas are absent from the repertoire of *bartamān-panthīs*, as seen, for example, in the following mantra: 'Through this practice with faeces, aversion and calumny are destroyed' (*E māṭi sādhane, hiṅsā, nindā hay kṣay*) (Jha 1995:96). The overcoming of aversion is of course connected with the cultivation of non-discrimination. Where lack of aversion

[18] The medical aspects of four moons practices cannot be dealt with here. A. Karim (1979/80) has written something on this. Also cf. Zvelebil 1973:31.

and the cultivation of love (the opposite of discrimination and calumny) are concerned, it is tempting to draw a parallel between the positive perception and ingestion of moons (be they one's own, another's or others'),[19] and the categorisation, and, indeed rendering of 'others' (*par*) as 'one's own' (*āpan*).

Another explanation given by *bartamān-panthīs* for the esoteric practice of the moons, which rests on a (partly) negative perception of such substances, is that 'poison destroys poison' (*biṣe biṣ kṣay*). Glosses of 'poison' as 'unholy' (*hārām*) or 'impure' are of less interest, and more likely to derive from opponents, than the implication that the poison at issue is the tendency itself towards loss (or excretion). For example, the esoteric practice of the moons is sometimes said to make its practitioners infertile. To complicate matters further, an allopathic principle opposite to this homeopathic action is also envisaged, according to which the tendency towards loss is counteracted by the act of ingestion.[20]

Several themes already familiar from the *bartamān-panthī* repertoire are therefore discernible in the case of four moons esoteric practice. One major theme is the restoration of wholeness; the aim of rendering into one's own (*āpan*) what is other (*par*), noted above, may be seen as an aspect of this. Similarly, loss from the body is redeemed by reabsorbing what is lost. The whole which was divided into male and female recovers completeness – the couple share their combined substances, or take in those of the other. In addition, what comes down (through the lower part of the body) is raised up (taken in through the mouth), and what comes out is taken back in. In one sense the endeavour of initiates is thus to reverse 'natural' downward, outward and fissiparous tendencies, with their inevitable concomitants of disease, decay and death. It is understandable therefore that *bartamān-panthī sādhanā* (and especially four moons practice) is susceptible to elaboration, by adherents and opponents alike, as the cultivation of a long and healthy life. One inflection of this theme is the alchemical pursuit of the immutable, immortal, golden body, while another is the pursuit of joy (*ānanda*) where restraint is conceived as a means to full enjoyment.[21] Aware of the hazards of the pursuit of immortality, others on the path of *bartamān* stress enjoyment of the here and now (*ihabād*) instead.[22] One of the connotations of *anurāgī*, a term which *bartamān-panthīs* sometimes apply to themselves, is 'enjoyer' or 'lover' (whether it be of life, of someone or of everyone).

In so far as esoteric practice is hierarchised and ordered into stages, the sphere of *bartamān-panthī sādhanā* as such tends to become identified with the final (*siddha*) stage, the sphere of *mānuṣ* as the perfected human being which transcends all prescriptions and stages. However, viewed from another perspective,

[19] What applies to the issuents of one's own body applies *a fortiori* to those of others.

[20] Another principle sometimes expressed is the idea of each moon reinforcing or nourishing its respective element in the body. Thus: '*Ras* increases *ras, rūp rūp,* and *māṭi māṭi*' (see Jha 1995:95).

[21] S. B. Dasgupta identifies the pursuit of immortality with the celibate Nāth tradition, and the cultivation of *mahāsukh* (supreme joy) with the Mahāyāna Buddhists who specialised in sexo-yogic practices (1969:247ff.).

[22] One of the Caryāpadas expresses an opposition between those *acintya yogīs* who have no fear of death, and others who practise alchemy (*ras-rasāyaṇa*) and presumably do fear it (Rānā 1981:55).

and parallel with the emphasis on *mānuṣ* as human being in the generic sense, is the tendency for *bartamān* to be identified with the preliminary gross (*sthūl*) stage. The *bartamān-panthī* emphasis on the senses, especially sight, in contrast to other less immediate epistemological strategies, was mentioned in connection with the cathexis on the gross. Yet while challenging the hierarchical yogic model of polarity within the individual's body with the more lateral model of male and female partners in esoteric practice, the latter may nevertheless come to be thought preliminary to the former. Thus the desire for the male to become female or androgynous (i.e. complete, as the female may be seen) may amount to a desire for autonomy, in practice (not always in theory) as an individual body. (Autonomy may also be of the couple conceived as one body.) The interiorisation to essences beyond normal vision is another example of this tendency. I recall a dispute between two practitioners, both of whom claimed to be in *bartamān*, which revolved around the unusual fact that one of them had no female partner. Stung by the scorn of his older and more established companion, the lone *sādhak* embarked on a defence to the effect that a woman is only needed at the preliminary, gross stage of esoteric practice, implying that, by means undisclosed, he had transcended this stage. In exasperation the other exclaimed: 'But *bartamān* **is** the gross (*sthūl*)!'[23] It is clear that the tendency to interiorise, noted in several earlier contexts, coexists with a process of exteriorisation. While concepts such as the 'I' (*āmi*), *mānuṣ*, and the guru are subject to interiorisation (from gross to subtle realities), they may also be exteriorised (when contrasted with *anumānik* entities), as an individual person, an ordinary human being or a living guru, as opposed to an image or disembodied deity, respectively.

It has not been my concern to mark out a distinct *bartamān-panthī* arena where esoteric practice is concerned. As stated earlier, there is no clear boundary around *bartamān* esoteric practice, and, in an important sense, oversystematisation and hierarchisation of its contents leads to the negation of *bartamān* itself. This is the force of the remark quoted above, that *bartamān* is gross. And needless to say, what is here called *bartamān* merges with other local, pan-Indian and even wider traditions. (In the absence of similar research on such communities, it is impossible to assess the extent of such overlap.) However, the determination of *bartamān-panthīs* in many contexts to define themselves against Yoga and Tantra (with both of which they share many practices) is not simply a question of pitting oneself in subaltern fashion against traditions legitimised by high Hindu culture. The articulation of such differences facilitates the constant recreation of a position which may be called *bartamān*.

Talking about practice (*hari-kathā*)

The importance of distinguishing practice (*sādhanā*) from talk about practice (*hari-kathā*) was mentioned earlier. Since no discussion on esoteric practice is

[23] Both these practitioners are Muslim gurus with many disciples. In other contexts, I have heard the guru who claimed that '*bartamān* is *sthūl*' elaborate stages of the *bartamān* path.

complete without consideration of *hari-kathā* (this being the path by which esoteric practice itself is approached), a few remarks on this complex subject are pertinent here.

I was frequently told that there are only two worth-while pursuits in life: one is doing the esoteric practice and the other is talking about it. Such talk is often known as *hari-kathā*, which an outsider would gloss as 'god-talk' (literally 'talk about Hari', that is, Viṣṇu), but which, especially in Bagri, tends to mean talk about esoteric practices (*sādhanā*).[24] Like the term itself, *hari-kathā* is normally encoded. As can be imagined, the difficulties in speaking directly about esoteric practice except in an intimate relationship are immense, and there are many aphorisms exhorting secrecy. As the term *hari-kathā* indicates, much of the terminology drawn on is superficially Vaishnava. However, as was noted earlier, a more pertinent gloss on *hari-kathā* is derivable from the meaning of *hari* as 'woman'. The one who steals (*haraṇ kare*) is called Hari, and a woman's creative power is related to her ability to steal substance from men. In a song (no. 25) beginning: 'Where will you find Hari, except in your own house . . . ?' (*Hari kothā pābire khuje, rayeche tor gharer mājhe* . . .), Maṇi affirms that Hara and Hari (conventionally Śiva and Viṣṇu) are man and woman, and that 'there is no Hari apart from woman . . . (*nāri bhinna hari keu nāi* . . .). She is the bestower of liberation (*mukti-dātā*)'.

As discussed earlier, *bartamān-panthīs* emphasise direct perception rather than scriptural authority, and material substance (*bastu*) rather than words (*nām*). Yet, fortunately for the researcher, those on the path of *bartamān* enjoy words immensely, and their rhetoric is generally of a highly sophisticated order. However, it is usually emphasised that these are words and rhetoric of a particular kind. When *anumān* (the imagined, or conceived), which includes language, is based on *bartamān* (what one perceives with one's own senses) it is allowable (see p. 195).

Those in *bartamān* usually know many songs, sometimes collected from notebooks, sometimes from an oral source. Not all initiates sing, and many sing only to each other in *āśrams* or *ākhṛās*. However, the conversation and rhetorical interchanges of all *bartamān-panthīs* are in varying degrees guided and enriched by the ideas, images and structures of these often profound and hauntingly beautiful songs. In addition to songs, there are also treatises on esoteric practices, usually written in cryptically in verse, which are for recitation (or silent reading) rather than singing. Notebooks containing these are copied again and again by practitioners, often with devices for misleading any uninitiated reader who might accidentally come across them. Treatises and songs of the great gurus of the past (the *mahat*, or *mahājan*) are sometimes referred to as *śāstra* (scripture, treatise), a manoeuvre generally connected with positing a tradition even if only for a moment,

24 As usual with *bartamān-panthīs* no meanings are finally fixed. A guru I met in Rarh distinguished *hari-kathā* and *sādhu-kathā*, the former being talk of God (Hari), the latter (literally 'talk of the perfected ones') being concerned with living human beings (or human beings in *bartamān* – '*bartamāner mānab kathā*').

and with the intent to remove such songs from the possibility of amendment or criticism.

Bartamān-panthīs tend also to be familiar with a host of stories and myths, classical and folk, which they are adept at interpreting at various levels. To the annoyance of the more conventional, scriptural stories and theories are often so competently appropriated by *bartamān-panthīs*, that their glosses seem far more convincing, even to me, than the usual ones.[25] *Bartamān-panthīs* use the language of conventional religiosity (Hindu and Muslim) partly to legitimise and partly to conceal esoteric practices. However, whereas *bartamān-panthīs* of Muslim background are familiar with Hindu as well as Muslim rhetoric, Hindu *bartamān-panthīs* develop their own skills within the range of Hindu sectarian discourse, especially Vaishnava and Shakta. Thus, on the whole, Muslim *bartamān-panthīs* have a greater competence in the Hindu repertoire, in addition to the Islamic, than vice versa. This is perhaps a function of the minority status of Muslims in the state of West Bengal. At times, the discourse of conventional religiosity thus appropriated exacts its own price. As corrections in Rāj's manuscript reveal, the radical edge of some of his songs was lost in their being rendered acceptably Vaishnava in style. Lack of fit between the conventional phrases and *bartamān-panthī* meanings may necessitate either an elaboration of meanings (where one word has to serve several different purposes) or a reduction of meanings (where several words all mean the same thing). Meanings may in part be moulded by a story-line which proceeds in ways not always conducive to the *bartamān-panthī* exegesis. More seriously, especially in unmixed (Hindu or Muslim) lineages, *bartamān-panthī* thought and practice may in some respects come to diverge along Hindu and Muslim lines.

In *bartamān-panthī* glosses a tendency to dispose unceremoniously of the deities, saints, symbols and other appurtenances of orthodox (*anumānik*) religion is prevalent. To select at random from thousands of examples in my notes: Caitanya (the founder of Bengali Vaishnavism) may be variously treated as a historical figure, or as enlightened consciousness (the literal meaning of the word is 'consciousness'). Alternatively, Caitanya may be taken to refer to 'woman', or 'the menstruation' or even 'the erect *liṅga*' (which has become 'conscious'). The five great saints (the *pañcatattva*) of Bengali Vaishnavism are subject to any number of such interpretations. Nor are Allah and Mahammad immune from such treatment, although, as pointed out above, it is Muslim *bartamān-panthīs* who are more familiar with the original sources and therefore more talented in this sphere. B.G. was only momentarily disconcerted when once I asked the reason for his wearing a *tulsi*-bead necklace (*mālā*), while his guru Maṇi, from whom he claims to derive his sartorial habit, wore none. One of his many ripostes was to challenge me: 'What does *mālā* mean anyway? It means "*mā*" and "*lā*".' He was expecting me to derive the meaning 'woman' from '*mā*' (standard colloquial Bengali for 'mother'), and 'to take' (*laiyā*) from '*lā*'. *Mālā* therefore becomes 'one who takes a woman

[25] This, presumably, was what Rāmakṛṣṇa was referring to when he remarked: 'they go in for big talk and yet are (sexually) immoral' (*lambā lambā kathā kay, ābār byābhicār kare*) (Śrī 'Ma' 1388 BS [vol. V]:181).

[for *sadhanā*]'. As was noted earlier, the word 'guru' may be subjected to a similar kind of analysis, where '*gu*' connotes 'vagina', and '*ru*' 'phallus' (see p. 146). The effect of such glosses on the conventional meaning differs. Thus glosses such as the guru as 'vagina plus phallus', and Caitanya as 'menstruation', inevitably detract from the historical or institutional figure. However, other glosses would be viewed as enriching their conventional meaning, as, for example, in the case of Caitanya as 'consciousness'. Exploitation of polysemy in general is a popular *bartamān-panthī* technique. For example, the term *nabarasik* is susceptible to different meanings depending on whether the first component (*naba*) is taken to mean 'nine' or 'new'.[26] Puns (*yamak* or *śleṣa*)[27] are also common. While puns may effect sudden entry into an already established universe, they easily slide into incredibility and instead reveal the arbitrariness of meaning. On the one hand, this is exactly in conformity with the *bartamān-panthī* position on 'name'; but, on the other, the process can become like a fire, consuming any fixed position, including those which the *bartamān-panthī* speaker is endeavouring to keep constant at the time. At this point, appeals to substance will often be resorted to. Riddles (*prahelikā*) are also favourite devices. An example of the latter is the so-called *ulṭa-kathā* (paradox or enigma, see p. 66). This may be illustrated by the following saying, literally translated: 'The body where Kṛṣṇa is absent is Bṛṇḍāban' (*Ye dehete Kṛṣṇa nāi, se-i bṛṇdāban)*, a statement of paradox precisely because Bṛṇḍāban *is* Kṛṣṇa's dwelling place. *Ulṭa-kathā* provokes a search for new angles in order to resolve contradictions. When I confronted some Vaishnava (non-*bartamān-panthī*) friends with this phrase, one of them triumphantly came out with this explanation: 'My body is worthless, destitute of Kṛṣṇa, but such is his grace that he may make even such a body his abode (Bṛṇḍāban).' By contrast, a standard *bartamān-panthī* gloss on this phrase assumes the following equations: (a) Kṛṣṇa is black (that was his colour, and *kṛṣṇa* also means 'black' or 'dark'), and (b) black is the colour of lust (*kām*). So the meaning becomes 'The body which is without lust is Bṛṇḍāban.'

Where meanings other than standard colloquial Bengali are concerned, several different phenomena are to be distinguished. First, there are variations dependent on region, class, community (Hindu and Muslim) and so on, where initiation is not a factor. For example, *bartamān-panthīs* almost invariably explicate the word *ādhyātmik* (usually rendered 'spiritual' in textually based studies) in terms of the body,[28] or at most inner realities (usually indicating their body when speaking of these) rather than outer realities. Yet this interpretation is often voiced by non-initiates also, and is in any case not considered controversial. The case of the *bartamān-panthī* gloss on the phrase '*siddha-deha*' is rather different, in that there

26 *Nabarasik* may therefore mean one who takes new fluid (in whatever sense), one who takes the fluid of the nine doors (of the body), or finally (one of the) nine *rasiks* (including Caṇḍīdās and Rajakinī etc.).

27 *Yamak* refers to the use of a word more than once with different meanings. *Śleṣa* is the use of a word once but with more than one meaning.

28 For example, I was told '*ādhyātmik* is what relates to the body, rather than outside', or '*ādhyātmik* is *dehatattva* (the theory of the body)'.

is an awareness of a standard meaning being contested (which is not generally the case with *ādhyātmik*). While orthodox Vaishnavas tend to regard the *siddha-deha* as non-physical, *bartamān-panthīs,* who allow of no existence beyond the body, would oppose such a gloss, arguing instead that *siddha-deha* means the 'transformed' or 'perfected' (literally 'cooked') physical body. (These are all standard meanings of *siddha*.) Neither of these examples could be categorised as *sandhā-bhāṣā,* since the first case involves no awareness of a difference between conventional and intended meanings, and the second assumes an open debate, rather than a contrast between exoteric and esoteric meanings. *Sandhā-bhāṣā* and related topics have been briefly considered in chapter 2 (pp. 66–70). Meanings gained through initiation may vary according to stage of esoteric practice, guru and 'line', although related structures are characteristically fragile and ephemeral. To take the example of a guru speaking to two disciples (at different levels of esoteric practice) and one uninitiated person, there will be times when the conversation is understood two ways (the uninitiated person versus the rest being the most likely combination). At junctures, the guru's words may have four possible meanings, with only the guru understanding them all, the more advanced disciple understanding three and so on. The opacity of the conversation may also vary in the same way, with the uninitiated person suffering a greater degree of incomprehension and the guru least. Even more complex is a situation where initiates of different 'lines' embark on *hari-kathā*, since hierarchies of meaning are tenuous, to say the least, and by no means generalised. Each small group tends to develop a cluster of words and phrases to which its members attribute a special meaning, and which thus present a quasi-fixity parallel to that of the groups themselves. These may or may not be known to others, and may or may not be shared by them. However, such hierarchies are temporary islands in the flow of constantly fluctuating context. New meanings may evolve even within the course of a single conversation. *Hari-kathā* serves many purposes: to establish hierarchies of understanding, membership of particular 'lines' and separation from the uninitiated, to preserve knowledge while speaking of it, as a means of self-protection, and last but not least, for the sheer joy of it (*ānanda*).

As in many cultures, the realm of *bartamān-panthī* speech is dominated by men. However women are normally considered to be superior in esoteric practice, either because the practices are for various reasons easier for them, or because they are *svayaṅ siddhā* (perfected by themselves, without the necessity for esoteric practice). As mentioned earlier, *bartamān-panthīs* speak of two mouths (or faces), the upper and lower, that is, the one which eats and talks, and the penis or vagina.[29] Both mouths take in and give out. It is recommended that care be taken concerning what one eats (with either mouth), for otherwise one might die, bodily in the case

[29] On the equation between head and genitals see Kakar 1981:100. A common theme of Madhubani folk painting depicts Śiva with a face painted on the genital region (e.g. O'Flaherty 1980b: pl.10). A woman acquaintance on the *bartamān* path explicitly compared the face and the genitals. Pointing to her tongue she said: 'In the mouth is a *liṅga*. Females become male.' Moreover, the clitoris is called the *yoni nāsā* (the 'nose' of the vagina).

of the upper mouth, seminally in the case of the lower. While the upper mouth, the source of *hari-kathā,* is powerful in the case of men, the lower mouth is stronger in women.[30] These mouths are the two main sources of exchange, give and take (*len-den*), or buying and selling (*kenā-becā*), whether this be of words (*hari-kathā*) or substance (*bastu*). In one sense therefore *nām*, rejected in other circumstances, is reintroduced, albeit usually on a subordinate level. As pointed out above, this may be justified on the grounds that such *anumān* is based on *bartamān*. Esoteric practice is primary, and it is often said that, without knowing esoteric practice, one cannot speak *hari-kathā*, an idea which, for various reasons, is indeed generally borne out in practice. The inseparability of the two *liṅgas* (tongue and penis) is echoed in the idea that if there is anything wrong with one's practice (*sādhan-bhajan*), one's words will reflect this. A practitioner opined that emission of semen not only wounds the lotus (female genitals) but destroys the *ānanda*, which in turn renders one incapable of speaking *hari-kathā,* a model supporting the non-dualistic arguments of Marriott and Inden (1974, 1977), Marriott (1976) and Inden and Nicholas (1977). If the semen rises, one wishes to speak *hari-kathā*. A Muslim guru assimilated the *liṅga* to the tongue,[31] both being for *svād* (taste, enjoyment) that is, for esoteric practice (see p. 228). He added: 'All words are produced in the *kulakuṇḍalinī* [in the genitals]. They rise up and the heart decides whether to say something or not. If this knowledge (*jñān*) of the heart is not functioning, one talks rubbish – this is madness (*pāglāmi*).' And he repeated a common saying: '*Gān* (song) means *jñān* (knowledge).'[32]

This dual classification of the mouths ties in directly with the *anumān* versus *bartamān* division, where *nām* (the upper mouth) is demoted in favour of *bastu* (substance, from the lower mouth), just as man (in theory) is demoted in favour of woman. The greater importance attributed to the lower mouth over the upper mouth is, in one sense, consonant with the idea that '*bartamān* is the gross' (see p. 233). A guru who emphasised the bliss (*ānanda*) to be experienced in esoteric practice affirmed that this degree of bliss is unattainable when we are very old. 'How can we retain it? But like a cow chews the cud at night, so we will get *ānanda* by talking *hari kathā* with a few disciples.' The lower mouth is in one sense the realm of non-discrimination, and I was often told that all *yonis* are the same, as are all *liṅgas*. By contrast, lack of individuality is not characteristic of the face. A Muslim guru told me: '*Saṅsār* [worldly life] is the face. The five senses and beauty are there. It is deceptive (*māyā*). It is what makes us individuals.' In this way the relationship of singing and esoteric practice are hierarchised, an order which is reversed for the *bhadralok* and those composers who cater to their taste. One of these, a very popular songwriter called Bhabā Pāglā, writes (G. R. Cakrabartī 1995:119):

[30] Cf. the parallel idea that male and female essences (*sattā*) are in both man and woman, the former residing in the head, the latter in the genitals. Men are male because of the preponderance of male essence, and women female because of the preponderance of female essence (see *BBBG*:387).

[31] A new initiate told me that if one does *kumbhak* and squeezes the *liṅga*, the tongue increases correspondingly in length.

[32] The Bengali pronounciation of *jñān* is quite similar to *gān*.

It is song which is the highest *sādhanā* of all,
It needs no flowers or sandalwood.
No *mantra-tantra* [spells and rituals] are required . . .
Do the *sādhanā* which is singing . . .

This chapter concludes with an illustration of the power of *hari-kathā* from my fieldwork. It often happened that in the midst of what seemed conventional discourse, religious clichés exhausted of meaning would suddenly spring to life in a subversive and yet wholly convincing manner. Once I dropped in on a Jati-Vaishnava whom I had seen engaged in orthodox Vaishnava chanting on various occasions. My suspicion that he might be involved in *bartamān-panthī* practices on some level was confirmed when I learned that he had taken initiation (*śikṣā*) with a disciple of Maṇi Gõsāi. When I asked why he had taken initiation, he began: 'Ordinary people make love like hens and ducks [that is, for a very short time]. There is no joy (*ānanda*) in it.' He then came out with a current Vaishnava cliché, 'Caitanya came to save us from creation (*sṛṣṭi*) and to give us joy (*ānanda*).' Because of its context, this hit me like a revelation. The conventional meaning is that Caitanya came to save us from the sorrows of rebirth (*sṛṣṭi*), so that we would experience heavenly happiness. Here, however, *sṛṣṭi* refers to the creation of life in the womb. By retaining semen there is no creation, no rebirth (e.g. of the man in the womb of his wife) and the supreme joy of sexual intercourse is prolonged, perhaps indefinitely. The ability to evoke a sense of sudden realisation of the real meaning of conventional phrases is a weapon of great power for gurus on the path of *bartamān*. The example given is of an extremely basic level of *bartamān-panthī* discourse, but all the more interesting for the fact that it operates at the frontier of the *bartamān* and non-*bartamān* worlds.

CONCLUSION

To some extent the structure of this book was determined by the present state of (especially English language) scholarship on those called 'Bāul'. The first task was to outline and account for the confusion in such studies, and specifically in the use of the word 'Bāul' itself. A consideration of different perceptions of Bāuls from an historical perspective was followed by an attempt to relate these differing views to current contrasting perceptions of being Bāul in two rural areas of West Bengal. The decision to abandon use of the word 'Bāul' relates partly to the widely differing ways in which the word is still used, but also to the fact that, in the area of my focused fieldwork, it is used more of others rather than the self. *Bartamān*, on the other hand, is a term used by actors of themselves.

As has been shown, the category *bartamān* is in many senses constructed in opposition to *anumān*. *Anumān* in turn is identified with the knowledge of others, as opposed to one's own, and is characteristically identified with 'orthodox' ideology and prescriptions validated by reference to authorised scripture, Hindu or Muslim. The resultant reversal of and opposition to prevailing structures and hierarchies leads to a path which is 'against the current' (*ujān*) or 'reverse' (*ulṭo*). This of course coexists with a tendency, more or less avowed, to erect parallel, partly parasitic structures.

These oppositional features have led to the consideration of Bāuls, along with other 'minor religious sects', in the context of the subaltern studies project.[1] In his attempt to mount an 'immanent critique of caste [and hence] of all synthetic theories about "the unity of Indian society" ', Partha Chatterjee (1994:175) takes as his focus the community called Balarāmī, whose membership consists almost entirely of poor low-caste householders.[2] While conceding that (contra Dumont) the empirical evidence for low-caste opposition to caste hierarchies is voluminous,[3] his general conclusion is that popular opposing views are confined to the implicit. He cites as a 'mark of subalternity' their 'negativity' and 'failure to construct an alternative universal to the dominant dharma' (1994:181). I hope to have shown

[1] By definition, the term Bāul excludes all non-subalterns (for example, amateur Bāuls) in this context.

[2] In 'Caste and subaltern consciousness' (in Guha 1989, reproduced in large part in Partha Chatterjee 1994:181ff.). Chatterjee's material is taken from Sudhīr Cakrabartī 1986. See p. 182.

[3] See e.g., Appadurai 1986, Berreman 1971, Beteille 1983, Derné 1990, Juergensmeyer 1982, Khare 1984, Kolenda 1964, Mencher 1974, Lynch 1969, O'Hanlon 1985.

that the critique offered by those who figure in this book is far from implicit, and moreover that, in many contexts, it constitutes an opposition to all structures which divide person from person, not just caste. As such it constructs a universal around the category of the human being. As Chatterjee bases his analysis on communities who differ from many of those called Bāul, his discussion is least sound where they are concerned. For example, while hinting that Bāuls might indeed display 'a new universalist system', he proceeds to deny their relevance on the grounds that they 'live as mendicants outside society' (1994:186). This conclusion errs in two respects. First, those called Bāul may be householders as well as renouncers, or their status may be ambiguous. Even where they are renouncers, it is at best an oversimplification to state that they live outside society. Second, in exaggerating the separation between householders and 'mendicants', Chatterjee ignores the impact of the renunciatory model in all such 'minor religious sects' and even, as Sumit Sarkar has argued, in subaltern protest movements in general (1989b:314). A particularly clear example of this is provided by Khare's study of Lucknow Untouchable ideology, in which the ascetic and Brahmin represent unconditional egalitarianism and conditional hierarchy respectively. For Untouchable householders, it is the ascetic who is held up as the exemplar of the moral individual (1984:28). Where those called Bāul are concerned, a universalist stance based on the category of the human being (*mānuṣ*) may be related to two other factors. First, in the case of many Bāuls and *bartamān-panthīs*, we find not only the relativisation of householder life from the perspective of the renouncer (Dumont 1960), (or, in a less formal way, from that of other, possibly derivative, initiatory groups), but also the relativisation of renunciation itself. Second, an emphasis on the human being and the denial of divisions between person and person undoubtedly relates, in a mutually reinforcing way, to the close association and mutual influence of Hindus and Muslims within the community, most clearly in joint Hindu and Muslim lineages. The fact that Chatterjee's whole discussion proceeds from within the Hindu sphere, from a consideration of caste rather than from *jāti* (which would not exclude religious categories, and specifically Muslims) is easier to criticise than amend. It reflects the imprisonment of academic thinking within categories (especially English language categories) which all too often precludes us from apprehending alternative modes of thinking.

In connection with the Balarāmīs, Chatterjee comments that at issue here is only a 'revolt of the spirit' (1989:204). There is no 'practical insubordination of labouring bodies' (*ibid.*). Consideration of many of those called Bāul for whom renunciation of some kind traditionally provides a model, or even an option, might have suggested different possibilities, albeit not the kind likely to satisfy Chatterjee. The kind of productive labour engaged in by the rural poor is one of several means of livelihood specifically prohibited by renunciatory theory (see p. 134). This is one reason why renouncers tend to elude the definitional grids of the subaltern historians. Whereas Balarāmīs emphasise seminal emission for the purpose of procreation, and see 'woman' as the source of the male body's destruction, the model of renunciation encourages lack of or fewer progeny among those called Bāul, even householders, for the desirability of foregoing procreation if true independence from householder life is to be attained has long been understood by renouncers. Moreover, the development of control of male seminal emission within sexual intercourse, coupled with the cultivation of emotional and other subtle aspects of the relationship is conducive to a developing intimacy between the partners, and a more radical attitude to women than that found among the Balarāmīs. The confidence that often comes from a world of experience attainable through one's own efforts is found in householder as well as renouncer practitioners, as is seen in predominantly Muslim lineages where formal renunciation is rarely an option. Where those who figure in this book are concerned, Partha Chatterjee's tentative suggestion of 'the trace of an identity that is defined not by others but by oneself' (1994:197; 1989:206) constitutes a serious understatement.

The appropriateness or otherwise of classifying Bāuls or *bartamān-panthīs* as subaltern depends not only on the definition of these terms, but also on what is thought to constitute subalternity. In the first volume of the Subaltern Studies series Ranajit Guha defined 'the subaltern classes' as a residual category. 'The social groups and elements included in this category represent *the demographic difference between the total Indian population and all those whom we have described as the "elite"*' (Guha 1986 (1982): 8. Original italics). Considering the whole series, definitions may be substantive or relational, in which case the possibility of being subaltern in some contexts and not in others is allowed for. (Fieldwork experience suggests to me that this is almost invariably the case.) However it is defined, there is a tendency to see subalternity in terms of opposition, whether etically, as a group considered by the analyst to be in opposition to another, or emically, in terms of an oppositional mentality, defined for example in terms of submissiveness and defiance (Bhadra 1989:54).

At the beginning of the Subaltern Studies series at any rate, the majority of contributors were historians. As has often been pointed out, in so far as subalterns figure in historical records at all, it is precisely in occasional explosions of defiance against those to whom they have long been submissive. One advantage in including the so-called 'deviant orders' (Ramakanta Chakravarti), 'obscure religious cults' (S. B. Dasgupta) or, more politely, the 'minor religious sects' (P. Chatterjee) as 'subaltern' is that the focus is thereby shifted from moments of rebellion, to a more quotidian oppositional stance. Indeed, in the present volume, oppositional (*bartamān-panthī*) elements have been highlighted, not only through my interest in these aspects of the material, but also through the focus on Rāj Khyāpā and his followers, some of whose songs, writings and speech are particularly explicit in their antinomianism. Here of course two kinds of opposition should be differentiated, although in practice they may be found in combination: first, the familiar subaltern stance of potentially upwardly mobile communities who oppose not so much the system as their position in it; and second, a more radical opposition to the structures of differentiation themselves – in one sense, an opposition to oppositions. This latter is the characteristic *bartamān* mode.

In their oppositional stance, *bartamān-panthīs* (and the vast majority of those called Bāul) differ from sectarian movements with primarily caste-based constituencies such as the Balarāmīs and the Matuas (Sekhar Bandyopadhyaya 1995), although these may be or at least look *bartamān-panthī* at the beginning of their trajectories. In the case of Bāuls and *bartamān-panthīs*, the renunciatory model (especially in the broadest sense, connoting liminality, outsiderness) plays a crucial role, for householders as well as renouncers, for those technically Muslim as well as Hindu. This is seen in a greater distancing from considerations of birth group – all the more so if the ideal of non-procreation is followed. Since anyone can in theory become Bāul or *bartamān-panthī*, their primary opposition is clearly not to any particular class, caste or religious community. Indeed, many of the orthodox-orthoprax Hindus and Muslims to whose ideas and practices *bartamān-panthīs* are opposed belong to dominant local groups (Guha's heterogeneous third category of the élite, 1986:8), from which not a few *bartamān-panthīs* also recruit.[4]

While those in *bartamān* are definitely conscious of a 'we'[5] identity, especially in connection with esoteric practice, their 'us' identity consists in more-or-less routinised opposition to orthodoxy-orthopraxy (normally abstract rather than personalised). More entrenched positions among *bartamān-panthīs* may in part be viewed as precipitates of equally entrenched configurations of dominant culture(s) which oppose and are opposed by them. Thus intolerance and persecution by reformist Islamic movements may sustain a profoundly oppositional identity in the case of 'Muslim' *bartamān-panthīs*. In some circumstances, this may crystallise in class terms, where indigent fakirs pit themselves against more prosperous and conventionally religious Muslims (Isherwood 1990). In the case of predominantly Vaishnava lineages, low-caste recruits may infuse *bartamān-panthī* anti-caste ideology with a specific antipathy towards upper-caste society, fuelled by the experience of discrimination and prejudice. This, taken to its extreme, may result in the sects with caste-based constituencies mentioned above. It is pertinent to recall here the individually sung songs of *bartamān-panthīs*, in contrast to those not only of orthodox Vaishnavas whose tradition is to sing collectively, but also of sects like the Matuas, where group singing is associated with the fostering of collective caste identity (Bandyopadhyay 1995:167). While the analyst would discern at times in *bartamān-panthī* oppositional stances both we-they and us-them distinctions, such divisions are rarely substantialised, and indeed are usually subverted by a critique of all self–other categories (*āpan-par*) and a concomitant emphasis on humankind (*mānuṣ*). To use the phraseology of Kampf, we find counter-tradition both in the sense of the 'tradition which opposes', as well as in the sense of 'that which opposes tradition' (quoted in Kailasapathy 1987:411).

After fieldwork in rural Bengal, I find the notion of subaltern consciousness 'eternally frozen in its structure of negation' as unconvincing as does Partha Chatterjee

[4] And to which they may still belong in varying degrees. Of course, as a general rule, this overlapping sphere marks the upper social limit for *bartamān-panthīs* (and Bāuls), and the lower limit for their opponents.

[5] Eriksen (1993:67) inspired by Sartre (1943).

(1994:197), and as an anthropologist would attribute its currency to the historian's necessary reliance on written documents. Whether or not Bāuls or *bartamān-panthīs* are to be counted subaltern, they certainly cannot be characterised in this way. Clearly it would be absurd to view the *bartamān-panthī* material entirely in terms of reactions to various orthodoxies-orthopraxies, and to deny that anything is ever conserved or perpetuated apart from oppositional tendencies. And this is apart from the fact that the expression of creativity and dissent must itself have a traditional basis of some kind. However, as has been shown, there are problems in conferring a 'life in history' on Bāuls or *bartamān-panthīs*, as Chatterjee advocates for subaltern culture (*ibid.*). Not only is this at odds with their own enterprise, but, for this very reason, they tend to leave behind few traces on the river of life, to paraphrase K. Sen's Bāul (1961:104).

One argument of this book has been that the more identity crystallises in terms of householder or renouncer structures, the less convincing are claims to be *bartamān* or Bāul. In these respects *bartamān* is an anti-identity identity, an anti-group group, which is why those in *bartamān* often simply call themselves human beings (*mānuṣ*). It is a category denying category, which is one reason they call themselves 'mad' (*bāul, khyāpā*). *Bartamān* may even loosely be rendered the 'here-now', for it connotes cathexis on the body, affirmation of the present, and, more specifically, a rejection of we–they structuring, either in space (religious or caste-based communities, etc.) or in time (lineages by blood or initiation). The intent to subvert identity as such is evidenced by a conscious eclecticism or bricolage, and, in general, a cavalier attitude to traditional contents and structures. The tendency to invert these works either towards their nullification or their unification into a whole.

So how is one to approach the question of *bartamān-panthī* identity? The first step of taking initiation with a *bartamān-panthī* guru is potentially of great significance in this connection. Yet, as discussed earlier, there are contradictions inherent in attempts to perpetuate and routinise being in *bartamān* (or *bāul*) even through specifically *bartamān-panthī* guru–disciple structures. On the one hand, opposition can itself become habitual, eventually undermining the authority of *bartamān-panthī* gurus. On the other hand, unquestioning devotion to the guru may be equally doomed to failure in terms of *bartamān,* as in the case of Hem Khyāpā, Rāj's disciple. Guru–disciple based communities or lineages are at best provisional. Esoteric practice is a clear criterion for being in *bartamān* in both emic and etic terms, although, as evidenced from *bartamān-panthī* opposition to Tantra, it is not sufficient. A kind of *bartamān* identity also evolves, I suggest, through the recurrence of what O'Hanlon has called 'distinctive practices' (1988:197).

My argument is that walking on the path of *bartamān* often sets in train events and processes potentially conducive to the growth of alienation from conventional society on the one hand and a kind of autonomy on the other. The fact that Bāuls move through, or in some sense inhabit a greater variety of social statuses and contexts than others of their socio-economic class leads to the relativisation of, and, frequently, alienation from such statuses and contexts. It may also reinforce a habit of relativising, opposing and subverting. As has been discussed earlier, the emphasis on kin generated by the guru weakens blood connections, and householder status is opposed and relativised by that of renouncer. The category Bāul has often been constructed with reference to the institutional guru and guru-derived lineages. Yet even in theory the authority of *bartamān-panthī* gurus is undermined in a variety of ways. It is as if, for some, at some crucial point, the spell has been broken, and claims of authority, of a clearly circumscribed 'we' group can no longer be taken seriously.

It may be useful to consider this matter in the light of standpoint theory (Harding 1987), which proposes that the perspective of the subordinated or marginalised is informed by a double hermeneutic. In complementing the top down (or inside out) dominant point of view with that of the bottom up (or outside in), it is purportedly less distorted, more complete. Whatever the merits of this argument, *bartamān-panthīs* actually embody a variety of stand-points, for they move through different statuses and identities: from householder to renouncer life and then perhaps to some indeterminate state. Some *bartamān-panthīs*, such as Rāj, have also seen life from several distinct angles through being declassed. I know of *bartamān-panthīs* who have both Hindu and Muslim persona, their identity changing according to convenience as they travel. Finally, in esoteric practice there is at least the attempt at gender reversal, interpreted more or less literally. In general, it could be argued that the ability to see oneself both as self and other is a prerequisite for the *bartamān-panthī* assault on this primary distinction.

An orientation towards material, immediate and perceptible realities, especially the body, comprises another category of distinctive practice. In addition to its negative definition in opposition to *anumān,* the word *bartamān* also has positive connotations of focus on material substance (*bastu*), esoteric practice and a general tendency to bring everything – practice, ideology, exegesis – back to the living human being, (in)dividual[6] or pair. This orientation, coupled with a weakening of group boundaries, is arguably connected with a strengthening of a sentiment of autonomy.

Bartamān-panthī esoteric practice entails the cultivation, knowledge of and control over one's body. One's own body and, in varying degrees, that of the partner, increasingly constitutes one's focus, as the site of transformation and authentic experience. The microcosm (the body) is identified with and imbued with the value of the macrocosm (the universe). My argument is that the emphasis on the microcosm, and the cathexis on the human body in esoteric practice, in effect renders categories such as caste, sect and religion insubstantial and even absurd to *bartamān-panthīs*. A determination to cathect on to the self (especially the body or substance of the body) rather than being defined by others, is discernible even among very poor, uneducated and recently initiated *bartamān-panthīs*. (Along with

[6] In general I agree with Marriott's arguments for the term 'dividual', especially in a South Asian context. At times I have used the clumsy form '(in)dividual' in order not to foreclose other possibilities. This will be discussed below.

practice, talking about practice (*hari-kathā*) constitutes a distinctive *bartamān-panthī* practice. Increasing familiarity with encoded, secret language, often deployed with considerable rhetorical skill, fosters relativisation and dislocation from conventional realities and representation, and from those – especially former kith and kin – who know nothing else.) Caste-based sects, such as the Matuas and Balarāmīs, differ from *bartamān-panthīs* in their lack of body-centred practices, as well as being firmly family and caste oriented. The shift of boundaries from categories of caste and religious community to those of the (in)dividual or couple on the one hand, and the whole of humanity (*mānuṣ*) on the other, further undermines the tendency to posit we–they/us–them distinctions.

The cathexis on material substances is of course opposed to the less accessible realities offered by those in *anumān*, whether external (e.g. deities) or internal (an allegedly immaterial[7] self or soul). The characterisation of *bartamān* in certain contexts as 'gross' (*sthūl*) may be read in the light of an opposition to such alleged realities, access to which requires mediation, authority or revelation. Yet cathexis on the body is also orientation to self, to thoughts, feelings and experience in general, and esoteric practices may also encourage the enhancement of affective and sensory faculties. In this respect the tendency to inwardness triumphs over that to outwardness. However, for *bartamān-panthīs*, while the inner may be subtle, it is far from immaterial. As shown, they normally identify the source of consciousness (the 'I') with *rajaḥ-bīj* (male and female generative essences). In many contexts clear equivalences are drawn between these two terms (as well as with *mānuṣ*), thus, in one sense, 'materialising' the whole discourse. In this connection the equation drawn by Duddu between matter (*bastu*) and Self/self (*ātman*) should also be borne in mind (p. 189). The emphasis on substance is reflected in the common self-appellation of *bastubādī*, usually translated as 'materialist'. The high value placed on material substances is particularly clear in the case of the four moons practices. The ingestion or other use of the four moons may appear antinomian, in the sense that these are regarded as excreta by conventional society (Hindu or Muslim). But, in fact, *bartamān-panthīs* see these substances as valuable secretions, as nutritional, and sometimes of great potency. The positive valuation of matter by *bartamān-panthīs* has been interpreted by some authorities in terms of continuities from older materialist (Lokāyata) traditions. As has been mentioned earlier, the fact that the term 'Lokāyata' means both 'materialism' and the 'philosophy of the people' suggests that such materialism was more widespread than generally thought. Indeed, in contrast to colonial and postcolonial obsessions with the 'spiritual East', several commentators have stressed the general materialism of sub-continental culture (see p. 192–3). It was not always clear to me how far *bartamān-panthī* radicalism consisted in their novel couching of commonly held (but subversive) assumptions in prestigious high Hindu and Muslim terminology,

[7] Although *bartamān-panthīs* construe the matter in oppositional terms, those they classify as being in *anumān* do not necessarily conform to this view. The important point is that *bartamān-panthīs* emphasise continuities between such inner realities and 'gross' ones, whereas those in *anumān* tend to emphasise discontinuity, or inaccessibility of some other kind.

or alternatively how far they were introducing listeners and neophytes to a new universe.

An initial impetus for this study was to relate two apparently disparate aspects of the life and thought of *bartamān-panthīs*: namely the emphasis on non-discrimination between person and person, and the single-minded cultivation of the body through *sādhanā*. The logic of this has partly been outlined above. However, in *bartamān-panthī* ideology, these two apparently disparate elements are linked through the notion of love. In *bartamān-panthī* texts, esoteric practices involving the cultivation of love with a partner of the opposite sex are directly related to the divinisation of the human being and human body, at the expense of transcendent deities and images. Love also dissolves the divisions between 'I' and not-'I', both on the level of substances and of persons. The association between non-dualism (*advaita*) and love is parallel to that drawn between discriminatory distinctions and ill-will. While the dissolution of we–they distinctions is most usually effected through interiorisation, so that *par* (others) become *āpan* (one's own), the same result is achieved through the alienating transformation of *āpan* into *par*. However the former notion identifies all with the self, and is therefore associated with love and communitas (Turner 1969), which partly explains its predominance, whereas the latter is suggestive of alienation. I suggest that the four moons practices, whether performed alone or with a partner, involve a shift or erasure of boundaries between self and not-self. Such practices necessitate a radically altered attitude to one's own and, even more, another's moons from the conventional, an attitude which might be characterised as love. It is tempting to relate this to a similar inclusiveness of the 'we' in the social body.

A striking example of the different worlds inhabited by *bartamān-panthīs* and conventional Hindus and Muslims is their contrasting attitudes to menstrual (and other female sexual) fluids (see chapter 9). The high value placed on such substances by *bartamān-panthīs*, as a 'moon' to be used in different ways, can be variously accounted for. These practices may be seen in hierarchical terms as the absorption of the substance and qualities of a superior being – on the pattern of devotees drinking water in which the guru's feet have been washed, or, less commonly, using the guru's excrement in various ways. Female fluids may be considered to be (or to contain) substances valuable to the male practitioner. The practices may constitute an attempt by the male to achieve balance and ultimately androgyny. Or they may be construed as a means of achieving equilibrium or even identity (*samatā*) between the partners. However the menstrual and other fluids are used, and whatever the gloss, a radically different attitude to women from that of conventional society is involved. And this, of course, is true of esoteric practices with a female in the first place.

It has been argued in this book that alongside the notion of the male practitioner requiring a similarly incomplete and imbalanced woman to complement him and form a whole is another: namely that women are complete in themselves, that is, they embody, or are capable of achieving, androgyny and wholeness within themselves. Through a woman, or by becoming woman(ly), the male practitioner may attain or recover wholeness and autonomy. In this connection it should be remembered that in *bartamān-panthī* ideology 'woman' is the personification of love, and is often said (especially by men) to have no distinction of birth group. My argument here is not that these notions are invariably advantageous to women *bartamān-panthīs*, although on average their position is better than others of their socio-economic class. The women I worked with tended to see themselves as much as individuals (as opposed to a class) as do the men. Like men, they experience the necessity to work to change themselves – a view of them expressed also by men in other contexts. Yet, as has been shown, the concept of the autonomous yet loving woman is capable of truly radical inflection, into a woman who both speaks and shits, that is, an agent who is also an ordinary, unidealised woman (see p. 184). This contrasts with the wider Tantric tradition (Hindu and Buddhist) where women are normally extolled because they are embodiments of a/the goddess (see Shaw 1994:39–47).

It is interesting to note the correspondence of these distinctive *bartamān-panthī* practices with Duddu Śā's list of Bāul characteristics: lack of group formation (*sampradāy*), reverence for the human being, focus on material realities and especially the body, and close association with women (see chapter 4).

A characteristic Bāuls and *bartamān-panthīs* tend to share with many others in the sub-continent is the dream, in Ramanujan's words, of freedom from context. They tend to see themselves and be seen by others as outsiders to a culture where 'context-sensitivity rules and binds' (1990:54). Those called '*bāul*' and those defining themselves as in '*bartamān*' are aspirers to, or in varying degrees, achievers of that freedom from context. Ramanujan contrasts the general pattern, that is, 'a necessary sequence in time with strict rules of phase and context ending in a free state', with that of *bhakti*, which, he asserts 'defies all contextual structures'. In *bhakti*, 'every pigeonhole of caste, ritual, gender, appropriate clothing and custom, stage of life, the whole system of homo hierarchicus . . . is the target of irony' (*ibid.*). Arguably, these two patterns combine in *bartamān-panthī* culture. In this, the notion of stages coexists with their negation, a denial of contextual structure at any level. A tendency to move from gross to subtle combines with a cathexis on the gross, as representing the here-now (*bartamān*).

This parallels the dual concept of *mānuṣ,* as the human being in the generic sense and as the perfected human being. While the former entails the denial of conventional discriminatory structures which separate person from person, the latter potentially generates differentiation through the transformation of (in)dividuals or pairs in esoteric practice. Not that these two aspects are unconnected. Thus the 'perfected one' (*sādhu*) transcends all discriminatory structures; and *mānuṣ* in the latter sense (as *sādhu*) is characterised by the vision of *mānuṣ* in the former (generic) sense.

While Rāj's notion of the 'I' (the *āmi*) represents the cathexis on inner realities, a movement, albeit strategic or preliminary, towards a 'self' in preference to externals, the *bartamān-panthī* notion of *mānuṣ* may have either external or internal referents. As the psycho-physical organism (of the self and all others) it stands opposed to deities, images and Allah on the one hand, and, on the other, to any divisions within humankind. High valuation of the human being, which at times is inflected as the divinisation of the human being, is a traditional subcontinental theme – Jain, Buddhist and Hindu.

The status of *mānuṣ* in *bartamān-panthī* eyes is clarified by the use of the same word in the context of the material essence and source of life, *rajaḥ-bīj*. As stated above, *bartamān-panthīs* appear to operate with a materialised notion of non-dualism, where the notions of *mānuṣ, āmi* and *rajaḥ-bīj* are equated in many contexts. While these point to the source of identity on a personal level, on a social level they are used to discredit boundaries between person and person. *Rajaḥ-bīj*, unlike that more elusive inner reality, the *āmi* (unless they are identified with each other), is potentially perceptible by the senses. It too is most often universalised and used to cut across divisive categories. Thus the same *rajaḥ-bīj* as the origin of all humankind (or all life, or indeed all) is a *bartamān-panthī* cliché, as is the notion that the entire universe consists of the joyful play (*līlā*, characterised by *ānanda*) of *rajaḥ-bīj*, the male and female essences.

Rāj and other *bartamān-panthīs* emphasise interiority and subjectivity (the *āmi*), both in the sense of a turning inwards, and of reliance on one's own experience and judgement as opposed to that of others. While interiorisation may appear to analysts as a retreat from a hostile world into narcissism, *bartamān-panthīs* clearly experience it as an empowering strategy. Control of one's destiny is thereby removed from powerful beings such as god(s) and the religious and social élite and restored to the self. This strategy evades the submission–defiance polarities discussed by the Subaltern Studies collective in favour of potential or actualised non-dependence.

What is interesting in the present context is that here the most subjective is the least 'individual' (in the sense of a unique, bounded entity). As Rāj constantly argued, the essence of the 'I' (*āmi*) is that it transcends distinction, it is the same in everyone. Here there are no distinctions between one self and another. Nor, finally, is there any opposition between the self and the collectivity, the latter being drawn much more widely than normal to approximate to the whole. There is no concern to mark a periphery to such a collectivity, and to do so would be to limit it. It is the artificial boundaries drawn within it which are a matter of concern and objection to *bartamān-panthīs*. It may be loosely characterised by them simply as all, as all living beings, or as all human beings, especially in contexts where divisions within humanity are being opposed.

The Western notion of the individual, with its academic and popular connotations of an indivisible, bounded unit has been considered inappropriate in the South Asian context by Marriott, and specifically in the context of householder society by Dumont. Marriott's alternative, 'dividual' (1976), has the merit of reflecting South Asian notions of permeability to others (e.g. through pollution) and of constant change and transformative possibilities (e.g. through action, and, specifically in the present context, through *sādhanā*). The concept of the dividual is especially appropriate to a hierarchical system, where each person is seen as part of a larger whole, rather than an independent entity.

Where Dumont's assertion that renouncers are the only true individuals in Indian society is concerned, *bartamān-panthīs* often reach the same conclusion as scholars such as Burghart (1978), namely, that the society of renouncers is as subject to structures and authority as that of householder life. In identifying both these worlds and attempting to evade or transcend both, it could be argued that it is *bartamān-panthīs* who are, or become, the most 'individual', in Dumont's sense. In a sense their negation of divisions within humankind is parallelled by a lack of divisibility in their construct of the person. Certainly, in distinguishing themselves from their original birth groups (and at times even from the society of renouncers), and in cathecting on to their own experience, something that scholars and Bengali householders and renouncers would all see as a strong sense of individuality may be fostered. For, in practice, *bartamān-panthīs* are constantly differentiating themselves against those they see as mystified by false identities. While Rāj uses the *āmi* concept in a non-individualistic way in his songs, he was widely judged, especially by his detractors, to be a self-willed individual who wished to define himself and his life, even in defiance of his only suppporters, his disciples.[8] Rāj's trajectory may parallel the forging of a sense of individuality through opposition in the case of the low castes and minorities (Khare 1984).

Yet denial of structure can also look like encompassment. What from the perspective of structure looks like an individual breaking away may appear to be an encompassing manoeuvre from another point of view. This is why some of those who sever all such connections may subsequently be revered as perfected (*siddha*). Any person within a hierarchy is by definition precluded from representing the whole, since they are a part of the whole. In the context of being in *bartamān*, individuality, potential or actualised, should arguably be viewed as the self-sufficiency resulting from wholeness, from the realisation of the macrocosm within the microcosm of the body. The identity between the individual and the whole (as opposed to the collectivities of caste, religion etc.) can be seen as an inflection of the classical *ātman–brahman* equation (see also Khare 1984 on this pattern in relation to Camar ideology.) Such an individuality is not primarily defined against other individuals – the emphasis on wholeness attenuates the importance of boundaries in favour of the totality of content. This is perhaps why the positive assertion of equality (between such individuals) is comparatively insignificant in *bartamān-panthī* discourse. Of greater importance for them is the denial of inequality asserted by others (which is senseless to those obsessed by wholeness). *Bartamān-panthīs* tend to talk of everyone being the same, or one (*ek*), which connotes identity rather than equality.

The unit can be replicated at many levels: the individual, the pair, the totality of perfected ones (*sādhu-samāj*), or the whole of humanity. For example, the *āmi*

[8] Brooks makes a similar point in connection with Tantrics (1990:134).

may connote the male–female pair, who together form an androgynous whole. One couple I worked with, Rāj's disciple's disciples, define themselves in this way. They regard their physical, mental and emotional states as closely intertwined, and anticipate dying together. The different 'levels', as we would see them, are not in a relationship of hierarchy and encompassment. Their relation is one of identity. As quoted earlier, 'The microcosm is both *within* and like the macrocosm, and paradoxically also contains it' (Ramanujan 1990:51).

While there is a great deal to be said for the notion of the dividual (and not only in South Asia), it seems clear that more scope is allowed for some kind of non-contingent individuality, even in traditional Bengali householder life, than such theories allow for. In fact, it seems to be the case that concepts of an immutable base to each person are more accessible (perhaps increasingly) to South Asian householders in general than is thought to be the case. A particularly explicit example is provided by Khare's material on north Indian Untouchable ideology. This links what is normally assumed to be a high Hindu notion – that of the non-contingent self (*ātman*) – and everyday social formulations. The association results in the fundamentally egalitarian construct of the 'moral individual' (1984:52), epitomised by the ascetic. North Indian ascetic reformers define the individual in terms of the self (*ātman*) within each person. This self in turn is characterised by indivisibility (*akhaṇḍatā*), permanence (*nityatā*), completeness (*purṇatāḥ*), consciousness (*caitanyatā*) and autonomy (*svātantrya*) (Khare 1984:55). What is of interest here is the way that such *ātman* concepts are popularised and projected into the sphere of everyday life, thus offering, alongside the dividual, a notion of the individual. This notion is used not only to subvert the notion of *jāt* and *varṇa*, but also to encourage an increasing sense of autonomy. Untouchable ideologues appear to share with *bartamān-panthīs* an acute sensitivity to the dangers inherent in positing oppositional groupings, a wisdom arguably inspired by renunciation (in the broadest sense) and its relativisation of all householder categories. Emphasising the relatively self-sufficient individual (as opposed to the dividual who is part of a whole, a group of some kind) may constitute an alternative, non-communal strategy for sabotaging discrimination.

In the Bengali context, songs of *bartamān-panthīs* such as Rāj clearly contribute to the spread of such ideas. In addition, they emphasise the accessibility of the self by materialising and relating it to the body, while still identifying it as the source of consciousness, as, for example, in Duddu's song where *ātman* and *bastu* (matter) are identified. However, as pointed out above, in abolishing hierarchical distinctions, boundaries between one individual and another are also denied. Such formulations derive authenticity from philosophical arguments concerning the convergence of absolute reality with worldly life, as opposed to situating the former at the end of series of progressions in time. These have been elaborated in *bhakti*, with its defiance of contextual structures, and in Tantric notions of the identity of *saṅsāra* (the endless cycle of existences) and *nirvāṇa* (liberation). Non-discriminatory ideals of *bartamān-panthīs* gain further legitimacy by their use of the term 'non-dualism' (*advaita*) with its high Hindu philosophical connotations.

As Béteille (1986) has pointed out, there are various kinds of individualism, and modernity is not their only source.

The same can be said for humanism. In situating and cutting notions such as humanism down to size, some theorists have ethnocentrically presumed that there is only one kind of humanism. A further assumption that universalising notions are invariably hegemonic in their intention or effects (Butler 1992: 7–8) can result in a quietistic attitude to all manner of parochialism and prejudice, and the masking of genuine radicalism. In the South Asian context, acquiescence in the face of (Hindu) chauvinist and (Islamic) fundamentalist arguments that secularism, humanism and feminism invariably derive from the West, that India is a 'religious country' and so on, has been disturbingly prevalent. It is ironical that the advent of the iconic, spiritual Bāul has contributed to such notions. One of the intentions of this book has been to highlight a possibly 'higher-order universalism' of 'non-players' (Nandy 1988:xiv).

Bartamān-panthī ideas are communicated through their songs and conversation, especially *hari-kathā*. Despite the importance of groups based on guru–disciple relationships, and the society of adepts in general, transmission of ideas and practices are by no means confined to these. The least routinised individuals, who approximate to the lone, wandering Bāul, if only in the eyes of others, tap into immensely powerful stereotypes of the trans-social renouncer. They offer a constant critique of established religious traditions and authority to the wider society from which they recruit, privileging instead the human being, and each person's body-centred experience. They also offer an alternative view of women. The fact that their ideals are imperfectly realised and at times contradicted is probably true of all ideals. They have undoubtedly contributed to the development and fostering of indigenous radicalism in Bengali communities, and arguably to the receptivity of Bengalis to radical ideas originating from outside South Asia, such as Western forms of secularism and feminism, and Marxism.

GLOSSARY

The glossary focuses on key terms used in the text, and especially some of the ways in which these terms are used by *bartamān-panthīs*.

Adhikār: competence, qualification, authority. (*Adhikārī:* one who is competent, qualified, authorised.)

Adhyātmik/ādhyātmik: The usual translation for this, as 'spiritual', is at best misleading. *Bartamān-panthīs*, as well as many uninitiated rural Bengalis, render it 'inner' or 'to do with the body, or bodily substance'. Tantric connotations of 'individualistic' and 'esoteric' are also relevant to *bartamān-panthīs* (Goudriaan and Gupta 1981:8).

Anna: A sixteenth part of a rupee; 16 annas connotes completeness, fullness.

Anumān: Literally meaning 'inference', and more colloquially 'guesswork', this term is opposed to *bartamān*. More generally *anumān* refers to 'orthodox' or conventional precepts and practices (Hindu or Muslim, householder or renouncer). The adjectival form is *ānumānik.*

Anurāg: Devotion, love. An important term in Bengali Vaishnavism, and one used of their path and themselves (*anurāgī*) by some (especially Vaishnava) *bartamān-panthīs.*

Ārop(a): The attribution of the qualities of one thing or person to another.

Aṭal: This adjective means literally 'unwavering, steady, constant, unperturbed, resolute' etc. In *bartamān-panthī* discourse it carries extra connotations of seminal retention.

Āul: The first of the series *āul, bāul, darbeś, sā̃i,* especially current in Rarh, which may be rationalised in terms of stages, or different 'lines' or *sampradāy*. In the former sense, it means either the stage before or the first stage of esoteric practice. In the latter sense it is often associated with a *sampradāy* called the Kartābhajās.

Avatār: Descent (of a deity) in bodily form.

Baidhik: Of *bidhi* (conventional or orthodox religious prescriptions and observances). See also *baidik.*

Baidik: Of the Veda (in this context, authorised scripture, Hindu or Muslim – see *bed*). *Baidik* and *baidhik* (adjectival forms of *bed* and *bidhi*), are often confused, sometimes unwittingly and sometimes deliberately. An anti-*baidik* position is sometimes softened into an anti-*baidhik* one for the benefit of those who can tolerate and even applaud the rejection of conventional religion, but within the general framework of what they construe to be 'Vedic' (*baidik*).

Bairāgī: A Vaishnava renouncer; also applied to Jati-Vaishnavas.

Bairāgya: Indifference to worldly concerns; renunciation (especially of Vaishnavas). Sometimes also used, in contexts where one would expect '*bairāgī*', as a title (or part of a title) of Vaishnavas and Jati-Vaishnavas (either simply 'Bairāgya' or 'Dās Bairāgya').

Bairgī: Colloquial (and often derogatory) form of *bairāgī*.

Baiṣṇab: See 'Vaishnava'.

Bartamān: The path of direct knowledge, and by extension of unorthodoxy. Opposed to *anumān*. (The older spelling, used by Rāj for example, is *barttamān*.)

Bartamān-panthī: Follower of the path of *bartamān*. Often identified with *bāul*.

Bastu: A 'thing, material; substance; matter; truth' etc. For *bartamān-panthīs*, *bastu* (as 'thing') is opposed to *nām* ('name'), and it often refers to primordial matter, especially in the sense of the basic male and female essences (*rajaḥ-bīj*).

Bed: Veda: that is, any orthodox scripture, including, for Muslims on the path of *bartamān*, the Koran and Hadith.

Behāl: '*Be*' is a privative; '*hāl*' means both the plough and the rudder of a boat, reflecting the most common occupations in a fertile, riverine land, such as Bengal. '*Behāl*' therefore means 'without plough (rudder)', hence 'poverty', 'indigence', as well as a state of being 'aimless', literally 'rudderless'. It also refers to the esoteric practice associated with the patchwork coat (*behāl*), which has Islamic connotations in Bengal. Poverty (another meaning of *behāl*) is embraced by *fakirs* (which also means 'indigent').

Bhadralok: Literally 'gentlefolk'. Although the term is well established by the latter half of the nineteenth century, its nature and usefulness as an analytical category are disputed. Whereas for scholars such as Broomfield the *bhadralok* constituted a 'status-group' in the Weberian sense (Broomfield 1968:5ff.), for those such as S. N. Mukherjee it denotes a *de facto* social group or class (1993:72–3, 131–2). The latter argues against bhadralok society being viewed as a traditional caste-based élite, on the grounds that it was not confined to the upper three castes, and that the vast majority of the upper castes supposedly comprising that élite were in lowly and poorly paid positions (Mukherjee 1993: 136–7). Partha Chatterjee (1994:35) settles for 'middle class' as a rendering, while admitting to 'literati' and 'intelligentsia' also.

Bhajan: Worship, service, reverence; glorification of a deity (especially in devotional songs); a type of devotional song.

Bhaṇitā: The *bhaṇitā* identifies the one who speaks (*bhaṇā*), i.e. the author. This is thus the 'signature' or 'idiograph' of the author of a song, etc. In the case of songs, the *bhaṇitā* typically comes at the end, often in the penultimate line. Frequently the name of the guru, and/or the female partner also figure.

Bhek: Vaishnava renunciation (*sannyās*); the garb of the Vaishnava ascetic; disguise, dissimulation.

Bhek-dhārī: A 'wearer' of bhek. A Vaishnava renouncer.

Bidhi: Conventional or orthodox religious prescriptions and observances. '*Bidhi-mārg*' (the path of *bidhi*) is opposed to *rāg-mārga*.

Bīj: Seed, semen; (root)-cause. For those in *bartamān*, the primary meaning is semen or sperm.

Bindu: Vital drop (male and female). In the male it usually means sperm (or something within this). The *bindu* of the female is associated with the menstrual fluid, rather than with orgasm.

Brahma(n): The absolute, the ground of all being. Important meanings for *bartamān-panthīs* include seminal fluid (or something within this), or the male and female essence (*rajaḥ-bīj,* that is, menstrual and sexual fluids).

Brāhma: (Anglicised as 'Brahma' or 'Brahmo'). Member of a prestigious reform movement of Bengal (the *Brāhma-samāj*), founded in the first part of the nineteenth century by Ram Mohan Roy and including members of the Tagore family.

Braja: Place of the love sports of Kṛṣṇa and the *gopīs* (cowherdesses) especially Rādhā.

Caitanya: A charismatic early sixteenth-century Vaishnava leader, often regarded as the founder of Bengali Vaishnavism.

Darbeś: Despite Islamic connotations (cf. Dervish), many Bāuls of non-Muslim origin call themselves *darbeś*, especially in the Rarh area of West Bengal (not all Darbeś would call themselves Bāul). Especially in Rarh, 'Āul, Bāul, Darbeś, Sā̃i' are often cited either as stages on the path, or as separate 'lines'.

Dharma: Now used as an equivalent for 'religion', the term *dharma* connotes both what is, and what is appropriate to do.

Dīkṣā: In a broad sense this refers to any kind of initiation. In a narrow sense it denotes the first initiation by *mantra*, taken by a wide variety of householders in Bengal. Those in *bartamān* will have taken a further initiation (formally or not) known as *śikṣā*. Finally renouncers (whether they be *bartamān-panthī* or not) take *sannyās* or (in Vaishnava terminology) *bhek*, which is regarded as another initiation. Unless specified to the contrary, *dīkṣā* refers to the preliminary initiation in this book.

Ḍor-kaupīn: The loin cloth (and the thread around the waist which secures it). It normally signifies celibacy and renunciation.

Dotārā: A two-stringed lute, played with both hands, especially popular in Bagri rather than Rarh.

Ekak-sādhanā: *Sādhanā* practised alone, without a partner of the opposite sex.

Ektārā: A one-stringed lute used as a drone. Played usually with only one hand, it forms an integral part of the image of the iconic, spiritualised Bāul, and is popular in Rarh.

Fakir: Apart from its specifically Islamic connotations, *fakir* can refer to any kind of renouncer, especially mendicants. It also means 'indigent'.

Gauṙīya-vaiṣṇava: In a literal sense, this means the Vaishnavism of Gauṙ (that is, Bengal), and thus would include many on the *bartamān* path. However, it often bears the more restricted meaning of 'orthodox' Bengali Vaishnavas, thus excluding those on the *bartamān* path.

Geruyā: A non-permanent dye consisting of a kind of pink-orange coloured earth applied to colourless cloth.

Ghar: Literally 'house(hold)', 'lineage', this applies also to the descendants by initiation of a guru. 'Rāj's *ghar*' thus refers to all those who wish to claim descent (or to whom are attributed descent) from Rāj. As with the word '*lāin*' ('line'), lineal connotations are usually attenuated, and it comes to mean any grouping of initiates who are considered to be related through initiation, or other links.

Goṣṭhī: Literally 'family, kindred, class, collection', this also applies to the descendants by initiation of a guru. Often used in the same sense as *ghar*.

Guru-bhāi: Brother through initiation from a common guru. (As is the case with 'blood-lineages' it may also refer loosely to the 'cousin brother' – that is where the guru's guru is common, etc.)

Guru-bon: Sister through initiation from a common guru. Also sometimes 'cousin sister' through initiation (see *guru-bhāi*).

Guru-mā: The wife or female partner of the guru.

Hari-kathā: Literally 'god-talk' (Hari is a name of Viṣṇu). *Hari* also means 'woman/women' to many initiates, and for *bartamān-panthīs, hari-kathā* refers to discussion about esoteric practices which usually involve a female partner, often in 'coded' language.

Hiṅsā: In the Bengali dictionary, *hiṅsā* means 'killing, slaughter; malice, spite, malevolence; (loosely) envy, jealousy' (*SBED*). In *bartamān-panthī* usage it connotes a divisive, discriminatory force, the opposite of love (*prem*).

Jal-cal: Those castes whose water is acceptable to Brahmins and the 'clean' (*sat*) Śūdras, *jal-acal* castes being those whose water is not acceptable to these higher castes.

Jat/Jati Vaishnava *(Jāt-baiṣṇab/Jāti-baiṣṇab):* A complex category which comprises, generally speaking, those for whom 'Vaishnava' functions, either positively or despite themselves, as a caste identity. They may be differentiated from those for whom the identity 'Vaishnava' co-exists with a separate caste identity, such as Brahmin, Kayastha etc. They also differ from those Vaishnavas who have renounced householder life and along with it caste identity of any sort. Traditionally the progeny of any inter-caste (or otherwise discernibly irregular) union were consigned to this 'caste'. Such people are 'Vaishnava through having lost caste' (*jāt hāriye vaiṣṇava*). In other words, 'Vaishnava' has become their caste identity by default. Jat Vaishnavas can marry anyone in theory (although there may be problems with entrants from the very low castes), just by making the incomer a Vaishnava. For a man, this 'conversion' involves formally taking *bhek* (Vaishnava *sannyās*), hence the loss of original caste identity and the (often contemptuous) label *bairgī*, a corrupted form of *bairāgī* (Vaishnava renouncer). There are Jat Vaishnavas whose forefathers converted the whole family, including children, to Vaishnava *dharma*, and lost their caste identity (a complex matter, since some of their descendants might later wish to reclaim it). While nowadays Jat Vaishnavas are generally *jal-cal*, their reputation may be tarnished by the 'illicit' relationship which often allegedly propelled them into the Jati Vaishnava fold, and by accusations of subsequent looseness in sexual relations. Not a few Bengali Jat Vaishnavas are in highly respected positions in society, such as judges etc.

Jīb (jīva): In conventional usage, *jīb* denotes any living being, but especially animals, as opposed to human beings. For *bartamān-panthīs* it usually indicates an uninitiated or undeveloped person.

Jotdār: Proprietor of agricultural land.

Kul/kūl: *Kul* means 'family, lineage, society, class, species' and thus groups in general. *Kūl* means 'shore, bank of the river, refuge'. In Bengali these have the same pronunciation, and *bartamān-panthīs* often use one or other spelling to cover all these meanings separately or together, as, for example, in the idea of *kul/kūl* as the refuge provided by groups (which *bartamān-panthīs* are forced or choose to leave). Another important reference is to women as a refuge (*āśray, kūl*) – women are often likened to rivers in *bartamān-panthī* thought. Transcription and translation of these terms involve inappropriate restriction of meaning.

(Kula)-kuṇḍalinī: A dormant energy at or near the bottom of the spine represented as a coiled and sleeping serpent. The practices associated with the arousal and raising upwards of this latent energy are associated with Shakta tantra and yoga.

Līlā: *Lilā* means 'love-making, erotic sports, pleasure, dalliance'; also the (incomprehensible) 'acts of god(s) or other divine beings' and 'manifestation, expression'.

Liṅga: The male generative organ.

Mānuṣ: Human being (either in a general sense, or in the sense of a perfected human being, one who has realised her/his potential as a human being).

Mārphat: The final (and most superior) of four Sufi or Fakiri stations (*mokām*), the others being *śariyat*, *tarikat*, *hakikat* (see Cashin 1995:118ff.). *Mārphatī* and *śariyatī* may denote unorthodox (fakirs) and orthodox Muslims respectively.

Māṭi: *Māṭi* literally means 'earth, clay, the world' etc., and is a *bartamān-panthī* code word for faeces (one of the four moons). *Māṭi* may also be assimilated to womanhood by *bartamān-panthīs,* through *mā* meaning 'mother'.

Māyā: The phenomenal world, delusion, attachment, infatuation, compassion etc.

Melā: Festival or fair.

Mūl-bastu: Primary matter, usually referring to semen or to *rajaḥ-bīj* (the generative essences of female and male).

Mūrti: Form, body, incarnation. Image (usually statue) of a deity.

Mūrti-pūjā: Image worship.

Par: *Par* means 'another' or 'different' as opposed to *āpan* – 'one's own (people)'. It may also mean 'supreme', 'absolute' and 'God'. The *bartamān-panthī* association of the word *par* with women calls on both these conventional meanings.

Pīṭhasthāna: A sacred 'seat' of the goddess, where the different parts of the Hindu goddess Satī's body are said to have fallen. The story goes that Satī died of mortification, and Śiva wandered distracted with grief with her body on his shoulder, endangering the order of the universe. Viṣṇu came behind him and cut the body away in pieces (see Sircar 1973).

Prāṇāyām: Breath control as prescribed in the *yoga* system. Used by *bartamān-panthīs* to denote any practices involving the breath.

Praśiṣya: A disciple's disciple, etc.

Pūjā: Worship, adoration; often ritualised worship.

Purbāśram: The earlier householder life of a renouncer.

Rāg: Literally 'passion', but with many other esoteric meanings. The *rāg-mārg* (path of *rāg*, or esoteric path) is opposed to *bidhi-mārg* (the path of conventional, esoteric religion), this latter being regarded either as worthless, or as a preliminary phase.

Rajaḥ: The menstrual flow, dust, the second of the three qualities (*guṇas*) etc. For those in *bartamān* it primarily denotes the first of these. Alternatively it may refer to other sexual fluids of the female, and is regarded as the generative female essence.

Rajaḥ-bīj: The generative essences of female and male.

Ras: A term with a whole complex of connotations which cover the physical, sensual, aesthetic and affective. In the path of *bartamān* there is an additional emphasis on physiological alchemy (*ras-rasāyan*). *Ras* means (among other things), (any) fluid, especially a liquid solution of anything hard; exudation; flavour, taste; mucus or phlegm, semen. A special *bartamān-panthī* meaning is: urine (as well as semen) or indeed any exudation from the body, especially any fluid produced 'of itself', rather than one produced through activity (in this sense *ras* is opposed to *rati*, the fluid produced in love-making). In aesthetics it means strong attachment or love; or sentiment expressed in writing. Additional meanings are (in Vaishnavism) a manner of worship; inner significance; (sense of) humour, fun, banter; mercury etc. When used to refer to one of the 'four moons', *ras* generally refers to urine.

Ras-rati: This may refer to the male and female sexual fluids (one or two moons), to the sexual fluids and urine (three moons), or to bodily fluids in general.

Rasik: There is no English equivalent for this term, which derives from *ras*. Commonly the term means 'capable of comprehending the inner or true significance, and the flavour (of); versed in the art of love-making; witty, humorous' (*SBED*). As used by *bartamān-panthīs* it usually refers to those engaged in (or accomplished in) their type of esoteric practice, with the emphasis being on the flow of *ras* (whether this be physical or emotional) and on the more alchemical side of esoteric practice.

Rasikā: A female *rasik*.

Rati: *Rati* is wife of the god of love, Madan, and related to this is its meaning of (various) female sexual fluids or other substances. It also may mean fluids produced in love-making, and thus may come to mean (in a restricted fashion) semen. As one of the 'four moons', *rati* denotes sexual fluids. For a discussion of the complexities of the term *rati,* see R. P. Das (1992:402ff.).

Rūp: Literally 'form, shape, beauty, kind, colour', etc., *rūp* is a *bartamān-panthī* code word for *rajaḥ* (the menstrual fluids).

Sādhak: One who is engaged in esoteric practice, whether or not of householder or renouncer status. Usually translated in this book as 'practitioner'.

Sādhan/sādhanā: Usually this means systematic and austere practice towards a goal. In the *bartamān-panthī* context, it refers to more or less systematised esoteric body-centred practices, normally involving a partner of the opposite sex. Elements of 'sexo-yoga', various usages of bodily substances and exudations, including physiological alchemy may all be included here.

Sādhan-bhajan: This phrase refers to practices one does for oneself (*sādhan*) and for another (*bhajan*), typically one's partner in esoteric practice. *Bhajan* conventionally means 'worship'.

Sādhu: One who is 'realised', 'perfected' in (a particular) esoteric practice, and who may be either a householder or a renouncer. '*Sādhu*' generally means a *sannyāsī* (renouncer) in South Asia, but for *bartamān-panthīs* the meaning is generally wider. Often translated here as 'adept'. In some contexts '*sādhu*' may take on the 'intentional meaning' of 'women' (in general), or 'a woman suitable for esoteric practice'.

Sādhu-samāj: The community (or society) of *sādhus*. Contrasted with the society of householders, or those who are not 'perfected' (depending on whether *sādhu* is taken to mean renouncer or 'perfected one'). See '*sādhu*'.

Sādhu-sabhā: An assembly of *sādhus*.

Sādhu-saṅga: Associating with adepts, a practice which may be advocated before initiation (when one is looking for a guru), as well as afterwards. (It can also mean practising esoteric practice with a woman or women. See '*sādhu*').

Sahaj: This literally means 'being born together with' (*saha* + *ja*), and by extension 'innate, inborn, hereditary, original, and natural'; also 'co-emergent' (Guenther), 'simultaneously arisen' (Kvaerne). In modern Bengal, *sahaj* also means 'easy', 'simple' and 'plain'. *Bartamān-panthīs* often describe their esoteric practice as *sahaj*, often in the context of pointing out how difficult it is! They also speak of the search for the *sahaj mānuṣ*.

Sahajiyā: A term used of many so-called 'Bāuls', but rarely used by *bartamān-panthīs* themselves. Its use effects a lineal connection between such Bāuls and the so-called 'Buddhist Sahajiyā' and 'Vaishnava Sahajiyā'. Sahajiyā is very largely a scholarly category.

Sā̃i: A contraction of *svāmī* (lord), cf. *gosvāmi* and *gosā̃i* (or *gõsāi*). The term is applied as an honorific, especially for one's guru (in any sense). Especially in the Rarh area, '*sā̃i*' is used (in contradictory and fluctuating fashion) to indicate not only the highest stage (*siddhi*) but also one of four 'lines', 'houses' or even *sampradāy*, the other three being *āul, bāul* and *darbeś*.

Samādhi: Although this generally denotes 'a meditational state, trance or reverie', *bartamān-panthīs* tend rather to use the word in its sense of 'tomb' or 'mausoleum'.

Samāj: This usually means 'society, community' etc. *Samāj* is also used by *bartamān-panthīs* to refer to a tomb or mausoleum (*samādhi*).

Sampradāy(a): Tradition, sometimes translated as 'sect'.

Sandhā-bhāṣā: 'Intentional language', that is, language which has one (or more) literal meanings, but intends another meaning or meanings.

Sannyās: Renunciation (of householder life).

Sannyāsī: One who has taken formal rites of renunciation (*sannyās* or *tyāg*).

Saṅsār: The world, the earth. Also, worldly life, that is, the transient world of birth and death as well as the world of the householder.

Śariyat: Islamic scripture, law, and practices legitimised through this. (See also *mārphat*.)

Śikṣā: Literally means 'practice, instruction, training' and in the *bartamān-panthī* context the reference is to esoteric practice. *Śikṣā*, as an initiation into esoteric practice, is differentiated from (and follows) *dīkṣā*, in the sense of mantra initiation (see *dīkṣā*).

Śiṣya: (Male) disciple. (*Śiṣyā* = female disciple. *Śiṣya-praśiṣya* = disciples and their disciples etc.)

Smārta: 'Mentioned in (of) *smṛti*' (a category of scripture), and thus by extension 'normative' or (for *bartamān-panthīs*) 'orthodox'.

Thānā: Police Station area. Administrative subdivision of districts.

Tyāg(ī): See *sannyās(ī)*.

Udāsīn: 'Disinterested, unattached; unaffected . . . indifferent to worldly interests; practising stoical asceticism' (*SBED*).

Vaishnava/*Vaiṣṇava/Baiṣṇab:* A follower of the (Hindu) god Viṣṇu (Biṣṇu), or one of his 'incarnations', especially, in the Bengali context, Kṛṣṇa.

Yogī: A practitioner of *yoga*, in its various senses. *Yoga* is most often categorised by *bartamān-panthī* initiates as *ekak sādhanā*, as against *yugal sādhanā*, that is a system of practice followed by a person alone, as against one undertaken with a partner.

Yoni: The female sex organs, specifically the vagina. For *bartamān-panthīs* this is the place of birth and death (related to seminal emission).

Yugal-sādhanā: Esoteric practice of a male and female together.

BIBLIOGRAPHY

English and French

Ahmad, Aijaz, 1992, 'Orientalism and after: ambivalence and cosmopolitan location in the work of Edward Said', *Economic and Political Weekly*, 25 July 1992, 98–116.

Ahmed, Rafiuddin, 1981, *The Bengal Muslims 1871–1906: a quest for identity*, Oxford University Press, Oxford.

Amin, Shahid and Chakrabarty, Dipesh, 1996, *Subaltern studies IX: writings on South Asian history and society*, Oxford University Press, Delhi.

Anderson, J. D., 1962, *A manual of the Bengali language*, Frederick Ungar Publishing Co., New York.

Appadurai, Arjun, 1986, 'Is homo hierarchicus?' *American Ethnologist*, 13, 745–61.

Appadurai, Arjun, Korom, Frank J. and Mills, Margaret (eds.), 1991, *Gender, genre and power in South Asian expressive traditions*, University of Pennsylvania Press, Philadelphia.

Archer, W. G., 1971, *Kalighat paintings*, Her Majesty's Stationery Office, London.

Arnold, David and Hardiman, David (eds.), 1994, *Subaltern studies VIII: essays in honour of Ranajit Guha*, Oxford University Press, Delhi.

Avalon, Arthur, 1972 (1913), *Tantra of the great liberation* (translation from the Sanskrit, with introduction and commentary by Avalon), Dover Publications, New York.

Avalon, Arthur (ed.), 1969 & 1970 [1914 & 1915], *Principles of tantra: the tantratattva of Śrīyukta Śiva Candra Vidyārṇava Bhaṭṭācārya Mahodaya*, 2 parts, Ganesh and Co., Madras.

Bagchi, Prabodh Chandra, 1975 (1939), *Studies in the Tantras*, University of Calcutta.

Bahl, Kali Charan, 1981, 'Forms of the Indian notion of sexuality and an interpretation of the Mymensingh ballad of Kajalrekha', in *Women, politics and literature in Bengal*, ed. Clinton B. Seely, South Asia Series, Occasional Paper No. 30, Asian Studies Centre, Michigan State University, 101–17.

Bandyopadhyay, Sekhar, 1995, 'Popular religion and social mobility in colonial Bengal: the Matua sect and the Namasudras', in Rajat Kanta Ray (ed.), *Mind, body and society*, 152–92.

Banerjee, Sumanta, 1989, *The parlour and the streets: elite and popular culture in nineteenth century Calcutta*, Seagull Books, Calcutta.

Barnett, Steve, 1977, 'Identity choice and caste ideology in South India', in K. David (ed.), 1997, *The new wind*, 393–414.

Barnett, Steve, Fruzzetti, Lina and Östör, Akos, 1976, 'Hierarchy purified: notes on Dumont and his critics', *Journal of Asian Studies*, 35:4, 627–46.

Basu, Kedarnath, 1888, 'On the minor Vaishnava sects of Bengal', *Journal of the Anthropological Society of Bombay*, 1:8 (1886–89), 477–504.

Basu, Ranu, 1976, 'Some aspects of the composition of the urban elite in Bengal, 1850–1872', in W. M. Gunderson (ed.), *Studies on Bengal*, South Asia Series, Occasional Paper No. 26, Asian Studies Centre, Michigan State University, 107–23.

Bayly, C. A., 1986, 'The origins of svadeshi (home industry): cloth and Indian society 1700–1930', in Arjun Appadurai (ed.), *The social life of things: commodities in cultural perspective*, Cambridge University Press, 285–321.

Berreman, Gerald, 1971, 'The Brahmanical view of caste', *Contributions to Indian sociology*, n.s. 5, 16–23.

Béteille, André, 1983, *Homo hierarchicus, homo equalis: the idea of natural inequality and other essays*, Oxford University Press, Delhi.

1986, 'Individualism and equality', *Current Anthropology*, 27:2 (April), 121–34.

Bhadra, Gautam, 1989, 'The mentality of subalternity: Kantanama or Rajdharma', in Guha (ed.), *Subaltern studies VI*, 54–91.

Bharati, Agehananda, 1970 [1965], *The Tantric tradition*, Rider and Co., London.

Bhattacharjee, G. P., 1973, *Renaissance and freedom movement in Bangladesh*, Minerva Associates, Calcutta.

Bhattacharya, B. K., 1979, *West Bengal District Gazetteers: Murshidabad*, Government of West Bengal, Calcutta.

Bhattacharya, Deben, 1969, *The mirror of the sky*, George, Allen and Unwin, London.

Bhattacharyya, Asit Kumar, 1962, 'Akshay Dutta, pioneer of Indian rationalism', in *The rationalist annual*, R.P.A., London.

Bhattacharya (Bhattacherjee), Bholanath, 1977, 'Some aspects of the esoteric cults of consort worship in Bengal: a field survey report', *Folklore*, Calcutta, 18:10 (October), 310–24; (December), 385–97.

Bhattacharyya, Deborah P., 1981, 'Madness as entropy: a Bengali view', in C. B. Seely (ed.), *Women, politics and literature in Bengal*, South Asia Series, Occasional Paper No. 30, Michigan State University, 31–40.

1986, *Pāglāmi: ethnopsychiatric knowledge in Bengal*, Syracuse University,

Bhattacharya, J. N., 1896, *Hindu castes and sects*, Calcutta.

Bloch, Maurice, and Parry, Jonathan (eds.), 1982, *Death and the regeneration of life*, Cambridge University Press, Cambridge.

Bose, Manindra Mohan, 1930, *The post-Chaitanya Sahajiya cult of Bengal*, University of Calcutta.

Bose, Sanat Kumar, 1961, 'The Bauls of Birbhum', in B. Ray, 1961, *Census 1961*, West Bengal, DCH Birbhum, 52–3.

Briggs, George Weston, 1938, *Gorakhnāth and the Kānphaṭā Yogīs*, Y.M.C.A. Press, Calcutta.

Brooks, Douglas Renfrew, 1990, *The secret of the three cities: an introduction to Hindu Sakta Tantrism*, University of Chicago Press, Chicago, IL.

1995, 'Esoteric knowledge and the tradition of the preceptors', in Lopez (ed.), 1995, *Religions of India*, 609–26.

Broomfield, J. H., 1968, *Elite conflict in a plural society: twentieth-century Bengal*, University of California Press, Stanford, CA.

Burghart, Richard, 1976, 'Bairāgī maṇḍals', *Contributions to Nepalese Studies* 3, 63–104.

1978, 'Hierarchical models of the Hindu social system', *Man* (n.s.), 13, 519–36.

1983a, 'Renunciation in the religious traditions of South Asia', *Man* (n.s.), 18, 635–53.

1983b, 'Wandering ascetics of the Rāmānandī sect', *History of Religions*, 22:4, 361–79.

1990, 'Ethnographers and their local counterparts in India', in R. Fardon (ed.), 1990, *Localizing strategies*, 260–79.

Butler, Judith, 1992, 'Contingent foundations: feminism and the question of "postmodernism" ', in J. Butler and Joan W. Scott (eds.), *Feminists theorize the political*, Routledge, New York and London.

Cantlie, Audrey, 1977, 'Aspects of Hindu asceticism', in I. M. Lewis (ed.), *Symbols and sentiments*, London, Academic Press, 247–67.

Capwell, Charles, 1974, 'The esoteric belief of the Bauls of Bengal', *Journal of Asian Studies*, 33:2, 255–64.

1986, *The music of the Bauls of Bengal*, Kent University Press, Kent, OH.

Carstairs, G. Morris, 1970 (1958), *The twice-born: a study of a community of high-caste Hindus*, Hogarth Press, London.

Cashin, David, 1995, *The ocean of love: middle Bengali Sufi literature and the Fakirs of Bengal* (thesis), Association of Oriental Studies, Stockholm University, Stockholm.

Chakrabarty, Dipesh, 2000, 'Radical histories and question of enlightenment rationalism: some recent critiques of *Subaltern Studies*', in V. Caturvedi (ed.), *Mapping subaltern studies and the postcolonial*, 256–299. (Originally published in *Economic and political weekly,* 30:114 (8 April 1995), 751–9.

Chakravarti, Ramakanta, 1985, *Vaiṣṇavism in Bengal 1486–1900*, Sanskrit Pustak Bhandar, Calcutta.

Chakravarti, Suchindra Chandra, 1969, *Philosophical foundation of Bengal Vaiṣṇavism*, Academic Publishers, Calcutta.

Chakravarti, Sudhir, 1980, 'Minor religious sects of Nadia', *I.C.S.S.R. Research Abstracts Quarterly*, 9 (January–June), 28–37, Delhi.

Chartier, Roger, 1984, 'Culture as appropriation: popular cultural uses in early modern France', in S. L. Kaplan (ed.), *Understanding popular culture: Europe from the Middle Ages to the nineteenth century*, Mouton, Berlin, New York, Amsterdam, 229–53.

Chatterjee, Partha, 1989, 'Caste and subaltern consciousness', in Ranajit Guha (ed.), *Subaltern studies VI*, 169–209.

1992, 'A religion of urban domesticity: Sri Ramakrishna and the Calcutta middle class', in Partha Chatterjee and Gyanendra Pandey (eds.), 1992, *Subaltern studies VII*, 40–68.

1994 [1993], *The nation and its fragments: colonial and postcolonial histories*, Oxford University Press, Delhi.

1996 [1995] (ed.), *Texts of power: emerging disciplines in colonial Bengal*, Samya, Calcutta.

Chatterjee, Partha, and Pandey, Gyanendra (eds.), 1992, *Subaltern studies VII: writings on South Asian history and society*, Oxford University Press, Delhi.

Chatterji, Suniti Kumar, 1970 [1926], *The origin and development of the Bengali language*, vol. I, George Allen and Unwin, London.

1978, *Select writings*, vol. 1, Vikas, New Delhi.

Chattopadhyaya, D. P., 1959, *Lokāyata: A study in ancient Indian materialism*, People's Publishing House, New Delhi.

1972 [1964], *Indian philosophy: a popular introduction*, People's Publishing House, New Delhi.

1990 (ed.), *Cārvāka/Lokāyata: an anthology of source materials and some recent studies*, Indian Council of Philosophical Research (New Delhi) in association with Ṛddhi-India, Calcutta.

Clark, T. W., 1967, 'Encounter and growth in Bengali culture: a survey of modern Bengali literature', in Edward C. Dimock, Jr (ed.), *Bengal: literature and history*, Occasional Paper No. 6, Asian Studies Center, Michigan State University, 83–91.

Clifford, J. and Marcus, G. E., 1986, *Writing culture: the poetics and politics of ethnography*, University of California Press, Berkeley, CA.

Daniel, Sheryl B., 1983, 'The tool box approach of the Tamil to the issues of moral responsibility and human destiny' in Keyes and Daniel (eds.), 1983, *Karma*, 27–62.

Daniel, E. Valentine, 1984, *Fluid signs: being a person the Tamil way*, University of California Press, Berkeley, CA.

Das, Paritosh, 1988, *Sahajiyā cult of Bengal and Pancha Sakhā cult of Orissa*, Firma KLM Private, Calcutta.

Das, Rahul Peter, 1990, 'Ancient Indian theories on the female role in conception compared with Ancient Greek and Graeco-Arabic (Yūnānī) theories', paper read for 3rd International Congress on Traditional Asian Medicine, Bombay, 4–7 January 1990.

1992, 'Problematic aspects of the sexual rituals of the Bauls of Bengal', *Journal of the American Oriental Society*, 112:3, 388–432.

1997, *Essays on Vaiṣṇavism in Bengal*, Firma KLM Private, Calcutta.

Das, Veena, 1982 [1977], *Structure and cognition: aspects of Hindu caste and ritual*, Oxford University Press, Delhi.

1986 (ed.), *The word and the world: fantasy, symbol and record*, Sage Publications, New Delhi.

1989, 'Subaltern as perspective', in Ranajit Guha (ed.), *Subaltern studies VI*, 310–24.

Dasgupta, Alokeranjan and Dasgupta, Mary Ann (translators), 1977, *Roots in the void: Baul songs of Bengal*, K. P. Bagchi and Co., Calcutta.

Dasgupta, Shashi Bhusan, 1969 [1946], *Obscure religious cults*, Firma K. L. Mukhopadhyaya, Calcutta.

Dasgupta, S. N., 1975 [1922], *A history of Indian philosophy*, 5 vols., Motilal Banarsidass, Delhi.

Das Gupta, Uma, 1975–76 'Santiniketan and Sriniketan: a historical introduction', *Visva-bharati Quarterly*.

Datta, Rajeshwari, 1978, 'The religious aspect of the Bāul songs of Bengal', *Journal of Asian Studies*, 37:3, 445–55.

David, K. (ed.), 1977, *The new wind: changing identities in South Asia*, Mouton and Co., The Hague.

Day, Lal Behari, 1970, *Bengal peasant life* (Calcutta), based on 1878 edn. (First published in 1874 as *Gobinda samanta: the history of a Bengal peasant.*)

De, S. K., 1961, *Early history of the Vaiṣṇava faith and movement in Bengal*, Calcutta.

1962 (1919), *Bengali literature in the nineteenth century (1757–1857)*, Firma K. L. Mukhopadhyay, Calcutta.

Delmonico, Neal, 1995, 'How to partake in the love of Kṛṣṇa', in Lopez (ed.), 1995, *Religions of India*, 244–68.

Denton, Lynn T., 1991, 'Varieties of Hindu female asceticism' in Leslie (ed.), 1991, *Roles and rituals*, 211–31.

Derné, Steve, 1990, 'The Kshatriya view of caste: a discussion of Raheja's *The poison in the gift*', *Contributions to Indian Sociology*, 24:2, 259–63.

Dimock, Edward C. (Jr), 1959, 'Rabindranath Tagore – "the Greatest of the Bāuls of Bengal"', *Journal of the Asiatic Society*, 29:1, 33–51.

1963, *The thief of love: Bengal tales from court and village*, University of Chicago Press, Chicago, IL and London.

1966, *The place of the hidden moon: erotic mysticism in the Vaiṣṇava-sahajiyā cult of Bengal*, University of Chicago Press, Chicago, IL and London.

1989, *The sound of silent guns and other essays*, Delhi.

Doniger, W. and Smith, B. K. (eds.), 1991, *The laws of Manu* (with Introduction and notes), Penguin Books India, New Delhi.

Dumont, Louis, 1957, 'For a sociology of India', *Contributions to Indian Sociology*, 1, 7–22.

1960, 'World renunciation in Indian religions', *Contributions to Indian Sociology*, 4, 33–62.

1970, *Homo hierarchicus: the caste system and its implications*, Weidenfeld and Richolson, London.

Dutt, G. S., 1931, Appendix on the indigenous dances of Bengal, *Census of India 1931,* (vol. V, part 1, *Bengal and Sikkim*).

Eliade, Mircea, 1954, *Le yoga, immortalité et liberté*, Payot, Paris.

1958, *Yoga: immortality and freedom*, trans. Willard R. Trask, Bollingen Series, Pantheon Inc., New York.

1962, *The forge and the crucible* (trans. from the French by Stephen Corrin), Rider and Co., London.

Eriksen, Thomas Hylland, 1993, *Ethnicity and nationalism: anthropological perspectives*, Pluto Press, London/Boulder, CO.

Fabian, Johannes, 1983, *Time and the other: how anthropology makes its object*, Cambridge University Press, Cambridge.

Fardon, Richard (ed.), 1990, *Localizing strategies: regional traditions of ethnographic writing*, Scottish Academy Press, Edinburgh, and Smithsonian Institution Press, Washington, DC.

Feher, Michel *et al.* (eds.), 1989, *Fragments for a history of the human body*, Pt. 2, Zone Press, New York.

Flood, Gavin D., 1992, 'Techniques of body and desire in Kashmir Śaivism', *Religion* 22, 47–62.

Fuller, C. J., 1992, *The camphor flame: popular Hinduism and society in India*, Princeton University Press, Princeton, NJ.

Fuller, C. J. and Spencer, Jonathan, 1990, 'South Asian anthropology in the 1980s', *South Asia Research*, 10:2, 85–105.

Ganguly, Suranjan and Ginsberg, Allen, 1994, 'On Baul poetry: an interview and six poems', *Michigan Quarterly Review*, 33:2 (Spring), 350–9.

Garrett, J. H. E., 1910, *Bengal District Gazetteers: Nadia*, Calcutta.

Gerow, Edwin, 'Rasa as a category of literary criticism', in Rachel Baumer and James R. Brandon (eds.), *Sanskrit drama in performance*, Honolulu, University Press of Hawaii, 226–57.

Ghosh, J. C., 1976 (1948), *Bengali literature*, Curzon Press, London.

Ghosh, S. N., 1981a, *Census of India (1981), District Census Handbook, Nadia District, West Bengal*, The Superintendent, Government Printing, West Bengal.

1981b, *Census of India (1981), District Census Handbook, Birbhum District, West Bengal*, The Superintendent, Government Printing, West Bengal.

1981c, *Census of India (1981), District Census Handbook, Murshidabad District, West Bengal*, The Superintendent, Government Printing, West Bengal.

1981d (ed.), *Census of India (1981): household population by religion of head of household (West Bengal)*, The Superintendent, Government Printing, West Bengal.

Ghurye, Govind S., 1953, *Indian sadhus*, Popular Book Depot, Bombay.

Gold, Ann Grodzins, 1989, *Fruitful journeys: the ways of Rajasthani pilgrims*, Oxford University Press, Delhi.

Gold, Daniel, 1987, 'Clan and lineage among the Sants: seed, substance, service', in Karine Schomer and W. H. McLeod (eds.), 1987, *The Sants*, 305–27.

Gordon, Leonard A., 1974, *Bengal: the nationalist movement 1876–1940*, Columbia University Press, New York.

Goudriaan, Teun, and Gupta, Sanjukta, 1981, *Hindu Tantric and Śākta literature, A history of Indian literature*, vol. II, Otto Harrassowitz, Wiesbaden.

Govinda, Anagarika, 1959, *Foundations of Tibetan mysticism*, Rider and Co., London.

Granoff, P., 1986–92, 'Tolerance in the Tantras', *Journal of Oriental Research*, Madras, 56–62: 283–302

Grierson, G. A., 1903, *Linguistic survey of India*, vol. V(1), Office of the Superintendent of Government Printing, Calcutta.

Guenther, Herbert V., 1973 [1968], *The royal song of Saraha: a study in the history of Buddhist thought*, Shambala Publications, Berkeley, CA.

Guha, Ranajit (ed.) 1986 [1982] *Subaltern studies I: writings on South Asian history and society*, Oxford University Press, Delhi.

1986 [1983], *Subaltern studies II* . . . Oxford University Press, Delhi.

1989 [1984], *Subaltern studies III* . . .

1990 [1985], *Subaltern studies IV* . . .

1987, *Subaltern studies V* . . .

1989, *Subaltern studies VI* . . .

Guha-Thakurta, Tapati, 1992, *The making of a new 'Indian' art: artists, aesthetics and nationalism in Bengal, c.1850–1920*, Cambridge University Press, Cambridge.

1996, 'Recovering the nation's art', in Partha Chatterjee (ed.), 1996, *Texts of power*, 63–92.

Gupta, Sanjukta, 1991, 'Women in the Śaiva/Śākta ethos', in Leslie (ed.), 1991, *Roles and rituals*, 193–209.

Gupta, Sanjukta, Hoens, Dirk Jan and Goudriaan, Teun, 1979, *Hindu Tantrism*, E. J. Brill, Leiden and Cologne.

Haberman, David L., 1988, *Acting as a way of salvation: a study of rāgānugā bhakti sādhanā*, Oxford University Press, Oxford.

Halbfass, Wilhelm, 1980, 'Karma, *apūrva*, and "natural" causes: observations on the growth and limits of the theory of *saṃsāra*', in O'Flaherty (ed.), 1980a, *Karma and rebirth*, 268–302.

Haq, Muhammad Enamul, 1975, *A history of Sufi-ism in Bengal*, Asiatic Society of Bangladesh, Dacca.

Harding, Sandra, 1987, *Feminism and methodology*, Indiana University Press, Bloomington, IN.

Hawley, John Stratton, 1988, 'Author and authority in the *bhakti* poetry of North India', *Journal of Asian Studies*, 47:2, 269–90.

Hawley, John Stratton and Wulff, Donna Marie (eds.), 1986 [1982], *The divine consort: Rādhā and the goddesses of India*, Beacon Press, Boston, MA.

Hayes, Glen A., 1995, 'The Vaiṣṇava Sahajiyā traditions of medieval Bengal', in Lopez (ed.), *Religions of India*, 333–51.

2000, 'The necklace of immortality: a seventeenth century Vaiṣṇava Sahajiyā text', in D. G. White (ed.), 2000, *Tantra in practice*, 308–25.

Heesterman, J. C., 1982, 'Householder and wanderer', in T. N. Madan (ed.), *Way of Life*, 251–71.

Hess, Linda, 1987, 'Kabir's rough rhetoric', in Schomer and McLeod (eds.), *The Sants*, 143–65.

Hess, Linda and Singh, Shukdev (trans; essays and notes by Linda Hess), 1986 [1983], *The Bījak of Kabir*, Motilal Banarsidass, Delhi.

Hiltebeitel, Alf (ed.), 1989, *Criminal gods and demon devotees: essays on the guardians of popular Hinduism*, State University of New York Press, Albany, NY.

Hobart, Mark, 1990, 'Who do you think you are? The authorised Balinese', in Richard Fardon (ed.), 1990, *Localizing strategies*, 303–38.

Hobsbawm E. and Ranger, T., 1983, *The invention of tradition*, Cambridge University Press, Cambridge.

Hunter, W. W., *A statistical account of Bengal*, Trubner and Co., London:

1875a	Vol. I,	*24 Parganas and Sundarbans.*
1875b	Vol. II	*Nadiya.*
1876a	Vol. III	*Midnapore and Hugli (including Howrah).*
1876b	Vol. IV	*Bardwan, Birbhum and Bankura.*
1876c	Vol. VII	*Maldah, Rangpur and Dinajpur.*
1876d	Vol. VIII	*Rajshahi and Bogra.*
1876e	Vol. IX	*Murshidabad and Pabna.*
1876f	Vol. VI	*Chittagong Hill Tracts, Chittagong, Noakhali, Tipperah, Hill Tipperah.*
1877	Vol. V	*Dacca (and Bakerganj, Faridpur and Maimensingh).*

1881, *Imperial Gazetteer of India* (vol. II), Trubner and Co., London.

1897, *Annals of rural Bengal*, Smith, Elder and Co., London.

Inden, Ronald B., 1986, 'Orientalist constructions of India', *Modern Asian Studies*, 20:3, 401–46.

1990, *Imagining India*, Basil Blackwell, Oxford.

Inden, Ronald B. and Nicholas, Ralph W., 1977, *Kinship in Bengali culture*, University of Chicago Press, Chicago, IL.

Isherwood, S., 1990, 'Diversity within Islam: an instance from Eastern India', *Anthropology Today*, 6:6, 8–10.

Jha, Sakti Nath, 1995, '*Cāri-candra bhed*: use of the four moons', in R. K. Ray (ed.), 1995, *Mind, body and society*, 65–108.

Juergensmeyer, Mark, 1982, *Religion as social vision: the movement against untouchability in 20th-century Punjab,* University of California Press, Berkeley, CA.

Kailasapathy K., 1987, 'The writings of the Tamil siddhas', in Schomer and McLeod (eds.), 1987, *The Sants*, 385–411.

Kakar, Sudhir, 1981 [1978], *The inner world: a psycho-analytic study of childhood and society in India*, Oxford University Press, Delhi.

1986 [1982], *Shamans, mystics and doctors: a psychological inquiry into India and its healing traditions*, Oxford University Press, Delhi.
1990 (1989), *Intimate relations: exploring Indian sexuality*, Penguin, Harmondsworth.
1991, *The analyst and the mystic: psychoanalytic reflections on religion and mysticism*, Viking, London.
Kakar, Sudhir and Ross, John M., 1986, *Tales of love, sex and danger*, Oxford University Press, Delhi.
Kane, P. V., 1941, *History of the Dharmaśāstra*, vol. II, Bhandarkar Oriental Research Institute, Poona.
1963, *History of the Dharmaśāstra*, vol. IV, Bhandarkar Oriental Research Institute.
Kapferer, Bruce (ed.), 1976, *Transaction and meaning: directions in the anthropology of exchange and symbolic behaviour*, I. S. H. I., Philadelphia, PA.
Karim, Anwarul, 1979/80, 'Folk medicine in Baul practice and their system of birth control', *Folklore*, Kushtia, Bangladesh, 26–38.
1980, *The Bauls of Bangladesh: a study of an obscure religious cult*, Lalan Academy, Kushtia, Bangladesh.
Kaviraj, Gopinath, 1927, 'Some aspects of the history and doctrines of the Nathas', in Gopinath Kaviraj (ed.), *The Princess of Wales Sarasvati Bhavan Studies*, vol. VI, Government Sanskrit Library, Benares, India, 19–43.
Keyes, Charles F. and Daniel, E. V. (eds.), 1983, *Karma: an anthropological inquiry*, University of California Press, Berkeley, CA.
Khare, R. S., 1984, *The untouchable as himself: ideology, identity and pragmatism among the Lucknow Chamars*, Cambridge University Press, Cambridge.
Kolenda, P., 1964, 'Religious anxiety and Hindu fate', *Journal of Asian Studies*, 23:71–82.
Kopf, David, 1969, *British Orientalism and the Bengal Renaissance: the dynamics of Indian modernization, 1773–1835*, University of California Press, Berkeley, CA.
1979, *The Brahmo Samaj and the shaping of the modern Indian mind*, Princeton University Press, Princeton, NJ.
Kripalani, Krishna, 1980 revd edn [1962], *Rabindranath Tagore: a biography*, Visva Bharati, Calcutta.
Kuchertz, Joseph, 1975 'Origin and construction of the melodies in Baul songs of Bengal', in *Yearbook of the international folk music council*, vol. VII, UNESCO (ed. Bruno Nettl), 85–91.
Kumar, Nita (ed.), 1994, *Women as subjects: South Asian histories*, University Press of Virginia.
Kvaerne, Per, 1977, *An anthology of Buddhist Tantric songs: a study of the Caryāgīti*, The Norwegian Academy of Science and Letters, Universitetsforlaget, Oslo-Bergen-Tromsø.
Larson, Gerald James, 1980, 'Karma as a "sociology of knowledge" or "social psychology" of process/praxis' in O'Flaherty (ed.) 1980a, *Karma and rebirth*, 303–16.
1990, 'India through Hindu categories: A Sāṁkhyā response', *Contributions to Indian Sociology*, (n.s.), 24:2, 237–50.
Larson, Gerald James and Bhattacharya, R. S. (eds.), 1987, *Sāmkhya: a dualist tradition in Indian philosophy*, Princeton University Press, Princeton, NJ.
Leslie, Julia (ed.), 1991, *Roles and rituals for Hindu women*, Pinter Publishers, London.
Lopez, Donald S. (ed.), 1995, *Religions of India in practice*, Princeton University Press, Princeton, NJ.

Lorenzen, David N., 1972, *The Kāpālikas and Kālāmukhas: two lost Śaivite sects*, University of California Press, Berkeley, CA.
1989, 'New data on the Kāpālikas' in Hiltebeitel (ed.), 1989, *Criminal gods*, 231–8.
Lupsa, Michèle (introduction, trans. and notes), 1967, *Chants à Kālī de Rāmprasād*, Institut Français d'Indologie, Pondichéry, no. 30.
Lynch, Owen M. (ed.), 1969, *The politics of untouchability: social mobility and social change in a city of India*, Columbia University Press, New York.
1990, *Divine passions: the social construction of emotion in India*, University of California Press, Berkeley, CA.
MacDonell, A. A., 1969 [1929], *A practical Sanskrit dictionary*, Oxford University Press, Oxford.
Madan, T. N. (ed.), 1982, *Way of life, king, householder, renouncer: essays in honour of Louis Dumont*, Vikas, New Delhi.
1987, *Non-renunciation: themes and interpretations of Hindu culture*, Oxford University Press, Delhi.
1992 (ed.), *Religion in India*, Oxford University Press, Delhi.
Mahapatra, Piyushkanti, 1971, 'The Baul cult', *Folklore* (Calcutta), (April), 126–33; (May), 167–75; (June), 218–28; (July), 258–67; (August), 296–310; (September), 333–49.
Mahdihassan, S., 1991 [1977], *Indian alchemy or rasayana: in the light of asceticism and geriatrics*, Motilal Banarsidass Publishers Pvt., Delhi.
Majumdar, Bimanbehari, 1969, *Kṛṣṇa in history and legend*, University of Calcutta.
Majumdar, D., 1975, *West Bengal District Gazetteers, Birbhum*, Government of West Bengal, Calcutta.
1978, *West Bengal District Gazetteers, Nadia*, Government of West Bengal, Calcutta.
Majumdar, Dipak and Roberge, Gaston, 1979, 'The Bauls: communicators and artists', *National Journal for the Performing Arts of Bombay*, 1–14.
Majumdar, R. C., 1971, *History of ancient Bengal*, Calcutta.
Mallik, Bhaktiprasad, 1972, *Language of the underworld of West Bengal*, Sanskrit College, Calcutta.
Maloney, Clarence, Aziz, K. M. Ashraful, and Sarkar, Profulla C., 1981, *Beliefs and fertility in Bangladesh*, Dacca, The International Centre for Diarrhoeal Disease Research, Bangladesh.
Marglin, Frederique Apffel, 1982, 'Types of sexual union and their implicit meanings', in Hawley and Wulff (eds.), *The divine consort*, 298–315.
1985, *Wives of the God-King: the rituals of the Devadasis of Puri*, Oxford University Press, Delhi.
1990, 'Refining the body: transformative emotion in ritual dance', in Owen Lynch (ed.), *Divine passions*, 212–36.
Marriott, McKim, 1976, 'Hindu transactions: diversity without dualism', in B. Kapferer (ed.), 1976, *Transaction and meaning*, 109–42.
1989, 'Constructing an Indian ethnosociology', *Contributions to Indian Sociology* (n.s.) 23:1, 1–39.
1990 (ed.), *India through Hindu categories*, Sage Publications, New Delhi.
Marriott, McKim, and Inden, Ronald B., 1974, 'Caste systems', *Encyclopaedia Britannica*, Macropaedia, vol. III, 982–91.
1977, 'Towards an ethnosociology of South Asian caste systems', in Kenneth David (ed.), 1977, *The new wind*, 227–38.

Masson, J. Moussaief, 1976, 'The psychology of the ascetic', *Journal of Asian Studies*, 35:4, 611–25.
1980, *The oceanic feeling: the origins of religious sentiment in India*, D. Reidel, Dordrecht.
Matilal, B. K., 1990, *The word and the world*, Oxford University Press, Delhi.
McDaniel, June, 1989, *The madness of the saints: ecstatic religion in Bengal*, University of Chicago Press, Chicago, IL.
McDermott, Rachel Fell, 1995, 'Bengali songs to Kālī', in Lopez (ed.), 1995, *Religions of India*, 55–76.
Mencher, Joan P., 1974, 'The caste system upside down, or the not-so-mysterious east', *Current Anthropology*, 15: 4, 469–92.
Mishra, Vijay C., 1987, 'Two truths are told: Tagore's Kabir', in Schomer and McLeod (eds.), *The Sants*, 167–80.
Misri, Urvashi, 1986, 'Child and childhood: a conceptual construction', in Veena Das (ed.), *The word and the world*, 115–32.
Mitra, Asoka, 1953, *The tribes and castes of West Bengal*, West Bengal Census (1951), West Bengal Government Press, Alipore, West Bengal.
Moffat, Michael, 1990, 'Deconstructing McKim Marriott's ethnosociology: an outcaste's critique', *Contributions to Indian Sociology* (n.s.) 25:2, 215–63.
Monier-Williams, M., 1960 [1899], *A Sanskrit–English dictionary*, Clarendon Press, Oxford.
Mukherjee, Prithwindra, 1985, *Les fous de l'absolu: chant baul*, Editions Findakly, Paris.
Mukherjee, Radhakamal, 1966, *A history of Indian civilisation*, vol. II, Hind Kitabs, Bombay.
Mukherjee, S. N., 1993, *Calcutta: essays in urban history*, Subarnarekha, Calcutta.
Mukherji, Tarapada, 1963, *The old Bengali language and text*, University of Calcutta.
Nandy, Ashis, 1988 [1983], *The intimate enemy: loss and recovery of self under colonialism*, Oxford University Press, Delhi.
Needham, Joseph, 1954, *Science and civilisation in China*, vol. I, *Introductory orientations*, Cambridge University Press, Cambridge.
1956, *Science and civilisation in China*, vol. II, *History of scientific thought*, Cambridge University Press, Cambridge.
1974, *Science and civilisation in China*, vol. V, *Spagyrical discovery and invention*, pt. 2, *Magisteries of gold and immortality*, Cambridge University Press.
1983, *Science and civilisation in China*, vol. V, pt. 5, *Physiological alchemy*, Cambridge University Press, Cambridge.
Needham, Rodney, 1975, 'Polythetic classification: convergence and consequences', *Man* (n.s.), 10, 349–69.
1979, *Symbolic classification*, Goodyear, Santa Monica, CA.
Nicholas, R., 1982, 'Sraddha, impurity and relations between the living and the dead', in T. N. Madan (ed.), 1982, *Way of life*, 367–79.
O'Connell, Joseph T., 1982, 'Jāti-Vaiṣṇavas of Bengal: "Subcaste" (Jāti) without "Caste" (Varṇa)', *Journal of Asian and African Studies*, 17:3–4, 189–207.
1990, 'Do *bhakti* movements change Hindu social structures? The case of Caitanya's Vaiṣṇavas in Bengal', in Bardwell L. Smith (ed.), *Boeings and bullock carts: studies in change and continuity in Indian civilization,* vol. IV, *Religious movements and social identity*, Chanakya Publications, Delhi, 39–63.

1985 (ed.), *Bengal Vaiṣṇavism, Orientalism, Society and the Arts*, South Asia Series, Occasional Paper 35, Asian Studies Center, Michigan State University.

O'Flaherty, Wendy Doniger, 1973, *Asceticism and eroticism in the mythology of Śiva*, Oxford University Press, Oxford.

1980a (ed.), *Karma and rebirth in classical Indian traditions*, University of California Press, Berkeley, CA.

1980b, *Women, androgynes and other mythical beasts*, University of Chicago Press, Chicago, and London.

O'Hanlon, Rosalind, 1985, *Caste, conflict and ideology: Mahatma Jotirao Phule and low caste protest in ninteenth-century Western India*, Cambridge University Press, Cambridge.

1988, 'Recovering the subject: subaltern studies and histories of resistance in Colonial South Asia', *Modern Asian Studies*, 22:1, 189–224.

1991, 'Issues of widowhood: gender and resistance in colonial Western India', in Douglas Haynes and Gyan Prakash (eds.), *Contesting power: resistance and everyday social life in South Asia*, University of California Press, Berkeley, CA, 62–108.

O'Hanlon, Rosalind and Washbrook, David, 1992, 'After Orientalism: culture, criticism and politics in the third world' *Comparative Studies in Society and History*, 34:1, 141–67.

Okely, J., 1983, The *Traveller-gypsies*, Cambridge University Press, Cambridge.

Olivelle, Patrick, 1992, *Saṃnyāsa Upaniṣads: Hindu scriptures on asceticism and renunciation*, Oxford University Press, New York, Oxford (Transl. with introduction and notes).

1993, *The āśrama system: the history and hermeneutics of a religious institution*, Oxford University Press, Oxford.

1995, 'Ascetic withdrawal or social engagement', in Lopez (ed.), 1995, *Religions of India*, 533–46.

O'Malley, L. S. S., 1908, *Eastern Bengal District Gazetteers: Chittagong*, Calcutta.

1910, *Bengal District Gazetteers: Birbhum*, Calcutta.

1916, *Bengal District Gazetteers: Rajshahi*, Calcutta.

Openshaw, Jeanne, 1994, "Baūls' of West Bengal: with special reference to Rāj Khyāpā and his followers', Ph.D. thesis, School of Oriental and African Studies, University of London.

1995, 'Rāj Kṛṣṇa: perspectives on the worlds of a little-known Bengali "guru" ', in R. K. Ray (ed.), 1995, *Mind, body and society*, 109–51.

1997a, 'The radicalism of Tagore and the "Bāuls" of Bengal', *South Asia Research*, 17:1, 20–36.

1997b, 'The web of deceit: challenges to Hindu and Muslim "orthodoxies" by "Bāuls" of Bengal', *Religion*, 27:297–309.

1998, ' "Killing" the guru: anti-hierarchical tendencies of "Bāuls" of Bengal', *Contributions to Indian Sociology,* 32:1, 1–19.

Östör, Ákos, Fruzzetti, Lina and Barnett, Steve (eds.), 1983, *Concepts of person: kinship, caste, and marriage in India*, Oxford University Press, Delhi.

Parish, Steven M., 1997 [1993], *Hierarchy and its discontents: culture and the politics of consciousness in caste society*, Oxford University Press, Delhi.

Parry, Jonathan, 1982, 'Sacrificial death and the necrophagous ascetic', in Bloch and Parry (eds.), *Death*, 1982, 74–110.

1989, 'The end of the body', in Feher *et al.* (eds.), 1989, *Fragments*, 491–517.

1994, *Death in Banaras*, Cambridge University Press, Cambridge.

Paul, H. C., 1973a 'Bāul-poets on chāri-chandra (or four states of the mind)', *Journal of the Asiatic Society of Bangladesh*, 1–53.

1973b, 'Bāul poets on the mystic letters', *Journal of the Asiatic Society of Bengal*, 81–96.

Peabody, Norbert, 1996, 'Tod's *Rajast'han* and the boundaries of imperial rule in nineteenth-century India', *Modern Asian Studies*, 30:1, 185–220.

Pinney, Chris, 1988, 'Representations of India: normalisation and the "other"', *Pacific Viewpoint*, 29:2, 144–62.

Potter, Karl, 1963, *Presuppositions of Indian philosophy*, Prentice Hall, New Jersey.

Prakash, Gyan, 1990, 'Writing post-Orientalist histories of the third world: perspectives from Indian historiography', *Comparative Studies in Society and History*, 32:2, 383–408.

1992, 'Can the "subaltern" ride? A reply to O'Hanlon and Washbrook', *Comparative Studies in Society and History*, 34:1, 168–84.

Qureshi, Mahmud Shah, 1977 (trans., introduction and commentary), *Poèmes mystiques Bengalis* (*chants Bāuls*), Collection Unesco d'Oeuvres Représentatives, Bangladesh.

Rahim, M. A., 1967, *Social and cultural history of Bengal*, vol. II (1576–1752), Pakistan Historical Society, Karachi.

Ramanujan, A. K., 1973, *Speaking of Śiva*, Penguin, Harmondsworth.

1990, 'Is there an Indian way of thinking? An informal essay', in Marriott (ed.), *India through Hindu categories*, 41–58.

1993 [1981], *Hymns for the drowning: poems for Viṣṇu of Nammālvār*, Penguin, India.

Ray, B., 1961, *Census 1961: West Bengal. District census handbook: Birbhum*, Government Printing, Calcutta, West Bengal.

Ray, Benoy Gopal, 1965, *Religious movements in modern India*, Visva Bharati, Santiniketan, West Bengal.

Ray, Manas, 1994, *The Bauls of Birbhum: a study in persistence and change in communication in cultural context*, Firma KLM Private, Calcutta.

Ray, Rajat Kanta (ed.), 1995, *Mind, body and society: life and mentality in colonial Bengal*, Oxford University Press, Delhi.

Raychaudhuri, Tapan, 1988, *Europe reconsidered: perceptions of the West in nineteenth century Bengal*, Oxford University Press, Delhi.

Risley, H. H., 1891, *Tribes and castes of Bengal*, vol. II, Bengal Secretariat Press, Calcutta.

Roy, Asim, 1983, *The Islamic syncretistic tradition in Bengal*, Princeton University Press, Princeton, NI.

Sannyal, Hitesranjan, 1981, *Social mobility in Bengal*, Papyrus, Calcutta.

Salomon, C., 1979, 'A contemporary sahajiyā interpretation of the Bilvamaṅgal-Cintāmaṇi legend, as sung by Sanātan Dās Bāul', in R. L. Park (ed.), *Patterns of change in modern Bengal*, South Asia series, Occasional Paper No. 29, Michigan State University, 97–110.

1991, 'The cosmogonical riddles of Lalan Fakir' in Arjun Appadurai *et al.* (eds.), *Gender, genre and power in South Asian expressive traditions*, University of Pennsylvania Press, Philadelphia, 267–304.

1995, 'Bāul Songs' in Lopez (ed.), 1995, *Religions of India*, 187–208.

Sarkar, R. M., 1990, *Bauls of Bengal, in the quest of man of the heart*, Gian Publishing House, New Delhi.

Sarkar, Sumit, 1985, 'The Kathamrita as a text: towards an understanding of Ramkrishna Paramhamsa', *Occasional Papers on History and Society*, No. XXII, Nehru Memorial Museum and Library, New Delhi.

1989a, ' "Renaissance", Kali-yuga and Kalki: constructions of time and history in colonial Bengal', paper presented at International Round Table of Historians and Anthropologists, Bellagio.

1989b, 'The conditions and nature of subaltern militancy' in Guha (ed.), 1989 (1984), *Subaltern studies III*, 271–320.

1989c,'Kalki-avatar of Bikrampur: a village scandal in early twentieth century Bengal', in Guha (ed.), *Subaltern studies VI*, Delhi, 1–53.

1990/91, 'Ramakrishna and the Calcutta of his times', *The Calcutta psyche,* India International Centre Quarterly, 17:3–4, New Delhi, 99–121.

1992, 'Kaliyuga, chakri and bhakti: Ramakrishna and his times', *Economic and Political Weekly* (18th June), 1543–66.

1998, *Writing social history*, Oxford University Press, Delhi.

Sartre, Jean-Paul, 1943, *L'être et le néant*, Gallimard, Paris.

Schendel, Willem van, 1984, *Madmen of Mymensingh: peasant resistance and the colonial process in Eastern India, 1824 to 1833.* ZZOA Working Paper No. 47. University of Amsterdam.

Schomer, Karine and McLeod, W. H. (eds.), 1987, *The Sants: studies in a devotional tradition of India*, Motilal Banarsidass, Delhi.

Schoterman, J. A. (ed. and introduction), 1980, *The Yonitantra*, Manohar, Delhi.

Sen, Amiya, P., 1993, *Hindu revivalism in Bengal: 1872–1905: some essays in interpretation*, Oxford University Press, Delhi.

Sen, Asok, 1987, 'Subaltern studies: capital, class and community' in Guha (ed.), *Subaltern studies V*, 203–35.

Sen, Dinescandra, 1928, *East Bengal ballads*, vol. III, pt. 1, University of Calcutta.

1932, *East Bengal ballads*, vol. II, pt. 1, University of Calcutta.

Sen, Kshitimohan, 1929, 'The Bauls and their cult of man', *Visva Bharati Quarterly*, 410–31, January.

*c.*1935, *Medieval mysticism of India*, Luzac and Co., London (trans. from the Bengali of 1930).

Sen, Kshitimohan, 1952 & 1953, 'The Bauls of Bengal', in *Visva Bharati Quarterly*, in 4 parts: vol. XVIII, pt. 2, 122–46; Part 3, 273–82; Part 4, 294–306; Vol. XIX, Part 1, 57–74; rendered into English by Lila Ray.

1961, *Hinduism*, Penguin, Harmondsworth.

Sen, Sukumar, 1971 [1960], *History of Bengali Literature*, Sahitya Akademi, New Delhi.

1977 [1971], *Chandidas*, Sahitya Akademi, New Delhi.

Sharma, K. N., 1990, 'Western Sociology with Indian icing', *Contributions to Indian Sociology* (n.s.) 24:2, 251–7.

Shaw, Miranda, 1994, *Passionate enlightenment: women in Tantric Buddhism*, Princeton University Press. Princeton, NJ.

Siddiqui, Ashraf, 1976, *Bangladesh District Gazetteers: Kushtia*, Dacca: Government of Bangladesh.

Silburn, Lilian, 1988, *Kuṇḍalinī, the energy of the depths: a comprehensive study based on the scriptures of nondualistic Kaśmir Śaivism*, translated by Jacques Gontier, State University of New York Press, Albany, NY.

Sinha, Surajit, 1968, 'Vaishnava influence on a tribal culture', in Milton Singer (ed.), *Krishna: myths, rites and attitudes*, University of Chicago Press, Phoenix, 64–89.

Sinha, Surajit and Saraswati, Baidyanath, 1978, *Ascetics of Kashi, an anthropological exploration*, N. K. Bose Memorial Foundation, Varanasi.

Sircar, D. C., 1973, *The Śākta Pīṭhas*, 2nd revd. edn, Motilal Banarsidass, Delhi.

Snellgrove, D. L., 1959, *The Hevajra Tantra: a critical study* (part 1), Oxford University Press, London.

Spivak, Gayatri Chakravorty, 1988, 'Can the subaltern speak?' in Cary Nelson and Lawrence Grossberg (eds.), *Marxism and the interpretation of culture*, University of Illinois Press, Urbana and Chicago, IL, 271–313.

Steinkellner, Ernst, 1978, 'Remarks on Tantristic hermeneutics' from *Proceedings of the Csomo de Körös memorial symposium*, ed. Louis Ligeti, Akadémiai Kiadó, Budapest, 445–58.

Tagore, Rabindranath, 1931, *The religion of man* (Hibbert lectures of 1930), Macmillan, London.

1971 [1922], *Creative unity*, Macmillan, London.

Tambiah, S. J., 1982, 'The renouncer: his individuality and his community', in T. N. Madan (ed.), 1982, *Way of Life*, 299–320.

Thapar, Romila, 1978 'Renunciation: the making of a counter-culture?' in R. Thapar, *Ancient Indian social history: some interpretations*, Orient Longman, New Delhi, 63–104.

1979 'Dissent and protest in the early Indian tradition' in *Studies in History*, 1:2, 177–95, New Delhi.

1982, 'The householder and the renouncer in the Brahmanical and Buddhist traditions', in T. N. Madan (ed.), 1982, *Way of life*, 273–98.

1985, 'Syndicated moksha?' *Seminar*, 13, 14–22.

1989, 'Imagined religious communities? Ancient history and the modern search for a Hindu identity', *Modern Asian Studies*, 23:2, 209–31.

Thurman, Robert A. F., 1988, 'Vajra hermeneutics' in Donald S. Lopez Jnr. (ed.), *Buddhist hermeneutics* (Studies in East Asian Buddhism 6), University of Hawaii Press, Honolulu, 119–48.

Tofayell, Z. A., 1968, *Lalan Shah and the lyrics of the Padma*, Ziaunnahar, Dacca.

Trawick, Margaret, 1990a, *Notes on love in a Tamil family*, University of California Press, Berkeley, CA.

1990b, 'The ideology of love in a Tamil family', in Owen Lynch (ed.), *The politics of untouchability*, 37–63.

Turner, V. W., 1969, *The ritual process – structure and anti-structure*, Aldine, New York.

Urban, Hugh B., 1999, 'The politics of madness: the construction and manipulation of the "Baul" image in modern Bengal', *South Asia,* 22:1, 13–46.

Van der Veer, Peter, 1987, 'Taming the ascetic: devotionalism in a Hindu monastic order', *Man* (n.s.) 22:4, 680–95.

Van Meter, Rachel R., 1969, 'Bankimcandra's view of the role of Bengal in Indian civilization' in David Kopf (ed.), *Bengal: regional identity*, Occasional Paper No. 9, Asian Studies Centre, Michigan State University, 61–72, East Lansing, MI.

Vaudeville, Charlotte, 1987a, 'Sant Mat: Santism as the Universal Path to Sanctity', in Karine Schomer and W. H. McLeod (eds.) 1987, *The Sants*, 21–40.

1987b, 'The Shaiva–Vaishnava Synthesis in Maharashtrian Santism', in Karine Schomer and W. H. McLeod (eds.), *The Sants*, 215–28.

Venkatraman R., 1990, *A history of the Tamil Siddha cult*, Ennes Publications, Madurai, India.

Visuvalingam, Sunthar, 1989, 'The trangressive sacrality of the Dīkṣita: sacrifice, criminality and *bhakti* in the Hindu tradition', in Hiltebeitel (ed.), *Criminal gods*, 427–62.

Wali, Maulvi Abdul, 1898, 'On curious tenets and practices of a certain class of faqirs in Bengal', *Journal of the Anthropological Society of Bombay*, 5:4, 203–19.

Wayman, Alex, 1974 [1973], *The Buddhist Tantras: light on Indo-Tibetan esotericism*, Routledge & Kegan Paul, London.

1991 [1977], *Yoga of the Guhyasamājatantra: the arcane lore of forty verses*, Motilal Banarsidass Publishers Private, Delhi.

White, David Gordon, 1984, 'Why gurus are heavy', *Numen* 31, 40–71.

1995, 'The ocean of mercury: an eleventh-century alchemical text', in Lopez (ed.), *Religions of India*, 281–7.

1996, *The alchemical body: siddha traditions in medieval India*, University of Chicago Press, Chicago, IL.

2000, *Tantra in practice*, Princeton University Press, Princeton, NJ.

Wilden, Anthony, 1980, *System and structure*, Tavistock Publications, London.

Wilson, H. H., 1841, *A sketch of the religious sects of the Hindus*, Asiatik Researches, vols. XVI and XVII, Bishop's College Press, Calcutta.

Winternitz, M., 1933, *History of Indian literature*, University of Calcutta.

Wise, J., 1894, 'The Mohammedans of Eastern Bengal', *Journal of the Anthropological Society of Bombay*, part III.

Wittgenstein, L., 1958, *Philosophical investigations* (trans. G.E.M. Anscombe), Blackwell, Oxford.

Zvelebil, Kamil V., 1973, *The poets of the powers*, Rider and Co., London.

Bengali

Bandyopādhyāy, Asit Kumār, 1990, *Bāṅlā sāhityer sampūrṇa itihās*, Modern Book Agency, Calcutta.

Bandyopādhyāy, Cārucandra, 1339 BS, '*Bāul*' in *Prabāsī* (Māgh and Phālgun), 497–503, 632–7.

Bandyopādhyāy, Somendranāth, 1967, *Bāṅlār bāul: kābya o darśan*, University of Calcutta Press.

Bandyopādhyāy, Tamonāś, 1391 BS, *Param guru Bhabā Pāglā* (Part 1), Mahāśaktir Āśray, Bhabār Bhabānī-mandir, Kālnā, Barddhamān District, West Bengal.

Bhaṭṭācārya, Aśutoṣ, 1958, *Bāṅglā maṅgal kābyer itihās*, Mukherji and Co., Calcutta.

Bhaṭṭācārya, Aśutoṣ, 1977 [1966], *Baṅgīya lok-saṅgīt ratnākar* (4 vols.), A. Mukherji and Co., Calcutta.

Bhaṭṭācārya, Kṛṣṇa (ed.), n.d., *Bibartta bilās granthaḥ: baiṣṇab o āul sampradāyer nigūṁh tattvābalī*, (attributed to Akiñcan Dās), Tārācād Dās and Sons, Calcutta.

Bhaṭṭācārya, Upendranāth, 1388 BS [1364 BS] *Bāṅlār bāul o bāul gān*, Orient Book Company, Calcutta, (abbreviated in the text as *BBBG*).

Cakrabarttī, Bihāri Lāl, 1307 BS, Baiśākh, *Granthābalī*, Abināś Cakrabarttī, ed., B. B. Dhar Company, Calcutta.

Cakrabartī, Haridās, 1395 BS [1388 BS], (*Ḍamar tantra-mūl*) *Pāñcabhautik cikitsā*, Cintāmanikuñja, Baṙa Pāthak Bāṙī, Baubājār, Nabadvīp.
Cakrabartī, Gopikā Rañjan, 1995, *Bhabāpāglār jīban o gān*, Bangla Academy, Dacca.
Cakrabartī, Mukundarām, 1975, *Caṇḍīmaṅgal*, ed. Sukumār Sen, Sahitya Akademi, New Delhi.
Cakrabartī, Rāmākānta, 1997, '*Paścimbaṅge bāul-dharma biṣayak adhyayaner bibhinna dhārā*', in Sudhīr Cakrabartī (ed.), 1997, 56–82.
Cakrabartī, Sudhīr, 1985, *Sāhebdhanī sampradāy: tāder gān*, Pustak Bipaṇi, Calcutta.
1986, *Balāhāḍi sampradāy ār tāder gān*, Pustak Bipaṇi, Calcutta.
1989, *Gabhīr nirjan pathe*, Ananda Publishers, Calcutta.
1990 (ed.), *Bāṅlā dehatattver gān*, Pustak Bipaṇi, Calcutta.
1992a, '*Bāṅlār bāul*' in *Deś*, 18 January 1992, Calcutta, 31–38.
1992b, *Brātya lokāyat Lālan*, Pustak Bipaṇi, Calcutta.
1997 (ed.), *Dhrubapad: Bāṅlār bāul phakir* (annual publication), Krishnanagar, Nadiya, West Bengal.
Caudhurī, Ābul Āhasān, 1988, *Kāṅāl Harināth Majumdār*, Bangla Academy, Dacca.
1990, *Lālan Śāha: 1774–1890*, Bangla Academy, Dacca.
1992, '*Cālacitra: baṅlādeśer bāulder*', in *Deś*, 18 January, Calcutta.
1998 (ed.), *Kāṅāl Harināth Majumdār: smārak-grantha*, Bangla Academy, Dacca.
Dās, Ajit, 1986, '*Jāt baiṣṇaber kathā*', *Bāromās*, Nababarṣa edn, Calcutta.
Dās, Haridās, 501 Śrīcaitanyābda (2nd edn) *Śrīśrīgauṙīya-baiṣṇab-abhidhān* (2 vols.), Śrīharibol Kuṭir, Nabadvīp, West Bengal.
Dās, Jñānendra Mohan, 1979 (2nd edn), *Bāṅglā bhāṣār abhidhān*, Sāhitya Saṅsad, Calcutta.
Dās, Motilāl and Mahāpātra, Piyuṣakānti, 1958, *Lālan Gitikā*, University of Calcutta.
Dās, Paritoṣ, 1978, *Sahajiyā o gauṙīya baiṣṇab dharma*, Firma K. L. M. (Private) Ltd., Calcutta.
Dās, Pūrṇa, 1986, '*Āmār chele-belā*' in *Ānanda Bājār Patrikā*, 18 May, Calcutta.
Dās, Sunīl, 1984, *Bhārati: itihās o racanāpañji*, Calcutta.
Dās Brahmacārī, Madan Mohan (ed. and trans.), 1389 BS, *Sahajiyā dalan: o śrīśrīcaitanya prem-dharmmer dīkṣā śikṣāgurur mīmāṅsā* (2 vols.), Śāntipur, West Bengal.
Dās Mahānta, Anurāgī, 1356 BS, *Gaur bhagabān*, Koṭā Natun Ākhṙā, Barddhamān.
Datta, Akṣay Kumār, 1870 (pt. 1) and 1883 (pt. 2) *Bhāratabarṣīya upāsak-sampradāy*, Binay Ghoṣ (ed.), 1969, Calcutta. (Abbreviated in text as *BBUS*.)
Ghoṣ-Dās, Rameś Candra (compiler and ed.), 1289 BS, *Bhāber gīt*, Aurora Press, Calcutta.
Gosvāmī, Jayaguru, 1972, *Cāraṇakabi Mukundadās*, Rabindra Library, Calcutta.
Gupta, Amit, 1983, *Bāṅlār lok-jībane bāul*, Saṅbād, Calcutta.
Hak, Khondkār Riyājul (ed.) 1976, *Lālan sāhitya o darśan*, Muktadhārā, Bangladesh.
Hārādhan (Baiṣṇab Ṭhākur), n.d., *Āśray siddhānta candroday bā svarūp dāmodar gosvāmīr kaṙcā*, Śrīmaṇīndranāth Adhikārī, No. 2, Government Colony, Malda District, West Bengal.
1391 BS, *Bhekāśrita tattva nirūpaṇ grantha*, (10th edn), Śrīmaṇīndranāth Adhikārī, No. 2, Government Colony, Malda District, West Bengal.
Haṭha Yoga Pradīpikā (see Sarasvatī, Svāmi Ýogeśvarānanda).
Islām, Mayhārūl, 1366, *Kabi Pāglā Kānāi*, Dacca.
Jayānanda, *Caitanya-maṅgal*, Bimanbehari Majumdar and Sukhamay Mukhopadhyay (eds.), 1971, The Asiatic Society, Calcutta.

Jhā, Śakti Nāth, 1983, '*Āul*', in *Saptāha*, 16:27, Calcutta.

1985, 'Murśīdābād jelār bastubādi musulmān bāul sampradāyik samāj, sāhitya ebaṅ darśan', Ph.D. dissertation (Calcutta University).

1985/86, '*Bāul darśane bhāratīya bastubāder upādān*', *Anik*, December 1985 and January 1986, Khagra, Murshidabad, West Bengal.

1991 (ed.), '*Jāt gela, jāt gela bale*', special bulletin of *Raurab*, Berhampore, Mursidabad.

1993a, *Bāul sanāktakaraṇ samasyā o Lālan*, Sucana Cultural Centre, 20 July 1993, Calcutta 24.

1993b, '*Lālaner gāne ātmajaibanik upādān*', *Smaraṇikā*, Paścim Baṅga Lālan Melā Samiti, Kadamkhāli, Bhīmpur, Nadia, West Bengal.

1993c, '*Sāmpradāyikatā o maulabāder pratibādī bāul āndolan*', *Bhāgīrathī*, Goyāl-jān Sebā Samiti, Baharampur, 1400 Śāradīyā Saṅkhyā.

1995, *Phakir Lālan Sā̃i: deś kāl ebaṅ śilpa*, Saṅbād Prakāśak, 57/2d, College Street, Calcutta.

1997, '*Gupta deha sādhanā ebaṅ tār samāj-tattva*', 91–104, in S. Cakrabartī (ed.).

1999, *Bastubādī bāul: udbhab, samāj saṅskṛti o darśan*, Lok-saṅskṛti o ādibāsī saṅskṛti kendra (Tathya o saṅskṛti bibhāg, Paścim Baṅga Sarkār), Calcutta.

Jhā, Śakti Nāth and Ghaṭak, Maitreya (eds.), 1997, *Bāul-phakir dhvaṅser āndolaner itibṛtta* in *Bartikā*, July–September 1997 (major contributor of articles, S. N. Jhā). Series editor Mahāśvetā Debī, Calcutta.

Kavirāj, Gopīnāth, 1983 [1975], *Tāntrik sādhanā o siddhānta* (2 parts), Barddhmān University, West Bengal.

Karīm, Ānoyārul, 1977, *Rabīndranāther śilāidaha*, Folklore Research Institute, Kushtia, Bangladesh.

Majumdār, Pārijāt (ed.), 1999, *Kāṅāl Harināth smārak-grantha*, Jāgarī, Calcutta.

Miśra, Manulāl, 1318 BS, *Bhāber gīter byākhā saha sahaj tattvaprakāś bā sanātan sahaj satya dharmer ādi itihās*, Calcutta.

1332 BS (3rd edn), *Kartābhajā dharmer ādi bṛttānta bā sahajtattva prakāś*, Calcutta.

Mitra, Sanat Kumār (ed.), 1382 BS, *Kartābhajā dharmmamat o itihās* (2 parts), Sāhitya Prakāś, Calcutta.

Mukhopādhyāy, Āditya, 1988, *Dharma o saṅskṛtir āloke bāul*, Sarat Publishing House, Calcutta.

Mukhopādhyāy, Harekṛṣṇa, 1961, *Baiṣṇab padābalī*, Sāhitya Saṅsad, Calcutta.

Mukhopādhyāy, Prabhāt-kumār, 1355 [1343] BS, *Rabīndrajībanī* (part 2), Visva Bharati, Calcutta.

Mukundarām (*see* Cakrabartī).

Nāg, Aruṇ (ed. and commentary), 1389 BS, *Saṭīk hutom pyācār nakaśā*, Subarṇarekhā, Calcutta.

Nāth, Śarat Candra, 1341 BS, *Dīn Śarater bāul gān*, Pabitra Rañjan Sarkār, Calcutta.

Pāl, Basantakumār, 1332, '*Phakir Lālan Sāh*', in *Prabāsī* (Śrābaṇ, 497–504).

Pāl-Deb-Mohānta, Satyaśib, 1990, *Ghoṣapāṛār satīmā o karttābhajā dharma*, Pustak Bipaṇi, Calcutta. (The author is a leading guru of the *kartābhajās*.)

Pāṇḍā, Biṣṇupada, 1388, *Kabi Bihārīlāl Cakrabartī o bāṅlā gītikabitār dhārā*, University of Calcutta.

Pāṭhak, Sunīti Kumār, 1982–4, '*Bāul khõje maner mānuṣ*' in *Mātṛbāṇī* (5 parts), Calcutta.

Rahmān, S. M. Lutphar, 1983, *Lālanśāh: jīban o gān*, Bāṅlādeś Śilpakalā Ekāḍemī., Bangladesh.

Rājā, Āli, 1324 BS, *Jñān-sāgar*, Ābdul Karim Sāhityabiśārad (ed.), Baṅgīya Sāhitya Pariṣad, Calcutta.
Rāmakṛṣṇa Paramahaṅsa (see 'Śrī Ma').
Rānā, Sumaṅgal, 1981, *Caryāgiti pañcāśikā*, Firma K.L.M. Private, Calcutta.
Rāy, Mahendranāth, c.1292 BS, *Akṣay Kumār Datter jibān bṛttānta*.
Rāy, Nihār-rañjan, 1980 (3rd edn), *Bāṅālir itihās, ādi parba*, vol I, Calcutta.
Saralā Debī (and Akṣay Kumār Maitreya), 1302 BS, '*Lālan Phakir o Gagan*' in *Bhārati*, Calcutta, pp. 275–81.
Sarasvatī, Svāmi Yogeśvarānanda, 1987, *Haṭha Yoga Pradīpikā* (ed. trans. commentator), Sibānanda Yogāśram, 471 Netājī Colony, Calcutta 10.
Śarīph, Āhamad, 1370 BS, '*Bāul tattva*' in *Bāṅlār ekāḍemī patrikā*, 7:4, Dacca, Bangladesh.
Śāstrī, Hara Prasād, 1959 (1st edn c. 1917), *Bauddha gān o dohā*, Baṅgīya Sāhitya Pariṣad, Calcutta.
Sen, Jaladhar, 1320 & 1321 BS, *Kāṅgāl Harināth* (2 parts), Calcutta.
Sen, Kṣitimohan, 1352 BS, *Bāṅlār sādhanā*, Biśvabidyāsaṅgraha, Biśvabhāratī Granthālay, Calcutta.
1397 BS (1st edn 1356 BS), *Bhārate hindu-musalmāner yukta sādhanā*, Biśvabhāratī Granthabibhāg, Calcutta.
1993, *Bāṅlār bāul* (1949 Līlā baktṛā), University of Calcutta Press.
Sen, Sukumār, 1948, *Bāṅgālā sāhityer itihās*, part 1, Modern Book Agency, Calcutta.
1975 (ed.), *Caṇḍīmaṅgal* (Mukundarām), Sahitya Akademi, New Delhi.
1983a [1963] (ed.), *Caitanya caritāmṛta* (Kṛṣṇadās Kabirāj), Sahitya Akademi, New Delhi.
1983b [1957], *Baiṣṇab padābalī*, Sahitya Akademi, New Delhi.
Siṅha, Kālīprasanna (see Nāg, Aruṇ).
Śrī 'Ma', 1388 BS [1339 BS], *Śrī Śrī Rāmakṛṣṇa Kathāmṛta* (5 vols.), Śrīma'r Ṭhākurbāṛī, Calcutta.
Ṭālib, Muhammad Ābu, 1976 CE, *'Lālan cariter upādān: tathya o satya'* in Hak (ed.), pp. 1–61.
Ṭhākur (Tagore), Rabīndranāth, 1290 BS *'Bāuler gān'* in *Bhārati*, Calcutta, 34–41.
1312 BS, *Bāul*, Majumdār Library, Calcutta.
1337 BS, Introduction to *Hārāmaṇi* (vol. I), M. Mansur Uddīn (ed.), Calcutta.
1383 BS, *Gorā*, Viśvabhāratī Granthan-bibhāg, Calcutta. (*Gorā* was serialised in *Prabāśī* from 1314–16 (1907–10)).
1386 BS *Rabīndra racanābalī: janmaśatabārṣik saṅskaraṇ* (The collected works of Rabindranath: birth centenary edition), West Bengal Government, Calcutta, vol. III.
1395 BS [1343 BS], *Patraput*, Viśvabhārati Granthan-bibhāg, Calcutta.
1397a BS, *Śiśu bholānāth*, Viśvabhārati Granthan-bibhāg, Calcutta.
1397b BS [1329 BS], *Lipikā*, Viśvabhārati Granthan-bibhāg, Calcutta.
Uddīn, Mahammad Mansur (ed.) *Hārāmaṇi*, vol. I, 1383 BS [1336], Muktadhara, Dacca.
(ed.) *Hārāmaṇi*, vol. V, 1390 BS [1368], Bangla Academy, Dacca, Bangladesh.
1980 (ed.), *Bāul gān: Kṣitimohan Sen Śāstrī saṅgṛhīta*, Hāsi Prakāśālay, Dacca.

GENERAL INDEX

NAME INDEX

(With two exceptions, initials are substituted for the names of living Bāuls/*bartamān-panthīs*, for reasons of confidentiality. Those known primarily by their forename, including Bāuls/*bartamān-panthīs*, are listed under forename rather than title. Names of groups are included in the general index.)

Ahmad, Aijaz, 21–2

Bagri (Bāgri), 75, 94–6
Bahl, K.C., 175, 219
Bandyopadhyaya, Sekhar, 243
Bangladesh, 51
Bayly, C.A., 88
Bengal, 75, 128, 252
Béteille, A., 252
B.G., 92, 96, 100, 132, 135, 137, 138, 172, 199, 204, 207, 214, 227, 231, 235
  on *bindu sādhanā*, 219, 220–1, 222–3, 224
Bhabā Pāglā, 238–9
Bhabānanda, 194
Bhadra, Gautam, 242
Bharati, Agehananda, 67–9, 215
Bhaṭṭācārya, Upendranāth, 3, 24–5, 29, 39, 51–3, 54, 56, 58–9, 60–2, 63, 68, 71, 77, 79, 107, 112, 114–15, 118, 197, 204
  on *bindu sādhanā*, 221–2, 223–4
Bhattacharya, D., 66, 67
Bhattacharyya, D.P., 78, 181
Bhattacharya, J.N., 3, 19, 23, 50
Bihāri Lāl (Cakrabarttī), 31, 177
B.N., 83–4, 88, 89
Briggs, G.W., 221
Broomfield, J.H., 19–20
Burghart, R., 125–7, 250

Caitanya, 23, 24, 104, 131, 136, 142, 146, 149, 153, 181, 187, 190, 198, 223, 235–6, 255, 239, 255
  as a Bāul, 97, 101
Cakrabartī, Sudhīr, 30, 44, 50, 111, 113, 182, 240–2
Cantlie, A., 130, 212
Capwell, C., 71
Caudhurī, Ābul Āhasān, 72, 129
Chakravarti, Ramakanta, 95, 176, 199
Chartier, R., 10
Chatterjee, Partha, 21, 60, 182, 240–4
Chattopadhyaya, D.P., 176, 192–3, 195

Das, Rahul Peter, 203, 214, 216, 221–2
Das, Veena, 126–7
Das Gupta, Uma, 50
Dasgupta, A. and M.A., 5, 61
Dasgupta, Shashi Bhusan, 27–8, 38, 52, 66, 111, 213, 215, 232
Datta, Akṣay Kumār, 3, 24–5, 26, 51, 229
D.D., 91, 102
D.G., 103, 172, 175, 186, 212, 231
Dimock, E.C., 1, 56–7, 58–9, 111, 147
Duddu Śā, 31, 108–10, 148, 189, 196, 246, 248, 251
Dumont, L.
  on caste, 240
  on Hinduism, 11
  on renunciation, 125–7, 241, 250
Dutt, G.S., 50

Eliade, M., 67, 69, 70

Fabian, J., 195
Flood, G., 221
Foucault, M., 14, 195

Gagan Harakarā, 37–9
Ginsberg, A., 4
Gold, D., 128, 146
Guha, Ranajit, 242, 243
Guha-Thakurta, Tapati, 30
Gupta, Sanjukta, 4, 147, 213

Haq, Md. Enamul, 25, 57, 59, 111, 191
Harding, S., 245
Harināth Majumdār/Kāṅāl Harināth/Phikir Cā̃d, 29–30, 31, 52–4

UNIVERSITY OF CAMBRIDGE
ORIENTAL PUBLICATIONS PUBLISHED FOR THE
FACULTY OF ORIENTAL STUDIES

1 *Averroes' commentary on Plato's Republic*, edited and translated by E. I. J. Rosenthal
2 *FitzGerald's "Salaman and Absal"*, edited by A. J. Arberry
3 *Ihara Saikaku: the Japanese family storehouse*, translated and edited by G. W. Sargent
4 *The Avestan Hymn to Mithra*, edited and translated by Ilya Gershevitch
5 *The Fuṣūl al-Madanī of al-Fārābī*, edited by D. M. Dunlop (out of print)
6 *Dun Karn, poet of Malta*, texts chosen and translated by A. J. Arberry; introduction, notes and glossary by P. Grech
7 *The political writings of Ogyū Sorai*, by J. R. McEwan
8 *Financial administration under the T'ang dynasty*, by D. C. Twitchett
9 *Neolithic cattle-keepers of south India: a study of the Deccan Ashmounds*, by F. R. Allchin
10 *The Japanses enlightenment: a study of the writings of Fukuzawa Yukichi*, by Carmen Blacker
11 *Records of Han administration.* Vol. I *Historical assessment*, by M. Loewe
12 *Records of Han administration.* Vol. II *Documents*, by M. Loewe
13 *The language of Indrajit of Orchā: a study of early Braj Bhāṣā prose*, by R. S. McGregor
14 *Japan's first general election, 1890*, by R. H. P. Mason
15 *A collection of tales from Uji: a study and translation of "Uji Shūi Monogatari,"* by D. E. Mills
16 *Studia semitica.* Vol. I *Jewish themes*, by E. I. J. Rosenthal
17 *Studia semitica.* Vol. II *Islamic themes*, by E. I. J. Rosenthal
18 *A Nestorian collection of Christological texts.* Vol. I *Syraic text*, by Luise Abramowski and Alan E. Goodman
19 *A Nestorian collection of Christological texts.* Vol. II *Introduction, translation, indexes*, by Luise Abramowski and Alan E. Goodman
20 *The Syraic version of the Pseudo-Nonnos mythological scholia*, by Sebastian Brock
21 *Water rights and irrigation practices in Lajih*, by A. M. A. Maktari
22 *The commentary of Rabbi David Kimhi on Psalms cxx–cl*, edited and translated by Joshua Baker and Ernest W. Nicholson

23 *Jalāl al-dīn al-Suyūṭī.* Vol. I *Biography and background*, by E. M. Sartain
24 *Jalāl al-dīn al-Suyūṭī.* Vol. II *Al-Tahadduth bini'mat allāh*, Arabic text, by E. M. Sartain
25 *Origen and the Jews: studies in Jewish–Christian relations in third-century Palestine*, by N. R. M. de Lange
26 *The Vīsalaḍevarāsa': a restoration of the text*, by John D. Smith
27 *Shabbethai Sofer and his prayer-book*, by Stefan C. Reif
28 *Mori Ōgai and the modernization of Japanese culture*, by Richard John Bowring
29 *The rebel lands: an investigation into the origins of early Mesopotamian mythology*, by J. V. Kinnier Wilson
30 *Saladin: the politics of the holy war*, by Malcolm C. Lyons and David Jackson
31 *Khotanese Buddhist texts* (revised edition), edited by H. W. Bailey
32 *Interpreting the Hebrew Bible: essays in honour of E. I. J. Rosenthal*, edited by J. A. Emerton and Stefan C. Reif
33 *The traditional interpretation of the Apocalypse of St John in the Ethiopian orthodox church*, by Roger W. Cowley
34 *South Asian archaeology 1981: proceedings of the sixth international conference of South Asian archaeologists in western Europe*, edited by Bridget Allchin (with assistance from Raymond Allchin and Miriam Sidell)
35 *God's conflict with the dragon and the sea. Echoes of a Canaanite myth in the Old Testament*, by John Day
36 *Land and sovereignty in India. Agrarian society and politics under the eighteenth-century Maratha Svarājya*, by André Wink
37 *God's caliph: religious authority in the first centuries of Islam*, by Patricia Crone and Martin Hinds
38 *Ethiopian Biblical interpretation: a study in exegetical tradition and hermeneutics*, by Roger W. Cowley
39 *Monk and mason on the Tigris frontier: the early history of Ṭur 'Abdin*, by Andrew Palmer
40 *Early Japanese books in Cambridge University Library: a catalogue of the Aston, Satow and Von Siebold collections*, by Nozumu Hayashi and Peter Kornicki
41 *Molech: a god of human sacrifice in the Old Testament*, by John Day
42 *Arabian studies*, edited by R. B. Serjeant and R. L. Bidwewll
43 *Naukar, Rajput and Sepoy: the ethnohistory of the military labour market in Hindustan, 1450–1850*, by Dirk H. A. Kolff
44 *The epic of Pabūjī: a study, transcription and translation*, by John D. Smith
45 *Anti-Christian polemic in Early Islam: Abū 'Īsā al-Warrāq's "Against the Trinity"*, by David Thomas
46 *Devotional literature in South Asia: current research, 1985–8. Papers of the fourth conference on devotional literature in New indo-Aryan languages*, edited by R. S. McGregor

47 *Genizah research after ninety years: the case of Judaeo-Arabic. Papers read at the third congress of the Society for Judaeo-Arabic Studies*, edited by Joshua Blau and Stefan C. Reif
48 *Divination, mythology and monarchy in Han China*, by Michael Loewe
49 *The Arabian epic: heroic and oral storytelling*, volumes I–III, by M. C. Lyons
50 *Religion in Japan: arrows to heaven and earth*, edited by P. F. Kornicki and I. J. McMullen
51 *Kingship and political practice in colonial India*, by Pamela G. Price
52 *Hebrew manuscripts at Cambridge University Library: a description and introduction*, by Stefan C. Reif
53 *Selected letters of Rabindranath Tagore*, edited by Krishna Dutta and Andrew Robinson
54 *State and court ritual in China*, edited by Joseph P. McDermott
55 *Indian semantic analysis: the* nirvacana *tradition*, by Eivind Kahrs
56 *The Syraic version of the Old Testament: an introduction*, by M. P. Weitzman
57 *The cult of Asharah in ancient Israel and Judah: evidence for a Hebrew goddess*, by Judith M. Hadley
58 *The transformation of nomadic society in the Arab East*, edited by Martha Mundy and Basim Musallam
59 *Early Muslim polemic against Christianity: Abū ʻĪsā al-Warrāq's "Against the Incarnation"*, edited and translated by David Thomas
60 *Seeking Bāuls of Bengal*, by Jeanne Openshaw